Caesar Ate My Jesus

Caesar Ate My Jesus

A Baby Boomer's Reflection on Spirituality
in the American Empire

Meg Gorzycki

RESOURCE *Publications* • Eugene, Oregon

CAESAR ATE MY JESUS
A Baby Boomer's Reflection on Spirituality in the American Empire

Copyright © 2017 Meg Gorzycki. All rights reserved. Except for brief quotations in critical publications or reviews, no part of this book may be reproduced in any manner without prior written permission from the publisher. Write: Permissions, Wipf and Stock Publishers, 199 W. 8th Ave., Suite 3, Eugene, OR 97401.

Resource Publications
An Imprint of Wipf and Stock Publishers
199 W. 8th Ave., Suite 3
Eugene, OR 97401

www.wipfandstock.com

PAPERBACK ISBN: 978-1-5326-1849-9
HARDCOVER ISBN: 978-1-4982-4410-7
EBOOK ISBN: 978-1-4982-4409-1

Manufactured in the U.S.A.   MAY 30, 2017

This book is dedicated to my parents, Tom and Judie,
my first teachers, who brought children into the world
with so much faith, so many dreams, and their sleeves rolled up.

Contents

Acknowledgments | ix

1   The Boom and Bust of Spirit | 1
2   The Kingdom of Controversy | 15
3   The Military Industrial Crucifix | 32
4   Pope John Kennedy | 47
5   The Quicksand of Vietnam | 65
6   Dissent | 83
7   Civil Rights | 106
8   Sex and the Kingdom | 126
9   The Dignity of Labor | 149
10 Banksters and Creditmeisters | 164
11 Born-Again Caesar | 179
12 A View from Distant Shores | 200
13 Post-Cold War Caesar | 220
14 In Excelsis Deo | 242

Bibliography | 259

Acknowledgments

It is not possible in this life to thank all the people who formed me in my youth. Many died before I realized the important role they played shaping my attitude towards humanity, God, intellectual development, and spiritual maturity. I was blessed as a child to be surrounded by adults who did not try to be children, and who made no apology for taking their faith and the spiritual and moral formation of me and my peers seriously. Their integrity, compassion, wisdom, and willingness to set boundaries that others criticized made hard lessons in growing up bearable, and gave me a sense of sacred purpose.

    I am especially grateful to my precious brother Joe, whose wit and discernment inspired every chapter. Many thanks to my dear sister Martha and dear brother Tony for their creative ideas and fresh perspectives. I also appreciate the love of my thoughtful and caring sisters Louise and Terri. I am grateful to Roberta Hoffman who encouraged me to think about this work from the Jewish perspective. Many thanks also to the boomers who helped me think through our experiences and what they mean: Don McLeod, Joe McBride, Sophie Clavier, Jim DeBruycker, Pam Howard, Greg Vanderheiden, Barb Haber, John and Cynthia Pugliaresi, and Sondra Arnsdorf. Thanks to Samar Haddad for her support, and to Barb Zurek for being my colleague.

1

The Boom and Bust of Spirit

Introduction

THIS BOOK IS A reaction to what the hell happened. It is about how soaring faith in the belief that America is God's right hand on earth lost altitude when confronted with the facts about our values and the agendas they bred. Boomers were weaned on unyielding assurance that we lived in the most virtuous nation on earth, and were repeatedly told that we, as a "Christian nation," represented the hope of all humanity. It is about growing up in a climate of confidence that prosperity was inevitable in part because we held fast to Judeo-Christian traditions, and then having to face the disturbing reality that such traditions were not necessarily prophylactics against war, corporate greed, political corruption, racism, sexism, and all manner of personal vanity that led individuals to exploit others.

This book is about how historical events and social change challenged the nation's understanding of what it means to be a "Christian nation." It is about what happened to our spiritual capital when our government and religious leaders stood at the cross roads of serious moral dilemmas and led us down the paths of militarism, materialism, and nationalism. This monograph explores the reality that the American way of life has been so often in conflict with America's own spiritual teachings. It is a response to the various ways America has interpreted the will of God, and how those interpretations have impacted the way we bring the Kingdom of God to bear in our lives and the world around us.

The material rush of affluence that swept boomers along from cradle to college taught us to be optimistic about the future, and that big science, the democratic process, and faith in God made prosperity a sure thing. Boomers were assured that the future was secure for anyone willing to get educated, work hard, and obey the laws. Boomers raised in religious households and who attended parochial schools often assimilated the notion that civic authority was bestowed by God, and only the worthiest among the worthy could have it.

Along the way to prosperity and making the world a better place, boomers encountered segregation, race riots, war, Watergate, the sexual revolution, banking scandals, and religious fundamentalism. These events lit political and theological fires in our own back yard and in our own churches and synagogues. Many boomers entered their retirement years with a great deal of sadness and cynicism. They felt that the nation's morality and democracy were degraded by civic and religious authorities who betrayed America's commitment to justice and love of neighbor for thirty pieces of silver. Senior boomers are disappointed by different things. Some who achieved their material dreams feel empty and unfulfilled. Some feel alienated in the workplace because their expertise became or was suddenly devalued. Others are distressed because the commitment to make the world a better place was readily disposable when more profitable things came along. These things have worn our spirits. They have troubled my own. This book, however, is not a requiem for hope and spirituality, it is a rallying cry.

Booming Possibilities

Baby boomers were fortunate children. They were born into a nation that endowed them with extraordinary opportunities. Americans were affluent following World War II (WWII) and proud to be part of a society in which most folks agreed that it was everybody's duty to promote public decency, and to give everyone a chance for self-improvement. The 76 million people born in the U.S. between 1945 and 1964 were taught to believe that their country was the leader of the free world and that it was engaged in the noble business of creating a new world order based on democracy and capitalism. The boomer generation witnessed and participated in technological and social revolutions that have had profound consequences for the U.S. and the world.

Boomers were the first generation to never have known a world without nuclear weapons. They were raised in an economy that depended heavily on producing and selling weapons. As Boomers grew up, so did the Interstate Highways System, which enabled mass mobility and its way of life. They were the first generation to be born into modern suburbs, and to grow up with indoor shopping malls.

Boomers were the first generation raised on a steady diet of television, and thus the first children targeted by television's incessant barrage of advertising. Commercials stimulated our cravings for treats and toys. Sophisticated marketing techniques helped to create a nation of consumers willing to assume debt to satisfy their appetites for things they thought would bring them wholeness and well-being.[1] They taught us that it was normal to want material things all the time, and that it was OK to constantly indulge ourselves. Boomers and their descendants have never lived without Madison Avenue's constant reminder that we would be sexier, more powerful, more secure, and better than others if we bought what we were told to buy.

Television, once the hope of idealists who believed the medium would be a conduit of learning and enlightenment, was readily corrupted. For the sake of reaping vast fortunes, TV executives and their sponsors gave the public "what they wanted." On the whole, the public did not want mind-expanding talk shows and documentaries. We were mesmerized by cartoons, situation comedies, variety shows, and melodrama. Boomers were a generation that could sing jingles for beer and cigarettes but struggled to name our own senators or to find Vietnam on a map.

Television also transformed politics. The oldest baby boomers were in first grade during the 1952 presidential election, in which the first televised ads and debates appeared. Many politicians thought that television was a passing fad that did little to the advance candidates. Skeptics about the new technology quickly changed their minds, especially after Madison Avenue's slick advertising agents proved that people's attitudes and behavior could be shaped by manipulating images and sentiment.[2] At present, Political Action Committees (PACs) collect millions of dollars from corporate and individual donations that are used to craft campaign ads targeting viewers' sentiments and emotions.[3]

Boomers saw mass corporate media proliferate and consolidate into the hands of just a few entities. The monopolization of media has a huge impact on what we know and what we believe about ourselves and our world. Its tendency is to reduce the scope of perspectives and opinions rather than to expand it.[4] Developments in digital communication boomer's lifetime have made instant global communication possible. This ability to connect with others has enhanced the interdependence of distant and diverse nations. Boomers and

---

1. Motivational research during the 1940s laid the groundwork for modern advertising, which targeted the consumer's anxieties, fantasies, and sense of worth. Packard's *The Hidden Persuaders*, 1957, was among the first scholarly works to document how marketing exploited our desires and anxieties.

2. Brader, *Campaigning for Hearts*, 2.

3. Jamison, *Packing the Presidency*, 417–421.

4. Both Chomsky's *Media Control* and Bagdikian's *The New Media Monopoly* provide an analytical discussion of corporate media, and trace the monopoly's development.

their descendants are more aware than their grandparents were of how their global neighbors live. They have access to mountains of information about how their decisions as voters and consumers impact people in foreign nations. The digital revolution, however, has not necessarily improved what Americans know about the world and how power operates behind closed doors. High schools and institutions of higher education do not routinely require students to complete courses that look critically at mass media or what it means to be a well-informed citizen.

Boomers have seen scientific revolutions in agriculture and the consolidation of corporate food production. Corporate farms have not only monopolized production, but altered the very genetic composition of plants and animals. As family farms were swallowed whole by agribusinesses, mass production techniques introduced hormones and anti-biotics to improve crop and livestock production, at great risk to public health.[5] Modern farming techniques contribute to the increase of allergies and other diseases, and corporate policies on patented seeds threaten farmers with decreased access to all seeds.[6] As seeds become the intellectual property of corporations, it is often our brothers and sisters in developing nations that suffer hunger the most as such seeds are costly.[7] Boomers were also the first children to enjoy breakfast cereals with sugar contents that tipped 50 percent, and to grow up on diets laden with high contents of fat, carbohydrates, and sodium.[8] Fast food became a staple at the cost of soaring obesity rates.[9]

Boomers watched Americans go to the moon and learned of great scientists who mapped galaxies that nobody knew existed. They were the beneficiaries of and sometimes participants in medical revolutions, such as vaccines, transplants, and psychotropic drugs that help us manage depression, anxiety, and other disorders. As school kids, my peers and I were proud of America's assistance to non-developed nations, and wanted to join the Peace Corps. We aspired to bring education, medicine, shelter, food, and sanitation to countries in want. Lots of boomers believed that they were part of something larger than themselves—something global and humanitarian.

I recall seeing the "Blue Marble" for the first time when I was 14. It is the picture of earth taken from space by the Apollo 17 crew, and features the whole planet with its continents and oceans beneath a soft swirl of clouds. A friend told me that the image humbled her, and made her feel small. The

5. Silbergeld, *Chickenizing Farms*, 89–108.
6. Pringle, *Food, Inc.*, 2–7.
7. Shiva, *Stolen Harvest*, 7–10.
8. Moss, M. *Salt, Sugar, Fat*, 7–12.
9. Schlosser, *Fast Food Nation*, 240–43.

sense of being small did not humiliate or distress her, but filled her with the understanding that she was part of something greater than herself and that she did not have to figure everything out or have all the answers. My reaction in 1972 to the image was different. I was not as awestruck as others. In retrospect, the image seemed mundane, almost unimpressive because I learned to expect society to produce exceptional things as a matter of course. Despite the anti-climactic sensation I had, the Blue Marble eventually caused me to feel vulnerable and to recognize the fragility of existence on earth.

Bubbles Bursting

Boomers have never known an America without poverty. While many boomers ascended to splendid heights of prosperity, others suffered from relentless deprivation and indifference in urban ghettos, on Native American reservations, and in rural counties. In 1959, 22.4 percent of Americans—roughly 40 million—lived in poverty.[10] John Kenneth Galbraith's *The Affluent Society*, documented the rise of America's prosperity.[11] Michael Harrington's *The Other America*, opened our eyes to the suffering of the poor, and exposed its underlying racism.[12] Fighting poverty ultimately became priorities in both Presidents John F. Kennedy's and Lyndon Johnson's administrations.

As boomers came of age, they learned that color and gender played a profound role in people's access to education, jobs, legal representation, and visibility in the media. In 1945, the government was a white man's world. By 2015, nearly 20% of Congress was female, and 30% of the House and 6% of the Senate consisted of racial minorities.[13] Congress, however, is still a country club, as it is populated largely by millionaires.[14] With Congressional help, financial institutions and corporations transformed the economy of 1950—an economy that was relatively stable and offered decent compensation to working class American—into an economy that is more volatile and less generous to the working class.[15]

Importantly, boomers were not raised to think of their country as an empire. We had to learn that on our own. In our youth, we had little awareness of how industrial expansion translated into covert CIA activities, war, and fiscal

10. DeNavas-Walt and Proctor, *Income and Poverty*, 12.
11. Galbraith, *Affluent Society*, 2–3.
12. Harrington, *Other America*, 6.
13. Bump, "The New Congress," lines 8–10.
14. Hunter, "Wealth of Congress," lines 2–13.
15. Reich, *Supercapitalism*, 50–87.

policies.[16] We were sheltered from obscene facts about what Americans have done to indigenous populations at home and abroad in order to stimulate progress. Boomers were not raised to think critically about the presumptions that grounded our values. As kids, we did not learn that "progress" was not necessarily progress from all perspectives. School curriculum of the 1950s and 60s enforced the assumption that bankers, industrialists, and government officials would never willfully harm us. We grew up assuming that the rest of the world wanted to be like the U.S. in every way because, without question, we were the best.

It took boomers a while to understand the ways of empire and their impact on the American dream and society's moral conduct. Painful experiences of discrimination, corruption, and greed prompted many to question their own and the nation's character. American support for foreign dictators who plundered their nation's resources and savagely oppressed their own people raised questions about America's commitment to peace and justice.

As the last half of the twentieth century dissolved the idealistic lens through which boomers had seen their lives, many pondered the possibility that they had been used by secular and religious authorities to inflict suffering, death, and destruction for the sake of empire-building and protecting private interests. Many became cynical toward religion and all things that smacked of piety, spirituality, and philosophical tenets on love and brotherhood. In the end, there was no Age of Aquarius. All the time Americans spent in church on Sundays, being born again, or dropping LSD to achieve nirvana did not derail American imperialism nor purge Americans hearts of xenophobia, sexism, racism, and contempt for the poor.

What happened to the love, mercy, and empathy Americans were supposed to have as a Judeo-Christian society? What happened to the belief that a higher power called upon us to put the well-being of others ahead of our pursuit of earthly treasures? What happened to the Jesus who called upon the faithful to love one's enemies, serve the poor, and walk humbly in the presence of God? Did the communists foil our sacred mission by infiltrating our homes and houses of worship and exchanging our real Bibles for ones that were phony and corrupted?

Flip Wilson, as his cross-dressed character, "Geraldine," used to exclaim, "The devil made me do it!" I'm not with Flip on this one. I think that Caesar ate my Jesus. Each time an elected official made it possible for the rich to exploit the vulnerable, or went to war to "save face," Caesar took a bite. He nibbled away every time a preacher lined his pockets by preaching bigotry, and each time the average Joe and Jane placed their neighbors in harm's way so that they

---

16. Perkins *New Confessions*, 1–3.

could get ahead. American Christianity has been an advocate of nationalism and materialism. At times, the rhetoric of politicians, corporate executives, clerics, and citizens on Main Streets across the land so closely paralleled that of ancient tribal priests presiding over human sacrifice, that it seemed as if the Jesus who was about humility, charity, and mercy was swallowed whole by a greater god.

Who or What is Caesar?

In this book, "Caesar" represents people and institutions who have the power to determine laws, policies, and the distribution of rights, resources, and information. Caesar is not neutral; he operates for the benefit of himself and his associates. Caesar is the personification of imperialism in the material sense, and the colonization of conscience in the psychological and spiritual sense. Caesar always casts himself in a positive light. His agenda may be to fortify national security, expand the economy, bring democracy to the oppressed, or "make America great again." Caesar may use the rhetoric of a pastoral and pious figure, but his actions often betray his lack of empathy for others.

Importantly, everyone has the potential to be Caesar. He wears many faces and might be a celebrity, a journalist, an evangelist, a scientist, a school board member, or a soccer mom. He is of any class, gender, faith, and color. He believes that some human beings are naturally entitled to keep others in a state of ignorance, debt, and fear "for their own good." He is the one ready to use religion to manipulate others, but not to humble and improve himself.

This text argues that Caesar's empire is not the same as the Kingdom of God. That seems obvious, but the point bears repeating. At the Democratic National Convention in 2016, Vice-President Joe Biden declared, "We are America. Second to none. And we own the finish line."[17] The exhilarated crowd roared with approval. The declaration stunned me. If America "owns the finish line," then, where and what is the Kingdom of God?

Caesar is all about empire, and empires are material in nature. They are concerned with the acquisition and management of resources, wealth, and people. When WWII crippled industries in most of the developed world, it left the U.S. relatively unscathed and in a position to dominate global economic and political affairs. To protect its new status, America built hundreds of military bases and nuclear missile silos all over the world.[18] Boomers inherited a nation that had achieved unprecedented power to subdue, destroy, or renew

---

17. Schultheis, "Joe Biden," lines 1–7.
18. Vine, *Base Nation*, 3.

the world. Many believed that God spared the U.S. during the war so that the U.S. could re-build the world anew in its own image.

A society that sees itself as "Christian," or at least as a nation that takes its spirituality and sacred teachings seriously, presents a special problem to those who build and run the empire. The problem is how to assure the faithful that spirituality, sacred teachings, and empire are all compatible. Historically, the state has used religion to win public support for its causes, from wars against Native Americans to modern regime changes. This poses a dilemma for the faithful. For some, living in the empire is a very real crisis. On one hand, they see their loyalty to the state to as injurious to others and their spiritual integrity. On the other hand, they see disloyalty to the state as injurious to their physical security, liberty, and well-being.

Serving Two Masters

The dilemma of maintaining loyalty to two lords is an old one, but it was what boomers—and everyone else—were asked to do. Jesus taught his disciples that nobody can serve two masters without hating one and loving the other, and that one cannot serve both God and mammon.[19] When Jesus was asked the question of whether it was right for the Jews to pay Roman taxes, Jesus replied that people should "Render therefore to Caesar the things that are Caesar's, and to God the things that are God's."[20] As a Catholic kid sitting in Church, I disliked this part of the Gospel because it was ambiguous. It did not specifically enumerate what belongs to Caesar. How were grown-ups—let alone children—supposed to know who owned what? Ultimately, the faithful of each generation are left to activate their consciences and discern for themselves the matter of what belongs to whom.

Some Christians believe that if they lived according to the Gospel in the real world, they would never survive. They argue that "turning the other cheek" would allow terrorists to conquer the nation. They insist selling all that one owns the sake of storing heavenly treasure leaves everyone poor and helpless, and if we become our brother's keeper, we will enable his laziness. Perhaps these assertions are true. Yet, there is plenty of sin to go around. We have done business with terrorists, and created a society in which even those working 40 hours a week cannot afford to support a small family, and in which our elders are neglected and abused.

---

19. Matt. 6:24.
20. Matt: 22:16–21.

When implored to serve two masters, boomers have witnessed and partaken in some of the greatest resistance to Caesar. On matters of race, Caesar directed us to abide by prevailing attitudes and conventions for the sake of social stability. He was supported by Christian white supremacists who challenged the authority of Federal laws by terrorizing civil rights workers and bombing African American churches. Sacred teachings directed us to dissent from these time-honored norms for the sake of decency and justice. Reverend Martin Luther King Jr. (MLK) challenged people to see Christ in the eyes of the segregated and oppressed.[21] On the matter of war, Caesar urged us to smite the enemy in Vietnam. He was enjoined by many Protestant and Catholic clerics alike who felt strongly about ridding the world of communists.[22] Cardinal Francis Spellman was an adamant cold warrior who was instrumental in covert CIA operations in Latin America and fiercely committed to U.S. victory in Vietnam.[23] Many Jews wanted the U.S. to be tough on communism in Vietnam so that it would not creep into the Middle East.[24] Others preached love of one's enemies and charity for the stranger. Dorothy Day, co-founder of the Catholic Workers, preached pacifism.[25]

Boomers received lots of directives about how they should activate faith in the world. Christian Reconstructionists and evangelicals directed Christians to take control of secular government and to create theocracies governed by righteous men until Jesus returned to rule the earth.[26] Theologian Harvey Cox told the faithful that they were part of "God's permanent revolution in history," who were obligated to renew the modern urban environment.[27] Pope Paul VI told Catholics to roll up their sleeves and get busy with work of healing and feeding the world.[28] Jews held that their advocacy of civil rights was grounded in far more than legal principles, and taught that it was the duty of the faithful to respect human rights because all were created in the image of God.[29]

Boomers got double messages. While told that we had to feed the hungry, heal the sick, and tend the poor, we were also told that we deserved the best that temporal life had to offer. While told that we had to glorify democracy, we

21. King, "Why Am I Opposed," 5–14.
22. Quinley, "Protestant Clergy," 45–47.
23. Cooney, *The American Pope*, 231–235; 298–299.
24. Klinghoffer, *Vietnam, Jews, and the Middle East*, 155–56; 212.
25. Roberts, *Dorothy Day*, 164.
26. Martin, *With God on Our Side*, 353–55
27. Cox, *The Secular City*, 206.
28. Paul VI, "Pastoral Constitution," lines 23–32.
29. Henkin, "Judaism and Human Rights," 436–38.

were directed to kill or punish people who freely chose other political systems. As members of temples and churches, we were told to be modest in want, but popular culture constantly told us to consume to our heart's delight.

Boomers learned to obey secular and religious authorities without question. We believed that these leaders were, by virtue of their position, trustworthy and committed to our safety and well-being. Millions of us grew up ignorant of the reality that elected officials, police officers, teachers, and clerics broke laws and abused the vulnerable. It took years before some folks could admit that our authorities engaged in deplorable acts with great regularity. Once we were innocent and called each other liars if somebody said that a policeman, president, or priest was a bad man. That was a long time ago.

Our leaders elevated and then dashed our faith in democracy and in the ideals for which America stood. John F. Kennedy inspired us to advance economic progress locally and abroad. He conveyed the notion that Washington was wholesome and humbly in the service of justice and decency. Richard Nixon urged us to renew law and order. He reached out to Cold War enemies such as China and the Soviet Union. Ultimately, Kennedy's womanizing tainted his image, while the Watergate affair convinced Americans that Washington was a cesspool of men gone mad with ambition. Boomers learned that nice guys could be naughty. They learned that both Kennedy and Nixon relied on mob money and political favors to get elected.[30] They learned that the line between heroes and villains is not always clear, and that we are all susceptible to Caesar's temptations. The ambiguity of the difference between good guys and bad guys had a paralyzing effect on our spirituality. If not our experts, public servants, educated professionals, and clerics, who would help us steady our moral compass?

Boomers from Nazareth

The Gospel of John tells readers that when Philip announced that the one of whom the prophets spoke was Jesus of Nazareth, Nathanial scoffed, "Can anything good come out of Nazareth?"[31] The comment was an insult to the provincial town that had no standing as a center of cultural achievement or political power. Metaphorically, most folks are from Nazareth who are routinely ignored by powerful individuals for lack of high office, fame, or academic credentials. Yet, each generation has a prophetic voice that offers its own unique perspective on the gap between our professed ideals and the way

---

30. Stone, R. *Nixon's Secrets*, 64; 12; 126–27;152–154.
31. John 1:46.

we live. The prophetic often urge us to engage in acts of dissent when the gap between professed ideals and actual conduct becomes unbearable.

Boomers' experiences supply us with narratives about spirituality worth studying. During the Cold War, Americans were taught lots of things about what God wanted from them. They were told to hate Russians because they were atheists. They were told that God wanted regime changes, racial and sexual discrimination, that God blesses capitalism, and wants the U.S. Constitution to be aligned with the Bible. Boomer's experiences teach us that even the most pious among us can be blinded by fear, vanity, power, and greed. They teach us that Caesar cannot always be trusted to tell us the truth, nor can he be relied upon to teach us how to be slow in judgment and critical in thinking.

Some think that it is pointless to talk about spirituality because it leads to unresolvable arguments. Some are embarrassed by their faith and are silent about it. Others approach God by way of public consensus and believe whatever is sanctioned by popular opinion. Lots of boomers I know have given up on serious conversations about spirituality, politics, and public morality because they feel trapped by political correctness. In my own experience growing up Catholic, I learned that the authenticity and vitality of our spirituality depends on our openness to debate, our capacity to feel shame when we have errored, and our willingness to confront conventional wisdom when appropriate. The Second Vatican Council jolted Catholics with the news that God wanted more than a full house at Mass every Sunday. He wanted the faithful to think deeply and engage their consciences. He wanted us to be his eyes, ears, and hands on earth.

Weary of religious controversy and hateful religious rhetoric, many Americans have thrown the spiritual baby out with institutional religion's bathwater. For some, it has become too painful to openly revere God because he has been appropriated by terrorists, pedophiles, fortune-seeking evangelists, and insincere politicians. It is not time to toss the spiritual baby, however, because the stakes are too high.

The argument over the meaning and proper place of religion and spirituality in our lives are still worth having for two reasons. First, human beings by nature question the purpose of existence and the nature of moral conduct. Whether adequate or not, religion remains a source of answers. Second, we live in a world wherein God has been politicized. Over the last several decades, political figures have brought God into the debate about public policies and affairs of state. We now live in a world wherein religious zealots want to create nations "ruled by God," and are willing to kill those who stand in their way. As long as people bring their faith into our civic relationships, we need to know enough about these faiths to speak intelligently about them. Without this, our criticisms are hollow and cheap.

Purpose, Lexicon, and Organization

This book is response to the disillusionment and cynicism that so many baby boomers have experienced. It was inspired by my encounters with peers who are bitterly disappointed in America's secular and religious leaders, and overwhelmed by a strong sense of moral disorientation. As my peers and I approach our last years on earth, lots of us find that we are spiritually troubled. I believe that there is good reason to be troubled by religious zealotry, intolerance, and abuses of authority. I sense, however, that spiritual angst prevails because Americans by definition (or so it seems) are not very quiet, contemplative people. When we apply our mental energy, we typically focus on solving material problems and innovations that will succeed in the market. We do not generally spend hours each day reflecting upon how our egos generate our own misery, nor meditate on channeling God's love in our lives.

The issue at the center of this book is how Caesar, in all his forms, challenges our spirituality and the morality that may proceed from it. It is about crossroad moments when people chose to go along with or to contest Caesar. It is about our struggle to invigorate the Kingdom of God in our lives.

The purpose of this book is to affirm the proposition that our lives have a sacred purpose, and that the purpose has immediate moral implications for our earthly lives. It is intended to prompt reflection on and conversations about the role of spirituality in our private and public lives. This text is also offered to inspire readers to improve their knowledge of themselves and the world, so that they are less likely to be victims of propaganda. This book is not about how to achieve absolute certainty about Jesus' identity, salvation, or God's will. I am still overwhelmed by the mystery of God. I do however, know a little bit about faith and hope and how they are influenced by others. I know what it means to incrementally have a change of heart and to adjust my ways of thinking for the better.

I invite readers to think about their own spirituality, and to examine the conditions they impose on their own love, empathy, fairness, and mercy. This book is offered with hope that readers will think about how American materialism and militarism blur the image of God as they look outside and inside themselves, and how dissent and learning might bring God into better focus.

There are some terms that regularly appear in this text that are used in special ways. References to "the Gospel" in this book regard the known scriptures that document the life and teachings of Jesus of Nazareth. These include texts that are not included in the orthodox canon, such as *Thomas, Andrew, Mary,* and *James*. My treatment of the Gospel shows a preference for a contextual and metaphoric approach to scripture, and recognizes Jesus as a prophetic figure who challenged the letter of the law with the intent of arousing the divinity within us. All biblical references are taken from the *New Oxford Annotated Bible: With the Apocrypha* (RSV) unless otherwise noted.

In this text, spirituality refers to a mystical and sacred property of self that is a source of wisdom and transcending experiences. It represents an intangible glue that binds all of creation and eternity together. It is also an instinctual impulse towards empathy. Spirituality is not the same a "religion," which originates from the concept of being "being bound" to a community or to God in a way that requires conformity to certain rules and rituals.[32] Religion binds people to creeds and allows its highest ranking members to expel others and deny them God's blessing. Spirituality is not the property of religious institutions, yet, historically, it has been both enhanced and corrupted by religious institutions.

The "prophetic voice" in this text is the voice of dissenters and spiritual mentors who call attention to the gaps between our love of God and the way we think and behave. The prophetic voice illuminates hypocrisy and speaks truth to power. Prophetic voices differ from priestly voices, as the priestly voice is the one calling us to serve the letter of the law. The priestly voice is largely the advance guard of manmade institutions, and so serves to justify and augment their authority. The priestly voice often defends prevailing norms long after those norms have proven detrimental to our spirituality.

The organization of the text is both chronological and thematic. Chapter Two takes up the meaning of "the Kingdom of God," which is a vital, re-occurring concept in this text. It is a term that has been and continues to be interpreted in various ways. Each interpretation bears its own moral implications. It is no small matter, then, that certain interpretations have eclipsed others in the long legacy of Christianity. Chapter Three introduces the values and world views that gave us Cold War militarism and nationalism. Subsequent chapters take up specific topics, including: John F Kennedy; the war in Vietnam; dissent; the sexual revolution; the Christian Right; the end of the cold War, and the post-cold War era. The chapters are somewhat chronologically arranged. This book is not a comprehensive survey of American history, but it relies heavily on historical narratives to bring readers into the seminal and pivotal events of the past for a second look their significance from a spiritual perspective. The last chapter offers thoughts about sustaining hope and spirituality.

---

32. "Religion," Online Etymological Dictionary.

This text is not meant to be a comprehensive memoir. I disclose certain memories because they were important in my life. I do not speak for all baby boomers. We all have a spiritual story to tell, so this narrative is only one of millions. Readers will see many references to Catholicism in this text. They are here because Catholicism formed my first beliefs about God and spirituality. Catholicism was my entry point to God and spirituality, but it is not my destination. Like all man-made religious institutions, the Church stands for something that transcends its own doctrines. I believe that there is one God of many revelations and one love with many incarnations. I do not speak for all Catholics. This text is not a plea for religious conversion. With respect to all, I believe that it is better to abandon one's religion in order to recover one's spirituality than to embrace a religion that cripples and corrupts spirituality.

This text is offered with the hope that readers will be moved to participate in the difficult conversations about the role and meaning of spirituality, religion, and morality in our political and secular institutional operations. It is offered with the hope that in exploring boomers' experiences, readers might be inspired to renew their own spirituality. Though Caesar will always be with us and always impose his narrative on the world, it is still possible to activate the love of God in the way we see, hear, feel, think, and live.

2

The Kingdom of Controversy

Pearly Gates and Earthly States

Few theological concepts are more compelling and troublesome than the Kingdom of God. Societies have been willing to kill and die for it. Some have restricted individual liberties and free thinking for the sake of obtaining it. The Kingdom of God is a concept that pre-dates the birth of Jesus of Nazareth. It excited great expectations in ancient Jewish society and continues to arouse passions in the contemporary world. To complicate matters, people have used the terms "Kingdom of God" and "Kingdom of Heaven" interchangeably. Both terms are found in the Gospel, and so challenge theologians to determine the difference. The way people define this complex term has serious implications for how they see the world, themselves, and their moral obligations.

It is easy to project our own ideas onto complex theological terms such as the Kingdom of God, but that approach to sacred texts often leaves readers at the shallow end of the spiritual pool. The Bible uses the term as symbol and metaphor so, literal interpretations are problematic.[1] I was raised to believe that the Kingdom of God is a physical place in the sky, but I do not know for sure if that is the case. Perhaps the most mystical understanding of the Kingdom of God is that it is a disposition and way of life, or the self that remains when the love of God has replaced the ego. Some may argue that this belief is inseparable from the claim that human beings can be made perfect on Earth. I do not believe that, but I do believe that we all can live in, and be an expression of God's grace, even when we are not perfect. I have found that perfection is a slippery slope as it is defined in so many different ways by various authorities.

---

1. Perrin, *Jesus and the Language*, 22–29.

How people see the Kingdom of God matters. When viewed as a heavenly estate reserved only for those who have adopted the "true" creed, the Kingdom loses lots of its mystical qualities and takes on a legalistic essence. It readily lends itself to the projection of zealots who see it as a club for individuals who attach the "will of God" to agendas that are materialistic and imperious.

The Kingdom of God is mentioned in both Hebrew and Christian scriptures. Like many theological terms, its meaning is wrapped in the author's language and the context in which the term was used. It is also flavored by the meaning of metaphors, myths, and symbols widely used by the community that produced the document.

In Hebrew Scriptures, the term "Kingdom of God" appears infrequently, but clearly denotes God's eternal sovereignty over all creation.[2] As residents of the Ancient Near East, the Israelites assimilated existing theologies that characterized gods as keepers of the physical world. In that world, God's sovereignty was not symbolic, it was material. Gods were the source of feast, famine, war, peace, life, and death. The God of Israel was very much like an earthly sovereign, and provided His people with the law. He was a tribal God, and did not extend equal protection to foreign civilizations.

The Jewish hope that God would end the oppression of his people in a summative battle between God and his enemies gave the Kingdom of God a concrete and apocalyptic dimension.[3] Prophets such as Isaiah and Jeremiah articulated the people's yearning for God's final intervention whereupon he would establish an earthly regime led by a descendant of King David. The Kingdom of God in this sense is physical and occupies a specific point in linear time.

The Jewish expectation that God will save his people from his enemies and create the Kingdom of God is central to Jewish literature of the Intertestamental Period, (420 BCE to 30 CE.).[4] This era encompasses the Greek rule of Judea, the Maccabean Revolt, and the Roman conquest of the Jewish Hasmonean Dynasty. As cultures collided in Judea, the Jews confronted the problem of maintaining orthodoxy while being occupied by a polytheistic empire. They also grappled with the challenge of maintaining their faith under the leadership of their Jewish brethren, the Hasmoneans, who many found corrupt.[5] It was during this period that Jewish authors penned the Apocrypha and Qumran writings, popularly known as the *Dead Sea Scrolls*. These texts

---

2. Vanhozzer, et. al, *God's Kingship*, 420–421.
3. O'Neill, "Kingdom of God," 130–141.
4. Ladd, "Kingdom," 169–171.
5. Flusser, *Judaism*, 7–12.

offer thoughts about the Kingdom of God that stray from the notion that it is a realm on earth.

The term "Apocrypha" refers to that which is "secret" or "hidden." The authors are unknown and the texts do not appear in all canons of the Bible. Apocryphal literature is charged with hopes that a messiah will soon deliver the Jews from oppression and wickedness. Roughly 30 percent of the Qumran texts consist of materials that are considered to be biblical, while the remainder consists of writings that represent rabbinic and early Christian writings.[6] Many of the authors of the Dead Sea Scrolls believed that they were living in the time just before the Day of Atonement, and composed revisions of existing Hebrew texts to reflect their eschatological hopes for a messiah who would appear in their lifetime.[7] Some hold that the Apocryphal literature introduces the concept of resurrection and eternal life as a motif for the exaltation of the righteous one who calls the faithful to renew their devotion to God, but who is persecuted and martyred instead.[8] In some respects, the Intertestamental Period was similar to contemporary America, whereby people were ensnared in political power struggles and faced competing theologies regarding the Kingdom of God, the messiah, and salvation.

Some believe the *Dead Sea Scrolls* are the sacred scriptures of the Essenes, a Jewish sect to which John the Baptist may have belonged.[9] The Essenes believed they represented true Judaism, a community undefiled by what they believed was priestly corruption in Jerusalem. They believed the faithful were becoming too worldly, and looked to the coming of God's Kingdom on earth to restore purity of faith. The Essenes practiced baptism, communal living, celibacy, and preached penitence and poverty. They spoke of an "end of time" as the termination of an evil in human history. They believed that the soul, not the body, was eternal, while the Pharisees believed that the righteous would be resurrected in body after death. These sects differed from the Sadducees, who did not believe in life after death, and so did not conceptualize the Kingdom of God as a post-mortem residence.[10]

The Essenes bore their suffering with confidence that the righteous would be rewarded in life after death.[11] They also held that all kings were ordained by God and served God's purpose. The Dead Sea Scrolls refer to an anointed servant who would suffer for the sake of righteousness to make many

---

6. Flint, *Dead Sea Scrolls*, xx-xxi.
7. Eshel, *Dead Sea Scrolls*, 2-3
8. Nickelsburg, *Resurrection, Immortality,* 67-118.
9. Collins, *Lives of Great Religious*, 33-35.
10. Ibid. 35-39.
11. Zeitlin, "Essenes," 102.

righteous, but did not recognize this anointed one as the sacrifice offered for the atonement of the many.[12] As theologian Mary Beavis has observed, the Kingdom of God was conceptualized at the time of Jesus' ministry as something external, yet Jesus speaks of the Kingdom as something internal, and present immediately to those who can comprehend it.[13]

The Gnostic Within

While Pharisees, Sadducees, and Essenes wrestled with matters of the messiah and his kingdom, the philosophical tenants of Gnosticism were seeping into Judaism, and would thus influence early Christian thought. Gnosticism is a world view and philosophical approach to life. Some believe that it contains elements of Eastern religions, such as Buddhism and Persian mysticism.[14] The term "gnosis" refers to "knowledge," more specifically, the *intuitive* knowledge about *the divine within*.[15] Gnosticism proposes that the sacred purpose of humanity is to realize oneness with God. A Gnostic "messiah," therefore, would then be a special prophet or teacher who helped people reach this goal.

The Gnostic Gospels are part of the Nag Hammadi library, which was discovered in an Egyptian cave in 1945. The texts were originally written in Greek and composed between 50 and 400 C.E. They include the Gospels of *Thomas*, *Philip*, *Andrew*, and *Mary*. They contain many of the sayings and stories about Jesus that are found in the four canonical Gospels. They also include material not found in the canon, and often portray Jesus as an enlightened teacher or spiritual guide rather than as a sacrificial lamb offered to pay for the sins of all mankind.

The Gnostic envisioned the Kingdom of God as an aspect of self that has been awakened. One who *knows* is one who intuitively grasps the "reality" that the true self originates in and is one with God, and one who senses the eternity of one's spiritual self.[16] The Kingdom in the Gnostic view is a metaphor for a state of consciousness or psychological disposition towards the world. In the Gospel of *Thomas*, Jesus announces that the Kingdom was not in the sky or in the sea, but rather, It "is within you and it is outside you."[17] In the *Secret Book of James*, Jesus cautions his followers, "Do not allow the kingdom of heaven to

---

12. Collins, 121.
13. Beavis, "Kingdom of God," 105–106.
14. Pagels, *Gnostic Gospels*, xxi-xxii.
15. Ibid. 119-41.
16. Davies, "Christology," 664–665.
17. Meyer, M. W. "*Gospel of Thomas*", 19.

wither."[18] The instruction is similar to the canonical parable about the wheat that falls on rocks, is devoured by weeds, and falls on fertile soil.[19] In the Gnostic view, the Kingdom is something that has to be diligently cultivated, and it is vulnerable to ruin. It is something co-created by God and humanity.

As history reveals, Jesus was a real burr in the theological saddle of Jews who held high hopes for a messiah who would restore the Davidic kingdom. He was not instantly recognized as the harbinger of the Kingdom of God, and his identity was as perplexing as his message. Jesus ministered to a community awash in theological turmoil. The Essenes, Pharisees, and Sadducees quarreled with each other. Greek, and Eastern philosophies creeped into Judaism. The priests called for strict fidelity to Mosaic Law and public atonement for sins, while prophetic voices echoed Amos and Hosea, calling for compassion and justice and an end to the exploitation of the poor by the rich.[20]

Jesus' assaults on religious hypocrisy and defense of the poor and vulnerable were consistent with the prophets. They acknowledged the reality that obedience to the law can conceal a great many sins. One who is fastidious in observing rules and rituals may yet neglect mercy, charity, and justice.[21] Jesus' statements about the Kingdom of God as a dynamic aspect of one's self affirm that those who love God are spiritually and morally transformed.[22] This view of the Kingdom is the essence of baptism or being born again, or having a radical transformation of personhood.

Rabbi Hyman Enelow wrote, "The Jew is a religious being," and observed that the originality of Jesus lay in his insistence that religion be a personal matter, *a state of being* wherein "religion and personality became one."[23] He wrote of Jesus:

> His message was not, 'Make me, or my word, the means of your religion.' It was, 'Let religion be to you and with you what it is to me and with me, a means of personal life, an expression of personal relationship with God, of filial self-identification with God. 'The Kingdom of Heaven,' he said according to the Sayings of Jesus discovered recently, 'is within you . . . [24]

---

18. Meyer, M. W. "The Secret Book of James," 12.
19. Mark 4:3–11.
20. Wiley, *Original Sin*, 17.
21. Matt. 23:13–28.
22. Pagels, *Beyond Belief*, 48–52; Luke 17:20–21; M. W. Meyer, "Secret Book of James," 12.
23. Enelow, *A Jewish View*, 4–6.
24. Ibid., 27.

This is the Jesus that speaks to the transcendent properties of faith, which are so very difficult to translate into institutional formulas and literal language.

John the Baptist's proclamation that "the kingdom of God's is at hand" has been widely interpreted as a signal that God's son had come to earth and it was time for the faithful to repent their sins and get serious about salvation.[25] As a Catholic, I learned that the Kingdom was "at hand" because God had intervened in human history to provide a bridge—Jesus as a sacrificial lamb—between sinful humanity and heaven. Whereas this view holds that God's salvific activity in the world is represented in the sacrifice of his only son, the Gnostic view is that God's salvific activity in the world is human activity that is perfectly aligned with God's love. This is not to say that as a Catholic youngster I was not taught to be good and to do good deeds, but the behavior served as evidence that I embraced the Catholic doctrine on salvation and not evidence that I came to be one with God in a mystical way.

The Jews and Gentiles who heard Jesus' teaching did not always dispute the idea that Jesus represented divine activity in the world, but they fought over what that meant. Jewish and Gentile converts to Christianity brought their own culture to bear on their understandings of the Gospel. Some had political agendas, others were mystical. Jesus' teachings on the Kingdom of God ultimately tore communities apart.[26] For the sake of civil peace and continuity of faith, something had to be done to resolve religious conflict. In the end, conflicts were "resolved" by a priestly elite who institutionalized the idea that the Kingdom of God is celestial real estate to which one has access only if they said so.

Take a Right at Nicaea

The first four centuries of Christianity witnessed scores of violent confrontations between bishops over doctrines concerning the Kingdom, the divinity of Jesus, bodily resurrection, and the authority of clerics. In the end, Roman emperors themselves became entangled in the controversies. From 307 to 391 C.E. emperors from Constantine to Theodosius fought against, negotiated with, maneuvered, exiled, imprisoned, and allied with various Christian bishops who had taken sides against each other on doctrinal matters.[27] The Roman state was compelled to intervene in Christian matters because civil wars, regardless of their basis, weakened the empire.

---

25. Mark 1:15.
26. Rubenstein, *When Jesus Became God*, 1–9.
27. Galvão-Sobrinho, *Doctrine and Power*, 2–3.

Rome had once persecuted Christianity, but as converts increased, the empire had an incentive to legalize it. By the time Constantine became emperor in 306, signs of imperial decline were writ large from east to west. Hostile tribes chewed at Rome's frontiers, citizens revolted against excruciating taxation, government corruption soured public morale, and arguments between religious sects loosened the weave of social cohesion. Constantine's *Edict of Milan*, 313 legalized Christianity, but did not make it the official religion of state, nor did it decide whether Jesus was divine. Some bishops embraced Arianism, the belief that Jesus was a lesser deity than God because he was born after God created all things.[28] Frequent and bloody conflict over the matter necessitated an imperial decision.

Constantine called for the Council of Nicaea in 325, where bishops resolved the Arian controversy with a creed that defined orthodox Christianity. It asserted that: Jesus is of one in being with God, and became man in order to win salvation for all; the dead shall be resurrected and judged; and, that all who accept Jesus' sacrifice on the cross as the atonement for sin will enter the eternal heavenly Kingdom. The emperor approved the creed, but the Arians did not.

As Christians continued to fight, waves of Huns swept across the central Asian steppes. They pushed the Goths deep into Rome's eastern regions, where they made contact with bishops and adopted Christianity. The Roman emperor Valens permitted refugee Goths to live in the empire in exchange for badly needed military service. The arrangement lasted for two years until famine struck. While Goths starved, greedy Roman food brokers set outrageously high prices for food, and triggered a revolt that left Valens dead and the Goths in control of a large portion of the Eastern Roman Empire.[29]

Understanding the urgency for political unity and stability, Theodosius made Christianity the empire's official religion. The *Edict of Thessalonica*, 380 announced that both the Eastern and Western empires would follow the Nicene Creed, and that all bishops in the empire would yield to the unique authority of the Bishop of Rome, the pope. It asserted that all other faiths were "demented" and subject to destruction by the state.[30]

The Nicene Creed established the Church's doctrine regarding the Kingdom of God, but it did not determine which of the many Christian scriptures in circulation were authentic and credible. Since these texts offered a variety of perspectives on Jesus' identity and teachings, there was a need to decide which were aligned with doctrines in the Nicaean Creed and which were heretical.

28. Hanson, R. P. *Search for Christian*, 3–8.
29. Kulikowski, *Rome's Gothic Wars*, 131.
30. Ehler and Morrall, *Church and State*, 6–7.

The Kingdom and the Canon

The biblical canon as we know it today is generally the product of three types of activity. The first was the informal filtering of texts by local churches, whereby materials about Jesus that were deemed "heretical" lost circulation. The second activity was a formal process of approval of existing texts undertaken by several councils of bishops, including: Rome 382; Hippo 393; and Carthage 397, 419. The early Christian community was tasked with determining the authenticity of anonymous works, and with creating a set of teachings that was cohesive in its perspective and regard for Jewish traditions that were ultimately used by Christians to explain Jesus.[31] A third activity concerns the difficult processes of translating and transcribing materials for future generations, which were undertaken before and after the canon was established.[32] By the end of the fifth century, the Catholic Church had a creed, an official canon of scripture, and had established a governing hierarchy led by the pope. It had also declared itself the "one true faith."

The canonical Gospels use both terms the "Kingdom of God" and the "Kingdom of Heaven," and by way of common use, many believe that these terms designate the same thing. As the canon offers more than one image of "the Kingdom," it can be argued that perhaps the Kingdom of God is not necessarily the same thing as the Kingdom of Heaven. The canon does make clear, however, that faith in these Kingdoms must improve the believer's moral conduct.

The canon includes the teaching that the Kingdom of God is within us, which is prominent in the Gnostic Gospels. The modern Catholic Church respects the notion that the Kingdom of God is an integral part of the human person transformed by faith, as is reflected in its teachings during and subsequent to Vatican II that called upon the faithful to activate their faith in tangible ways for the improvement of society.[33] Luke's reference (17:21), however, is somewhat of a Gnostic island in a sea of competing views that focus intensely on the Kingdom of God as something external and exclusive. It is envisioned and as a catch of fish that will be sorted so that the bad will be thrown away and the good salvaged, and as wheat is separated from weeds that will be

---

31. Fredriksen, *From Jesus to Christ*, 5–8.

32. McDonald's *Biblical Canon* studies these processes, and the controversies that attended them.

33. Vatican II was the Second Ecumenical Vatican Council held between 1962 and 1965. For a comprehensive reading of issues and procedures, see O'Malley *What Happened at Vatican II*. In addition, Germillion *The Gospel of Peace and Justice* contains multiple encyclicals on peace, justice, and social responsibility. They inspired many boomers who were involved with the Civil Rights and Anti-war Movements.

burned.[34] The Kingdom imposes obligations to God, and failure to meet these obligations warrants punishment. This is relayed in the parable of the master who takes a journey after leaving talents to his servants. When the master returns, he praises the two servants who multiplied the number of talents, and scorns the foolish servant who buried the talents for safe keeping.[35]

As I child I learned that the Kingdom of God was about my final judgement and whether I was worthy of heaven. The priest and sisters who instructed me at St. Bridget School gave me the impression that Jesus was a sneaky kind of savior. I had to be vigilant every day, or I would get caught in the act of sin and spoil my entire salvation. This was reinforced by the parable of the virgins who missed the wedding banquet as their lamps ran out of oil while they waited for the groom.[36] Orthodox Christian teachings of the Kingdom of God require the faithful to accept Jesus' crucifixion as the sacrifice that redeemed mankind, and the resurrection as evidence that Jesus is Lord and has conquered death. Lots of Christians never get beyond the literal interpretation of these events, and regard the more mystical interpretations as heresy. Paradoxically, heretical teachings sometimes illuminate very meaningful things about the mystery of our sacred purpose and being one with God.

The Cross and the Kingdom

The spectacular assertions that Jesus was literally God, let himself be murdered, and then physically rose from the dead for the purpose of redeeming mankind has aroused much skepticism. Historians are confident that a person known as Jesus lived in ancient Judea during the early first century, was a teacher, and was executed. Yet, even at the time of his trial and crucifixion, Jesus own disciples were perplexed about the meaning of the ordeal.

The canonical Gospels make clear that the disciples were troubled by Jesus' arrest and compliance with his executioners. When the Sanhedrin arrived to incarcerate Jesus, Peter himself drew a sword in protest.[37] At that time, he appears to have no awareness that Jesus' arrest might be part of God's plan to redeem the world. When Jesus was tried and condemned to death, the disciples withdrew from him in fear for their own lives. They did not stand beside Jesus confident that they were standing on holy ground or the moral side of a conflict. Further, Peter denied knowing Jesus, and none of the ca-

---

34. Matt. 13:26–43; 47.
35. Matt. 25:14–30.
36. Matt. 25:1–13.
37. John 18:10.

nonical Gospels report that the disciples gathered at the cross to honor their murdered rabbi. In the aftermath of the crucifixion, the disciples struggled to understand its meaning. Like other prophets, their Jesus was dead. What did his death mean in light of his teachings?

For Catholics, the assertion that the cross is literally the altar upon which Jesus died for the remission of sins is a source of real shame. On more than one occasion, I sat through Masses and Stations of the Cross during the season of Lent, thinking to myself that salvation was somewhat futile. I was never going to be worthy of heaven. The game was rigged. Jesus was born perfect; I was not. He was God; I was not. I quietly rebelled and argued to myself, "If I am such a terrible person, and my sins are so bad that Jesus had to get beaten and nailed to a cross, then why was I created in the first place?"

The nuns and priests told me and my classmates that Jesus would help us achieve perfection, and that the Holy Spirit would make us strong. So, on I went into a world where I knew I would combat sin every day, regularly lose the battle, go to confession, say my prayers, and start the fight all over again. The cross was where things got personal with me and Jesus. The cross was required because of "original sin," and the best I could hope for was that Jesus would find my repentance sincere and my efforts to imitate his goodness sufficient. Yet, regardless of how well I did, I would, by nature, be a sinner—a creature that by design could not achieve enlightenment and so had to settle for salvation—a kind of spiritual bailout.

Like my mother, who was pious in many ways, I felt that I owed Jesus some time on the cross. As a kid I put pebbles in my shoes and learned to endure physical pain to prove my devotion to God. I offered headaches and menstrual cramps to Jesus. As a child, it was difficult to look at the crucifix and avoid my own indictment: "*Look at how he suffers! How could you do that to poor Jesus?*" I prayed for the courage to accept my own martyrdom should it be necessary. I thought that there was no greater insult to God than to reject the sorrowful son of God, whose head was crowned with thorns and whose hands and feet were pierced by thick and heavy nails. I believed that each time I disobeyed God, I was hurting Jesus all over again. The cross seemed to damn me at the same time it redeemed me.

Had the theology of creation been different, we might have been taught that we were born in a state of grace. Had Christianity emerged in a different place and time, I might have been taught that I need not feel cursed because I was born human. This would not have eliminated the value of Jesus, but it would have cast his teachings, death, and resurrection into new light.

While the Gnostics held that Jesus was spiritual and messianic in in the way of an enlightened teacher, they did not think that he suffered and died for the forgiveness of sin. Gnostics had no concept of original sin. In the *Mary*, Jesus tells his disciples that sin is nonexistent, and that only when they *act in discord* with their nature do they commit what were known as sins.[38] This suggests that Jesus's message was at least in part about rousing his follower's awareness that they were by nature a part of God and eternity, and as such were by divine nature not sinful, but *chose* to be sinful.

The Gnostics held that mankind was ensnared in the material world, which was evil, and so needed a savior from the spiritual realm who could light the path to illumination in the spirit world. Gnostics regarded Jesus as that kind of savior.[39] Some Gnostics even believed that Jesus's death on the cross was "apparent" but not "real," as Jesus never fully took human form."[40] In the *Second Treatise of the Great Seth*, Jesus indicates that he died in appearance only, and was laughing at his executioners' ignorance.[41] This view was ultimately condemned as heresy as it posited that Jesus' human form was an illusion. Heresy aside, this mockery of death underscores the theological proposition that the spirit is immortal and thus, in the mystical sense, that death itself is an illusion. The mysticism of Jesus' willingness to accept the cross lies partially in the assertion that one cannot kill what is eternal and non-material in essence.

Mythologist Joseph Campbell opined that Jesus went to the cross not because God demanded ransom for humanity's sins, but because he accepted the consequences that befall people who are so thoroughly wedded psychologically and spiritually to the Kingdom of God, that their physical existence is a rather marginal experience. Jesus, he argued, was so completely one with the spirit world, that negotiating with Caesar for his life was ridiculous.[42]

Campbell suggests that Jesus' was aware that the essence of his faith could not be contained in, expressed by, or governed by law. Campbell rejected the idea that Jesus was a blood offering to atone for sins, and replaced it with the idea that Jesus welcomed his crucifixion as a man who would rather die than espouse politically correct doctrines that had no spiritual authenticity. What was rendered to Caesar on the cross was his physical flesh. What was rendered to God was his mind, will, soul, and eternal spiritual essence—and that was rendered long before the Romans arrested him.

As a metaphor for what happens to the ego once the individual has given oneself over to God, the cross connotes a level of spirituality that anyone, not

38. Roukema, *Jesus, Gnosis, and Dogma*, 82.
39. Pagels, *Gnostic Gospels*, 129–131.
40. Yamauchi, "Crucifixion," 7.
41. Robinson, *Nag Hammadi*, 154.
42. Campbell, *Hero's Journey*, 155.

just Jesus, can achieve. The idea that Jesus was not God incarnate, but someone who achieved a form of enlightenment had already been floated in the first century. It reappeared in the work of Walter Rauschenbusch, the nineteenth century architect of the Social Gospel, who claimed that Jesus' identity was an "achievement" and not "an effortless inheritance."[43] Like all mortals, he argued, Jesus had to struggle with temptation and moral options, and learn from mistakes. From this perspective, Judaism is Jesus' entry point to God and his destination point was oneness with God.

This theological scenario differs from the one I inherited, which posits that Jesus was always one with God, but took human form long enough to preach and be executed. I knew as a child that if I questioned Jesus' divinity, the nuns might skid right off their kneelers and have to work overtime to correct my apostasy. As a child the Jesus who was also God seemed brotherly and friendly until somebody made a mistake, and then he became the mercurial judge who sent sinners to the fiery furnace of hell. It seemed odd that a God who created all people out of love would burn people for eternity because they struggled with orthodoxy.

Philosopher Thomas Sheen argues that the scandal of Jesus' trial and execution was not that the prophet was killed, but that the disciples lost faith in what he proclaimed.[44] Their failure to embrace the eternity that the crucified Jesus represented, and their lack of faith in eternal life locked the disciples in fear. As reported in the Acts of the Apostles, the threat of arrest and execution initially paralyzed their ministry. This allegedly changed after Peter's epiphany and the apostles' Easter experience.

Resurrection and the Kingdom

Historians have documented the ministry and crucifixion of Jesus, but the matter of resurrection relies only on Christian texts recorded long after Jesus' death. Early followers of Jesus were troubled by Jesus' death and its implications for Jesus' teachings about the Kingdom of God. Jesus had not accomplished what the Jews expected the messiah to accomplish, yet the he personified the essence of Jewish teachings which fervently embraced the notion that the people were always in the presence of God. What narrative would compel others to follow Jesus as did those who knew him and welcomed him as a fulfillment of the prophets?

---

43. Rauschenbusch, *Theology*, 151.
44. Sheehan, *The First Coming*, 102–03.

Orthodox teaching holds that Jesus rose from the dead, appeared to his disciples over the course of 40 days, and then was physically assumed into heaven. The canonical Gospels report that Mary Magdalene was first to see the risen Jesus, and in Luke, the risen Jesus appears to Peter.[45] After Jesus' death, Peter and other disciples see Jesus while fishing at the Sea of Galilee.[46] The Acts of the Apostles report that Jesus made frequent appearances after his resurrection. The New Testament canon presents these appearances as literal and concrete, not metaphoric. The Gnostic version of events is different. In *Mary*, Mary Magdalene sees Jesus in a vision, which is consistent with the Gnostic understanding of resurrection as a spiritual event rather than a physical one.[47] The Gnostics held that spiritual maturity enabled individuals to see the mysticism of the resurrection, and that not all who had known Jesus were capable of that level of understanding.[48]

The resurrection narrative was a late addition to the canonical Gospels that were written 30 to 70 years after Jesus' death.[49] During that time, members of the Jesus movement within Judaism were deciphering Jesus and his message. Christianity had already begun to take form before the matter of Jesus' resurrection was "resolved" by way of institutional doctrine. Orthodox Christianity teaches the resurrection narrative as a historical event, but others argue that the resurrection narrative was a means of coming to grips with the cognitive dissonance that swept over the disciples in the wake of Jesus' death.[50] The decision to define the resurrection as a physical event rather than a metaphoric event helped Jesus' followers justify their confidence that he was the messiah who would eventually establish an earthly kingdom, even though that earthly kingdom was not immediately forthcoming.

The Church's doctrine on resurrection had a political function and it ultimately paved the way for Caesar to subordinate spirituality to his own agenda. By placing Peter in the physical presence of the risen Jesus and declaring his conversion to the notion that Jesus was indeed the son of God whose death made it possible for sinners to enter the eternal Kingdom of God after death, the Catholic Church gave Peter a tremendous amount of authority. It gave Peter and his heirs a dominant role in how Jesus and his message would interpreted for thousands of years. By way of having contact with the physically risen Jesus, Peter represents a tangible link between the messiah in heaven and

---

45. Luke 24:12–31.
46. John 21:1–18.
47. Pagels, *Gnostic Gospels*, 11–17.
48. Ibid., 22–27.
49. Koester, *Introduction*, 64–65.
50. Jackson, H. "Resurrection Belief," 422–25.

the faithful on earth. Early Church patriarchs and their Catholic successors held that only those who meet Peter's criteria will be regarded as legitimate evangelists. They also reserved the priestly right to define the Kingdom of God, its allies, and its enemies.

Peter's Paradigm

The Catholic Church believes that its authority is derived from Peter. Because of Peter's faith, Jesus gave Peter the keys to the Kingdom of Heaven and announced that Peter is the rock upon which Jesus will build his church. Jesus added that whatever Peter would bind on earth would also be bound in heaven.[51] In the Catholic tradition, all popes are descendants of Peter and thus inherit the keys to the Kingdom. This understanding of religious authority creates a paradigm—which I call "Peter's paradigm"—that places a human institution between God and the faithful. It is an old paradigm of faith, one that similar to the religion of the Pharisees. It is a paradigm that is given to legalism and disinclined to regard the Kingdom of God as a metaphor. It is a paradigm that has serious implications for how the faithful interpret and articulate their spirituality in the world.

Peter's paradigm relies on religious authorities to guard the faith against heresy, preside over institutional rituals, and perpetuate the one true faith by ordaining only those in step with institutional doctrines. The priestly class act as "middle men" between the individual and God. They have the power to forgive or not forgive sins, and to withhold the sacraments from the faithful under certain conditions. Peter's paradigm holds that when speaking on matters of faith and morals, the pope is infallible.

Peter's paradigm is at ease with behaviors that Jesus did not exhibit, including the administration of capital punishment to those who offended God or his representatives. Indeed, Peter's judgment had lethal effects. Readers learn in the Acts of the Apostles that the disciples and their followers lived in a communal arrangement that required the wealthy to sell their possessions so that all might live equally. Peter was especially adamant about this. When a man named Ananias deceived Peter and withheld a parcel of land, Peter confronted him and the man died on the spot. Peter then interrogated the man's wife, Saphhira, who had conspired with her husband to "test the Spirit of the Lord," and she too instantly fell dead.[52] The fate of Ananias and Saphhira is bewildering in light of Jesus' instruction to Peter that he forgive sinners not

---

51. Matt. 16:13–20.
52. Acts 5:1–10.

seven times, but "seventy times seven."[53] There is no record in the canonical Gospels that anyone died as a result of being confronted by Jesus with his or her sins. Rather, they were forgiven and restored to the community.

Peter's paradigm endows the priestly class with an exalted social position, which the disciples sometimes exploited. On one occasion, members of the community drew attention to the neglect of the widows and bid Peter to assist in the distribution of food for them. The twelve apostles then directed others to attend the matter, telling them that, "It is not right that we should give up preaching the word of God to serve tables."[54] This response lacks the humility that Jesus expressed in his ministry as exemplified when he washed his disciples' feet.[55] It flies in the face of Jesus' teaching that those who are sincere about following him should be servant to all.[56] Not long after Jesus' departure, elitism in the Christian community was alive and well.

Peter's paradigm is concerned with rule and conformity. It is skeptical of the unsupervised conscience. It does not trust that a person could become one with God, as was suggested by Gnostics. In Peter's paradigm, the truth flows from the top down, from the executives in the institution's hierarchy to the masses below. Therefore, the faithful know the spirit because they have been instructed on what "spirit" means. The faithful are fortified in spirit not by awakening to a divine essence in their own person, but because they partake in the sacramental life of the institution. It is no surprise that for centuries Catholics wallowed in superstitions, for, without understanding mysticism and metaphor, the physical elements of rituals and sacraments themselves become endowed with supernatural powers.

Peter's paradigm often justifies the perpetuation of manmade, cultural norms at the expense of articulating love. It is vulnerable to cultural biases, hysteria, and human ignorance. Peter's paradigm made possible the persecution of "witches," the condemnation of Galileo in 1633 who dared assert that the universe was heliocentric, and blaming the Jews for the plague. Peter's paradigm prevails each time the faithful elevate the letter of the law above the spirit of the law. It is what Jesus confronted when he excoriated the high priests for their love of high office, their obsession the letter of the law, and their neglect of those in need.[57] It triumphs when religious authorities excommunicate, humiliate, or deny sacraments to those who call attention to the

53. Matt. 18:21–22.
54. Acts 6:1–3.
55. John 13:1–17.
56. Mark 9:35.
57. Matt. 23:1–39.

gap between the religious institution's professed love of God and the policies it advocates.

The canonical letters of the apostles that follow the Gospels confirm that Peter's paradigm has less of a quarrel with the state and cultural norms than with the individual's condition of sin. Paul admonished slaves to obey their masters, and directed women to obey their husbands.[58] He declared that the faithful should obey civic authorities, and that those who "resist what God has appointed" will "incur judgment."[59] Christianity's first evangelicals emphasized the need for the faithful to wage a personal war against sin. They did not urge the faithful to establish a theocracy. Even when Rome executed hundreds of Christians, the faithful astonished Caesar by welcoming martyrdom as an expression of their devotion to God and their rejection of the state's religion.[60]

Peter's paradigm raises the question of whether the faithful are right in following their consciences and spiritual intuitions in order to bring the Kingdom of God to bear on earth, or whether they ought to obediently conform to the directives of institutional authorities. The dilemma is not an easy one. Peter's paradigm offers the faithful a formula for salvation, clear rules, and a sense of moral certainty. Yet, it is vulnerable to the opinion of religious leaders who abuse their authority and yet are enshrined in a mystique that causes people to accept their opinions without question. On the other hand, one's conscience is sacred; it where our dialogue with God takes place. Yet, conscience is also vulnerable to the limits of one's understanding of matters and to egotistical interests.

Boomer Catholics have known Peter's paradigm and Gnostic perspectives. The Catholicism of my parents' generation was steeped in Peter's paradigm, and yet, especially after Vatican II, it called upon the faithful to bring the Kingdom of God to bear on social and political matters. Vatican II celebrated and encouraged people to use their conscience, which often placed Catholics in conflict with those who strictly obeyed the rules. Ultimately, the Church embraces both views of the Kingdom, so what's the fuss?

The problem is that Caesar has so often insisted on Peter's paradigm, even when it justifies war, discrimination, and hatred. The problem is that Caesar readily associates his agenda with God's even when it causes homelessness, hunger, illness, and injustice. The problem is that so many religious people believe that when Caesar tells us that our nation and way of life is so superior to others, they need not question the veracity and spiritual implications of such claims.

---

58. Col. 3:22; Eph. 5:22.
59. Rom. 13:1–7.
60. Bowersock, *Martyrdom & Rome*, 1–4.

Boomer's experiences reveal that Caesar's material ambitions often called upon the faithful to believe things about others that were not true, and to serve his agenda on the threat that our material world and national security would come tumbling down if we did not. Boomer's experiences also teach us that some of America's greatest moments occurred when dissenters challenged Caesar with their prophetic voices and civil disobedience. These stories offer some insights to the good we may do when we see the world for what it is, see ourselves for who we are, and open our hearts and minds to the possibility that we are Kingdom of God embodied if we want to be.

3

The Military Industrial Crucifix

God's Cold War

IN THE AFTERMATH OF WWII, the United States was poised to dominate the world's economic and political landscapes. It had emerged relatively unscathed by enemy occupation and carpet bombing, and it had lost roughly 350,000 lives—a mere fraction when compared to the tens of millions lost by the Soviet Union, Germany, Japan, and others. Many regarded the U.S. victory over Japanese and Nazi imperialism as proof that America's way of life, government, and economic system were favored by God.

The U.S. had established itself as a superpower in 1945, yet there remained one diabolical menace to God-loving civilization, and that was communism. For the next 46 years, the U.S. led its Western allies in the Cold War against communism wherever it existed. The Cold War was fought with an arms race, a space race, propaganda, and military interventions across the globe. It consumed billions of dollars that might have been used for education, health care, and other public services. It consumed millions of lives and compromised the trust that other nations had reflexively placed in America. Whether we spent our fortunes to preserve our lives, or whether we spent our lives to preserve our fortunes remains for historians to debate.

The conservative and militant posture Americans took toward communism during the Cold War represents a convergence of three beliefs deeply engrained in American thought long before the Soviets occupied nations behind the Iron Curtain. The first belief was America's conviction that the U.S. had a divine and salvific role to play in history. The Puritan announcement that the new society in America would be a "city on a hill" that radiantly exemplified

Christian virtue to the world, is among America's most enduring myths.[1] The second belief was that Marxist theory was inherently evil and misguided. Protestants, Catholics, and Jews joined the anti-communist crusade, each pointing to some theological or philosophical deficit in Marxist theory and practice.[2] Lastly, Americans believed in sacrificial realism, or the notion that in order to create a more perfect world, we must prune from the tree of civilization branches that are diseased and life-threatening.

The story of sacrifice is an old narrative, one that is found in sacred scriptures and myths around the world. This narrative is part of the human psyche, even if we are not conscious of it. Lots of boomers dutifully stood by Caesar during the Cold War with confidence that laying our lives on the line and taking other lives was the way to protect decency from atheistic depravity. The sacrifice of human life, however, seemed on many occasions to render unto Caesar things that did not belong to him and to undercut the very democratic principles we espoused. It also seemed to contradict the claim to being a Christian nation.

Abraham, Isaac, and America

The sacrifice narrative is central to the Judeo-Christian tradition. In Genesis, readers find the *Aqedah*, "the binding of Isaac," where, acting on God's will, Abraham is poised to kill his only son.[3] In the ancient world, human sacrifice was common, and so readers do not find Abraham protesting God's request.[4] Angry and vain gods needed to be fed and appeased for the sake of an abundant harvest or protection from one's enemies. To withhold sacrifice was an act of ingratitude and defiance. The blood offering was pragmatic as it was chiefly concerned with the physical survival of a people. Abraham took his knife in hand to prove his devotion to God. At the last minute, an angel from God intervened. Abraham was found pleasing to God, and so Isaac was spared. The meaning of this ancient episode is often debated, but it is hard to deny that it remains an archetype in modern American thought.

I was taught that Abraham's story signaled a shift in God's regard for human life. In exchange for Abraham's unyielding loyalty to the "one true God," God saved Isaac, who got to live and procreate, thus fulfilling God's promise

---

1. Gamble, *In Search*, 3–6.

2. Hertzog's *Spiritual-industrial Complex* documents how religion was drawn into the war against communism and was influential in foreign policy-making during the early years of the conflict.

3. Genesis 22:1–19.

4. McCarthy, D., "Symbolism of Blood," 166–68.

to Abraham that he would be the father of a great nation. The lessons from my youth about Abraham and Isaac emphasized how God's intervention made the Israelites special. They were allowed to flourish because as they were chosen to tell the world about their God. There are alternative interpretations to the story.

Philosopher Omri Boehm argues that Abraham took an ethical stand and disobeyed God.[5] He shifts the story from one in which God is testing Abraham to a story in which Abraham is testing God by asserting *his understanding* of the sacredness of life. Theologian Ronald Green observed that, "Although Judaism is unquestionably an ethical tradition based on the divine command, it is also a tradition of human autonomy and reason."[6] Abraham's test concerned his moral judgment and whether he would suspend his ethical reasoning if to act obediently meant annihilating his own flesh and blood.

The idea that a society must make sacrifices in order to do God's will is firmly fixed in the American psyche. Such sacrifices are often literal, and not metaphoric for our commitment to ethical reasoning. Americans do not always speak of sacrifice to "do God's will," but we do speak of sacrifice in order to achieve "a greater good." Many who cherish the Bible's teaching cherish the idea that the world can be made into a better place by killing political enemies, terrorists, and people who commit heinous crimes. There are, however, key differences between the *Aqedah* and notions of sacrifice that have prevailed since the Cold War.

Isaac does not play the same role in American mythology as he did in the biblical sense. In the Genesis narrative, Abraham's offering of Isaac's life would bring nothing to the Lord of all creation who was already all powerful and without want. Jewish tradition holds that Isaac is a symbol of martyrdom that is spiritually, and not materially sanctifying. This is not the case with Caesar. In worldly empires, Caesar calls for citizens to sacrifice their lives to defend a way of life, property, and wealth. To "defend a way of life" is to fight for resources and privileges to which a society feels entitled. In addition, God called Abraham to sacrifice his own son, and not the sons of others. Caesar routinely calls upon us to sacrifice the lives of others *and ourselves*. In the theological sense, Isaac plays a role in God's test of Abraham's devotion which is not destined to be tragic.[7] In Caesar's world, Isaac dies, or is obliterated economically, for he is in Caesar's world a mere object and a means to a material end.

The sacrifice narrative is key to the way many see the world. Readers of the Hebrew Scriptures find God smiting the enemies of his chosen people.

---

5. Boehm, "Child Sacrifice," 155–56.
6. Green, R. "Abraham, Isaac," 1.
7. Coats, "Abraham's Sacrifice," 389–400.

Yahweh did not behave as if war was evil. As scholars have observed, the commandment, "thou shalt not kill," was not a general prohibition against killing, but against certain kinds of killing, like taking of innocent life for personal gain.[8] The messiah that the Jews, and later Christians, expected would sweep away Israel's foes and establish a new kingdom. Thus, war was a way to sanctification and restoration. Jesus, however, offered no evidence that he would or wanted others to take up arms against their enemies. This has challenged the faithfuls' thinking about war. Are the faithful to take up the sword as did the patriarchs of ancient Israel, or are they to sheath their swords as Jesus directed Peter to do in the Garden of Gethsemane?

Just War

The Just War theory retains the notion that war can be sanctifying and restorative. It argues that when societies are confronted with evil so great that it threatens the lives and well-being of others, the people are justified in using physical violence to protect themselves.[9] The Catholic doctrine of Just War asserts that in order to engage mortal combat, threats to society must be very serious, long-range, and imminent. The Church also insists that all other options for conflict resolution have been attempted, that war must not replace one evil with another, and that there exists a strong chance of success.[10] Catholic doctrine also forbids wars of offense, wars for imperial ends, pre-emptive strikes, and the use of nuclear weapons. The Just War Theory does not resolve all controversies regarding the right interpretation of such things as "serious threats," "long-range," and "evil." However imperfect, Just War principles reject wars of conquest and war without restraint.

America waged many wars during the boomer's lifetime, but whether they were "just" is questionable. Some wars were confined to propaganda and bribery. Some involved coups and assassinations. During the Cold War the U.S. sought to make the world in its own image. Democratic process were no good unless they produced foreign leaders that met with Caesar's approval. In 1948 the Central Intelligence Agency (CIA) manipulated the outcome of balloting by purchasing votes, disseminating propaganda, and recruiting priests to spy on socialist candidates in Italy.[11] It was the beginning of a long history of Caesar's covert interventions in world affairs.

---

8. Solomon, "Judaism and Ethics of War," 295–98.
9. Ramsey, "The Just War," 8–22.
10. National Conference of Catholic Bishops, "The Challenge," 2–4.
11. Weimer, *Legacy of Ashes*, 29–30.

Caesar graduated to the next level by forcing legally elected national leaders from office. In 1951 Mohammed Mosaddeq, the democratically elected leader of Iran, was forced from office by the CIA. Mosaddeq wanted to nationalize the oil industry so that profits would flow to Iranians who struggled to build a modern nation. Investors in the Anglo-Persian Oil Company seethed with resentment, calling Mosaddeq "Moscow's puppet."[12] The coup brought the autocratic Pahlavi dynasty to power and seeded Iranian resentment of the U.S. that culminated in the 1979 revolution. Seeking to improve the distribution of wealth generated by his nation's resources, Jacobo Arbenz Guzman planned to nationalize land held by United Fruit. The company was a Rockefeller enterprise that had plantations all over Latin America, holding at one point 42 percent of tax-free Guatemalan land while leaving thousands of acres uncultivated.[13] The CIA coup left hundreds of Guatemalans dead, and landless peasants went hungry in a land of agricultural abundance.[14]

Caesar's conduct was not new. The U.S. had, after all, taken Hawaii by force and muscled its way across North America by killing Native Americans and placing them on reservations. During the Cold War, Caesar told Americans that the Soviets were poised to conquer the world, enslave the masses, and impose atheism if America did not act. Cold War doctrine taught my peers and I that it was better to be dead than red. For God and righteousness to prevail, somebody had to die. The Isaac that is bound for death in order to verify allegiance to a higher power and consent to that power's agenda is the one frequently referenced in this text.

During the Cold War, clergy from all religious denominations told Americans that God was a cold warrior. Reverend Reinhold Niebuhr, a popular Protestant theologian and spokesperson for realism in the early Cold War era, declared that, "the so-called free world must cover itself with guilt in order to ward off the perils of communism."[15] He believed that to sustain moral order in the world, decent societies had to do indecent things. So onward the faithful marched, resolved that if they bloodied their hands for a good cause, God would forgive them in the end.

---

12. Ibid., 92–105.

13. Schlesinger and Kinzer's *Bitter Fruit* provides a stark look at the intricacies of the U.S. led coup against Arbenz, while G. Colby's *Thy Will Be Done* examines the role of Rockefeller and the Christian missions that did his bidding throughout Latin America.

14. In 1954, two percent of the Guatemalan population held seventy-two percent of the land, and prior to the 1952 reforms, eighty percent of Guatemala's arable land was unused. Much of it was in the hands of American corporations, as noted in Gordon's "A Case History of Subversion."

15. Niebuhr, *Irony*, 4.

Truman and God

Most of the history lessons I received in my youth and college years left students with the impression that America's course of action during the Cold War was inevitable. The parade of events, speeches, treaties, and policies seemed to have a pre-ordained quality about them, and conveyed the notion that the U.S. instinctively pursued the right path with little need for debate. I often had the feeling that America's preeminence in the world was pre-destined, and it was futile to argue that the U.S. way of life was injurious to others because as a Christian and democratic nation, we somehow floated above decadence and vice.

One of Caesar's first assault on boomer's spirituality thus came in the form of our orientation to the world. Caesar taught us as youngsters barely able to read that America was the center of civilization and that God said so. Each morning at St. Bridget School, I stood with my classmates and said our prayers. Next, we stood with our eyes fixed on the American flag and recited the Pledge of Allegiance. These were daily rituals for eight years of my life. Children do not automatically grasp the important differences between God's will and Caesar's will, especially when the salute to the flag declares that we are "one nation under God." God and country were intertwined in my grade school mind. They blended like the marbling of vanilla and chocolate cake stirred together in one pan. One could not eat one and not the other.

Caesar's nationalism was not reserved for children learning to obey the law and assimilate a sense of national identity. Throughout the Cold War people of all ages were subjected to indoctrination that placed God on the same level as country. Thus, our obligations to the state became obligations to God. America's first Cold War president, Harry Truman, frequently reinforced the notion that God was unequivocally on America's side. His speeches and actions sometimes left the impression that the American God was very much like the bellicose and jealous God of ancient Israel.

President Truman did not trust the Soviets, nor believe it was noble to collaborate with them. He held that the best way to check Soviet expansion was by way of containment and collective defense.[16] He staunchly supported the North American Treaty Organization (NATO), initiated a pattern of robust military spending that went on even in times of peace, created the CIA and endowed it with a wide latitude of permission to conduct covert operations, and refused to collaborate with Soviets for the sake of balancing atomic power and deterring aggression. He did this in good Christian faith.

---

16. Spalding, *First Cold Warrior*, 24–32.

Religion was not incidental to Harry Truman. Though he engaged very little in formal religion, he prayed daily and relied on his Christian teachings to inform the ethical codes necessary for statecraft.[17] For Truman, the Cold War was a moral conflict. To advance the virtues of democracy and capitalism, he supported media campaigns, such as the *Voice of America*—a radio broadcast across the Iron Curtain. He culled the support of religious leaders who roused the faithful to fight communism, and appointed an ambassador to Vatican City, which solidified the diplomatic alliance between the Catholic Church and Washington.

Truman explicitly said that the Cold War was a Christian crusade. In his 1949 inauguration speech he stated that communism believed violence was the way to correct social problems, and that it rejected the idea that individuals have the moral and intellectual ability to govern themselves.[18] The Cold War, in Truman's mind, was noble not only because America championed democracy, but because it sought the material well-being of those in want and advocated freedom of worship. Truman opined that people can build a good society "if they follow the will of the Lord."[19] He said that, "We are under divine orders—not only to refrain from doing evil, but also to do good and to make this world a better place."[20] He denounced communism as a "terrible fanaticism," that "denies the existence of God," and stated that while we may not know the purpose of God, it is the nation's duty to fight for peace and the moral codes that separate it from communism.[21] Boomers were thus suckled with the paradox that peace was something won by war.

While addressing clergy gathered in Washington in the fall of 1951, Truman declared that "the whole human enterprise" was in danger, and that America's duty was to help preserve "a world civilization in which man's belief in God can survive."[22] He balanced his anti-communist rhetoric with cautionary instruction, stating that the nation must "struggle to maintain civil liberties," remain "open for self-criticism," and not be "led astray by self-righteousness."[23] It was a prophetic statement in some respects, but also hypocritical. At the time, racial segregation was enforced by law and lynching, and the U.S. was already on the road to Vietnam and the horror that would call for the sacrifice of so many innocent Isaacs.

17. Ibid., 205–208.
18. Truman, "Inaugural," paragraphs 12–20.
19. Truman, "Address in Spokane," paragraphs 8–9.
20. Truman, "Address at the Cornerstone," paragraph 9.
21. Ibid., paragraph 10.
22. Truman, "Address to the Washington," paragraph 26.
23. Ibid.

Truman's crusade against communism was not without moral compromise. The U.S. recognized that to restore Europe's economy and democracy, it had to include Germany. This required the "de-Nazification" of Germany. To this end, the U.S. assisted the allies with constructing a new German government and constitution, and prosecuted Nazi officials for war crimes and crimes against humanity. Complete de-Nazification, however, was nearly impossible. So many Germans had Nazi affiliations that to ban them all from public office would deprive Germany of the civil servants needed to run the nation. It was also difficult for Truman to ignore the reality that the U.S. needed European allies to halt Soviet expansion, and that many former Nazis were some of the best scientists and highly skilled spies in the world. These former Nazis were valuable assets in the battle against communism, and so, in step with political realism, Truman's administration relaxed its resolve to punish all former Nazis. Over 700 Nazi scientists who produced rockets, developed chemical weapons, and researched atomic energy were relocated to the U.S. where their services were applied in America's Cold War projects. Hundreds more were hired by the U.S. to spy on communists in Europe.[24]

Truman's affection for God and Christian morality did not lessen his desire to make the U.S. the mightiest nuclear force on the planet, nor to punish those who dissented from this objective. In October, 1945, he met with Robert Oppenheimer, "father of the atomic bomb," who was among a cadre of scientists who had serious moral concerns about the new weapon and a U.S. monopoly of the device. Like many others who created the bomb, Oppenheimer understood the horror of WWII's aerial carpet bombing, in which hundreds of thousands of civilians died as napalm incinerated their cities. He had already expressed his view that, "there was something wrong with a country where no one questioned that."[25]

Oppenheimer confided to Truman that he was remorseful about the use of atomic bombs against Japan, and felt as though he had "blood on his hands." Truman steamed that Oppenheimer was a "cry baby scientist," and scoffed, "Blood on his hands, dammit, he hasn't half as much blood on his hands as I have. You just don't go around bellyaching about it."[26] He said of Oppenheimer that he "never wanted to see that son of a bitch again."[27] For

---

24. Jacobson's *Operation Paperclip* and Lichtblau's *The Nazis Next Door* reveal the extent to which the U.S. used Nazis in its intelligence operations and what moral and legal obstacles had to be overcome to do so. Readers may also note that U.S. banks and industries invested heavily in Hitler's Germany following WWI and that many who did so had sympathy for Nazi ideologies, as noted in Black's *Nazi Nexus*.

25. Bird and Sherwin, *American Prometheus*, 291.

26. Ibid.

27. Ibid.

Truman and so many other Americans, including church leaders, the use of atomic bombs against Japan was a practical initiative in the course of war, and those who challenged that point were told to keep criticism to themselves and not to arouse division in the country.[28]

Oppenheimer is not only the "father of the atomic bomb," he was also among the first atomic scientists who dissented from Caesar's views of the new weapon. He favored collaboration with the Soviets to manage and control atomic weapons and opposed the development of new superweapons.[29] As Oppenheimer and his allies attempted to dissuade Truman from developing more powerful devices, Edward Teller, another physicist-parent of the atomic bomb, argued in favor of super-weapons and their proliferation. Truman opted for Teller's vision, and in 1952, the U.S. detonated a hydrogen bomb that was a thousand times more powerful than the bomb that leveled Hiroshima.[30]

Here, in the wee hours of the Cold War, the U.S. endowed boomers with a vital aspect of our identity and mission. We were Christian warriors. It was our God-given, patriotic duty to defeat the communists by any and all means. Present at the dawn of the Cold War were dissenters who rejected nuclear confrontations and stock-piling. They included scientists, housewives, doctors, students, and clerics who often made their stand with Bibles in hand. Caesar was a realist who saw their moralism as dangerous and naïve.

Eisenhower and the Iron Cross

Ironically, a five-star general in the U.S. Army and 34th President of the United States offered one of the nation's greatest prophetic speeches against militarism. Dwight Eisenhower was an avowed cold warrior who understood the intoxicating effects of war and what it did to men who inhaled it on the battle fields and in corporate board rooms. He correctly anticipated that the line between the just and the unjust war could easily be manipulated where Caesar smelled profit.

Eisenhower was a realist and a cold warrior, yet, he saw that massive military mobilization had an impact on the quality of life in America. In 1953, he declared that:

> Every gun that is made, every warship that is launched, every rocket fired signifies, in the final sense, a theft from those who hunger and are not fed, those who are cold and not clothed... The

---

28. Boyer, *By the Bomb's*, 193–95.
29. Wittner, *Struggle*, 157–60.
30. York, *Advisors*, 62–74.

cost of one modern heavy bomber is this: a modern brick school in more than 30 cities. It is two electric power plants, each serving a town of 60,000 population . . . We pay for a single destroyer for new homes that could have sheltered more than 8,000 people . . . This is not a way of life at all . . . Under the cloud of threatening war, it is humanity hanging from a cross of iron.[31]

Eisenhower had seen war up close. He had liberated Nazi concentration camps in WWII and led assaults which left thousands dead on the Western Front. He had observed the deprivations that leave civilians hungry, homeless, and willing to sell themselves for food and shelter.

Regardless of the cost of war, Eisenhower was pressed into military action. By the time he entered the White House, Mao Zedong had imposed communism in China, North Korea had invaded South Korea, the Soviet Union had produced atomic bombs, and Marxist revolutionaries were poised around the globe to advance their causes in the wake of decolonization. At that time, reductions of the defense budget drew accusations of being "soft on communism." Eisenhower was under pressure to push the Soviets back to Moscow, and thus liberate the Eastern Bloc.

During Eisenhower's administration, the CIA orchestrated covert activities that took hundreds of thousands of lives and resulted in regime changes across the globe.[32] In addition to supporting coups against Mosaddeq and Arbenz, Eisenhower approved aid to militia in the Philippines and Burma who brutally suppressed and murdered their own people. In 1954, following the defeat of the French colonial forces in Vietnam, the CIA assumed control of anti-Marxist partisans in North Vietnam. It was a giant step towards the American 20-year war in Vietnam. In 1959, the CIA removed the Dalai Lama from Tibet and supported Khampa tribesmen in their resistance to China's invasion. Patrice Lumumba, the democratically elected president of the Republic of the Congo, was assassinated by forces that included the CIA. The Congo (Zaire) was rich mineral deposits, including copper, diamonds, gold, and uranium. In its fight for independence from Belgium, the Congolese appealed to the U.S. for help, but the U.S. refused. Lumumba then sought Soviet aid, which sealed his fate. The U.S. supported Mobutu Sese Seko, a corrupt dictator who oppressed and murdered thousands of his own people.[33]

---

31. Eisenhower, "Chance for Peace," paragraphs 30–38.

32. Taubman's *Secret Empire* provides a detailed survey of the powerful roles of the CIA and the space program as a spy system during Eisenhower's administration, and Blum's *Killing Hope* chronicles CIA activity over the course of several presidents.

33. Weiner, *Legacy of Ashes*, 187–89.

The U.S. government was not above sacrificing civilian Isaacs for in the anti-communist crusade. During the Cold War, rural America and densely populated cities became targets in a series of secret testing of both biological and chemical agents. In 1952, the Mayor and City Council of Minneapolis approved "defense" tests during which the U.S. Army sprayed zinc cadmium sulfide over my home town. These "dustings" were "harmless," according to Army officials, and they were important to determine whether "smoke screens" could be used to hide targets from enemy aircraft.[34] Such tests were undertaken in other cities without the informed consent of their inhabitants. At the time, little was known about the effects of the florescent powder, but many in cities subjected to the experiments people complained about high cancer rates. In the 1960s, nerve gas was dispersed over Alaska, deadly bacteria was released over Hawaii, and other neurological toxins were tested in Florida and Maryland.[35]

To advance the cause of democracy and the American way of life, the U.S. government conducted other tests on human subjects unaware of what was being done to their bodies and minds. Populations were exposed to pathogens including Serrati (a pneumonia-like illness), Bordetella (whooping cough), and in the U.S. Army, thousands of soldiers were exposed to nerve gases, LSD, Sarin, and other toxins.[36] Prisoners, prostitutes, and army personnel were injected with chemicals and subjected to physical and mental torture for the benefit of improving U.S. intelligence and military operations.[37] These experiments were typically not discussed in boomer's history, science, or civics lessons. They were ignored. In less than a decade following the Nuremburg Trials, in which Hitler's doctors were prosecuted for subjecting people to bio-chemical experiments, American Caesars were behaving in ways that resembled the Nazis.

While Eisenhower was in office, the U.S. store of nuclear weapons increased from about 1,000 to roughly 23,000.[38] With the technology to pulverize whole cities with one bomb came the realization that armed confrontation might leave the victors with a world not worth owning. The U.S. therefore pursued two strategies. The first was to maintain a nuclear arsenal large enough to

---

34. Cole, *Clouds of Secrecy*, 60–64.
35. Chan, "U.S. Admits Bio-Weapons Tests," lines 1–7.
36. Veterans Health Initiative, *Health Effects*, 3–10.
37. Cole *The Eleventh Plague* and Moren *Undue Risk* document U.S. bio-chemical experimentation on unwitting and volunteer subjects at home and abroad. Both provide disturbing insights to the moral reasoning that justified these acts.
38. Ledbetter, *Unwarranted Influence*, 4.

intimidate the enemy and versatile enough to wage a limited nuclear assault.[39] The second was to train personnel of developing nations in the arts of repression aimed at keeping a lid on reform and revolution.[40] In 1946, the U.S. established the School of the Americas in Panama, which trained Latin American military personal for their future roles as leaders and soldiers south of the U.S. border who would take up the "good fight" for democracy and capitalism.[41] For the sake of defending democracy, assassins and government leaders in Latin American countries kidnapped, tortured, raped, and murdered tens of thousands of their own people with the blessing of the U.S. government and the support of its taxpayers.[42]

By the time Eisenhower left office, relations between private industry and government had become so intimate that it was difficult to tell where one began and the other one ended. In his farewell address, Eisenhower observed that, despite the need for national security, the U.S. also had to be vigilant against corruption and domestic threats to liberty. He stated:

> We annually spend on military security more than the net income of all United States corporations. This conjunction of an immense military establishment and large arms industry is new in the American experience. The total influence—economic, political, even spiritual—is felt in every city, every State house, and every office of Federal government. We recognize the imperative need for this development. Yet we must not fail to comprehend its grave implications. Our toil, resources and livelihood are all involved; so is the structure of our society. In the councils of government, we must guard against the acquisition of unwarranted influence, whether sought or unsought, by the military industrial complex . . . We must never let the weight of this combination endanger our liberties or democratic process. We should take nothing for granted. Only an alert and knowledgeable citizenry can compel the proper meshing of the huge industrial and military machinery

---

39. Kissinger, *Nuclear Weapons*, 4–5.

40. Prouty, *JFK: The CIA*, 183–86.

41. The School of the Americas (SOA) was relocated to fort Benning, Georgia in 1984, and was renamed Western Hemisphere Institute for Security Cooperation (WHINSEC) in 2001.

42. The School of the Americas Watch was established by Fr. Roy Bourgeois in 1990. It documents human rights abuses by graduates of the SOA and bases its objection to WHINSEC's existence on the Gospel's teachings regarding love and human dignity. Nelson-Pallmeyer *School of Assassins* and Gill, L *The School of the Americas* examine the controversy.

of defense with our peaceful methods and goals, so that security and liberty prosper together.[43]

Eisenhower was not describing the future, but something that already existed. Just as profiteers had had gouged taxpayers in past wars, corporations plundered the public's purse during the Cold War.[44] Eisenhower's objection to war and its adverse impact on America's material and spiritual life could easily have triggered accusations that he was un-American. The Oval Office and his reputation as a gifted general protected him against such assertions. Those who echoed his concerns in the 1960s, however, were not shielded by such prestige, and were readily labeled "un-American," "reds," and "traitors."

A Christian Nation . . . Maybe, Maybe Not

Here is a little sneak preview about the Cold War. The communist party has left the Kremlin and the Cold War is technically over. The Soviet Union was unable to bear the burden of its empire and collapsed. New commissars have emerged and Russia's teetering steps toward democracy have been shadowed by militant nationalism and ruthless mafia operations.[45] In cities from Vladivostok to St. Petersburg, billboards feature sassy ads for fashion and liquor. In the new Russia, evangelical churches and casinos both flourish. Jesus thrives alongside Ronald McDonald, Colonel Sanders, and the Marlboro Man.

The Cold War is no longer the basis of domestic and foreign policy, but the military-industrial complex lives on. The demise of the Soviet Union has not quelled Caesar's interest in empire in either the U.S or in Russia. It has not stopped American Caesars from accusing reformers of being communists. Islamic terrorism has replaced the Soviet Union as America's arch-enemy, and provides the military-industrial complex with a rational for its operations, and the staggering cost to keep the world safe for God and democracy.

To bring the Kingdom of God to bear on Earth in its most spiritual sense in 1950 would have been seen as unpatriotic. Nationalism during the Cold War and beyond made it very difficult for the average citizen to have empathy for our enemies and mercy for the masses that were placed in the crossfire of America's Cold War crusades. To activate the deepest spirituality at the heart of Jesus' teachings would have required Caesar to be humbled by powers

---

43. Eisenhower, "Farewell Address," lines 56–67.

44. Brandes *Warhogs* traces war profiteering from the colonial to the modern era, and provides a dimension of war not generally presented in school lessons about American history.

45. Hoffman, *Oligarchs*, 6–8.

greater than himself. Caesar and his people were not capable of that in 1950 and we may never be capable of that as a nation.

Baby boomers inherited the American tradition of bringing God into public life, but that did not necessarily make it Christian. Americans like to say that the U.S. is a Christian nation, but the claim is problematic. In boomer's lifetime lots of Americans hid their racial and sexual prejudices and hatred beneath the veneer of public courtesy. Color lines were enforced in real estate transactions, country clubs barred membership to "kikes" and "coons," and news media reported events from a white, male, Protestant perspective. The notion that the founders of the U.S. intended to create a Christian society is popular, but it is not accurate.

Not all who crossed the Atlantic and settled in the colonies of North America sought the new world to create a theocratic society. Certainly the Puritans of the Massachusetts Bay Colony were of that ilk, but there were thousands more who only wanted the chance to own land, discover gold, escape debt, and make fortunes in trade. The presumption that American forefathers explicitly designed a Christian nation is contradicted by the reality that the U.S. Constitution specifically states in the First Amendment that, "Congress shall make no law respecting the establishment of religion, or prohibiting the free exercise thereof." Thus, the U.S. does not embrace an official state religion.[46]

A second problem with the assertion that the U.S. is a Christian nation lies in the matter of demographics. In 2007, presidential candidate Barack Obama upset many Americans with the simple recognition that the numbers of non-Christian Americans are significant. "Whatever we once were," said the President, "we're no longer just a Christian nation; we are also a Jewish nation, a Muslim nation, a Buddhist nation, a Hindu nation, and a nation of nonbelievers."[47] In 1961, the year Obama was born, about 92 percent of U.S. citizens were Christian. In 2013 that number dropped to 78.4 percent, while 1.7 percent were Jewish, 0.6 percent were Muslim, and 0.4 percent were Hindu. In 1952, 75 percent of Americans reported that religion was very important in their personal life, while in 2012, 56 percent reported the same.[48] The numbers suggest that the 20th century was a diversifying and secularizing experience.

A third problem with the assertion that the U.S. is a Christian nation lies in the disparities between American values and conduct and the values and

---

46. Davis "America's True History" identifies the specific measures taken during the colonial era to prevent theocracies from taking hold and to preserving religious freedom.

47. Brody, "Obama to CBS News," lines 25–31.

48. Gallup Poll, "Religion," includes several tables that illustrate the data.

conduct espoused by the Gospels. Had Obama's remarks on America's Christian identity stemmed from these disparities, he *might* have said: "Look—people who live by the Gospel just don't go around stockpiling nuclear weapons and making massive amounts of money by selling military hardware to the world. That's not Christian. It is also not brotherly love when you force a regime change and kill innocent civilians, or prop up dictators who enslave and exterminate their own people. There is no future—no hope there. Nor is a nation Christian when it allows the rich to rob the poor by way of reckless speculation in the market. That is not what Jesus taught us to do." That would have been a different sermon than the one Americans got about demographics. Obama's remarks about demographics were aimed to improve civic cooperation among diverse religious groups. Many understand, however, the objectives of our cooperation are just as important as cooperation itself. They know that reaching a consensus does not alone make us moral.

As boomers' experiences illustrate, America has offered the world more than unbridled capitalism, atomic destruction, and tyrants who do corporate bidding in third world countries. It offered the world an alternative to Caesar. It offered the world prophetic leaders and dissenters, some who openly have preached the Gospel, others who have rested their case for an end to poverty, civil rights, peace, and de-armament on secular philosophical principles that honor human dignity. America offered the world political and social movements that in secular and spiritual language announced the oneness of humanity, and that our sacred calling is to love and be loved. These moments—these lessons—are among the most potent of boomer's lifetime.

4

Pope John Kennedy

A Catholic in the White House

As a toddler, I was taught to memorize the names of important leaders. My parents taught me that Pope John XXIII was the leader of the Catholic Church and that John F. Kennedy (JFK) was the President of the United States. Inevitably, I confused them and pranced around the house chanting "Pope John Kennedy." I had no idea why adults laughed when I did this and no awareness of the disquieting implications of what I said. Both leaders became iconic for Catholic boomers. Both inspired confidence in the idea that people could make the world a better place. While Pope John ushered modernism into the Catholic liturgy and social teachings, Kennedy spoke of scientific research, new medicines, volunteerism, and bringing peace to the world. Both seemed to want the Kingdom of God to be larger presence on earth. Kennedy was special in my home. He was America's first Catholic president.

Kennedy was the third U.S. President in the atomic age. Like many elected officials, he was often forced to choose between what he believed was moral and right and what would keep him in office. He understood the necessity to project a wholesome image to the masses while discretely indulging in the sins of the flesh to which he felt perfectly entitled. He was a womanizer who lied to the public, committed reckless acts that could have threatened national security, and supported militarism in part to reinforce his masculine image. He was not above smear campaigns to sour the appeal of those who ran against him.[1] He approved wire-tapping of political foes, approved assassination

---

1. Hersh *Dark Side of Camelot* has documented John F. Kennedy's sordid road to the White House, and exposed some of the entitlements to which the American elite take for granted.

plots, and initiated more military interventions than did Presidents Truman, Eisenhower, and Johnson.[2]

Despite his flaws, JFK remains a heroic figure for baby boomers, in part because the human psyche needs people who personify ideals. Without them, it is often difficult to see our way to a moral course of action. The emotional need for heroes often leaves us vulnerable to projecting substance where there is none, and to mistaking charisma for leadership. Kennedy, however, had both substance and charm. He not only supported policies that helped people improve their lives, he inspired many to be better than what they thought they could be. His legacy reveals that people need more bread to thrive. They need inspiration, optimism, and the feeling that they are part of something larger than themselves. JFK's special regard for public service resonated with something larger than self and rang with hope that Americans could overcome poverty and injustice.[3] A survey taken at the time of JFK's assassination revealed that 83 percent of Americans felt ashamed that such a crime could be committed in the U.S., and that 79 percent felt as though they lost someone "very close and dear" to them.[4] Many Americans felt confused and anxious about who would lead the nation. Many saw his untimely and brutal death as an assault on hope and confidence in the human capacity for goodness.

Kennedy's struggle with Caesar offers insight to what it means to embrace spirituality in the American empire. JFK may have fallen very short of the Gospel teachings in many instances, but it is the moments in which he flew in the face of Caesar that catches one's attention. In those moments we glimpse the possibilities of a prophetic voice and witness the tension between Caesar and the Kingdom of God; we see a conscience evolving, incrementally, but perceptibly, in ways that anyone could evolve.

Bear Any Burden

Kennedy was both baptized by the Catholic Church and bitten by Caesar. Through his veins coursed both the nutrients that fortify charity and compassion *and* the toxins that corrupt. He was a consummate politician and understood how to access power. He moved in elite social and political circles that were peppered with individuals who were racist, sexist, and anti-Semitic. He was a part of Caesar's world, one in which political favors were bought and

---

2. Patterson, *Kennedy's Quest*, 5.

3. Barnes *John F. Kennedy on Leadership* explores Kennedy's character and what made him an effective leader. Kennedy was sensitive to how others perceived his leadership and mindfully cultivated his skills.

4. Sheatsley and Feldman, "Assassination," 196.

sold, and one in which dishonesty was a means to an end. He understood what was expected of him as a cold warrior and champion of private enterprise. Over time, however, Kennedy showed signs of dissent from Caesar's agenda and values. In some ways, the Kennedy who took office in 1961 was not the same Kennedy who died in 1963.

In his inaugural address, Kennedy told the world that the U.S. remained committed to defending human rights, and to the expansion of democracy around the globe. He announced that the U.S. would "pay any price, bear any burden," and "meet any hardship . . . to assure the survival and the success of liberty."[5] Though he consistently warned that atomic war would be more terrible than anything known before, and sought a national shelter program, the U.S. added nearly 10,000 nuclear warheads to its arsenal during his presidency.[6]

When Kennedy took office, racism and poverty in the U.S. were blatant contradictions to the nation's commitment to human rights. Yet, when Americans thought of offenses to human rights, it pointed first to communism. JFK inherited the Cold War and understood that those who were labeled "soft" on communism were denounced in many circles as unmasculine and unfit for office.[7] Cold warriors did not allow their will to fight to become flabby by wishful thinking that adversaries meant no harm. JFK entered office as a strident cold warrior who, like other cold warriors, placed opposition to communism at the center of foreign policy. Those who criticized U.S. policy were labeled "anti-American," and routinely dismissed as irrational or irresponsible.[8] In 1963, when the French voiced its opposition to U.S. intervention in Vietnam, members of Kennedy's administration called the French "psychotic," and compulsively anti-American, while Kennedy declared that, "these bastards just live off the fat of the land and spit at us every chance they get."[9]

Though he never ceased being a cold warrior, Kennedy's dissent from Caesar on at least a few occasions reveal a man willing to challenge assumptions about the Isaacs Caesar wants to sacrifice for the sake of empire. When confronting U.S. Steel, segregationists, the Soviet Union, and his own advisors on the matter of Vietnam, he revealed the potential for the prophetic "no" to be heard above Caesar's much amplified "yes."

---

5. Kennedy, J. F. "Inaugural Address," lines 16–18.
6. Kristensen "How Presidents Arms," lines 26–27.
7. Cuordileone, "Politics in an Age," 544–45.
8. Friedman, "Anti-Americanism," 514.
9. Ibid., 509–510.

Made of Steel

One of the greatest challenges JFK inherited from the Eisenhower administration was the recession of 1958, in which over 7 percent of the labor force was out of work.[10] In general, conservatives favored policies that would keep industries strong, while liberals sought relief and reform. Conservatives were leery of government interventions as they placed more trust in the "natural" dynamics of the economy than in human interference with them.[11] They also feared that Kennedy would lend too much support to labor and pursue reform. Their worries bore fruit.

In April, 1962 Kennedy confronted U.S. Steel, whose executives had declared a price increase of $6.00 per ton. Other steel manufacturers followed suit. The action smacked of price fixing and an artificial inflation of cost. The price hike came on the heels of a labor settlement in which steel workers gained a 2.5 percent wage increase. Following this, Secretary of Labor, Arthur Goldberg and U.S. Steel worked out an agreement on prices that would be non-inflationary. In theory, increased profits would be used to upgrade mills. Roger Blough, Chairman of the U.S. Steel's Board of Directors, argued that production costs had increased 6 percent since 1958, and that the 3.5 percent increase in price would still not compensate for the dip in profits from $190 million in 1960 to $114 million in 1961.[12]

Kennedy's remarks following U.S. Steel's price hike targeted a single company and was an open criticism of what he believed was corporate greed. He described the price hike as "a wholly unjustifiable and irresponsible defiance of public interest," noting that the increase would inflate "the cost of homes, autos, appliances, and most other items for every American family."[13] The proposed price increase had implications for the cost of national defense, as steel is required to make planes, tanks, guns, and other necessities of battle. Kennedy also contradicted Blough, and reported that the materials required to produce steel had declined and that labor costs were essentially the same as they had been 1958. "In short," he said, "at a time when they could be exploring how more efficiency and better prices could be obtained . . . a few gigantic corporations have decided to increase prices in ruthless disregard of their public responsibilities."[14] The business community pounced.

---

10. Current Population Reports, "Labor Force," 10.
11. Gable, "The Politics and Economics," 559.
12. Godden and Maidment, "Anger, Language, and Politics," 321.
13. Kennedy, J. F. "News Conference," lines 14–16.
14. Ibid., lines 37–40.

Fortune magazine ran an editorial that excoriated the President, claiming that he was wrong about the cost of production, and that U.S. Steel was justified as the cost per ton had not increased in four years. The editorial referred to JFK's remarks as "demagogic," and a form of government harassment of business.[15] Senator Barry Goldwater (R-AZ) characterized Kennedy's reprimand as an attempt to "socialize the business of this country."[16] A poll of 6,000 business executives revealed that just two months after JFK's confrontation, 52 percent of respondents viewed him as "strongly anti-business."[17] The public, however, saw something redeeming in the president's speech. They gave him and his stand against U.S. Steel an approval rating of 58 percent.

U.S. Steel rescinded its price increase, but the episode raised the question of who was the rightful shepherd of the economy. Private companies argued they were the guardians of the nation's prosperity. After all, they reasoned, it was their ingenuity and expansion that employed the masses. Kennedy held that government was the guardian of public prosperity since it had the duty to protect the masses against inflation, monopoly, low wages, hazardous working conditions, and unemployment.[18]

Scholars note that Kennedy's anger toward U.S. Steel went beyond his concerns for the economy, and that JFK viewed U.S. Steel's actions as a challenge to his authority.[19] Privately, Kennedy snapped at his advisors that U.S. Steel "fucked us and we've got to try to fuck them . . . My father told me businessmen were all pricks, but I didn't really believe he was right until now."[20] Some perceive JFK's speech as a sign that he would not permit Caesar's industrial titans to bully the nation. Though JFK was a devout fiscal conservative, his battle with U.S. Steel suggests that he understood the potential for corporate greed to disrupt the market and that neutrality on the matter was dangerous.

Months after his dual with U.S. Steel, Kennedy undertook plans to alter taxation for the purpose of stimulating the sluggish economy. He outlined a tax structure that accelerated depreciation credit for businesses, and decreases in capital gains and corporate taxes. At that time, income tax for the

---

15. "Steel: Ides of April," 97–98. Henry Luce owned *Fortune* magazine, as well as *Time* and *Life*. He was an ally of CIA and fierce defender of American corporate power. See Douglass, *JFK and the Unspeakable*, 164.

16. Dallek, *"Unfinished Life*, 488.

17. Schlesinger, *Thousand Days*, 638.

18. Ibid., 485.

19. Godden and Maidment, "Anger, Language and Politics," 317.

20. Dallek, *"Unfinished Life*, 484.

top income bracket was about 90 percent.[21] Like other fiscal conservatives, he believed that economic growth and full employment were by-products of low corporate taxes. He appeared to have full confidence that when businesses were given tax breaks, they would reflexively use their profits to replace outdated machinery, develop new products, and employ more people.[22] Republicans feared JFK's policies would lead to inflation and bankruptcy. Ironically, tax breaks later became the cornerstone of Republican economics.

Had JFK lived long enough, he may have made several speeches against corporate greed. The fact that lots of boomers did live long enough to see spectacular acts of Wall Street piracy as the twentieth century ended and the twenty-fist began is owed to JFK himself. Had it not been for his dissent in 1962, the world as we know it might have been reduced to radioactive dust and rubble in a war over Soviet missiles in Cuba.

Caesar Goes to Cuba

Robert McNamara, former Secretary of Defense under Presidents John F. Kennedy and Lyndon B. Johnson (LBJ), revealed that during the Cuban Missile Crisis, the world came "closer than we knew at the time" to a nuclear holocaust.[23] Former Secretary of State Dean Rusk called the event the "most dangerous crisis the world has ever seen."[24] Some historians say that the crisis was resolved only by *defying* the traditional model of political decision-making, which focused on the imperative for one side to be victorious and the other side to be defeated.[25] Throughout most of the Cold War, the idea that adversaries could and should reach a "win-win" resolution to conflict was simply not politically correct, and that is part of what makes JFK's actions during the crisis worth a second look.

The Cuban Missile Crisis was rooted in the U.S. attempt to overthrow Fidel Castro, who had toppled Cuba's American-supported dictator, Fulgencio Batista. The Bay of Pigs mission flopped in part because JFK called off an air strike that would have crippled Cuban fortifications. An air strike, he reasoned, would compromise his ability to win concessions from the Soviets,

---

21. Blodget, "Truth about Taxes," lines 40–45.

22. Kennedy, J. F. "Address and Question," advocated tax reductions for personal and corporate income, and asserted that, Americans needed to spend more than 94 percent on their post-tax income to grow the economy.

23. Leonard and Blachurst, "I Don't Think Anybody Thought," lines 100–01.

24. Zeiler, *Dean Rusk*, 80.

25. Anderson, P. A. "Decision-Making by Objection," 216–221.

who were stockpiling nuclear bombs and threatening a war over Berlin. Hawks in the Pentagon and the CIA saw JFK's decision as an act of treason.[26]

To improve Cuban defenses, Castro accepted Soviet Premier Nikita Khrushchev's offer to install nuclear missiles in Cuba. Khrushchev did not inform the U.S. of the defense deal, which fed U.S. suspicions of Khrushchev's intentions.[27] On October 14, 1962, American spy planes photographed Cuba's missile installations, and for the next two weeks, the U.S. and the Soviet Union engaged in a nuclear showdown. Kennedy's advisors in the Executive Committee for National Security (EX-COMM) were eager for a pre-emptive strike and an invasion of Cuba. They believed that war with the Soviets was inevitable, and that the U.S. should attack first while they had the advantage.[28]

Caesar insisted that credibility and leadership rested on brute force. Air Force General Curtis Le May saw Cuba as a side show to the main event of forcing the Soviets from Eastern Europe, and he wanted the Navy and Strategic Air Command to surround Cuba, and "fry" it if necessary.[29] He argued that war was the only way to resolve the crisis, and to pursue a "political" resolution would send a message to U.S. allies that America was weak.[30] Le May was chafed not only about missing an opportunity to deliver a severe setback to the Kremlin, but about what was to him a pattern of civilian indifference to military expertise.[31]

General Maxwell Taylor supported military action in Cuba. Mindful that U.S. action in Cuba could trigger Soviet occupation of West Berlin, he was convinced that Soviet military bases in Cuba was categorically a different threat to the U.S. than was Castro's army on its own.[32] General David Shoup agreed with LeMay, stating that it would be best to smash the entire stock of missiles in one full-on assault. He fumed, "You go in there and friggin' around with the missiles. You're screwed . . . You've got to go in and take out the whole goddamn thing . . . ."[33] Others, such as Llewellyn Thompson, Kennedy's advisor on Russian affairs, insisted that any deal with the Soviets would be a

26. Stoll, *JFK Conservative*, 144–47.

27. Kennedy, R. F. *Thirteen Days*, 9.

28. The details of EXCOM's position on the crisis are captured on tape and explored in Stern's *The Week the World Stood Still*. The tapes reveal that Robert Kennedy's *Thirteen Days* portrays its author as the steady voice of peace throughout the ordeal, when in fact Robert Kennedy was at times very hawkish.

29. Stern, "Inside Story," Lines 54–57.

30. Dallek, *An Unfinished Life*, 555.

31. Coffey, *Iron Eagle*, 224–25, 370–71.

32. Ritter, *Dangerous Ground*, 117.

33. Ibid., 122.

defeat.³⁴ Robert F. Kennedy, the Attorney General, initially favored an invasion of Cuba, then later sided with Robert McNamara, who supported a naval blockade of Cuba. Congress was also combative. Senator William Fulbright (D-AR) reasoned that it would not be an act of war against the Soviets if only Cuba were attacked, while Senator Richard Russell (D-GA) opined that armed conflict was a sure thing, and that the U.S. should strike first.³⁵

Meanwhile in Moscow, Khrushchev and his advisors anticipated the worst. Fearing a U.S. invasion of Cuba, they argued about potential responses. Like JFK, Khrushchev was surrounded by hawks who pressured him to take a combative and uncompromising stance.³⁶ The official exchanges between the two world leaders embody the classic elements of rivalry: both did not fully trust the other; each believed the other aimed to out-maneuver him; both were cynical about claims that weapons were deployed for purely defensive reasons; each had placed the other in a category that was defined by assumptions; and, both believed that reason was on their side.³⁷

Both leaders had rattled sabers in each other's direction after the Bay of Pig's debacle in 1961. Khrushchev expressed his hopes that JFK would not permit the "flame of war ignited by interventions in Cuba to grow into an incomparable conflagration," and said that he remained committed to defending Cuba in the event of an attack.³⁸ JFK assured Khrushchev that the U.S. had no intentions to invade Cuba, and firmly reminded Khrushchev that thousands of Cuban refugees were fleeing what they believed was an oppressive government. He lectured the Premier, arguing that the "great revolution in the history of man, past, present and future, is the revolution of those determined to be free."³⁹ Khrushchev countered, asserting that, "people have been drowned in blood" during colonial wars, and that, the U.S. was seeking to restore its monopoly over Cuba so it could plunder its resources and get rich at the expense of the Cuban people.⁴⁰ He chided Kennedy for the hypocrisy of lecturing him on Budapest while the U.S. "crushed the independence in Guatemala by sending mercenaries."⁴¹

On October 22nd, Kennedy ordered U.S. ships to intercept Soviet ships bound for Cuba. Khrushchev's reply was forceful. The U.S., he declared, had

34. Pious, "Cuban Missile Crisis," 83.
35. Dallek, *Unfinished Life*, 557.
36. Zubok, *Failed Empire*, 143–50.
37. Gillespie, "Dialogical Dynamics," 140–46.
38. Khrushchev, "Telegram from Embassy, April 18" lines 27–30.
39. Kennedy, J. F. "Letter from President Kennedy," lines 51–53.
40. Khrushchev, "Letter from Chairman, April 22," lines 34–37.
41. Ibid., lines 201–04.

no right to control another nation's defense policies. Thus, on October 23, 1962, two superpowers stood eye to eye, braced for nuclear war. On that day, Bobby Kennedy secretly met with Soviet Ambassador, Anatoly Dobrynin, who denied that there were Soviet missiles in Cuba. Khrushchev's missive to Kennedy the following day revealed his fury and frustration. He said that the U.S. had no authority to interfere with relations between two sovereign nations, and insisted the JFK was not "declaring a quarantine, but rather . . . setting forth an ultimatum and threatening that if we do not give in to your demands you will use force."[42] JFK bluntly told the Premier that the Soviets had started the crisis by secretly dispatching missiles to Cuba after they were warned that such action would be regarded as a threat to U.S. security.[43]

By that time, Soviet ships were halted behind quarantine lines, but the matter of removing the missiles already installed remained problematic. Khrushchev's letter of October 26th was appeal for reason and an acknowledgement that an exchange of nuclear bombs would be a barbaric act of destruction that neither side could tolerate. He questioned whether Kennedy could actually believe Cuba and the Soviet Union could successfully attack the U.S., and whether Kennedy understood that, "you too will receive the same that you hurl against us."[44] We are "normal people," Khrushchev insisted, who want only peaceful competition between nations who embrace different ideologies.

On October 27th, just hours after the U.S. proposed a deal, a U.S. spy plane was shot down over Cuba. JFK's advisors had already decided that if U.S. planes were shot down over Cuba, the U.S. would attack Cuba. Rather than risk escalation, however, Kennedy ordered *no retaliation*. Later that night, Bobby Kennedy met with Dobrynin, and described the President's agony. He beseeched Dobrynin to convey the President's desperate position to Khrushchev. He stated that once the shooting started, the crisis would escalate, and perhaps the U.S. military would usurp President Kennedy's power.[45] Then, he offered a deal. The U.S. would withdraw missiles in Turkey and promise not invade Cuba if the Soviets would remove missiles from Cuba. The agreement would have to be kept secret, however, in order to assure the public that Kennedy did not capitulate to Moscow.

In the heat of conflict, some of the most powerful men in the world postured themselves like six-year old bullies in a sandbox. They insisted that they had the mightiest muscle and the most righteous cause in the fight. They

42. Khrushchev, "Letter from Chairman, October 24," lines 20–24.
43. Kennedy, J. F. "Telegram from the Department," lines 5–15.
44. Khrushchev, "Telegram from the Embassy, October 26," lines 80–94.
45. Hersh, *Dark Side*, 341–371.

played the game of brinksmanship and issued ultimatums to the point where an irreversible catastrophe was about to take place. The world I knew as a child nearly became a cinder in space because militant nationalists refused to see themselves in the face of their enemies. In the end, Kennedy and Khrushchev averted disaster not only because they were willing to reason, but because they were open to empathy.

Noah's Red Ark

Whether faith in God prevented two cold warriors from hitting each other with atomic bombs is debatable. The record is clear, however, that Kennedy and Khrushchev found their way to mutual empathy, and that in itself shifted the outcome of their confrontation. Kennedy and Khrushchev agreed that nuclear war was more than civilization could bear, as it would consume more Isaacs than sanity would allow. In the end, JFK *was not willing* to "bear any burden or pay any price" to keep Moscow in its place. In the words of his brother Bobby, JFK, "had no heart for a war that would inevitably kill children all over the world who knew nothing about the conflict and had no say about it."[46]

JFK, did not always abide by the teachings of the Catholic Church, and was adept at framing moral issues in secular terms.[47] His moral compass was, however, was spiritual inasmuch as he felt tremendously obligated to protect humanity and loathed the idea of nuclear war. Three years before he became President, he declared that the U.S. had to abandon its faith in "apocalyptic solutions" and rigid patterns of conflict resolution as the post-colonial world demanded new ways of defining peace, victory, and friend.[48] JFK's empathy for those who suffered was augmented by his own familiarity with pain. He suffered from Addison's disease, thyroid deficiency, colitis, and chronic back pain. In his youth, he was so sickly that many feared for his life. He was injured in the Pacific during WWII and, as a journalist in post-war Germany, saw the horrific effects of carpet bombing and deprivations caused by the cost of war.

In his remarkable book, *JFK and the Unspeakable*, James Douglass tells readers that during the missile crisis, Kennedy gave an interview to a French journalist, Jean Daniel. Kennedy told Daniel that, "I believe that there is no country in the world, including all the African regions . . . where economic colonization, humiliation and exploitation were worse than in Cuba, in part

---

46. Douglass, *JFK and the Unspeakable*, 26–27.
47. Carty, "Secular Icon," 139–142.
48. Kennedy, J. F. "Democrat Looks," 46.

owing to my country's policies during the Batista regime." He added, "To some extent it is as though Batista was the incarnation of a number of sins on the part of the United States," and "we shall have to pay for those sins."[49] The cold warrior had become repentant for the sins of his nation. That was a chapter deleted from boomers' history lessons. Daniel was on his way to Cuba where he was to interview Castro. JFK was confident that Daniel would relay his empathy. In the fall of 1963, Kennedy pursued secret dialogue with Castro in an attempt to repair relations. By that time, JFK's foreign policies had created serious enemies at home.[50]

On June 10, 1963, Kennedy delivered a speech at American University in which it was clear that the cold warrior had parted company with the most militant in Congress, the Pentagon, and CIA. While critical of Soviet conduct, he expressed abundant empathy for the Soviet Union. He said that while it was discouraging to find Soviet propaganda telling the world that the U.S. was poised to fight imperialist wars for the purpose of economically enslaving the world, the U.S. was not destined for war. He rejected the notion that peace was impossible, and asserted that since problems were manmade, so too solutions would come from human effort. He declared that, "no government or social system is so evil that its people must be considered as lacking in virtue," and he praised Soviet achievements in industry, science, and economics.[51] Unlike other American cold warriors in high office, Kennedy acknowledged the severity of Russia's sacrifices and losses in WWII, and gave Russians the credit they deserved for defeating the Nazis on the Eastern Front. He appealed to the world to see peace as a rational means of collective problem-solving. His remarks were predicated on his acceptance of co-existence with communism, a proposition many cold warriors found abhorrent and deserving of death.

At that time, many Americans did not understand Khrushchev or his country. Khrushchev was often portrayed as a buffoon in the media, and made to be the face of Godless communism. Americans, who generally understood little of Russian history, saw Russians as slaves of a state riddled with Byzantine idiosyncrasies. Many knew of Stalin's purges, gulags, and repression, and assumed that any successor of the dictator would follow his predecessor's footsteps.

---

49. Douglass, *JFK and the Unspeakable*, 73.

50. Leroy F. Prouty, Chief of Special Operations for the Joint Chiefs of Staff during Kennedy's administration, documented the evolution of the CIA's contempt for Kennedy in his book *JFK: The CIA, Vietnam and the Plot to Assassinate John F. Kennedy*. His accounts were dramatized in Oliver Stone's popular film *JFK*, 1991. The film's "Mr. X" is based on Prouty.

51. Kennedy, J. F. "Commencement Address," lines 78–89.

Few knew the world that shaped Khrushchev. They did not know the hard life of peasants living under Russian czars and aristocrats, nor did they comprehend the suffering caused by two German invasions, one in 1914 and the other in 1941. Americans did not know what it meant to live under Nazi occupation, to daily breathe the stench of carnage, and to live off of human flesh when livestock, granaries, and farms were reduced to wreckage and ash.[52] While the U.S. mourned the loss of less than half a million people in WWII, Soviets grieved the loss of over 26 million.[53, 54] Americans did not know the agony of Lieutenant General Khrushchev as he defended Kiev, Stalingrad, and Kursk against Nazi invaders in his homeland. They did not know of his loathing for Stalin's capricious and sadistic tyranny.[55] For many Americans, these things were irrelevant. Communists were evil, and that was all they needed to know.

Americans knew little about Khrushchev's philosophical side, and about his Christian upbringing. Despite his adoption of atheism, he used biblical metaphors to explain himself. In September, 1961, he wrote at length to Kennedy about his thoughts regarding their meeting and world affairs, and said:

> I often think how necessary it is for men who are vested with trust and great power to be inspired with the understanding of what seems to be an obvious truism, which is that we live on one planet and it is not in man's power—at least in the foreseeable future—to change that. In a certain sense there is an analogy here—I like this comparison—with Noah's Ark where both the "clean" and the "unclean" found sanctuary. But regardless of who lists himself with the "clean" and who is considered to be "unclean," they are all equally interested in one thing and that is that the Ark should successfully continue its cruise. And we have no other alternative: either we should live in peace and cooperation so that the Ark maintains its buoyancy, or else it sinks. Therefore we must display concern for all of mankind, not to mention our own advantages, and find every possibility leading to peaceful solutions of problems.[56]

---

52. Overy, *Russia's War,* 107, 183.
53. Ellman and Maksudov, "Soviet Deaths," 671–72.
54. Adams, *Best War Ever,* 5–6.
55. Taubman *Khrushchev* and Fursenko and Naftali's *Khrushchev's Cold War* describe Khrushchev's humble origins and ascent to power as one of Stalin's henchmen. His bravado was reckless, and his stubborn pursuit of ill-conceived policies caused his downfall. He bristled when others moralized about Soviet conduct, claiming they knew little about the hardships of Russian life. His moral code seemed to tolerate bloodshed more than hypocrisy.
56. Khrushchev, "Letter from Chairman Khrushchev, September 29," lines 358–370.

At the apex of the crisis, Khrushchev and Kennedy exchanged letters in which they articulated their thoughts about Cuban sovereignty, the global balance of power, the mobilization of nuclear missiles around the world, the intentions of the U.S. and Soviet Union, and the prospect of nuclear war. On October 26, 1962 Khrushchev penned the following to JFK:

> I can see Mr. President, that you are also not without a sense of anxiety for the fate of the world, not without an understanding of and correct assessment of the nature of modern warfare and what war entails. What good would war do you? You threaten us with war. But you well know that the very least you would get in response would be what you had given us; you would suffer the same consequences. And that must be clear to us—people invested with authority, trust, and responsibility. We must not succumb to light-headedness and petty passions, regardless of whether elections are forthcoming in one country or another. These are transitory things, but should war break out, it would not be in our power to stop it, for such is the logic of war . . .
>
> Only lunatics or suicides, who themselves want to perish and before they die destroy the world, could do this. But we want to live and by no means do we want to destroy your country. We want something quite different: to compete with your country in a peaceful endeavor. We argue with you; we have differences on ideological questions. But our concept of the world is that questions of ideology, as well as economic problems, should be settled by other than military means; they must be solved in peaceful contest . . .[57]

Khrushchev's words confirmed two things that cold warriors were unprepared to accept. First, they underscored the Soviet Union's desire to avoid a nuclear confrontation. Second, they demonstrated that Soviets appreciated the reality that what is satisfying in the heat of an emotional contest of will is not necessarily satisfying to long-range objectives. JFK was able to bring the crisis to a peaceful resolution not just because he was willing to compromise, but because he had the faith in Khrushchev's humanity. He believed that his adversaries shared his own empathy for a vulnerable planet. On the threshold of war, JFK said "no" to Caesar.

Just prior to the missile crisis, Kennedy had read Barbara Tuckman's *The Guns of August*. It explores how the arrogance of Edwardian aristocrats and industrialists contributed to the outbreak of World War I. The book profoundly

---

57. Blight and Lang, *Armageddon Letters*, 103–04.

influenced Kennedy during the missile crisis.[58] In particular, he was shaken by the inability of Europe's leaders to anticipate the scale of carnage and ruin wrought by modern industrial warfare. He was also disturbed by egotism that bred indifference to the slaughter. JFK did not wish to repeat 1914. In his anguish, he consulted with Pope John XXIII, who beseeched global leaders to "save peace," and to "spare the world the horrors of a war whose terrifying consequences no one can predict."[59]

Khrushchev did not ridicule JFK's moral languish, he shared it. He approved *Pravda's* (Soviet newspaper) headline of October 26, 1962 which was Pope John's appeal: "We beg all rulers not to be deaf to the cries of humanity." He sent a memorandum to the Pope in which he declared his respect for the Church as a servant to all people, and welcomed papal mediation in times of global crisis.[60] God works in mysterious ways. The atheist, it seems, had some sense of spirituality.

Pacem in Terror

Neither Kennedy nor Khrushchev were saints, but they both defied Caesar and proved that war is not inevitable. They taught us that there is something redeeming about empathizing with one's adversaries, and with leaving them an honorable way out of conflict. In his memoirs, Robert Kennedy noted that paying attention to unintended consequences, minding world opinion, and keeping the military under civilian control are vital in conflict-resolution.[61] McNamara confided years after the crisis that rationality cannot always save people from disaster. The belief that there is always somethings greater than oneself, and always the need to see matters from others' point of view, he said, are critical in conflict resolution.[62]

The Cuban Missile Crisis increased public awareness of the threat of nuclear war and prompted regulation. Kennedy and Khrushchev signed the Nuclear Test Ban Treaty of 1963, which prohibited nuclear tests in space, underwater, and on earth's surface. The crisis also inspired Pope John XXIII's *Pacem in Terris* which confronted materialism and militarism. It argued

---

58. O'Brian, *John F. Kennedy*, 793.Also see Robert Kennedy's *Thirteen Days*, 49.
59. Rychlak, "War Prevented," lines 41–47.
60. Hanson, E. O. *Catholic Church*, 10.
61. Kennedy, R. F. *Thirteen Days*, 85–98.
62. Blight and Lang, *Fog of War*, 59–86.

peace was not about stockpiling bombs, but healing wounds, and feeding the hungry.[63]

After the crisis, JFK continued to struggle with the question of what to render unto Caesar. He permitted the CIA to sabotage Cuban railroads, electric power plants, and factories.[64] He approved of chemical warfare against communist rebels in South Vietnam, and the 1963 coup which wrested President Ngo Dinh Diem from office.[65] The National Security Action Memorandum (NSAM) 263 (October, 1963) announced Kennedy's intentions to withdraw 1,000 American troops by the end of the year. His goal to end U.S. military involvement in Vietnam is supported by the fact that when his advisors reported that South Vietnam showed few signs of victory, JFK saw no point to increasing training and ground support for Diem's army.[66]

Some say JFK wanted to end the war because it was unwinnable, while others suggest he planned to withdraw troops as the South Vietnamese were showing signs that they could handle the war themselves. Other have said that if he really found interference with Vietnam objectionable, he would have opposed the coup against Diem, and allowed the South Vietnamese to broker its own peace with North Vietnam, even if it gave concessions to the North Vietnamese communists.

As James Douglass has observed, "John Kennedy's turn toward peace was not without reversals and compromises."[67] Indeed, JFK straddled two ways of being in the world, with one foot in Caesar's empire, and the other in the Kingdom of God. It seems as if the young executive was maturing while in office and growing into the skin of a prophetic leader, reminding us that the Kingdom of God does not emerge whole in any single generation, but evolves one insight and one judgment at a time.

For lots of boomers, Kennedy occupies a place that is usually reserved for philosophers, poets, and artists. Though an executive in one of the most powerful offices in the world, his thoughts and deeds often irritated Caesar. He lifted his prophetic voice over the crowing and cackling of cold warriors, giving Caesar an incentive to find a more compliant servant.

---

63. Pacem in Terris refers to "Peace on Earth," This was John XXIII's last encyclical. It bravely suggested that Marxism was not by definition the antithesis of Christianity, and invited the faithful to engage political life and to work with adversaries towards peace.

64. Douglass, *JFK and the Unspeakable*, 66.

65. Chomsky, *Rethinking Camelot*, 32, 90–91.

66. Scott, *Deep Politics*, 24–30, 32–37.

67. Douglass, *JFK and the Unspeakable*, 66.

Caesar Ate My Jesus

November 22, 1963

I was ill and home from kindergarten when Kennedy was murdered in Dallas, Texas. I watched the funeral with my grandmother. My father was at work, and my mother was in the hospital recovering from the difficult birth of my brother, Joe. As we viewed the black and white television images, my grandmother wept. I lay on my belly on the living room floor and drew pictures of the event and of the assassination itself. My mother retained these pictures and gave them to me many years later.

In school, I learned that Lee Harvey Oswald shot Kennedy. That story was standard in textbooks for decades, but my confidence in it faltered as I studied evidence to the contrary. At first, it was madness to think that Americans would kill their own leaders to advance their interests. That was the stuff of ancient Romans and modern dictators. It was bizarre to think that government authorities, law enforcement officers, and mobsters could conspire to hide the truth of an assassination by tampering with evidence, murdering witnesses, and extorting people. Everything I had learned in my youth about America indicated that my country was exceptional and was not in the same orbit as history's "less enlightened" societies. After studying history and talking with people who have served in the armed forces and intelligence community, the plausibility that John F. Kennedy was the victim of an American coup was no longer surreal.

For many Americans, the assassination was the beginning of a series of painful awakenings about how power operates. We learned that Caesar does not always tell the truth and that American Caesars are similar to Caesars ripped from history's headlines. Many became scholars who exposed hidden history and who endured Caesars' systematic efforts to discredit them as "malcontents," "wackadoodles," and "conspiracy nuts."

The first trickle of theories contesting the claim that Oswald acted alone did not come from anarchists who hated their America. They came largely from citizens who loved their country and the decency that JFK managed to articulate despite his weaknesses. The theories were written by highly educated individuals, such as attorneys Mark Lane and Jim Garrison, journalist Jim Marrs, and U.S. State Department analyst, Harold Weisberg.[68] They felt that official accounts of the assassination were insufficient, distorted, and that failure to confront contradictory evidence placed democracy in harm's way. Their research into the inconsistencies of the *Warren Report* and other materials were the first to illuminate flaws in the assertion that Kennedy was murdered

---

68. See Lane. M. *Rush to Judgment* (1966), Garrison *On the Trail of Assassins* (1988), Marrs *Crossfire* (1989), and Weisberg *Whitewash* (1965).

by a solitary lunatic. They also spoke to how the "lone nut" theory enabled Americans' stubborn denial that rogue elements in our democracy exist.

I stand with the 62 percent of Americans who believe that there was a conspiracy to kill President Kennedy, and that there still exists an official cover-up to prevent the public from knowing who orchestrated it and why.[69] Whereas monographs such as David Lifton's *The Best Evidence* and Dr. Charles Crenshaw's *Conspiracy of Silence* offer substantial forensic evidence that contradicts the *Warren Report*, books including Leroy Fletcher Prouty's *JFK: The CIA, Vietnam, and the Plot to Assassinate John F. Kennedy*, James W. Douglass' *JFK and the Unspeakable*, and Roger Stone's *The Man Who Killed Kennedy*, address the motives that Washington's power brokers had for killing Kennedy.[70]

It took me many years to appreciate the fact that scholarship has a place in our spiritual lives. It may seem bizarre to link studies of politics and history to spirituality, but for me it helped to sharpen the contrast between the material world and the Kingdom of God. My investigation of Kennedy's life and death forced me to respect the courage it took for common citizens, police officers, x-ray technicians, doctors, housewives, engineers, and journalists to contradict what FBI and Secret Service said about JFK's assassination. It compelled me to be a critical reader and to hold assertions to high standards of evidence. It taught me that just because something was in print did not make it true.

Eventually, I applied my lessons to other narratives of American history and to foreign affairs. A new world opened to me, and suddenly, American dissent and the complaints of people who lived under the boot heels of dictators the U.S. established in developing nations made sense. The U.S. was suddenly not the cosmic fountain of truth, and it was not the center of the universe. It hit me like a baptismal font over the head. What the sisters of St. Bridget told me as a child was true. God was at the center of our purpose on earth and I shared that purpose with everyone else on the planet, which made us brothers and sisters with a vested interest in the truth about how the world works and how our actions affect each other. Put in another way, our access to truth enhances our moral choices. Many Caesars compete to be the center of the universe, and they will marginalize, humiliate, threaten, damage, or kill those who resist. To secure his place in the material world, Caesar's first victim must always be the truth.

The trauma caused by Kennedy's death rings with something more than national grief for a fallen president. It resonates the utter disorientation that people feel when they lose heroes, and what happens when the personification

---

69. Craighill, "Poll," Line 1–19.
70. See bibliography for citations.

of hope and vitality is violently torn from our lives. The assassination left many Americans in a deep contemplative silence for a long time. People who were inspired by him still feel anguished decades later. Lots of boomers regularly muse, "I wonder what would have happened if Kennedy had lived and had a second term." The sadness and speculation suggest that people yearn for leaders who have a moral vision and a prophetic voice. They indicate that our spirits are kindled by what leaders do, and so seek their light.

For some, the grief over JFK's death is a special grief. It is the kind of grief that tempts people to stop grieving altogether, not because there are no more tragedies in the world, but because hope in humanity has been sucked from the air they breathe. Whether one believes the assassination was the work of a single deranged gunman, or the product of a conspiracy, it signaled an existential pivot in America. Evil had triumphed over goodness; insanity was victorious over reason; void had conquered vitality and charisma; and, the death of a president rattled democracy.

The existential crisis of JFK's death was essentially an intrusion of doubt into a world that was generally certain about the prevalence of a fixed universal moral order. In this order, nothing was random and God protected America because it was his special city on a hill. If JFK's assassin was a solitary lunatic, the universe seemed to be telling Americans that there is no such thing as an objective moral order. If the assassination was the result of a well-orchestrated conspiracy, then perhaps there was a moral order and it had been sabotaged by a Caesar that was too big to fight. For so many, JFK's death was the beginning of a spiritual crisis that engulfed the 1960s. At the heart of the crisis was whether the Kingdom of God, the better world that Kennedy envisioned, was so far beyond our grasp, that nobody, not even the faithful, should bother reaching.

5

The Quicksand of Vietnam

Texas-Sized Ambitions

KENNEDY'S DEATH MADE LYNDON Baines Johnson (LBJ), a long-time Kennedy foe, the nation's commander in chief. Since his days in the Senate, LBJ had nursed a deep hatred for the Kennedys and the political influence of their money. He resented JFK's Eastern Establishment roots and said Kennedy was just a "sonny boy" who never really did anything in Congress.[1] LBJ was JFK's running mate in 1960 largely because Democrats needed all the Southern votes LBJ could muster. Johnson had been a powerful Senate majority leader. He was adept at gathering information about fellow senators and using it to manipulate their positions on legislation. By 1963, there was movement to drop LBJ as Kennedy's vice-presidential running-mate in 1964, and it scalded the ambitious Texan who had ingratiated himself so well to so many Caesars, including oilmen, defense contractors, and Washington insiders.[2]

On one hand LBJ saw himself as Franklin Roosevelt's heir, a leader who would create the "Great Society" with welfare, civil rights legislation, Medicare, and public education. On the other hand, LBJ was a militant cold warrior whose time in Congress coincided with the fall of China to the communists and the Korean War. He fretted that he if did not stand up to the communists in Vietnam, he would be seen as cowardly, "an unmanly man."[3] He loved power and believed that for the sake of their own good, some folks needed to be bullied into doing things "the right way." He was also a man who

---

1. Dallek, *Flawed Giant*, 7.

2. Caro *Means of Ascent* chronicles Johnson's path to the White House, and along the road from 1948 to 1960, readers learn about how politics operate behind closed doors in America and the role of big money in the electoral process.

3. Dean, *Imperial Brotherhood*, 201.

craved the adulation of the masses whom he routinely despised.[4] Ultimately, Johnson's legacy and the nation were both ravaged by the war in Vietnam. The war caused many Americans to question the nation's morality, their own conscience, and claims that the U.S. was a Christian nation.

The war punctuated the reality that even when society holds itself to standards of just war, it can easily slip into an unjust war when the right propaganda is disseminated, and the right ego is threatened. It illustrated how difficult it has been to move a Christian nation away from Peter's paradigm toward the spirituality Jesus preached.

The People in the Photographs

In 1964, little Catholic first-graders in my class who pledged allegiance to the flag and prayed the "Our Father" could probably not find Asia on a map. By the time we reached fourth grade, we were hearing about brothers or cousins who died in a place called "Vietnam." By seventh grade, we were watching televised reports and reading magazines that were filled with horrible and shocking images of wounded soldiers, bodies floating in rivers, and bloodied peasants fleeing burning villages.

As a child, I did not know why Vietnam threatened my country. I studied geography in grade school and looked at textbook pictures of people from all over the world. I learned Asians were rice farmers who lived in thatched huts. I learned that they used animals and not tractors to do their work. The little Asian faces in the war pictures looked a lot like the ones my peers and I supported in our mission drives. I recall seeing the iconic photograph of Kim Phuc, the young girl running down a road near Trang Bang, South Vietnam with other crying children. They had been hit with napalm, an incendiary jelly that sets landscapes, buildings, and people on fire. The photo made me feel ashamed. The girl was naked and exposed to soldiers' eyes. She was in agony and she was vulnerable. I also felt a stinging heaviness in my chest like my heart was crying. I was thirteen at the time.

I knew only one person who was killed during the war, but his name is not etched in the Vietnam War Memorial in Washington, D.C. Gary died in training when an LCM-8 landing craft dropped its ramp on top of him and cut him in half, so he was technically not in the war. Two of the first veterans I met were proud to show me their collection of "trophies" they had taken from the war. They were the severed ears and fingers of their "kills." The mummified

---

4. Nelson, P. *LBJ*, and Hershman, *Power beyond Reason* address evidence that Johnson was manic-depressive, narcissistic, and obsessed with power.

flesh reminded them that they were alive—that they got the other guy before the other guy got them. Between swigs of brandy the veterans recalled episodes wherein the earth exploded and dismembered bodies were sent skywards. To the veterans, the owners of those ears and fingers were "gooks," nothing but loathsome objects in life. In death, the "gook's" body parts became treasured ornamentations of the victors' glory, and a testament of their numbness to mayhem.

Both of the veterans who showed me their war souvenirs were raised Catholic. I asked them once if their faith ever influenced the way they felt about killing people in Vietnam. "Hell no," one laughed. "Religion don't mean shit when you are in a mess of Cong who want to blow your head off—you just waste those motherfuckers before they waste you, and you let God sort it out."

One of the first times I wept over the war was when I encountered a picture in which an American solider held up the remains of a Vietnamese boy. The dismembered corpse dangled from a torn shirt, and the boy's shoulders, head, and single arm hung like a tangle of weeds dredged from the bottom of a lake. The pictures of Agent Orange's disfigured victims still arouse rage and grief. The U.S. used Monsanto's and Dow's Agent Orange (Dioxin) to defoliate forests and destroy food supplies. It afflicted American soldiers as well as Vietnamese civilians and troops. Since it resides in water and soil long after it is used, the morbidity and mortality caused by it was felt long after the war ended.[5]

Empathy was a cornerstone of morality in my household. When I wronged somebody, it was common for my parents to cross examine me with the question: "How would you feel?" At present, it is impossible for me to view images of people immolated with napalm or blown to pieces by Claymore mines and not ask, "What if that were my mother, my father, my brother, or my sister?" I learned to answer that question by remembering that the people in the photographs *are* my brothers and sisters.

Christopher Hedges has argued that war is "a force that gives us meaning."[6] He asserted that in war comes an inner fury to survive and an acuity of the senses. The emotional exhilaration of war is so potent that it affects people who are distant from battle grounds. It charges the adrenaline of policy-makers and everyone back home who has a stake in the war. War excites anticipations of windfall stock dividends from investments in planes,

---

5. Wilcox, F. A. *Scorched Earth*, describes the immediate and long-term effects of Agent Orange on fish, animals, and human beings, and also efforts to bring Dow Chemical and other companies to court as war criminals.

6. Hedges, *War is a Force*, 3–6.

ships, weapons, and all the accoutrement of war. War galvanizes national unity and a sense of purpose and identity.

War, as Hedges wrote, has two dimensions. The first dimension is mythic, which represents the way we frame the conflict and project meaning onto our role. In myth, good and evil are absolute and polar opposites. The mythos of war dictates that only one side can be virtuous, and must, for the sake of what is good and right, kill what is not virtuous. To be ambiguous about the righteousness of the enemy's cause or to waiver on whether he deserved death is to be treasonous.

In the mythic dimension, images of war are sanitized. Men do not cry out for their mothers as they bleed to death. They do not vomit as they wipe the entrails of their disemboweled friends from their faces. In the mythic dimension, there is no long-term morbidity and coast to war. The conflict is episodic rather than wholly integrated into society's foreign policies and economy. Seeing a war as an episodic event helps us pretend that war is not our systematic response to conflict, and imagine that it is an exception to how we respond to conflict. The role of the mythic dimension of war is to anesthetize our objections to it. It disguises the truth about war and its provocations, so that when Caesar rallies the nation to fight, people will gladly and proudly kill for him.

The second dimension of war is sensory. This is the real world in which men do cry for their mothers and sicken at the sight of a dismembered friend. This dimension is filled with the stench of chemicals and corpses. It is filled with searing screams of rape victims, desperate cries for mercy, and the endless percussion of guns and mortar. It is filled with hyperbolic bragging about "greasing Charlie" (killing Vietcong). It is a dimension in which one finds veterans of war too traumatized by combat to relate to their families and hold down a job. It is the dimension wherein public resources are siphoned away from education, health care, and law enforcement so it may compensate widows and orphans.

The mythical dimensions of the Vietnam War eroded as journalists, veterans, and government officials disclosed the truth about the conflict. When the mythic curtain of the war was opened, it shed light on the mythic aspects of American democracy. One could not, it seemed, expose one myth without exposing the other. Boomers and their elders who were raised to believe their government would never lie or engage in obscene acts against helpless populations had to face the reality that their government had indeed lied and committed atrocities. What many thought was a soundly moral intervention in 1965 became a sinful and senseless act of butchery by 1970.

From Advisors to Adversaries

The war in Vietnam began and ended as a failure of empathy. During WWII, the Vietnamese fought to win their independence not only from occupying Japanese armies, but from the French who had colonized the region in 1883. The French refused to leave and were defeated in 1954 at Dien Bien Phu. Eisenhower appealed to the British for help, claiming that Vietnamese resources such as tin and rubber were vital to the West, and that if communism prevailed in Vietnam, it would prevail over all of Southeast Asia.[7] The British declined the offer. The country was split along the seventeenth parallel. The North Vietnamese elected Ho Chi Minh, a communist, to be their president. Minh vowed to unite the North with South Vietnam, which had established a republic led by the American-backed Ngo Dinh Nhu. Eisenhower and JFK maintained a U.S. presence in Vietnam, but it consisted largely of CIA and military personnel who trained the South Vietnamese with the expectation that they would bear the burden of their own battles, as they repelled North Vietnam's attempts to annex them.

Kennedy's venture in to Vietnam was motivated in part by his promises to be a steely cold warrior. Keeping the promise was not easy. In 1961, Khrushchev ordered that the Berlin Wall be built, the Bay of Pigs invasion to overthrow Castro was botched, a coup occurred in the Congo, and communists were rapidly taking control of Laos. By then JFK had lost trust in his advisors, who did not always share his vision for peace and cooperation with Moscow.[8] Throughout his administration, JFK rejected the advice of hawks in the Pentagon who wanted the U.S. to send armed forces to Vietnam. Instead, he sent advisors and equipment to President Diem. JFK signed National Security Action memorandum (NSAM) 52, which renewed U.S. intentions to keep communism out of South Vietnam, but it did not call for combat troops.

Kennedy sent Vice-President Johnson to Vietnam in May, 1961 to assess the likelihood that Diem would prevail without a full-scale U.S. invasion. LBJ met with Diem, who was worried that the U.S. would allow South Vietnam to go the way of Laos. LBJ soothed Diem with promises of support that extended far beyond what JFK authorized, but that reflected what members of the Pentagon and CIA wanted.[9] LBJ knew that Diem was corrupt and unpopular, yet wrote in his report that, "The battle against communism must be joined in Southeast Asia with the strength and determination to achieve success there—or the United States, inevitably, must surrender the Pacific and

---

7. Moss, G. D. *Vietnam*, 37–38.
8. Fursenko and Naftali, *"One Hell of a Gamble,"* 127, and Moss, G. D. *Vietnam*, 37–38.
9. Newman, *JFK and Vietnam*, 70–72.

take up our defenses on our own shores."[10] His report stopped short of calling for an invasion, and suggested that such would not be desirable.[11]

Kennedy was in a hellish corner. In his inaugural speech he said that the U.S. dare not tempt its enemies with weakness, and that the U.S. would "bear any burden" in the defense of liberty, and now events were testing his resolve. He had also proclaimed that "civility is not a sign of weakness," and invited both superpowers to "explore what problems unite us instead of belaboring the problems which divide us."[12] Between the lines of LBJ's apocalyptic forecast of what would happen in Southeast Asia if the U.S. was not more aggressive and his cautious words about sending troops—which could have been insincere and duplicitous—was the implication that if Diem's government fell on Kennedy's watch, it would make Kennedy a failure.[13]

In October, 1963, JFK signed NSAM 263, which called for the removal of 1,000 military personal from Vietnam by the end of the year. On the day after Kennedy was buried, Johnson issued NSAM 273 reversing JFK's course.[14] There were about 1,600 advisors in Vietnam, and it was LBJ's turn to prove whether he would "bear any burden" to prevent communism from spreading in Asia.

Unlike JFK, Johnson was not a student of foreign affairs. He was vulnerable to short-sighted approaches to international conflict. He relied heavily on expert opinion, and reports from the field. The information he received was not always accurate. Caesar's officers, like military careerists of all times, have an interest in pandering to Caesar's ambitions. They often deliver glowing reports from the battlefields because they think that is what Caesar wants to hear. Generals Earle Wheeler, William Westmoreland, and Admiral Ulysses Sharp sent glowing confirmations that victory was inevitable. During Kennedy's administration, military officials and advisors often reported information that was exaggerated and contradictory.[15] Deception played a major role in the Vietnam tragedy, as generals continued to lie to presidents and presidents continued to lie to Congress and American citizens.[16]

10. Ibid., 90.
11. VanDeMark, *Into the Quagmire*, 10.
12. Kenney, "Inaugural Address," lines 48–50.
13. Historians Dallek, (1999); Hershman, (2002), Joesten, (2013) have abundantly documented Johnson's seething resentment of Kennedy and his class privilege. Roger Stone (2013) argues that Johnson had a motive for and a role in Kennedy's assassination.
14. See bibliography for NSAM 263 and NSAM 273.
15. Newman, *JFK and Vietnam*, 190–95, 223–31.
16. Ellsberg *Secrets* illustrates the scope of the Pentagon's deception and on how it impacted public opinion and political thinking. McMaster *Dereliction of Duty* exposes McNamara's exceptional confidence in himself, and how hubris and ineptness in the

THE QUICKSAND OF VIETNAM

At the close of 1963, it was clear that South Vietnamese could not repel the North by itself, and that many in South Vietnam saw the U.S. as a meddling empire. The 1964 presidential election was a year away, and LBJ feared defeat if appeared to be soft on Vietnam. Anxieties about being impotent were staples of Washington's culture, wherein men plumed their masculinity with aggressive posturing. LBJ's remarks about defeating the enemy were often sexualized and vulgar. He spoke of defeating the enemy by cutting off his "pecker."[17] In a meeting with advisors, he snorted, "Who the hell was this Ho Chi Minh, anyway, that he thought he could push America around?" He opened his trousers, wagged his penis in front of his pals and asked, "Has Ho Chi Minh got anything like that?"[18] This was an aspect of government leadership that the nuns of St. Bridget left out of my grade school civics' lessons.

In August, 1964, a destroyer off the coast of North Vietnam, was allegedly attacked. Despite murky veracity, LBJ leveraged the event to escalate the war. With minor dissent, Congress passed *The Gulf of Tonkin Resolution* that gave LBJ a blank check for waging war in Vietnam, and LBJ gladly authorized bombing raids against North Vietnam. In February 1965, thousands of American soldiers arrived in South Vietnam. By then, LBJ's advisors had lost respect for South Vietnam's army. The war was changing Vietnam. Brothels and bars proliferated. American aid intended for economic development was used to purchase goods to sell to Americans working in Vietnam—a practice that prolonged dependence on U.S. aid. With more dollars in its economy, Vietnamese officials inflated the prices of rent, permits, visas, and increased their investment in the enormously profitable opium trade.[19]

As military force seemed futile, Johnson wooed the North Vietnamese with financial incentives. In April, 1965, he offered Ho Chi Minh peace in exchange for a "Marshall Plan" for Southeast Asian. Minh rejected it as an imperialist ploy.[20] Increasingly, LBJ removed the Joint Chiefs of Staff from the decision-making process. They had failed to produce victory. Moreover, LBJ disliked their warnings about defeat. To maintain their good standing with their bellicose president, advisors were optimistic about the war. In turn, LBJ radiated confidence in victory. At the close of 1965, there were 200,000 U.S. troops in Vietnam, and the American death toll was 1,928.[21]

Pentagon and the presidents' administrations catalyzed disaster in Vietnam.
17. Schmidt, *Folly of War*, 281.
18. Darby, *Three Faces*, 158.
19. Herring, "People Quite Apart," 4–6.
20. Cohrs, "Towards a New Deal," 61.
21. "Statistical Information about Casualties," tables by year.

From Adversary to Terrorist

By 1966, protest against the war and Congressional inquiries put LBJ on the defensive at home. The U.S. Senate Foreign Relations Committee (Fulbright Committee) aired the complaints of generals, veterans, and presidential advisors concerning LBJ's management of the war and his lack of transparency to Congress. The hearings revealed the enormous scale of force and destruction needed to win, and caused the public to question the wisdom of the war. By the end of the year, nearly 400,000 American troops were in Vietnam and over 8,000 Americans had died.[22] In 1967, as negotiations failed and as the Vietcong increased their assaults, another 11, 363 Americans died.[23] Johnson found himself in the thick of political quicksand. Escalation threatened to draw China and the U.S.S.R. into the war. In August, McNamara, one of the architects of the war, testified before the Fulbright Committee that he had doubts that the U.S. would prevail.[24]

As the election of 1968 neared, Johnson was neck-deep in the quagmire. The Tet Offensive in January rocked LBJ's world. Vietcong guerrillas attacked over 100 cities in South Vietnam and occupied the U.S. embassy in Saigon. In the spring, Senator Eugene McCarthy (D-MN) and Senator Robert Kennedy (D-NY) announced their presidential candidacies and opposition to the war. Without a peace treaty in hand, LBJ's hopes for re-election were grim. On February 27th, CBS news anchor, Walter Cronkite, who had just returned from a tour of Vietnam, delivered a rare editorial to millions of viewers. He concluded that the war was unwinnable and that only way out was to negotiate, "as an honorable people who lived up to their pledge to defend democracy, and did the best they could."[25] Two days later, Robert McNamara, resigned.

As LBJ rallied his supporters, a massacre was afoot. On March 16, U.S. soldiers led by Lieutenant William Calley raped, mutilated, and murdered nearly 500 civilians in the village of My Lai.[26] Pictures of the atrocity appeared in *Life* magazine in November, 1969. The logic of war was plain in the pictures of bullet-filled women and children lying in a ditch: there were no lines between Vietnamese civilians and enemy soldiers. *Life* did not publish pictures of U.S. soldiers forcing their victims to perform oral sex on them, and shoving

---

22. Ibid.
23. Ibid.
24. Fry, *Debating Vietnam*, 115–120.
25. Bliss, *Now the News*, 35–51.
26. Turse *Kill Anything that Moves* and Bilton and Sims *Four Hours in My Lai* give readers a harrowing account of the massacre, and, perhaps more importantly, the conditions, values, and thought processes that ultimately lead to the atrocities and make them seem normal.

bayonets into the vaginas of their rape victims.[27] That aspect of the war, one so common in history, wherein men merge the thrill of orgasm with the rush of the kill, was censored.[28] Calley was tried for murdering Vietnamese civilians, and soldiers repeatedly stated that they were "just following orders."[29] Their petitions had the eerie ring of the Nuremberg Trials of Nazi war criminals. Calley was given a life sentence, but after serving three and a half years, he was pardoned by President Nixon in 1974.

On March 18, 1968, LBJ was in my home town of Minneapolis. He spoke to the National Farmers Union, telling folks that American blood was spilled for freedom and national security. He chided North Vietnam for refusing U.S. terms of peace, and called for a renewal of "patriotic support" for the right of others to determine their own government."[30] LBJ spoke with all the passion a man can muster knowing his cause is lost. He seemed delusional and oblivious to the fact that the U.S. prevented Vietnamese self-determination after the French left. Disillusioned and bitter, LBJ withdrew from the presidential race. In 1968, another 16, 899 Americans were killed in Vietnam.[31]

Richard and Henry Go to War

Nixon inched past Vice-President Hubert Humphrey (D-MN) in 1968 with less than one percent of the popular vote. He had campaigned on a law and order platform and promised to win the war with honor. To increase the odds of winning, he purloined details about secret peace talks from officials in LBJ's administration. If Democrats were to reach a peace agreement before November 5th, Nixon's hopes for the presidency would be dashed. Nixon needed to persuade South Vietnamese President Thieu that he would get a better deal if he delayed the settlement until after the election. The moment was ripe for intrigue. Enter Henry Kissinger, foreign policy consultant in both JFK's and LBJ's administrations—a man whose mind was as brilliant as it was imperious, and whose ego was as gargantuan as it was chauvinistic.[32]

Kissinger had participated in clandestine peace negotiations in Paris in 1967, but drifted away from the Democrats. In 1968 he was coordinating

---

27. Allison, *My Lai*, 27–50.
28. Weaver, *Ideologies of Forgetting*, 1–18.
29. Davidson, "My Lai Massacre," lines 18–19.
30. Johnson, "Remarks to Delegates," lines 128–46.
31. "Statistical Information about Casualties," tables by year.
32. Thimmesch, "How Kissinger Fooled," 48.

foreign policy research for Nelson Rockefeller, and playing both parties.[33] While gathering intelligence from Democrats close to the negotiations, and offering to provide Rockefeller with his own file on Nixon—a man Kissinger allegedly hated—he was also scheming to secure a place in Nixon's White House in the event of a Republican victory.[34]

In September, 1968, Kissinger learned of the Democrats' strategy for peace. The Vietcong would cease attacks against South Vietnam, accept a demilitarized zone, and move forward with peace talks if the U.S. stopped bombing North Vietnam. Kissinger relayed the news to Nixon. He also sent a letter to Humphrey in which he criticized Nixon and offered his service to Democrats. Nixon then offered Thieu better terms, so Thieu pulled out of the negotiations.[35] LBJ had halted bombing on October 31st, but the agreement upon which Humphrey hung his victory was in ruins. The wily Kissinger had done Nixon a great favor. He later became Nixon's National Security Advisor, and then Secretary of State.

Nixon urged Americans to stay the course in Vietnam as he had a secret plan for an honorable peace. His strategy was to reduce Ho Chi Minh's forces to a smoldering heap of rubble, or at least to frighten Ho Chi Minh into surrender by convincing him that he was a trigger-happy madman poised to use nuclear force.[36] Ho Chi Minh did not take the bait.

As support for the war atrophied, Nixon was in a bind. Massive bombing campaigns were politically costly, so Nixon opted for clandestine attacks. He widened the scope of secret bombing raids in 1969 hoping to destroy Vietcong supply lines in Laos and Cambodia. The incursions into Laos and Cambodia brought a tsunami of public outrage. Protests proliferated and the press amplified moral objections to the war. During ceremonies at Brown University, hundreds of students stood with their backs to Kissinger, who had been invited to receive an honorary degree. Kissinger bitterly grumbled, "Conscientious objection must be reserved for only the great moral issues, and Vietnam is not of this magnitude."[37] Here was vintage Caesar, taking control of the political narrative, and telling the world that the destruction, deception, desecration, and death manifest in the war did not meet the criteria of a "great moral issue."

As Hanoi refused to capitulate, Nixon reluctantly supported Vietnamization, whereby the U.S. transferred their combat role to the South Vietnamese. As this was under way, the U.S. took parting shots. In 1972, Nixon ordered

33. Hanhimaki, *Flawed Architect*, 21.
34. Hersh, *Price of Power*, 11–24.
35. Ibid., 18–19.
36. Sherry, *In the Shadow*, 312.
37. Hersh, *Price of Power*, 119.

the mining of North Vietnamese ports and massive bombing of North Vietnam. As the faithful celebrated Christmas in 1972, 36,000 tons of explosives were dropped on North Vietnam—more than all that fell between 1969 and 1971.[38] North Vietnam endured it. On January 23, 1973, a peace agreement announced the end of the war and the re-unification of North and South Vietnam. The Socialist Republic of Vietnam was declared in 1976. A 30 year episode in the Cold War was over.

Goodbye June Cleaver

Recently, I read "Made in Vietnam" on the manufacturer's label of a shirt I purchased. "That's curious," I thought: "Vietnam is communist country—we slaughtered a lot of people there to halt the expansion of godless Marxism—why are we doing business with communists?" In the end, the Vietnamese turned out to be the *good kind* of communist—the kind that likes to do business on American terms. Facing economic hardship and deprivations in technical and consumer goods, Vietnam normalized international relations in 1995. At that time, the U.S. had already enjoyed 16 years of normal trade relations with communist China. Kennedy's ghost looks on as former adversaries seem to have found that they are indeed united by common problems, and that those common problems concern barriers to prosperity.

The legacies of the Vietnam War are staggering. Approximately 58,000 Americans and at least one million Vietnamese, lost their lives.[39] About seven million tons of bombs were dropped on Vietnam—nearly five times as much as was dropped on Nazi Germany during WWII. In addition, over 19 million gallons of various toxic defoliants were used in the war.[40] The war cost about $500 billion dollars or roughly $2,204 per U.S. citizen.[41] The true cost to rebuild the farms, cities, and infrastructures, and to care for veterans on both sides, civilian casualties, and orphans, may never be known.

The war also made some folks rich. A sample of 36 defense firms shows that profits jumped from $471.5 million in 1960 to $1.2 billion in 1969.[42] There is always a lot of loot to be made in a war: weapons have to be stocked; buildings, roads, ports, and airstrips have to be built; oil and gas have to be supplied for ships, aircraft, and ground transportation; and, food and medical

38. Woods, *Quest*, 311–12.
39. Hirschman, et. al., "Vietnamese Casualties," 807–809.
40. Friis, *Essentials*, 163.
41. Hedges, *What Every Person*, 4–5.
42. Bohi, "Profit Performance," 724.

supplies must be sufficient. Caesar was tempted. Political consultant Roger Stone observed, "Where Kennedy saw a futile effort and unforgiveable death toll, Johnson saw an opportunity and a commitment to his donors."[43] LBJ's home state of Texas, after all, was and still is home to some of America's largest defense contractors.[44]

During the Vietnam War, the U.S. government contracted with Brown & Root, a subsidiary construction company of Haliburton, to whom LBJ had given special contracts when a young congressman in Texas. Eventually, hundreds of millions of taxpayers' dollars found their way to Brown & Root, and tens of thousands of Brown & Root dollars found their way to LBJ campaign.[45] As Brown & Root's contracts with the government approached $1 billion dollars in 1969, a young Congressman, Donald Rumsfeld (R-IL) wondered why his colleagues had expressed little interest in auditing the company.[46] The sweetheart deals were among the first of special contracts that would abuse tax payers by wasting resources, inflating the cost of services, and using profit to lobby for war.[47] LBJ's wife, Lady Bird Johnson, also profited from the bloodshed, as she was part owner of the company that made "tiger cages."[48] These steel grids were set over concrete pits that were five by eight feet and held three to five prisoners that were kept in chains.[49] Lady Bird's stock in Bell Helicopter also soared as thousands of "Hueys" were used in battle.[50] Vietnam taught us that even when war-mongers do not win, they can still generate profit for somebody.

The psychological impact of the war lingers in many forms. For some, Vietnam is a metaphor for the futility of war, and the folly of trying to force a way of life on others. For others it symbolizes the mistake of allowing public opinion to dictate how the nation fights its battles. When government executives compare Vietnam to other wars, they are not necessarily examining parallels to avoid war, but because they want to wage war without public scrutiny

---

43. Stone, R. *Man Who Killed*, 191.

44. Texas was in many ways ground zero for the military-industrial complex after WWII. Its oil, aeronautics, and construction corporations exercised considerable influence over the social and political culture of the now very conservative state, as documented in Cunningham *Cowboy Conservatism*.

45. Dallek, *Lyndon B. Johnson*, 46.

46. Stone, R. *Man Who Killed*, 192–93.

47. Disquieting facts about defense industries and profiteering are addressed in, Chatterjee *Haliburton's Army*, Rasor and Bauman *Betraying Our Troops*, and Carter, J. M. "War Profiteering."

48. Wells, *War Within*, 457.

49. Fridell, *Prisoners*, 72–73.

50. Stone, R., *The Man who Killed*, 46.

and accountability. President Ronald Reagan assured listeners that he was aware of the "Vietnam syndrome," and did not want the U.S. to get bogged down in a war in El Salvador.[51] In 1990, as President George H. W. Bush sent troops to Iraq, he declared, "I've told the American people before that this will not be another Vietnam . . . Our troops will have the best possible support in the entire world, and they will not be asked to fight with one hand tied behind their back."[52] To Caesar, Vietnam represents tactical and logistical blunders, not a lapse in morality.

Vietnam did not derail Caesar's imperious ambitions, but it did teach him to improve the way he manipulated the narrative of war. After the war, the U.S. military imposed limits on journalistic access to operations by creating press pools and directing coverage.[53] Journalists are "embedded" into military troops, and military officials censor their reports under the auspices of "national security."[54] Stories are told largely from Caesar's point of view, and the pictures they relay are highly sanitized. American Caesars learned that public trust is a matter of convincing people that from Isaac's sacrifice in war, comes something redemptive, even if what is redemptive is mythic.

The Vietnam War engendered cynicism towards America's commitment to decency and human rights. The war exposed Caesar's indifference to crimes against humanity. It made people question democracy and American morality. As my brother Tony said, "Vietnam was a huge turning point—it was the end of the June Cleaver era." To say goodbye to June Cleaver was to say goodbye to the belief that America's moral code was wholesome and incorruptible. It was to say good-bye to the idea that everything grown-ups said was true. Those farewells hit spirituality hard. Americans who had grown up assured that the U.S. was about the Christian business of "love they neighbor," were blasted by the reality that we did not seem to love others as much as we loved ourselves.

The Least of My Brothers

One of the songs we sang at Mass when I was in junior high school said, "Whatsoever you do to the least of my brothers that you do unto me."[55] It was meant to remind the faithful that our actions towards others were actions towards Jesus. When I sang, I had pictures in my mind of certain people that were "the

---

51. Reagan, "Remarks during a White House," lines 47–51.
52. Bush, G. H. W. "Address to the Nation Announcing Allied," lines 56–57.
53. Foerstel, *From Watergate*, 100.
54. Tuosto, "Grunt Truth," 20–31.
55. Willard F. Jabusch, "Whatsoever You Do," OCP, 2009.

least of my brothers." I pictured the single mother who lived down the street in a worn and tiny home; the elderly poor in my neighborhood whose teeth were missing and whose clothes were tattered and smelly; and I thought about the sick and orphaned who received money that my school collected for the missions. In my little kid's world view, I thought the "least" were only those who lived in poverty. I had not yet grasped that to be the "least" was not always to be poor, but to be despised. I was unaware at that time that popular culture had already taught me about who was the least. They were communists, Nazis, homosexuals, molesters, non-conformists, political dissenters, and criminals. None of these people were in my childhood prayers—though undoubtedly, they all needed them.

Ho Chi Minh was among the least. He was scorned because he did not accept the American Caesar's prescribed status for what LBJ considered puny people from third world countries.[56] Minh had worked in the U.S. from 1911 to 1919 and admired democracy. In France, he studied politics and socialism. Encouraged by President Woodrow Wilson's speeches about democracy and self-determination, he went to the Conference at Versailles in 1919 to present his case for Vietnamese liberation from France. He was flatly rejected by Western officials who held that colonial nations were unfit for self-governance. In 1954, nearly 90 percent of Vietnam's population were peasants who lived on small farms, without electricity, sanitation, modern medicine, and formal education.[57] From their perspective, socialism was better than colonial dictatorship. Though Minh used America's Declaration of Independence as the model for the Declaration of Independence for the Democratic Republic of Vietnam, Americans refused to see the battles of Hue and Da Nang in the same ways they saw the battles of Lexington and Saratoga.[58]

In his book, *In Retrospect* and in the documentary film, *The Fog of War*, Robert McNamara said he learned that it is vital to empathize with one's enemy.[59] He lamented that very few of the experts who advised the presidents had a deep knowledge of Vietnam's culture, language, and history. McNamara was Secretary of Defense not because he was an expert in Vietnam or statecraft, but because he was an expert in efficiency. In war, Caesar wants efficiency, which is defined by expeditiously subduing the enemy.

56. Kimmel, *Manhood in America*, 178.

57. For a concise overview of Vietnam's past, see Chapuis, *A History of Vietnam*. This text notes the historical animosity between Indochina and the Chinese, which is significant given the American belief that China and Vietnam would one day merge to form an Asian communist behemoth that would devour everything between the Pacific and the Mediterranean Sea.

58. Minh, "Vietnamese Declaration, 1945."

59. See McNamara *In Retrospect* and *The Fog of War*, directed by Errol Morris.

Whether LBJ was without empathy is debatable. Some suggests that LBJ took up the war because he saw himself as heir to the Southern tradition of caring for those burdened by injustice.[60] LBJ insisted that he had to stay the course of intervention because it was consistent with JFK's wishes as expressed in NSAM 52.[61] Others note that LBJ was determined not to be the first president to lose a war.[62] It has also been observed that in order for LBJ to get congressional support for his Great Society legislation, which included educational, nutritional, and public subsidy programs, he had to give hawks in Congress the war they demanded.[63] Ironically, LBJ's Great Society called for massive federal spending on behalf of public welfare, and was thus similar to the socialist path to Vietnamese welfare that Ho Chi Minh embraced. Johnson, it seems, could not see that each man was trying to do the same thing for his people in their own historical and cultural context, and within their own ideological framework.

Biographer Robert Dallek takes aim at LBJ's ego, which he believed clouded the president's judgment. He asserts that LBJ found it difficult to bear loss, and so created the expectation that his advisors would bring him nothing but good news from the front.[64] Vietnam reminds us that Caesar believes that the limits of one's own power makes one weak. In the Kingdom of God, however, it is the ego that makes us fragile. It is the ego that enslaves us to the fear of losing wars, wealth, fame, and power. It is the ego that keeps us focused on the approval of those we admire or need to advance our agendas, rather than on the flock we shepherd.

A Theology of Vietnam

In theory, a theology of a given subject should suggest what that subject might teach us about God and God's will. The Vietnam War contains some poignant moments that may lead us to a deeper understanding of the Kingdom of God and spirituality. Foremost in my mind is the reality that the presidents who lead the U.S. into the war were all Christians who publically espoused love of neighbor and devotion to God. These were men who, like many of the nation's military officers and statesmen, could quote the Bible. Despite their religious

---

60. Woods, "Dixies' Dove," 151–52.
61. Newman, *JFK and Vietnam*, 82–83.
62. Westheider, *The Vietnam War*, 12.
63. Nichter, *Lyndon B. Johnson*, 146.
64. Dallek, *Flawed Giant*, 309.

formation, these men not only pursued war, but defended it in ways that illuminated their low regard for fellow human beings.

Lots of folks who supported the war in Vietnam did so because they believed that the Vietnamese would be enslaved and oppressed if they did not have a government in our own image. It was charitable to want our Vietnamese brothers and sisters to have liberty and rights, yet our actions betrayed the limits of our charity. We justified rape, genocide, torture, and the contamination of an entire eco-system to drive Vietnamese sovereignty in a direction it did not favor. There is nothing in the Gospel that calls upon the faithful to shatter people's lives for the sake of sustaining a political and economic way of life. Vietnam asked Americans to ponder the question of what compelling objectives will separate them from their spirituality. It asked Americans to determine whether we actually possess the love and wisdom that is required to make life and death decisions for others.

I saw a photograph once that featured a priest saying Mass for a group of soldiers seated on the ground. The priest was wearing a chasuble that was made from camouflage-patterned fabric. On one hand, it conveyed the notion that the priest truly identified with the soldiers. On the other hand, the merging of the scared vestment with the iconic uniform of jungle warfare conveyed the notion that Caesar and God had become one. The image confirmed that somebody thought it was important to bring the sacraments to war. What remains troubling is that we seem to have made a sacrament of war in American culture.

There were plenty of clerics who saw soldiers as God's agents. Billy Graham, the lauded evangelical who advised American presidents for decades, said that he had no sympathy for ministers who wanted the U.S. to pull out of Vietnam.[65] Graham urged Nixon to bomb North Vietnam, ruin to its economy, and force its surrender.[66] Francis Cardinal Spellman was a crusader for victory in what many Catholics believed was a war against Satan's attempts to control the world, and Meir Kane articulated the Orthodox Jewish opinion that communism must be defeated as it was an immediate threat to Israel.[67]

LBJ held that the war in Vietnam was a just war, but that is debatable. The Just War doctrine confirms the right to life, the value of each individual, and the need to preserve life by force if necessary.[68] The Vietnam War pushed the envelope on righteous intervention and exposed some limitations of the Just War doctrine.

---

65. Williams, *God's Own Party*, 79.
66. Bothwell, *Prince of War*, 93–106.
67. Gill, J. K. *Religious Communities*, 97–99.
68. See Mattox, *St. Augustine and the Theory of Just War*.

First, in order to wage a just war, all other means of conflict resolution must be exhausted. The problems with that criteria are that both the "conflict" and the "exhaustion of other means" are often in the eye of the beholder. The Just War doctrine does not recognize the inherent superiority of any form of governance. It does not argue that democracy must prevail in all nations. It does honor preventative wars wherein tyrants are set to invade a country, but who gets to define "tyrants?" Ho Chi Minh was very popular in Vietnam, and U.S. officials say that if an election had been held in the 1950s, 80 percent of the Vietnamese would have supported him.[69] To Vietnamese, the U.S., was the tyrant, as it was fighting a colonial war and launching a preemptive strike at the same time. The Vietnamese seemed to be on the side of the Just War doctrine as it clearly vilifies a pre-emptive strike for economic or imperial ambitions.

Second, while the doctrine recognizes that economic exploitation can lead to war, it does not assert that economic exploitation *is itself* war. So much of the anti-communist rhetoric of the Cold War assailed the Soviet Union for turning human beings into slaves of the state, which is true in some ways, yet, the Just War theory does not vindicate military invasion based on this arrangement. If economic exploitation of the state or any other agency alone were enough to justify a military intervention, then—given the treatment of many workers in America—the U.S. might have to figure out how to invade itself.

Third, the Just War doctrine's assertion that perpetrators of war must secure the "likelihood of victory," is a very slippery slope. General Curtis Le May, who wanted to bomb Vietnam "back to the Stone Age," held that victory was a sure thing if the U.S. simply killed anybody capable of resistance. He was correct. The likelihood of victory increases when one has a stockpile of nuclear weapons and is not afraid to use them. Victory, however, becomes a relative concept if the victorious inherit an uninhabitable planet.

To say that the moral of the Vietnam story is that war is a bad thing that should never happen is trite and superficial. The theology of Vietnam teaches us the importance of listening to those who suffer, even when—and especially when—they tell you that your actions are the source of their suffering. It teaches us the importance of understanding our adversaries and empathizing with their needs, concerns, and fears. It teaches us to be slow in judgment because it is difficult to know every consequence of every action in the near and distant future. A theology of war teaches us that war devours more than lives and property. It teaches us that war ravages the humanity of both the vanquished and the victor.

69. Appy, *American Reckoning*, 20.

A theology of Vietnam teaches us that the assumptions we made about the Vietnamese did not permit Americans to see anything other than their own projections of the world. LBJ's approach to the war followed Peter's paradigm. It was unable to rise above political doctrines in order to see the least of our brothers and sisters. It was dualistic in its moral outlook, whereby all forms of Marxism were inherently evil, and all forms of democracy were inherently good. It was quick to punish those who "sinned," and slow to understand the "sinner."

When I think about America punishing other nations for "their sins," I think of when Jesus prevented the adulterous woman from being stoned. He did not argue that people had no right to take a life, nor did he say the woman was innocent. Instead, he revealed that those who were ready to kill the woman were themselves sinners.[70] As a child, I saw this story was a warning against hypocrisy, but it is much more. The faithful who were ready to stone the woman acted reflexively, and were encouraged by their peers. Jesus' intervention is thus a powerful invitation to resist mob mentality. In the Cold War, mob mentality was wrapped in the flag, and the flag was often hoisted higher than God.

As for defending righteousness with violence, I think of when the Romans came to arrest Jesus in the Garden of Gethsemane. Peter drew a sword and severed an ear from one of the soldiers. Jesus directed him to put away his weapon and told him, "Put your sword back into its place; for all who take the sword shall perish by the sword."[71] For many years, I thought that Jesus was telling his followers that those who exert violence against others, risk their own death by violence. There is more to the statement. Perhaps what Jesus meant was that something inside of us dies when we live by the sword. Perhaps "the sword" pertains to an aggressive state of mind wherein we are constantly poised to compete rather than cooperate, harm rather than help, and deceive rather than illuminate.

In the metaphoric sense, to die by the sword may be to extinguish that part of our humanity that is able to see the dignity of others, cooperate with others, and empathize with others. Symbolically, the sword is a summative thrust of ego. It represents the will to control, and to kill what cannot be controlled or possessed. The greatest act of dissent, therefore, may not be in one's refusal to wave the sword, but one's refusal to value the things that make swords our best friends. That was a lesson that even dissenters themselves confronted as protests and cultural revolutions proliferated in the 1960s, and as the temptation to take an eye for an eye presented itself.

70. John 8:1–10.
71. Matt.26:52.

6

Dissent

We Questioned

THE VIETNAM WAR AROUSED passions on all sides of the conflict. Opponents of the war were sometimes very quiet about their position, and sometimes they were not only publically very vocal, but aggressive in their protest. It was clear to me even in grade school that the demonstrations and editorials against the war were motivated by the belief that the war had crossed a moral line. Remonstrance typically did not lead with concerns about the cost of the war or the reality that the U.S. did not seem to be winning. Disapproval came from the gut as people's consciences told them that American conduct in Southeast Asia had strayed very far from American standards of decency.

As the details of mayhem, rape, and wonton destruction trickled into public awareness, people questioned the extent to which their own government was attempting to hide or distort the truth. For many, the war their first lesson in American imperialism. Some concluded that Washington's motives for intervention were neither honest nor honorable, and that executives in the White House and Pentagon could not be trusted. Some concluded that Cold War hawks had violated the Gospel and sacred teachings by insisting that God was on the side of American militarism.

Opposition to the Vietnam War represents some of America's most profound efforts to bring the Kingdom of God to bear on our relationships with others. Some demonstrations were forthright in calling for Caesar's accountability, and offered explicit resistance to the notion that Caesar had the right to appropriate Jesus as an ally in war. Some demonstrators bore witness to the reality that even those with noble intentions can take their protests to such levels of hate, destruction, and personal indulgence that they too become Caesar.

Atomic Dissent

Baby boomers did not invent dissent. American history is a series of dissent.[1] Dissent embodies the nation's imperative for liberty and the American "can do" attitude that had spurred Americans on to continuously make our world anew. It is an ancillary to our sense of individualism. Dissent is also part of society's on-going debate about the right relationship between the individual and the state, and the morality of national priorities and policies.

Dissent in the 1960s and 70s was infused with counter-culturalism. It was a feast for the mind and senses. Intellectuals wrote fresh works in social criticism, new theologies, and revisionist history. Some indulged in hallucinogens that facilitated journeys to uncharted regions of the psyche. Others designed what they believed would be utopian communities. Counter-culturalism and rebellion were ultimately commercialized. Peter Max made a fortune putting psychedelic imagery on everything from posters to plastics.[2] Merchants who privately cursed hippies happily took their cash for tie-dyed shirts and incense. When the trends shifted and the backlash against liberalism caught up with America in the 1980s, lots of folks looked back on the years of protest like a driver waking up from an alcohol-induced blackout. They wondered, "Did I hit anyone? Did I get to where I needed to go?"

America's experiences with dissent in the 60s and 70s are ripe with lessons about the challenge to activate one's spirituality in the American empire. They teach us that Caesar has an interest in repressing dissent and controlling the public's perception of reality. They teach us about the power of the media and stereotypes. They reveal that not all dissent is cut from the same cloth, as some was prayerful and peaceful and some was mindless and hedonistic. Finally, they teach us that even when dissenters do not prevail in the political sense, they often sustain the presence of the Kingdom of God.

Prior to the war in Vietnam, most Americans were optimistic about their ability to lead the world to democracy and prosperity. There existed a consensus that foreign policy rightfully aimed to extinguish and contain communism, and that few—if any—moral restraints applied to the endeavor. In the early years of the Cold War, Americans were largely unaware of Caesar's covert activities. Accounts of coups and civil wars abroad were reported in ways that hid CIA involvement. Folks believed that only traitors and communists used terms such as "imperialistic" to describe American activities.

The dissent that was so forcefully articulated in the 60s and 70s against war, however, began long before LBJ waded into the quicksand of Vietnam.

---

1. For an overview of this phenomenon, see Young's *Dissent*.
2. "Poster Artist Peter Max," 34–39.

The antecedents of the Anti-War Movement were lone voices in the wilderness. They were pacifists and scientists whose consciences were ignited when the first atom bomb exploded. They often echoed the anti-imperialism of generations past.

Truman justified the use of atomic bombs against Japan with the argument that in doing so, the invasion of Japan would be unnecessary, and hundreds of thousands of lives would be saved. Hawkish cold warriors thought that the bomb would shift the balance of power between the U.S. and the Soviets.[3] The bomb also brought some scientists great prestige, and some figured that the U.S. had to use the bomb to justify the gargantuan investment in atomic research. Before the U.S. dropped atomic bombs on Japan, scientists, including Leo Szilard, who had helped produce the weapons, petitioned the government against doing so.[4] Many on the Manhattan Project's team regretted creating the bomb, and correctly feared it would unleash a deadly arms race.[5] Scientists and scholars, not beatniks and hippies, were the first to object to nuclear proliferation. They were the fore-runners of the Anti-War Movement in the 1960s, and they were often punished for their efforts.

By 1954 a well of hope for peace and disarmament had sprung. The Korean War was over, Soviet dictator Joseph Stalin was dead, and Senator Joe McCarthy's reckless pursuit of communists in government and Hollywood had been censured. America's intelligentsia was inspired. In 1955, eleven renowned scientists signed the Einstein-Russell Manifesto. It illuminated the horror of nuclear war and called upon world governments to find peaceful solutions to conflict.[6] For his efforts, its co-author Albert Einstein was investigated by the FBI for his potential associations with communists.[7] In 1958, Linus Pauling, a founder of quantum chemistry, asked the United Nations to end to nuclear testing. His petition was signed by over 11,000 scientists from around the world.[8] The FBI spent 20 years spying on him and his associates.[9]

The general public joined scientists in their atomic dissent. In 1954, the U.S. Federal Civil Defense Agency instituted Operation Alert. Its purpose was

---

3. Alperhovitz, *Decision*, 127–32.

4. Berger, *Life and Times*, 77.

5. Rhodes *Making of the Atom Bomb* provides an extraordinary investigation into the motives for producing the atom bomb, the concerns it aroused, and the regrets it produced.

6. See "Russell-Einstein Manifesto."

7. Jerome, *Einstein File*, 228.

8. Hagar, *Linus Pauling*, 136.

9. Pauling speaks about his own conscience, faith, and activism in *Linus Pauling in His Own Words*.

to conduct civil defense drills. New York State made non-compliance with drills a crime. On June 15, 1955, a handful of protesters tested that law by refusing to participate. Led by Dorothy Day and the Catholic Workers Movement, the demonstrators held that since it was highly unlikely for anyone to survive a nuclear blast, it was wrong for the government to pretend otherwise by having such drills. Thirty-one people were arrested and faced a year in jail and $500.00 fine.[10] In the same year, Catholics, Quakers, and others participated in a prayer-chain for peace. It was the most vocal faith-based anti-nuclear initiative up to that point.[11] Reverend Norman Thomas sued the U.S. Department of Defense and the Atomic Energy Commission in 1958 to stop nuclear weapons testing. The case was dismissed as the court refused testimony from Japanese victims of atomic bombs.[12] Prayer did not prevent proliferation. In 1955, the U.S. had nearly 2,500 nuclear warheads and five years later they numbered over 4,000.[13]

Three events in 1957 intensified dissent. First, Harvard Professor, Henry Kissinger published *Nuclear Weapons and Foreign Policy*. He argued that limited nuclear war could be fought successfully without creating total war or mass retaliation.[14] Second, in September, the Soviet Union successfully tested the world's first intercontinental ballistic missile (ICBM), which could deliver a nuclear bomb without planes and pilots. Third, in October, the Soviets put the world's first satellite, *Sputnik*, into orbit around the earth. A space race thus enjoined the arms race.

As anti-nuclear activists labored for peace, academic dissenters criticized U.S. Cold War policies. One scholar opined as early as 1957 that the U.S. was so obsessed with moralism and a messianic spirit that its foreign policy had become inflexible and dangerously intolerant of national sovereignty.[15] Vietnam, it seems, was destined to prove the assertion was true.

10. Nepstad, "Disruptive Action," 99–100.
11. DeBenedetti, *American Ordeal*, 16.
12. Thomas, N. *Prerequisites for Peace*, 75–77.
13. Lundestad, *East, West, North, South*, 140.
14. Kissinger also observed that atomic science changed the way power is balanced. The territorial wars that once established the might of a nation, had been replaced by the possession of a stockpile of nuclear bombs. The stockpile, in theory, held external aggressors in check.
15. Thomas, M. L. "Critical Appraisal," 926.

Early Warning

Chugging through the waves of the South China Sea in November 1945, a group of American Merchant Marines received an order to transport 13,000 French soldiers to Vietnam. The Japanese had been expunged from Indochina, and France wanted its colony back. Crew members of the *Winchester Victory* sent a cable protesting the "use of this and other American vessels for carrying foreign combat troops . . . to further the imperialist policies" of a foreign country.[16] At the time of this first act of resistance to a war in Vietnam, many of the iconic personalities of Anti-War Movement were still in diapers. The protest confirms that in 1945 at least some Americans were uneasy about facilitating imperialism. Their story, however, was one I never encountered in formal studies of history.

Dissent against the war in Vietnam did not begin on campuses or with flamboyant rallies in the streets. It was born of what people with boots on the ground saw as they peered into what was left of Vietnam after WWII. It sprung from what military experts saw as they looked into the eyes of Vietnamese nationalists who were ready to die for their freedom. Historian Robert Buzzanco notes that in the 1950s, "several powerful and respected military leaders of the post-war era—especially Generals Matthew B. Ridgeway, James, Gavin, and David Shoup—rejected the notion that the United States could play a constructive role in Indochina."[17] Early dissenters included Vice-President Lyndon Johnson, Senators Mike Mansfield (D-MT), Wayne Morse (R-OR), and Ernest Gruening (D-AK). Within five years of deployment, warned JFK's advisor George Ball, the U.S. would have 300,000 soldiers fighting in rice paddies and jungles, never to be heard from again.[18] All of these dissenters believed that America had a duty to protect democracy, but held that Vietnam was peripheral to national security.

At the onset of the Anti-War Movement, civilian dissenters generally had confidence that if they simply exposed how the war violated democratic principles and humanitarian values, the U.S. would end hostilities. Prior to 1965, the Anti-War Movement was largely non-violent and populated by socialists, pacifists, conservatives, clerics, veterans, housewives, students, professors, state officials, and civil rights activists of all colors and faiths. Opposition to the war quietly percolated in academic and religious circles at a time when most Americans knew little about Vietnam. Organizations such as the National Committee for a Sane Nuclear Policy (SANE) and Women's

---

16. Appy, *Patriots*, 37.
17. Buzzanco, *Masters of War*, 9.
18. Perlstein, *Nixonland*, 102.

International League for Peace and Freedom (WILPF), demonstrated, while the Sisters of Notre Dame de Namur held prayer vigils and kneel-ins. Congregational minister and pacifist, A. J. Muste, pleaded with society to understand that the power to love made the power to destroy whole worlds unnecessary.[19]

On April 12, 1962, as the U.S. had military advisors on the ground in South Vietnam, Thomas Merton, a Cistercian monk, read a prayer before the House of Representatives. He petitioned the Almighty to save the United States from its obsession with power, and to "teach us to understand ourselves and our adversaries."[20] Merton also penned that the U.S. was incapable of making peace because Americans were reluctant to admit errors in their thinking, and mired in self-deception about their motives, which were greedy and self-righteous.[21] Merton called for the nation to confess its sins, but Caesar, still high on his victory over Axis powers in WWII and increasingly inebriated with the power he possessed, was not penitent.

The first major peep of public dissent against the war occurred April 17, 1963 when two organizations, the Women's Strike for Peace (WSP) and SANE held their annual Easter demonstration at which some carried picket signs opposing American involvement in Vietnam.[22] There were no crazed hippies burning the American flag at the event, and no national guardsmen pouncing on hysterical mobs. Instead, about 7,000 people gathered at the United Nations Plaza to support President Kennedy's *Test Ban Treaty* and Pope John XXIII's encyclical, *Pacem in Terris* (Peace on Earth).

College campuses provided fertile soil for dissent as many hosted army enlistment centers and allowed corporate representatives, such as those from Dow Chemical, (makers of napalm), to recruit students. Some had affiliations with the Institute for Defense Analysis, a think tank dedicated to weapons development. The democratization of college students that was achieved by the G.I. Bill and substantial increases in the enrollment of working class and minority students, had a liberalizing effect on campuses. Many students were very serious about academic success, but sensitive to discrimination and to the strident culture of conformity.[23]

The Student Peace Union (SPU) took up the anti-nuclear cause in 1959, while others pursued peace through organizations that were religious or socialist. Students for a Democratic Society (SDS) was formed in 1960 by students who saw themselves as heirs of a non-violent populist tradition

19. Muste, "Getting Rid of War," 85.
20. Merton, "Passion for Peace," 327–328.
21. Merton, "Roots," 96–104.
22. Farrell, *Spirit*, 172.
23. Horowitz, "1960s," 10–12.

committed to civil rights and fair labor practices. In its *Port Huron Statement*, SDS asserted that it was time to renew democracy, which had been corroded by racial bigotry, nuclear proliferation, and the abundance of the rich in the face of world hunger.[24] It called attention to the gap between the nation's reverence for justice and its tolerance of poverty and racism. It stated that the war in Vietnam was a symptom of a diseased corporate system, but rejected the Soviet option as a way forward.

Prior to 1965, dissenters from diverse professions, political views, and backgrounds had made three key points about the Cold War. Frist, a war in Indochina was militarily impractical. Second, nuclear proliferation was dangerous and immoral. Third, the imperious use of power was injurious to democracy. Even when combined, these assertions were not enough to throw LBJ off the bucking bronco of war. Only when the war consumed his political capital did he figure it was time to quit the rodeo.

Hey, Hey, LBJ

Caesars are often blinded by power and delusional in their sense of omnipotence. They are often inebriated by their own egos and believe that they alone may rightfully dictate the terms of a democratic process. Some offer evidence that LBJ came into the White House already toxic with narcissism and manic-depression.[25] It is said that he was obsessed by anti-Kennedy sentiments, and worried that others would see him as less deserving of high office than the sons of the wealthy Ivy League establishment. He was ruthless in his pursuit of dominance, and alternately self-pitying when he felt under-appreciated. When others got attention and praise he thought he should have, he punished them by cancelling programs or by cutting offenders from his circle of confidants. After being elected in his own right, LBJ enjoyed an approval rating of 64 percent and the majority of Americans supported U.S. actions in Vietnam.[26] In a year, the adulation lost its sheen.

Unwilling to accept defeat by a "third world" nation, LBJ dug in his Texas boot heals for as much war as Americans would tolerate. He believed that opposition to the war was the result of communist infiltration. He squandered the confidence Democrats had in the party's commitment to peace by offering

24. Hayden, *Port Huron Statement*, lines 5–18.

25. Hershman *Power beyond Reason* and Curtis *Hubris and the Presidency* expose the personal flaws of LBJ. In reality, others had similar personalities and thrived in America's political arena. This suggests that our political culture favors strong, aggressive egos, and those willing to ruin lives for the sake acquiring power.

26. Dallek, *Lyndon B. Johnson*, 172.

North Vietnam an olive branch in one hand and secret bombing raids on the other. LBJ believed peace would come on American terms only if the U.S. bombed North Vietnam to smithereens. He alienated fellow citizens by referring to "my troops" and "my planes" as if they were his personal property and the war was his private crusade.

The first major student demonstration against the war occurred in 1964. Led by the May 2nd Movement (M2M), it was not well-received as its members endorsed Marxism.[27] Opposition to the war shifted gears following the *Gulf of Tonkin Resolution*. Across the nation, people protested. At the University of California at Berkeley, students founded the Free Speech Movement (FSM) to fight the administration's suppression of political activism. Several FSM members had just returned from a summer in the South where they had worked for civil rights. They were highly educated and had assumed heavy adult responsibilities while risking their lives for a democratic cause. Like the SDS and M2M, the FSM held that democracy itself was imperiled by a lack of open debate on social issues, and by pressure to conform to traditional expectations without meaningful critique.[28]

In March 1965, *Operation Rolling Thunder* began a three-year operation that pounded North Vietnam with one million tons of bombs. LBJ averred that for the sake of ending aggression, it was necessary to inflict such horror. "I wish it were possible to convince others with words of what we now find necessary to say with guns and planes" he said; "armed hostility is futile."[29] The message was clear: North Vietnam would do what the U.S. wanted it to do, or the U.S. would murder its way to compliance. That spring at the University of Michigan, students held the first teach-in on Vietnam, with about 2,500 students attending. Universities across the country replicated the event, drawing tens of thousands more. They studied LBJ's narrative, alternative perspectives, and foreign policy.

LBJ also faced dissent from Congress and the Pentagon. In 1966, Senator William Fulbright (D-AR) began hearings on Vietnam. The televised proceedings revealed surprising fractures in support for Caesar's war. Lieutenant General James Gavin and former Ambassador to the Soviet Union, George Kennan—the man whose reports from Russia laid the foundation for the policy of containment—both challenged the legitimacy of U.S. aggression. General Maxwell Taylor, who had supported intervention, had become doubtful

---

27. Gitlin, *Sixties*, 180.
28. Eynon, "Community in Motion," 56–59.
29. Johnson, "Address at Johns Hopkins," lines 76–78.

about whether increased assaults would bring victory.[30] LBJ reacted to the hearings by placing Fulbright and his associates under FBI surveillance.[31]

In light of the war's mismanagement and moral turpitude, Security Advisor, McGeorge Bundy, Undersecretary of State, George Ball, and Press Secretary, Bill Moyers resigned. A year later, Robert McNamara left his position. At year's end, Senator Eugene McCarthy (D-MN) delivered a prophetic speech to his peers. He said the war was illegal, unwinnable, diplomatically disastrous, and morally wrong.[32] Recalling Rome's war against Carthage, he noted that while Rome was victorious, it suffered a mortal wound. War gutted the economy and upset social order so badly that reformers could not revive civil cooperation. The weight of greed and wars waged to satisfy it destroyed the empire. Like Rome, argued McCarthy, the U.S. preferred expediency over right judgment, ghettos over communities, disunity over shared purpose, and incredibility over integrity. McCarthy's message floated above political rhetoric in the stratosphere wherein the Kingdom of God lives—an altitude at which most Americans and Washington insiders were not yet ready to live.

By 1967 LBJ was in a pickle. Congressional hawks told the president that if he was going to bomb North Vietnam, he should go all the way with it. To do so, LBJ would risk war with China and the Soviet Union. Business executives worried that the war increased inflation and deficit spending.[33] War's carnage reached middle class homemakers who opened their *Redbook* and *Ladies Home Journal* magazines to review the latest meatloaf recipe only to find articles that detailed the mutilating effects of incendiary bombs on children.[34] Out of "Christian charity" some women adopted Vietnamese children who were victims of war.[35] Housewives known as the "napalm ladies" blocked shipments of bombs in San Jose and docks near Vallejo, California.[36] Lots of women strongly identified with Vietnamese mothers as they readily understood the helplessness of children and orphans.

LBJ's reaction to the horrors of war was less maternal. His obsession with winning made him defiant. He saw himself a victim of irrational dissenters who chanted at the White House gates "Hey! Hey! LBJ—how many kids did

---

30. Fry, *Debating Vietnam*, 55–74.

31. Woods, *LBJ*, 720.

32. McCarthy, E. "Senator Eugene McCarthy Crystalizes," 147–150.

33. A year by year account of the public's discontent with the war is found in Wells *War Within*.

34. Maraniss, *They Marched*, 72–74.

35. See Sachs *Life We Were Given*, which recounts "Operation Babylift" that in 1975 rescued 3,000 displaced Vietnamese children.

36. Wells, *War Within*, 84–87.

you kill today?" He isolated himself, became paranoid, and drank heavily. He told advisors that the Holy Spirit came to him in the wee hours of the day and told him which targets to bomb.[37] His conduct bore witness to the reality that messianic zeal can take the faithful to very dark places.

Kumbaya like Hell

While the Holy Spirit provided reconnaissance to LBJ, another Holy Spirit whispered dissent to concerned Americans. The war brought to the surface the old contest between the Gnostic paradigm and Peter's paradigm of the Kingdom of God. The Gnostic paradigm offered no solace for cold warriors. As a way of life, the Kingdom of God was incompatible with imperialism. American realism preached that the faithful could not bring the bounty of God's love to bear on "gooks" and "reds" because that gave comfort to the enemy and would threaten national security and democracy.

Peter's paradigm of the Kingdom of God accommodated cold warriors as it taught the faithful that the Kingdom of God was other-worldly. Peter's paradigm made the Kingdom of God remote, and in the space between heaven and earth Caesar assumed the role of God's middle man, who had an antidote for every objection to war. He appropriated Jesus for his agenda. Jesus, after all, had paid for everyone's past, present, and future sins. Caesar assured us that God needed good men to do bad things to avoid a greater evil. Lots of Catholics I knew took this position. While holding hands and singing Kumbaya in church, they were ever-ready to give the bad guy hell once the Mass was over.

Among the most bellicose in the Catholic community was Cardinal Francis Spellman, Archbishop of New York. As a young priest, he aspired to high ecclesial office and yearned to move in circles of secular power. He supported the CIA's coups and worked with FBI agents to undermine union leaders. When the Vatican II condemned nuclear war, Spellman publically opposed the position.[38] Spellman's adversary, Bishop Fulton Sheen, represented a more prophetic voice.[39] Sheen abhorred communism, yet, he held that peace on threats of nuclear annihilation was immoral. In 1967, he stepped away from the traditional Catholic compliance with the nation's crusade, called for

---

37. Hershman, *Power beyond Reason*, 213.

38. Cooney *American Pope* examines Spellman's life, ambitions, and political life. Spellman's career is an example how the lines between religious authority and Caesar have been blurred in recent history.

39. Winsboro, "Religion, Culture, and the Cold," 206–233.

an immediate end to the war, and appealed to the U.S. to reconcile with its Vietnamese brothers.[40]

The numbers of clerics willing to sign petitions to end the war increased as the war became more horrific. In 1965 the Protestant magazine, *Christianity in Crisis*, announced its opposition. Throughout the year, dozens of organizations such as the National Council of Churches, Fellowship of Reconciliation, and the Union of Hebrew Congregations passed resolutions calling for de-escalation and negotiation. Clergy and Laymen Concerned about Vietnam (CALCAV) participated in peaceful demonstrations, circulated petitions, and held prayer vigils. Its members included Jewish rabbis, Catholic priests, Protestant ministers, and theologians of multiple denominations. They shared the conviction that all political matters had moral implications, and that the Vietnam War was immoral.[41]

Religious dissent moved some to suicide. In Detroit, Michigan on March 16, 1965, Alice Herz, an 82-year old Holocaust survivor, poured cleaning fluid on herself and ignited it. She died ten days later. In a suicide note she told readers, "I did it to protest the arms race," and Johnson's "use of his high office to wipe out small nations."[42] Herz had imitated Thich Quang Duc, a Buddhist monk who self-immolated in June, 1963, in protest against Diem's persecution of Buddhists. In November, a 32-year old Quaker, Norman Morrison, sat down about 100 yards away from McNamara's office window at the Pentagon, soaked himself with kerosene and set himself on fire. He left memos condemning his government's determination to tell the rest of the world how it had to live.[43] Five days after Morrison's death, Roger La Porte, a 21 year-old member of the Catholic Worker, set himself ablaze outside the United Nation's library in New York.[44] He too was outraged by the war.

As the war intensified members of CALCAV, including William Sloane Coffin, Harvey Cox, John Bennett, Robert McAfee Brown, and Daniel Berrigan opted for civil disobedience. They participated in actions against the draft, demanded amnesty for conscientious objectors, and withheld taxes. They asked Dow Chemical to terminate their contract with the Defense Department, and helped to bring children maimed by shrapnel and napalm to the U.S. for medical treatment.[45]

40. Morgan, J. G. "Change of Course," 126.

41. Hall *Because of the Faith* meticulously traces ecumenical dissent and its contrast to conservativism.

42. Swerdlow, *Women Strike*, 130–31.

43. Mann, *Wartime Dissent*, 127.

44. Ibid.

45. Hall, *Because of their Faith*, 67.

In 1967 Father Phillip Berrigan and four others occupied the Baltimore Selective Service office and poured blood onto its files. Seven months later, Berrigan's brother, Father Daniel Berrigan led a break-in at the Catonsville, Maryland draft board. His group stole and burned 378 draft files. Berrigan said his actions articulated the Gospel, and that they were signs that the Catholic Church was engaged in the world.[46] Brown, a Presbyterian minister argued that to be passive about the war, made one an ally of executioners.[47] Reformed Church's Reverend Lee Kester declared that the religious justification of the war was a distortion of Christianity's purpose, and wrongfully deified democracy, and Episcopal Bishop James Pike charged that, "It is all right to tell Germans you can't obey orders, now how about Americans who say 'my conscience does not allow me to obey orders?"[48] Rabbi Arnold Jacob Wolf wrote that Jewish assertions that Jews had no place in public debate about the war was tantamount to the compliance of Jews awaiting deportation to Nazi death camps.[49] Coffin, Yale University's Chaplain, explained, "If we could pack the jails, Congress might act." NBC journalist John Chancellor noted that, "If men like this are beginning to say things like this, I guess we had all better start paying attention."[50] Ironically, Jesus had been speaking through the Gospels about peace and justice for centuries, but it took Coffin to get Chancellor's attention.

In his 1967 speech, *A Time to Break Silence*, MLK stated that the war not only laid waste to land and lives, but degraded the humanity of survivors on both sides. The sanctity of the Vietnamese family was desecrated and American soldiers were dehumanized as they became indifferent to torture, rape, mayhem, and murder.[51] He condemned war as an unjust way of settling differences. MLK's speech was denounced by 168 newspapers in the U.S., and caused LBJ to disinvite King to the White House. LBJ believed that King had betrayed him and joined the ranks of crackpots and communists.[52]

Seven months after MLK's speech, LBJ attended a service at in Virginia, and heard a sermon by Episcopal cleric, Reverend Cotesworth Lewis. The pastor declared that American Christians were appalled by the war in which "three times as many civilian casualties" as military died in a neo-colonial

---

46. Patton, "Rhetoric at Catonsville," 4.
47. Brown, R. M. "Dissent," 3
48. Yoder, "Protest," 54–55.
49. Staub, *Torn at the Roots*, 119.
50. Wells, *War Within*, 192.
51. King "Beyond Vietnam," lines 224–33.
52. Dallek, *Flawed Giant*, 467.

venture.⁵³ It took courage for Lewis to say those words in the presence of an American Caesar. Many congregations punished such preachers by withholding donations and firing clerics.

Life magazine rallied around LBJ. Its November 24, 1967 edition carried the article, *Daffy Datelines for a Critical Sermon*, which praised the White House Press Corps for providing "a gratifying guffaw" over the sermon. Members of the press posted mock datelines on White House bulletin boards. One read: "Washington—Secretary McNamara confirmed tonight that the Burton Parish Church had been added to its list of targets in the expanded air war."⁵⁴ The mockery bordered blasphemy. It was an odd thing to say in an era wherein churches were regularly bombed and vandalized because they supported the Civil Rights Movement. In Caesar's world however, where people learn to follow Caesar's cues on what is sacred and what is not, lots of folks do not recognize assaults against their own spirituality even when they see it.

Chicago

The 1968 Tet Offensive slammed defeat into American brains. Despite efforts to put a positive spin on the event, it confirmed the futility of U.S. operations. Peace talks began in Paris that year, but they did not alter LBJ's course. As the presidential election of 1968 approached, Eugene McCarthy and Robert Kennedy announced their bids for office based on a peace platform. Kennedy was murdered in June, leaving McCarthy as the lone peace Democratic candidate. Every bit Caesar until the bitter end, LBJ turned Humphrey's path to the nomination into a sadistic ordeal. After bullying Humphrey for years, LBJ told the Minnesotan that if he wanted the White House he would have to take his place as its cold warrior in chief. LBJ threatened to withhold support and see that funding for Humphrey's campaign would evaporate if he did not comply.⁵⁵ Thus came Caesar's Faustian bargain to Hubert.

The 1968 Democratic National Convention (DNC) in Chicago was a natural platform for dissent. Opposition to the war had reached a critical mass. The conflict had spilled over into Laos and Cambodia. LBJ had lied to the public and to Congress about the war, and government officials ignored critics and dissenters. During the DNC, rioting occurred in part because many stopped believing that their government listened to reason. Mayor Richard Daley ordered that barricades and barbed wire be erected to prevent

---

53. Woods, *LBJ*, 799.
54. Sidney, "Daffy Datelines," 38 B.
55. Solberg, *Hubert Humphrey*, 317–322.

protestors from getting near the convention center. Playwright Arthur Miller, who addressed the DNC, said, "It's a little frightening . . . being in this fortress trying to select a President, and I lament that . . . There is no contact between the powers that be and a lot of the people."[56] Protesters provoked cops, and cops baited protesters. The episode showed the world the limits of America's commitment to open debate.

To lots of folks, the scene in Chicago looked like revolution. For some it was a heroic stand against the establishment. For some it was a carnival of posturing. Roughly 10,000 Protesters faced over 20,000 police, National Guards, and U.S. Army personnel who tear-gassed and clubbed them.[57] Over 1,000 were injured and 662 were arrested.[58] In Chicago, whatever spirituality dissenters brought to the streets evaporated in blazing vulgarity and violence. Millions viewed the riot on TV and saw policemen beating unarmed protesters while others chanted: "the whole world is watching."[59]

Prior to 1965, media coverage of demonstrations against the war were scarce and tended to be treated as human interest. It tended to ignore substance and favor the spectacle. Big crowds, shocking confrontations, and celebrities got press; nuns praying the rosary for peace did not. Clean-cut and traditional, members of the Young Americans for Freedom were among the boomers that did not get the same press coverage as did their more raucous and colorful anti-war peers.[60] In the early years of the war, dissenters were largely depicted as deviant and misguided. Those who were anti-imperialists were dismissed as "reds." Those who were religious were regarded as "too idealistic." As press coverage of war and dissent increased, there erupted a battle over who would control the narrative. Conservatives wanted a narrative in the style of WWII coverage that lionized the U.S. as liberty's champion, and that portrayed demonstrators as anti-American. Liberals wanted a narrative that would hold authority accountable for transgressions against democracy and humanity. Everybody seemed to have hard time listening to each other.

56. Brown, W. R. "Television and the Democratic," 239.
57. Gitlin, *Sixties*, 331.
58. Moss, G. D. *Vietnam*, 266.

59. Gitlin *Whole World* chronicles the events of the protest in Chicago, but most importantly calls attention to how media exposure impacted protesters, and those who saw the confrontation on television. He argues that television media embodies its own ideology, which is often undetected, and designed to protect the status quo by reporting just enough dissent to sell the news, but not enough to expose how private interests dictate public policy.

60. Schneider *Cadres for Conservatism* makes the case that conservative young adults helped to retain the spirit of Barry Goldwater's republicanism throughout the 1960s and 1970s.

Television and newspaper executives saw profit in covering the outrageous and sensational. They managed the narrative about dissent by deciding which images to feature, which spokesperson to quote, and which perspective to take.[61] As demonstrations became more brazen and theatrical, networks and publications increased their interest but not necessarily their analysis.[62] They made spokespersons into celebrities, which inspired some to play to the cameras and to say things that their organizations did not believe. The celebrity effect inflated egos and fractured organizational unity. Media coverage reinforced stereotypes of dissenters that repelled mainstream Americans. Picturing dissenters as wild anarchists compromised the New Left's credibility. The caricatures of dissenters made it easy for others to dismiss their legitimacy. As long as dissenters were shaggy 19 year-olds throwing rocks at police, the Anti-War Movement could be dismissed a plaything of spoiled children.[63]

Nixon and the Liberal Bastards

Republicans capitalized on Chicago. Richard Nixon (R-CA), the law and order candidate, became our 37th President. Despite the failures of covert bombing, escalation of hostilities, international outrage, and unrest at home, the voters had elected a man who vowed to fight on until an "honorable peace" could be secured. Like LBJ, Nixon could not understand dissent. Like LBJ, he believed that antiwar activities were orchestrated by communists, and authorized the FBI and CIA to infiltrate dissenting organizations.[64]

By 1969 the left was disintegrating. SANE, CALCAV, SDS, and other groups found themselves at odds over objectives and strategies. Extremists in the SDS formed the Weather Underground and preached communist revolution. The Weatherman called for an end to the establishment, and as a new decade began, they inflicted terrorism in the form of bombings of government buildings and police stations. In October a nation-wide Moratorium to end the war was held. Over a half a million people participated in Washington, D.C. alone. Hollywood celebrities gave speeches, teach-ins were held, and people prayed for peace. Housewives, physicians, clergy, teachers, laborers, veterans, and people from all walks of life participated. Blinded by his determination not to lose face, Nixon saw the peace movement as reckless idealism,

61. Gitlin, *Whole World*, 140–75.
62. Ibid.
63. Bork, *Slouching*, 50–51.
64. Small, *Antiwarriors*, 61.

and referred to the broad constituency of dissenters as "liberal bastards."[65] He bluntly denied protests affected him, yet ordered his staff to find information that would discredit demonstrators.[66] In addition, some in his circle believed that the protests were damaging the peace process.[67]

By 1970 empathy on all sides of the conflict was fragile and worn. Then came the astounding invasion of Cambodia. The U.S. had already dropped two million bombs on Laos in its attempt to destroy the Ho Chi Minh Trail—the North Vietnamese supply line that ran along South Vietnam's western border—and was now intent on doing the same in Cambodia.[68] The escalation of the war sparked new waves of unrest on college campuses. On May 4, 1970, National Guardsmen at Kent State University in Ohio shot 13 people, killing four. Two days later, protesters were killed at Jackson State University in Mississippi. Nixon was short on sympathy towards the dead and instead fumed over young people's disrespect for the police.[69] The iconic photo of Mary Vecchio raising her arms in outrage over the dead body of Kent State student Jeffrey Miller cried for a rational that was not forthcoming. Earlier in the week, Nixon had referred to protesters as "bums," and said of the Kent State shootings that, "when dissent turns to violence it invites tragedy."[70]

As the White House braced itself for demonstrations scheduled for May 9th, 5,000 thousand soldiers were dispatched to Washington and 1,000 National guardsmen were deputized as police officers. At 4:30 AM on the day of the protest, a restless Richard Nixon took his valet, Manalo Sanchez for a visit to the Lincoln Memorial. There the President met with demonstrators and chatted mainly about sports and travel. He told his Chief of Staff, H. R. Haldeman, that he had also spoken about the "spiritual hunger which all of us have," and that the meeting was all about "the depth and mystery of life."[71] The spontaneous nocturnal encounter with students represented the part of Nixon that wanted so deeply to connect with youth as would a loving father. By that point however, many saw a deceitful Caesar in Nixon's paternal persona.

Nixon was raised in the Quaker tradition, in which piety, hard work, and charity were foremost. His father raised citrus trees and took on secondary work to make ends meet. Nixon knew what it was like to work hard in the

---

65. Wells, *War Within*, 386.
66. Hoff, *Nixon Reconsidered*, 228
67. Wells, *War Within*, 306–07.
68. Mirza, *Rise and Fall*, 422.
69. Langguth, *Our Vietnam*, 570.
70. Lytle, *America's Uncivil Wars*, 355.
71. Wells, *War Within*, 440.

dust and not have much to show for it.⁷² For folks of his generation and background, a college education was a treasure, and those had it were the luckiest people in the world. To squander such an opportunity for self-improvement was in Nixon's view a let down to the whole society.⁷³ Nixon had a good point, but students argued that they could not improve the world if they were busy destroying it.

Whatever spirituality Nixon had accessed during his conversation with the students seemed to disintegrate under the hail of bombs that would pulverize Cambodia, Laos, and Vietnam for the remainder of his presidency. In an interview in 1971, Nixon sounded delusional as he confided, "I rate myself as a deeply committed pacifist, perhaps because of my Quaker heritage from my mother."⁷⁴ At some level Nixon was aware of the existential and moral issues involved in the war. It was this awareness that so many dissidents hoped to tap as they made their objections known. Theirs was the hope that ultimately powerful individuals will be humbled by human suffering and shamed by atrocities they themselves have orchestrated. Theirs was the hope that humanity would somehow eclipse the ego and the attitudes that stood not only between themselves and war, but between themselves and the agendas that make war inevitable.

Growing numbers of elected officials were disturbed by events. Nixon's battle with dissenters thus graduated from one against "nutty" hippies to one against respected Congressional leaders. Convinced that the war was being fought on fraudulent terms, Daniel Ellsberg, former U.S. Marine and a Rand Corporation analyst once loyal to the cause, gave the Fulbright Committee 47 volumes of the *Pentagon Papers*.⁷⁵ The secret documents proved that, for years, U.S. officials had lied to Congress and the public about the war. They enraged Congressional members who felt that their authority had been usurped. They stoked the credibility of those who had expressed cynicism towards intervention all along.

Secretary of State Henry Kissinger called Ellsberg the "most dangerous man in America," and Nixon considered him a traitor.⁷⁶ Kissinger instigated the burglary of Ellsberg's psychiatrist, hoping to find something to discredit him.⁷⁷ Break-

---

72. Nixon's *Memoirs of Richard Nixon* is filled with sentimental and poignant stories that reveal the taproot of both his moral outlook and his ambitions.

73. Mazlish, *In Search of Nixon*, 95.

74. Wells, *War Within*, 477.

75. Herring *The Pentagon Papers* contains scores of government documents related to the war in Vietnam with helpful commentary for readers.

76. Sheinkin, *Most Dangerous*, 2.

77. Wells, *War Within*, 520. Ironically, the money to pay the burglars came from the

ins, wire-tapping, and deception were all in a day's work for Kissinger. He was obsessed with power and preferred the Machiavellian approach to government, wherein executives are not accountable to those they govern.[78] Nixon sued the *New York Times* which had published excerpts of the *Papers*. The Supreme Court found that the request to block publication of the *Papers* did not meet criteria for prior restraint. "Only a free and unrestrained press," wrote Justice Hugo Black, "can effectively expose deception in the government."[79]

Adding salt to Nixon's wounds, John Kerry, a veteran, testified before the Fulbright Committee. He had witnessed war crimes committed by American soldiers, and said that the U.S. exploited American soldiers for nothing.[80] For many veterans, dissent was the only moral way back to wholeness and forgiveness.[81] These veterans, often physically and psychologically maimed in combat, were punished for their dissent. Peers scorned them. Military personnel harassed them. People told them that they were a "disgrace to the uniform."[82] The uniform was Caesar's, and the men who wore it were told that it validated their manhood and made them an elite in their own superior society. Just as snakes shed their skin to renew their flesh, many veterans shed their uniforms and identities as soldiers to renew their humanity. Disinterested in the war's atrocities and unmoved by the moral implications of Kerry's report, Nixon had the FBI investigate Kerry.[83]

Jesus was Cool

In the sixties and seventies, protesters were caricatured as long-haired, bell-bottomed, sandal-footed, "kids." As the stereotype goes, they hated the police, and disliked hard work. My peers and I grew up believing that this image was an objective reality. The stereotype propelled a dualistic and over-simplified

---

federal budget for the Associated Milk Producers and was laundered through the organization People United for Good Government.

78. Kissinger's narcissism and paranoia, are laid bare in Hersh *Price of Power*. Hersh describes Kissinger's relationship with Nixon as "hostage," whereby Nixon compulsively needed flattery and Kissinger compulsively needed to provide it (p. 40). It is not hard to imagine this interfered with honest and objective conversations about weighty matters of state.

79. New York Times v. United States, 403 U.S. 713 (1971).

80. Schmitz, *Richard Nixon and the Vietnam*, 126.

81. Moser *New Winter Soldiers* offers interviews of veterans who dissented from the war and who struggled with their psychological well-being, patriotism, and sense of morality after witnessing and participating in horrific combat scenarios and atrocities.

82. Hunt, *Turning*, 99.

83. Bossie, *Many Faces*, 55.

way of seeing the world: young people hated war and older people liked war; people who opposed the war hated America, and people who supported the war loved America; those who conformed to mainstream culture were safe, and those who did not were dangerous. In my ten-year old eyes, hippies were curiously similar to Jesus. I pictured Jesus with long hair, a beard, a tunic, and sandals. He did not wear a crew-cut or wing-tips. Jesus liked to hang out with his friends and did not have a regular job. Jesus was about peace and love. He confronted hypocrisy. He was cool.

In 1968 I explicitly linked my religious formation with political attitudes. It was the year I consciously understood that God was not always on the side of authority. My classmates and I prayed that year for slain leaders, King and Robert F. Kennedy. Our prayers melded with those we uttered for peace. We prayed as earnestly as kids can pray that God put a stop to bigotry and killing, but prayer did not seem to work. I was bothered by the possibility people in Washington D.C. thought they were better than God. Through my youthful eyes, I could not determine whether it was God or man who was powerless to do anything about hate and war.

For many boomers, the sound of dissent was music. Modern liturgical songs, such as, "Whatsoever you do to the least of my brothers" provoked my young conscience.[84] Secular tunes such as: Edwin Starr's *War*;[85] Barry McGuire's *Eve of Destruction*;[86] Pete Seeger's *Last Train to Nuremberg*,[87] The Association's *Requiem for the Masses*;[88] Coven's *One Tin Soldier*[89] and, Phil Ochs' *I Ain't Marching Anymore*[90] captured my attention. They were serious songs. I was a serious Catholic kid. Eric Burdon and the Animals' *Sky Pilot* was a favorite. It tells the story of an army chaplain who blesses troops before battle, assuring them that God is on their side. A weary solider returns from the assault and remembers the words, "Thou shall not kill."[91] There was something magical about a rock song that referenced the Gospel. The idea that nuns, priests, rock stars, and folk singers like Bob Dylan and Peter, Paul and Mary were all saying the same thing inspired and legitimized my budding sense of social justice.

84. Willard F. Jabusch, "Whatsoever You Do," OCP, 2009.
85. Edwin Starr. *War and Peace*. Gordy, 1970.
86. Barry McGuire, "Eve of Destruction," Dunhill, 1965.
87. Pete Seeger, "Last Rain to Nuremberg," Columbia, 1973.
88. The Association, "Requiem,"1967.
89. Coven, "One Tin Soldier," Warner Brothers, 1971.
90. Phil Ochs, "I Ain't Marching Anymore," Electra, 1964.
91. Eric Burdon and the Animals, "Sky Pilot," MGM, 1967.

Leaders and Leadership

In my youth, I was inculcated with respect for leaders. I looked up to priests, teachers, coaches, and police officers. I put elected officials on pedestals. They represented decency. For me, their presence assured that order, safety, and fairness would prevail. Leaders were people who had a moral compass, and they were proud to be public servants. In grade school, leadership was an explicit part of the curricula. My classmates and I studied what made people leaders. We earned leadership positions in our classes, school safety patrol, and on athletic teams by proving that we were responsible, kind, fair, and self-disciplined. When we proved unworthy of trust, we were scolded and removed from our positions. My peers and I also knew that it was a shame to lose one's leadership position and that the worst kind of leader was one who felt no shame when he or she behaved badly. In my youth, it was outside the realm of possibility that someone could have authority and not be a leader.

My classmates and I also had the mildly cynical sense that leaders got to be leaders because they were "teacher's pets." Lots of boys and girls in my class mocked those who had leadership roles in Mass or a school event, and yet, most of us yearned to be recognized for that something special that set us apart from our classmates. It was a great source of pride to be an altar boy, the captain of a team, or milk monitor at lunch.

Aware of how leadership sometimes kindled arrogance, the nuns and teachers at St. Bridget constantly reminded students that with leadership came responsibility, and with responsibility came accountability. That was no small matter because accountability included answering to God. The nuns looked us square in the eyes and told us that good leaders think about others first. It was our duty as leaders to protect others, be a good role model, see that others needs were addressed, and to lift others up in times of sorrow and loss. Among the most tragic consequences of the war in Vietnam was that it convinced so many good people—so many devoutly religious and civic-minded individuals—that their own leaders and role models in high offices had made a mockery of public service and leadership.

During the sixties and seventies many leaders destroyed their own credibility. Government officials deceived the public. Military officers lied to their superiors. Journalists distorted the facts. Police and Guardsmen beat and killed unarmed people. Honors students in prestigious universities trashed public property and destroyed their professors' research. Anarchists targeted public officials for deadly bombings. In each instance, leaders found ways to justify the actions. That in itself was a wake-up call to my mind and spirit.

My Catholic formation profoundly influenced the way I reacted to these things. When I learned that U.S. presidents in my lifetime fought wars to "save face," I perceived the actions as both an abuse of Constitutional powers granted the executive and as a sin against humanity. When I read evidence that my taxes had funded dictators who treated their own people as disposable beasts of burden, I perceived the practice as both an abuse of the nation's wealth and as a sin against humanity. When I learned that some elected officials and judges were racist, I saw their attitudes as a slap in the face to principles of democracy and to God whose divine spark resides in all people. When I learned that my government lied to the nation about the motives for war, and of the obscene details of slaughter and sexual terrorism, I saw its conduct as defiance of civil rights and as a capitulation to evil. I have often thought about the war crimes committed by soldiers and the government that issued orders. Twenty years before LBJ began his bombing campaign, the world watched Americans prosecute Nazis for war crimes. In America, it seems, there is no Nuremberg.[92]

By the time I was 16, I no longer revered leadership like I did when I was 9 years old. The shift was more than "normal adolescent rebellion." Though I was rebellious—and my mother frequently told me I was "the limit"—the fact remained that leaders behaved badly. When they behaved badly, they placed spirituality itself in harm's way. When they fought wars for imperious and egotistical reasons, they legitimized the greed and vanity that is latent in all of us. As they lied to us, they helped to norm dishonesty. Their refusal to take seriously the thoughts of intelligent and credible dissenters diminished confidence in the democratic process and cooperation among people with diverse perspectives. The abuse of power and pillaging of public trust made decent citizens feel like they were suckers for following the rules.

When a 9-year old undergoes the shift from having complete trust and faith in leadership to being cynical by age 16, it is a contained crisis that threatens one individual's maturation process, and confidence in civility. When a whole society undergoes the same shift, it is a collective crisis that threatens the very moral outlook of that society, and undercuts the will of whole generations to cooperate and make sacrifices necessary for the good of us all.

Henry Kissinger was fond of psychoanalyzing dissenters and typically concluded that they were communist dupes or the off-spring of parents who were skeptics and moral relativists. He theorized that students rebelled against society because they had been spoiled by affluence, permitted to demand certainty without sacrifice, and then complain that they lived in a "spiritual

---

92. Nelson, D. *The War behind Me* presents a harrowing account of U.S. war crimes committed Southeast Asia. Military archives and interviews with veterans illustrate the U.S. government's indifference to the Geneva Conventions' protocols of war.

desert."[93] Kissinger demonstrated little empathy for those who felt that American culture was void of spiritual or moral substance. His family fled Nazi Germany in 1938, and as a student in the West, he studied the variables that made democracies vulnerable to fascism. An advocate of globalism, Kissinger saw the U.S. as the world's leader not because of its democracy, but because following WWII it had the military might to enforce peace and cooperation.[94] He was a realist who believed that for the sake of global stability, adversaries at home and abroad had to be kept in check, even when democratic rights and privileges were sacrificed for the cause.

From the perspective of the Nixons, and Kissingers of America, the U.S. was not a spiritual desert; it was saving the world from communist enslavement. Their commitment to use force—even to the point of threatening the use of nuclear weapons—raised questions about their sanity, morality, and their cause.[95]

Lessons of Dissent

People have very mixed feelings about dissent in the sixties and seventies. Some see it as a failure and an embarrassment. Some argue that it helped the nation see its moral shortcomings. Others lament that marches and acts of civil disobedience did not end imperialism, even though Nixon's administration admitted that protest tempered their actions in Southeast Asia.[96] The story of dissent, however, does not end with a whimper of shame. Those who called attention to the gap between the nation's espoused morality and its conduct, and who offered alternatives to Caesar's course of action still matter. They articulated our spiritual potential, and offer four important lessons about dissent.

First, dissenters taught us the importance of internal dialogues and examinations of conscience. Scholars note that, "Under the sway of ideology, men in the mass lose their capacity for internal dialogue, the inner conversation in which experience is related to conscience so that the aims and standards of conscience may be rethought in light of living evidence."[97] Boomers' experiences showed us that people at all points on a political spectrum are vulnerable to hysteria and demagoguery. Internal dialogues help us see the

93. Wells, *War Within*, 315–316.
94. Suri, *Henry Kissinger*, 1–2.
95. Ibid., 217.
96. Wells, *War Within*, 435.
97. Stevens, *God-Fearing*, 17.

potential consequences of assertions and actions, and to determine whether we have drifted towards Caesar and why we have done so. It is an opportunity to see that ideology is not the same as conscience.

Second, boomers' experiences reveal that internal dialogue and studies of conscience are enriched by learning. To empathize with others, we must know something about them. To know the truth about others we must sometimes scale Caesar's walls of propaganda. Many boomers can recall arguments they had over the war, and how excruciating it was to hear the opinions of people who were ignorant of the facts. Boomer's experience teaches us that partisans on all sides have an interest in spinning facts to suit their agendas, and that those who want the truth may have to work hard to find it.

A third lesson of boomers' dissent is that, even when dissenters' goals are not achieved, it is possible to bring the Kingdom of God to bear on earth. Dissenters offer us a prophetic voice. Like the prophet, dissenters are called not to be successful, but to be faithful. In bearing witness to the truth, dissenters compel empathy. Ironically, Caesar ostensibly went to war with empathy for the oppressed on his mind, and so the faithful is faced with the reality that the tormentor and the liberator are not always easy to distinguish. Prophets help others distinguish the two, and that distinction is vital to our moral decision-making, even if we do not achieve our goals.

Finally, dissenters reminded us that the quality of a society's leadership has an impact on public morality, national integrity, hope, and civility. In many respects, dissent, even in the extreme—perhaps especially in the extreme—was a cry for authentic and humane leadership. Dissent exposed the reality that American leadership suffered from its own priestly approach to the world. The priestly doctrine that America was without moral peer crippled its capacity to embrace all of God's children as true brothers and sisters. The priestly approach to leadership was reflexively hostile towards criticism and alternative perspectives. It tainted executive judgment. It prevented leaders from seeing that sometimes the least of our brothers holds the brightest light that shows the way forward.

7

Civil Rights

Across Third Street

When I think of the events that best represent American efforts to leaven the Kingdom of God into our public and political lives, the Civil Rights Movement shares a place with dissent against the war at the top of the list. This is because the Civil Rights Movement was both a political and a spiritual campaign. It was political inasmuch as it advocated legal reforms and called for a redistribution of power, representation, and rights. It was spiritual because it invited Americans to accept the proposition that everyone's well-being is connected to the well-being of the least and the despised in society. The Civil Rights Movement is filled with stories of prophetic individuals who would not permit Caesar to control the narrative about human dignity.

When I was five or six years old, I used the word "Nigger" within earshot of my mother. It was a word I heard my neighbors use. Enraged, she dragged me into the kitchen and scoured my mouth with a bar of soap and a washcloth. I sat on the steps near the back door, humiliated, crying bitterly, and bubbling at the mouth. One generally does not think about Minneapolis as an iconic city of the Civil Rights Movement, but it was ground zero for me. At the time of my oral cleansing, the Civil Rights Movement was gaining momentum and visibility. Both of my parents found racism repugnant. They explicitly taught me and my five siblings that it was our responsibility to "get along with everybody." My mother always said "It was "unacceptable for my children to defame other people."

My mother, who late in life became a peace activist and Associate of the Sisters of Notre Dame, grew up in Mankato, Minnesota, a small city of about 50,000. She told me that when she was young, people of color usually lived "on the other side of Third Street," literally across the railroad tracks that hugged the Minnesota River. There, she said, was were "the poorest people I knew." In the thirties and forties, tiny numbers of Lebanese, Native Americans, African Americans, and Mexicans represented Mankato's diversity. Mankato was discrete about its racism. As a child, mom thought that race-related problems were confined to the South.

My father grew up in different circumstances. He was the guy across the tracks. He grew up in Northeast Minneapolis under the grinding heel of poverty. His dad was an alcoholic who rarely held a job. My father often said that when he was a kid, "We didn't think about the color of your skin—we were poor, and if you were going to make it, you had to get along with everybody—blacks, Jews, Polacks—nobody was better than anybody else."

I had to take the matter of my foul mouth to the confessional, where Catholics report their sins, and then make acts of contrition. As a Catholic, I imagined the Civil Rights Movement was calling the nation to a collective confession, whereby it had to admit the sin of racism, and then make restitution. My classmates and I prayed routinely for civil rights leaders and wrote essays honoring them. As a youngster, I did not perceive that their message had implications for the American empire that went beyond ending discrimination against blacks. It took many years to understand racism's relationship to sexism, classism, militarism, and poverty. Society's denial of the connections were embedded in the sing-song history lessons that hid America's imperialism and caste system from view.

The few teachers who exposed American racism and its linkage to other offenses against humanity risked the ire of their peers and parent boards who favored a more patriotic rendition of the past. Mr. Falor, a former officer in the U.S. Air Force, was one of my public high school history teachers who sidestepped orthodoxy. I studied Native American History with him. It was an elective courses that drew about 25 students out of a class of 230. Only "nerds" and college-bound upperclassmen signed up with Falor. I was both. My class read Dee Brown's *Bury My Heart at Wounded Knee*.[1] It was the first history class I had taken that did not use a state-sanctioned textbook, and the first to prompt students to compare and contrast sources. As I read history from Native American perspectives, I saw that historical narratives are interpretative. I learned that by way of deleting certain voices from history books, Americans could see their nation as a moral paragon. Mr. Falor was not a Catholic school teacher, yet, he consistently demanded that students think about the suffering

---

1. Brown's book was published in 1970 and is a classic example of revisionist history, which proliferated in the sixties and beyond, and which aims to improve objectivity and representation of multiple perspectives in historical scholarship.

of others and the arrogance of those who inflicted the suffering. In his own way, he taught spirituality.

I cannot say that having my mouth washed out with soap for saying the word "Nigger" resolved all of my attitudes towards race. Like many of my peers, I struggled with prejudice. Everything in my upbringing, from religious sermons to parenting and athletic coaching demanded that I treat others with respect. Yet, there were peers who were openly hateful, bigoted neighbors, and relatives who used racial slurs. When pressed in public about my convictions, I stood firm on the side of justice. When pressed in private to laugh at a racist joke, I laughed.

My attitudes towards race and diversity were shaped by thousands of formal and informal experiences. I learned by listening to my parents' Nat King Cole albums as a child, and then later learning that Cole's 1956 variety show was cancelled because viewers were offended by a black man crooning alongside white women. I learned to laugh at what black comedians had to say about white culture, and to recognize the kernel of truth in the punch line. I learned by hearing my father's stories about his navy buddies of all backgrounds. I saw my father's pride in his decision as president of the school board to hire Mrs. Burger, the first Jewish teacher at St. Bridget School. I learned by listening to Mr. Miller, who taught Russian History without bashing America's Cold War enemy. I learned by reading Chaim Potok's novel, *The Chosen*, and discussing it with my high school math teacher, Mrs. Ziegenfuss.[2] I learned by playing sports with Native and African American teammates. I learned because the adults whom I admired were explicit in their expectation that I refrain from prejudice, and they were not afraid to take criticism for doing so. I was also profoundly influenced by what I saw on TV. Two movies in particular impressed me as an adolescent. To me, *To Kill a Mockingbird* and *In the Heat of the Night* are outstanding examples of how the arts bring to viewers the truth about our humanity, the possibilities of overcoming our troubled nature, and the good that comes from doing so.[3]

---

2. *The Chosen* is a coming of age story that explores the struggle for identity, and the individual's need for spiritual moorings, family, loyalty, and respect. The discussion my teacher and I had about that book were some of the first conversations I had about the Jewish faith with a member of that faith.

3. *To Kill a Mockingbird*, directed by Robert Milligan (1962; Hollywood, CA: Universal Studios home entertainment, 2012), DVD. *In the Heat of the Night*, directed by Norman Jewison (1967, Beverly Hills, CA: MGM, 2008), DVD. Other films that confronted racism impressed me as an adolescent, including *Gentleman's Agreement, Sayonara, West Side Story, A Patch of Blue*, and *Guess Who's Coming to Dinner*. See bibliography.

CIVIL RIGHTS

Finch and Tibbs

To Kill a Mockingbird is set in Alabama during the Depression. It is a story about Atticus Finch, a lawyer defending a black man wrongfully accused of raping a white woman. It is also about Finch's children who struggle to comprehend the adult world and decency. Like Tibbs, Finch, (played by Gregory Peck), is smart and gutsy. He is a widower who loves his daughter "Scout" and his son "Jem," and takes their moral formation seriously. The story is told from Scout's point of view. I identified with her, because she was curious and rebellious. She and I shared contempt for social customs that kept girls imprisoned in dresses, prevented them from climbing trees, and shut children out of adult conversations.

In *To Kill a Mockingbird*, Finch is admired for his principles and not for preventing racism to prevail in the halls of justice. Despite his iron-clad defense of Robinson, the defendant is found guilty. Finch's virtue lies mainly in the fact that, while he knows it is unlikely that a jury of twelve white men would find a black man innocent of raping a white woman, he is honor-bound to provide a stellar defense. Finch is revered by the black community, whose representatives, including a minister, watch the trial from the courtroom's balcony, and rise to their feet when Finch leaves the room.

Finch's moral potency had little effect on the mob that gathered at the jail with intent to lynch Robinson. It is not until Scout appears, calls the men by their names, and mentions something kind about them that the rabble dispersed themselves. The scene suggests that reason and law alone cannot achieve morality, and that shame keeps malice in check. Ultimately, Robinson is killed while trying to escape. It puzzled me because it seemed to reinforce the stereotype that blacks do not respect the law. When I was older, I saw that Robinson lost faith in the law and chose the manner of his death for the sake of his own dignity. He preferred to take 17 bullets in flight, rather than be electrocuted in captivity.

Sidney Poitier played Detective Virgil Tibbs in the film *In the Heat of the Night*. He was smart, gutsy, handsome, and on the right side of justice. Rod Steiger played Bill Gillespie, a stereotypical Southern sheriff whose racism and arrogance re-enforced my negative childhood perceptions of the South. In the story, a wealthy industrialist, Phillip Colbert, who planned to open a factory in Sparta, Mississippi is murdered. On the presumption that a black man with lots of cash in his pocket must be a criminal, Gillespie arrests Tibbs while he awaits a train. When Tibbs reveals his identity as a homicide detective from Philadelphia, Gillespie seeks his assistance in solving the case. As Tibbs clears another suspect wrongfully accused of the crime, the sheriff's ineptitude is revealed, and Gillespie wants Tibbs to leave town. Tibbs remains, however, after Colbert's widow tells Sparta's mayor that she will pull the factory and the much needed jobs out of town if Tibbs is off the case.

Tibbs's suspicions fall on Eric Endicott, a rich cotton plantation owner who opposed the factory because it would give decent-paying jobs and the status that goes with it to blacks. During an inquiry, Endicott swats Tibbs across the face, and was slapped forcefully in return. The scene was shocking in 1967, but I was with Tibbs all the way. Endicott presses Gillespie on what he will do about the exchange and snarls that in the past he could have had Tibbs shot for such an act. By then, Gillespie's racism has mellowed, and he replies that he does not know what he is going to do about it. After questioning Endicott, Tibbs is cornered by a gang of white thugs and Gillespie rescues him.

As the investigation unfolds, the two men wrestle with their own prejudices, and the reality that their cooperation has placed them in jeopardy. Gillespie's partnership with Tibbs warms when Gillespie has Tibbs visit him in his home. In their conversation, the sheriff asked Tibbs if he ever got lonely. Tibbs replied, "No lonelier than you, man." Outraged by the idea of sharing the same vulnerability as a black man, Gillespie called Tibbs "boy," and declares that he does not need his pity. Gillespie's struggle to see Tibbs as a brother under the skin is fully exposed, as is the sheriff's alienation from others. His pride will not allow him to take comfort from Tibbs, though he clearly needs it.

In the end, Gillespie turned a corner. Initially driven to respect Tibbs for his material utility in solving the murder, he learns to respect him as a man. Had Tibbs been unable to crack the case, or trembled in Endicott's presence, it is possible that Gillespie would not have changed his attitude. The worlds of Tibbs, Gillespie, and Finch are a worlds where laws and justice are pliable and relative. In this world, white officers decide when to enforce the law and white juries hear evidence selectively. The films revealed that in Caesar's world there is a difference between respect for a white man fighting for a black man's justice on white man's terms, and respect for a black man fighting for justice on any terms.

Faith in the Street

One morning in 1966, I discovered a pile of bloody towels in the flowerbox by the back door. Frightened, I asked my mother what had happened. The previous evening, my parents had hosted a study club in which parishioners joined Father McCarthy for a discussion of Vatican II. While they met, a fight broke out in the street in front of my house. The men broke up the fight while the women tended the injured who had been struck with baseball bats and broken bottles. I asked my mother what the fight was about. She replied, "Well, they were fighting because the black kids and the white kids just don't know how to get along."

The fact that my parents were engaged in a study of faith when teenagers were beating each other bloody in my front yard now seems like a metaphor. Those who are on a spiritual journey are not called to live above the fray, but to insert themselves into the material world to witness the Kingdom of God. The faithful gathered to study and pray that night did not cease to study and pray when they broke up the fight. They simply continued their study of the Gospel by doing what the Gospel asked. They bound wounds, comforted the frightened, and made peace.

There was no question at St. Bridget School that God was on the side of civil rights, but for many Americans, segregation was more than custom; it was divinely ordained. American realism dictated that folks from different races would always live in conflict. On that premise, preachers recruited God to vindicate racism. Pious segregationists claimed that mixed marriages would soil the white race.[4] They quibbled that segregation was not necessarily discrimination, and that segregation was acceptable because famous people believed in it. They wrote that integration was a communist plot to destroy America and declared that the president invited the wrath of God by appointing Negros to government positions.[5] They believed integration corrupted the Kingdom of God by attaching secular meaning to it.[6]

The Civil Rights Movement is sometimes presented as a legal contest waged with assertions about morality, rather than a moral struggle waged with assertions about the law. In reality, religious faith was foundational to the movement. Churches were among the first to host civil rights meetings and sponsor organizations. Religion provided the movement with its cause, structure, inspiration, and resilience.[7] In 1942, Reverend George Hauser, James Farmer, and Byard Rustin created the Congress for Racial Equality (CORE). The founders were deeply religious. They embraced Mahatma Gandhi's teachings on non-violence as a strategy to win civil rights and as a principle for

---

4. Butler examines 72 sermons delivered in the U.S. between 1955 and 1965 in "God Preachers, and Segregation." They reveal a legacy of twisted logic and Christian preference for a hateful and vengeful God.

5. Dicky 1958 book, *Bible and Segregation*, is his interpretation of Genesis and the origin of races. He held that God sent the Great Flood to punish humanity for violating racial purity and breeding outside "their kind."

6. Ellis, "Segregation," 6–9.

7. Morris *Origins of the Civil Rights Movement* applies sociological scholarship to understanding the secular and religious cornerstones of the modern Civil Rights Movement.

living.[8] Decades prior to the tumultuous sixties, activists of this ilk orchestrated peaceful sit-ins and demonstrations.

In 1955, Martin Luther King Jr., a 26-year old Baptist Minister, organized the Montgomery bus boycott. The boycott lasted a year and inspired several ministers, including Ralph Abernathy, Fred Shuttlesworth, Joseph Lowry, and MLK to create the Southern Christian Leadership Conference (SCLC). It called for an end to discrimination, non-violent protest, and was open to blacks and whites. SCLC's success was due in part to Ella Baker, former National Director of the National Association for the Advancement of Colored People (NAACP). Baker confronted sexism in the movement, and focused on the task of community building. In 1960, she helped students at Shaw University in North Carolina found the Student Non-Violent Coordinating Committee (SNCC).[9] SNCC worked with CORE to build interracial cooperation, organize non-violent protests, and played a major role in voter registration drives.

Like other denominations, Catholics were Christians divided by a common Bible. While some felt the Scriptures rallied them to integration, others held that they justified racial segregation. Catholics were in turmoil over civil rights. In 1958, the American Catholic Bishops formally condemned segregation, and called for justice.[10] Despite this, some priests were ordered not to challenge state laws on segregation and some were vehemently racist.[11] Many criticized nuns and priests who joined public protests, and pontificated that their jobs were to administer the sacraments or to be on their knees praying.[12] Largely liberal on social issues, Catholics gave President Johnson nearly eighty percent of their votes in 1964.[13] The leftist Catholic magazine, *Ramparts*, criticized American attitudes towards race. It regularly countered the conservative Catholic opinions found in sources such as William F. Buckley's, magazine, the *National Review*.[14] Buckley himself was openly racist. As the "advanced race," he argued, whites were entitled to establish the laws of civility.[15]

---

8. Morris, *Origins*, 120–38.
9. Payne, "Ella Baker," 885–899.
10. McCormick and Connors, *Facing Ethical Issues*, 56–57.
11. McMahon, *What Parish*, 144–45.
12. McGreevy, "Radical Justice," 230.
13. Steinfels, "Roman Catholics", 357.

14. Burns, "No Longer Emerging," 321–333. A lively and colorful account of the short-lived *Ramparts* and its impact on Catholics and the general public is found in Richardson *A Bomb in Every Issue*.

15. Judis, *William F. Buckley* 138.

Writing for *Ramparts* in 1963, Thomas Merton criticized the nation's conceptualization of freedom, and accused the nation of having little interest in human liberty and in the human person unless the individuals in question had something to buy or sell.[16] Merton was on to something. Civil rights was linked to economics. The African American cause meant little to some people not just because of good old fashioned racism, but because blacks had little in the way of material wealth to offer Caesar. Perhaps if they had they possessed the gold, diamonds, uranium and copper that, for example, that the Congo possessed, their petitions would have been taken more seriously. In many respects, it was not until great numbers of blacks registered to vote that Caesar took African Americans seriously. If not the gravity of their cause, at least the potential loss of votes tugged at Caesar's heart.

Quiet Them Down

Civil rights was a cause that could end political careers. In 1960, presidential candidate, JFK walked a fine line on civil rights. He publically supported civil rights to gain minority and liberal support, but tread cautiously on the matter of legislation, as he needed Southern votes. Kennedy had supported the 1957 Civil Rights Act which called for a commission to study civil rights violations and advance voting rights. The bill initially permitted the Attorney General to prosecute civil rights violations. LBJ, as Senate Majority Leader saw that as a problem for Democrats itching to secure the presidency in the 1960. Having little love for what he called the "nigger bill," LBJ engineered a compromise. The section that authorized federal enforcement was gutted before the final vote. Johnson saw the issue of civil rights as a matter of patronage rather than as one of justice. In a discussion over the bill, he said that, "These Negroes are getting pretty uppity these days, and that's a problem for us, since they've got something now they never had before: the political pull to back up their uppityness. Now we've got to do something about this—we've got to give them a little something, just enough to quiet them down, not enough to make a difference."[17] At the time JFK and LBJ won the election, neither one was a zealot on behalf of the people LBJ publically called "the Nigras."

In the spring of 1960, while MLK was jailed in Atlanta, JFK called King's wife, Coretta, to express his concern. Subsequently, JFK's staff distributed two million pamphlets calling upon blacks to vote for Kennedy because, unlike his opponent, Richard Nixon, he had compassion for King. Initially, MLK

---

16. Merton, "The Black Revolution," 8.
17. Caro, *Master of the Senate*, 955.

supported Nixon, but after JFK's phone call, he directed his community to elect Kennedy.[18] In his inaugural address, JFK attacked poll taxes, literacy tests, and obstacles to voting rights. During his first two years in office, however, the young executive seemed unwilling or unable to move civil rights legislation forward. Impatience and conflict sizzled in many communities as the delay wore on.

Initially, JFK fought segregation on legal grounds, arguing that Brown v. Board of Education, which banned segregation in 1954, had to be upheld at the state level.[19] To court favor with Southern Democrats, however, he appointed five openly racist judges to federal courts. These included William Cox of Mississippi, who called black plaintiffs "chimpanzees."[20] Many Southerners saw no legitimacy in Supreme Court decisions. Only the state, they claimed, had the right to determine laws on integration. JFK was also irritated by demonstrations, especially when they required federal intervention in states that were already resentful that he, and not Nixon, was in the White House.

In May, 1961 a group of CORE and SNCC volunteers boarded busses heading from Washington, D.C. to New Orleans to protest the segregation of interstate transportation. When Freedom Riders reached Anniston, Alabama, a mob tossed a bomb into the coach, forcing riders from the burning vehicle into the hands bullies who beat them. The flaming Greyhound bus and bloodied volunteers made headlines nation-wide. To quell Southern anxieties, JFK's administration quietly worked out an agreement with NAACP, CORE, SNCC and the SCLC. They would stop the Freedom Rides in exchange for private foundational money to launch voter registration campaigns.[21]

In 1962, James Meredith, an African American undergraduate, arrived at the University of Mississippi. Governor Ross Barnett went on TV to declare, "We must either submit to the unlawful dictates of the Federal government or stand up like men and tell them never!"[22] As 2,500 protesters clashed against 23,000 National Guardsmen and Federal Troops, hundreds were injured and two were killed. Barnett, who taught Sunday school, declared that "God was the original segregationist," and that integration was "genocide."[23]

While Meridith confronted Barnett, Cesar Chavez and Delores Huerta formed United Farm Workers (UFW). Like CORE and SCLA, they were dedicated to non-violence and saw the relationship between racism, poverty, and

18. Lemann, *Promised Land*, 114.
19. Brown v Board of Education of Topeka, 347 U.S. 483 (1954).
20. Dallek, *Unfinished Life*, 494.
21. Meir and Rudwick, *CORE*, 173–74.
22. Braden, *Oral Tradition*, 119.
23. Davis, *Weary Feet*, 244.

militancy. Laborers who picked crops seasonally were forced to work over 40 hours a week for less than a dollar an hour, no pensions or benefits, and no access to decent housing and sanitation.[24] As a Catholic, Chavez held that the Church had a duty to support the strikes and petitions of the workers. Catholics were typically divided. Some accused the UFW of being a communist front. Some withheld contributions to their parishes and bishop's appeals when they found their local priests and nuns participating in UFW rallies. My recollection of Chavez's movement takes me to childhood summers void of grapes. My parents were supporting the UFW's strike and so boycotted them. Grapes were a treat in my household, and my family enjoyed them only in July and August. Though I missed their refreshing sweetness, I accepted my mother's explanation that we had to "go without things sometimes because people were not being fair to their workers."

Stepping Forward, Stepping Back

By 1963, some civil rights advocates had grown skeptical about MLK's non-violence and cynical about Washington's commitment to civil rights. Growing numbers of African Americans turned to alternatives, including Muslim's Elijah Muhammad's black supremacy, which taught that whites were devils and that the Christian Bible was "poison."[25] In April, MLK was arrested demonstrating in Birmingham, Alabama. While behind bars, he heard that some white clerics found his defiance of a ban on demonstrations "untimely and unwise." His response, a *Letter from a Birmingham Jail*, justified his dissent. He challenged the assertion that the non-violent protests should be "condemned because they precipitate violence," and compared it to "condemning a robbed man because his possession of money precipitated the evil act of robbery."[26] He noted that the Negro community was told generation after generation to wait for justice as indignities and assaults were heaped upon them, and said, "We must come to see that human progress never rolls in on wheels inevitability; it comes through the tireless efforts of men willing to be co-workers with God, and without this hard work time itself becomes an ally of the forces of social stagnation."[27]

---

24. Ferriss and Sandoval *The Fight in the Fields* traces the ordeal of migrant workers in the twentieth century and addresses the role that Catholicism played in the UFW's work.
25. Berg, *Elijah Muhammed*, 59.
26. King, *Letter*, 8.
27. Ibid., 9.

Violence over civil rights intensified during JFK's term. In 1960, sin-ins produced 3,600 arrests, and three years later, the Birmingham campaign alone produced nearly 15,000 arrests.[28] Law-abiding protesters were arrested on specious charges and ruthlessly beaten by police. On June, 11, 1963, National Guards confronted Governor George Wallace at Alabama University where he blocked the entrance of black students. The next night, JFK addressed the nation, and decried the disparities between the rights and opportunities afforded blacks and whites. He announced, "We are confronted primarily with a moral issue . . . As old as the Scriptures." He enumerated the disadvantages of being black and pointed to the hypocrisy of demanding democracy abroad while stifling it at home.[29]

For every step forward, it seemed there was a terrible step back. Just hours after JFK's speech, NAACP field director Medgar Evers was shot dead in Mississippi. The elation of King's *I have a Dream* speech and March on Washington in August fell two weeks later, as dynamite exploded in the Sixteenth Street Baptist Church in Birmingham. The blast decapitated 14 year-old Cynthia Wesley, killed three other girls, and injured 22 others. A stained glass window on the lower floor survived, and "only the face of Jesus was gone."[30] Perhaps the assailants wanted to be sure Jesus would not bear witness to their crime.

From Neshoba County to Atlantic City

In the summer of '64 Mississippi was the epicenter of both hope and rage. The Civil Rights Act was poised for a vote. Millions of Americans were still poor, still victims of discrimination, and still without the vote. Though 45 percent of Mississippi's population were black, just 5 percent of blacks were registered voters. The KKK was a forceful presence in the state. They burned churches, bombed homes, and intimidated blacks who sought to vote. Many in the south resented the presence of civil rights workers and labeled them "communists" and "agitators."[31]

In the summer of 1964, CORE and SNCC participated in *Freedom Summer*, a campaign to register voters and to educate the poor in Mississippi. Over one half of the volunteers were white students from Ivy League universities and many were motivated by religious convictions. For many, the experience

28. Wirmark, "Nonviolent Methods," 118.
29. Kennedy, J. F. "Civil Rights Address," lines 30–49
30. Carter, D. T. *Politics of Rage*, 176–79.
31. Harvey, *Freedom's Coming*, 198.

was inspiring. For others, it resulted in a crisis of faith. The experience opened volunteers' eyes to "third world" conditions in their own back yard, and to the discrete racism of their own religious leaders and teachers. Among the volunteers were two Jews from New York, Andrew Goodman and Michael Schwerner. Both had been drawn to the movement by their faith.[32]

Goodman and Schwerner were joined in Mississippi by fellow CORE member James Chaney, an African American Catholic who organized voting registration events. They were part of a team sent to Mississippi to investigate the arson of a church used for a Freedom School. The men were abducted in Neshoba County on June 21st, beaten, and shot by Klansmen. During the search for the three men, officers found the remains of several missing African Americans left to rot in isolated woodlands and swamps.[33] The corpses bore witness to the reality that people could go missing in good Christian parishes without too much concern from the local law. The disappearance of Schwerner, Chaney, and Goodman magnified the urgency of federal legislation, and on July 2, LBJ signed the Civil Rights Act. A month later, the bodies of the three CORE workers were uncovered in an earthen dam. Eighteen were arrested for the crime, but, claiming a lack of evidence against the defendants, the state refused to prosecute. Federal authorities then pressed charges of conspiracy to violate civil rights laws. Only seven were convicted, including Deputy Sheriff Cecil Price. Jurors received death threats from the KKK and the longest sentence imposed was six years. Judge Cox issued sentences ranging from 3 to 10 years claiming, "They killed one nigger, one Jew and a white man . . . I gave them what I thought they deserved."[34]

The summer of 1964 saw riots and white backlash against integration. Bathers were beaten on Florida's beaches, and a hotel manager in St. Augustine poured acid into a swimming pool in which black and white bathers swam.[35] Some riots were sparked by police brutality. In Harlem, a six-day melee began when police shot James Powell, a black, unarmed, 15-year boy. Powell witnessed a building manager hose a group of black kids who had been sitting on the steps of his building. The boys retaliated by throwing bottles and garbage can lids at the manager. Powell had joined the fray.[36]

32. Cagin and Dray *We Are Not Afraid* provides a rich narrative on Goodman, Schwerner and Chaney and the events that unfolded in the summer of 1964. Also see McAdam *Freedom Summer*.

33. Watson, *Freedom Summer*, 191–211.

34. Ibid., 159.

35. Photographs of this and other confrontations in 1964 appear in *Taylor*, "1964: Civil Rights Battles."

36. Shapiro, F. *Race Riots* documents the Harlem riots with eyewitness accounts and insights to the religious community's efforts to obtain justice and keep the peace.

In preparation for the fall election, CORE formed the Mississippi Freedom Democratic Party (MDFP). It selected delegates for the 1964 Democratic convention to be held in Atlantic City, New Jersey. The MFDP declared that their black delegates—not the white delegates selected by white Democratic Party officials—had the right to represent Mississippi. It argued that blacks had been excluded in the primaries and thus were not represented. The confrontation threw the convention into the national spotlight. LBJ had set his mind on making the convention a mandate for his Great Society—a series of federal programs aimed at lifting people out of poverty. He regarded the MFDP initiative as an unjustified challenge to his ambitions.[37] Race riots, FBI clashes with the KKK, war in Vietnam, and dissent, swarmed around LBJ like gnats that would not let him breathe. Wanting desperately to be elected in his own right and not remembered as an accidental president, he had to work out a compromise that would please liberal Democrats while not alienating conservative Democrats.

On August 22st, television networks aired live coverage of the MFDP's appeal to the Credential Committee, which would decide which delegates to seat. Several representatives from the MFDP, including Fannie Lou Hamer, a sharecropper and CORE volunteer, were slated to speak. Hamer, shocked viewers with her graphic description of how she and others had been arrested and beaten for trying to register to vote. LBJ had been monitoring the program and panicked when he saw her. Hamer's accounts rang with moral authority capable of cracking fragile Democratic unity. LBJ had the networks pre-empt the broadcast for a presidential announcement—an update on national events that was so paltry many believed its sole purpose was to hijack Hamer's speech.[38] LBJ spared no paranoia to secure power. He had FBI surveillance placed inside MLK's hotel room and in store fronts rented by CORE and SNCC volunteers. He held that Kennedy fans and communists conspired to sabotage the election.[39] LBJ demanded that his Vice-President would have to be someone "who would kiss my ass on a hot summer's day and say its smells like roses."[40] In line for the job was Minnesotan Hubert Humphrey.

To clinch the nomination, LBJ pressed Humphrey to negotiate a settlement. He hinted that Humphrey's place as his running mate depended on success. As LBJ's advance guard, Humphrey demanded that the Democratic Party and the MFDP seat only two of the MFDP delegates. The compromise suggested that in the future, the Democratic Party would refuse to seat a state

---

37. Dickerson, *Dixie's Dirty Secret*, 96–97.
38. Donaldson, *Liberalism's Last*, 218.
39. Dallek, *Flawed Giant*, 174–75.
40. Ibid., 181.

delegation that was not integrated. LBJ's pal Walter Reuther was called in to manage MLK. As President of the United Auto Workers, Reuther had considerable influence over organizations that funded civil rights initiatives. He made it clear that the well would run dry if MLK did not approve the agreement.[41] Once more, white Caesars had set the terms of black progress. Johnson went on to defeat Goldwater, and signed the Voting Rights Act in 1965 that banned literacy tests and provided for bi-lingual ballots. His administration's battle with racism, however, was not over.

Plymouth Avenue

In February, 1965, Malcom X was assassinated by members of the Nation of Islam. After preaching hatred for whites, he had converted to Sunni Islam and opened himself to dialogue with MLK and others urging non-violence. He had come to believe that Black Nationalism wounded the humanitarian essence of the civil rights cause, and that blacks and whites should work together to bring about a world truly dedicated to respect for human dignity—something much larger than civil rights.[42] His death punctuated the rift between those who sought justice through interracial and peaceful collaboration and those who did not.

In the spring of 1965, my mother was invited to join a group of Catholic activists who would march from Selma to Montgomery with MLK. My mother declined, as she did not want to leave five children with a baby sitter for a week. On March 7th, demonstrators met Sheriff Jim Clark's mob of deputized citizens, who assaulted marchers with clubs, tear gas, and rubber hoses wrapped with barbed wire. Dozens were injured. Days after the event, civil rights worker, Viola Liuzzo, a 39 year-old housewife and mother of five, was shot while driving near Selma. She had broken a Southern taboo by offering a ride to Leroy Morton, a 19 year-old African American activist. In a speech to the New York Police Department's Holy Names Society, William Buckley, Jr. said that Liuzzo violated the unwritten rules about white, liberal, activism in the South. The South, he pontificated, could not be blamed for doing what it did. The audience burst into applause and cheering.[43]

Increasingly, the riots became deadly. In August, 1965, 34 people died in the Watts neighborhood of Los Angeles when rioting broke out following an argument between a white policeman and a black motorist. In 1966,

---

41. Skipper, *Showdown*, 132–33.
42. Morrow, "Malcolm X," 221.
43. Bridges and Coyne, *Strictly Right*, 90.

hundreds were injured and several died in riots in Cleveland, St. Louis, San Francisco, and Chicago. In July, 1967, 26 people died in Newark riots, and another 43 perished in Detroit. Racial unrest impacted white support for civil rights. While white support for equal job opportunities doubled between 1940 and 1963, nearly two thirds of whites disapproved of the Freedom Rides and King's March on Washington.[44] Minnesota's Hubert Humphrey, who had done so much to inch Democrats forward on the matter of civil rights, paled as race riots came home to his land of lakes. He toured many of the cities hardest hit by the melees, walked through decaying housing units and neglected neighborhoods, and remarked, "It's no wonder that some people are part animal. They have to be to survive."[45]

When I was a kid, Minnesotans' boasted of Minneapolis's diverse population, because it was home to Italians, Poles, Irish, Germans, Scandinavians, and Jews. In those days, we were proud that Lutherans lived peacefully beside Catholics. In 1960, 96.8 percent of Minneapolis' 482,872 residents were white.[46] Minneapolis' history is scarred by bigotry. In the early 20th century, many of Minnesota's most lucrative industries, such as iron mining, lumbering, grain milling, and banking were closed to Jews.[47] Discrimination persisted in housing as well. As Mayor of Minneapolis from 1945 to 1948, Humphrey commissioned a study that found that 63 percent of firms did not hire Jews, blacks, or Japanese Americans. In 1947, the Joint Committee for Employment Opportunity was formed in my home town and had 46 organizations working with local businesses to end discrimination. Two years later, Minneapolis was recognized by the National Conference for Christians and Jews for improving business policies.[48] Despite these efforts, Jim Crow was alive and well from International Falls to Albert Lea.

On August 3, 1966, blacks attacked businesses along Plymouth Avenue in North Minneapolis. They threw rocks through windows and looted shops. Most of the commercial buildings along Plymouth Avenue were owned and operated by Jews, who's German and Eastern European ancestors fled poverty and oppression at the turn of the twentieth century. African Americans who lived in the neighborhood complained that the Jews inflated the prices of inferior goods and provided no jobs for them. During the week of July 21, 1967, riots erupted again on Plymouth Avenue, and the National Guardsmen were called in to restore order.

44. Haines, *Black Radicals*, 45–46.
45. Sidney, "L.B.J.'s Ombudsman," 36.
46. U.S. Census Bureau, "Table 24: Minnesota."
47. Weber, "Gentiles Preferred," 168.
48. Ibid., 180–81.

The Near North Community, where Plymouth Avenue runs east-west, is less than three miles from where I grew up. As a child, I went there to compete in sports. Racial tension was real even for eleven year-old girls playing basketball. Most of the teams of inner city Catholic schools were white. Ascension School, located in the Near North was an exception. Closer to Plymouth Avenue, the school had more African American and Native American families than St. Bridget. As with St. Bridget, Ascension School was next to the church, and the adults that chaperoned activities saw their work as a ministry. They intervened when kids got rough or sassy. They explicitly taught sportsmanship and respect for other teams and their communities.

It was common for Ascension's Monsignor William Coates to be in the stands at the basketball games. He loved people and he celebrated youth. Most kids liked the attention of adults when they were competing. To see a priest at the game was a big deal. Coates made folks feel like family. When riots broke out in his parish during the 1960s, he served on the Mayor's committee to resolve the conflict. Years after my days in Ascension's gym, my father worked with Coates as an ordained deacon at the Church of the Ascension. He was proud to be a part of Ascension's parish, and often said he felt more love at Ascension than he felt in other more affluent, more homogenous parishes.

Plymouth Avenue met the rest of Minneapolis when the school district implemented its desegregation programs in 1970s. Pursuant to state guidelines that set a maximum enrollment of minority students at a Minneapolis public school at 30 percent, bussing programs were implemented on elementary and secondary campuses. At that time, over 80 percent of Minneapolis Public Schools' 55,000 students, and ninety percent of the faculty were white.[49] The desegregation initiative called upon schools to create magnet programs and then directed principles to invite students interested in them to be bussed to the magnet campus. About 11,000 students were bussed in the first year of the program, and the district increased its recruitment of minority teachers.

Bussing drew many complaints, and the price tag was considerable. Transportation, teacher training, and enforcement cost tax payers millions of dollars annually. The first school pairing alone coast about $500,000.[50] Some felt that bussing contributed to higher standards of learning, while others thought that it disrupted communities. Teachers complained that they were being asked to do things for which they were ill-prepared. I missed the bussing program at Patrick Henry, but my brother, Joe, did not. He noted that students wasted hours of time in cross-town travel, and that many saw the program as a joke. Students were bussed in, he said, "but at the end of the day they were

---

49. United States Commission on Civil Rights, *School Desegregation*, 2.
50. Ibid., 15.

bussed right back to the impoverished and depressed neighborhoods where they came from—don't you think they resented the hell out of that?"

Affirmative Action evolved by way of executive orders, amendments to the 1964 Civil Rights Act, and federal enforcement programs throughout the sixties and seventies. It helped many to get out of poverty, but did not resolve enduring anxieties about race and justice. It called for hiring quotas, enrollment standards for universities, and time-tables by which institutions would reach their diversity goals. It irritated state and local officials who felt the federal government was abusing its authority in futile attempts to engineer society. Critics charged that it was expensive, displaced white male workers, lowered incentives for workers to excel, and decreased academic standards. Some say it resulted in reverse discrimination. Others opined that it spawned a culture of entitlement and dependency.[51]

By the late 1960s, the Civil Rights Movement had assumed a new militancy. The Civil Rights Act and Voting Rights Act had not lifted African Americans out of urban or rural poverty, and had certainly not expunged racism from the hearts of bigots ready to offend and discriminate against them. In 1966, Stokely Carmichael called for Black Power. He reasoned that integration was problematic because, while it paved a path for some blacks to escape the ghetto, it did not transform society, which he believed was morally mangled by capitalism.[52] James Forman, former member of SNCC and the Black Panther Party, denounced capitalism and said the U.S was the most barbaric country in the world. He called on blacks to lead a global revolution against white oppression.[53] In 1966 Oakland residents Huey Newton and Bobby Seale formed the Black Panthers. The Panthers openly disparaged capitalism. Their platform called for decent housing, full employment of black men, good schools, an end to police brutality, and the exemption of black men from military service.[54]

Black Power and Black Panthers brought white anxieties to the surface. Some felt that blacks had achieved enough by way of legislation and public assistance, and that agitators were simply ungrateful. It was clear by 1967 that liberal Americans were generally amenable to the idea that such a wealthy nation should give minorities a wider slice of the prosperity pie, but they did not want the dessert menu altered. Morally bankrupt or not, capitalism would prevail.

---

51. Curry *Affirmative Action Debate* and Beckwith and Jones *Affirmative Action* capture the arguments on all side of the Affirmative Action controversy.
52. Carmichael, "What We Want," 137–44.
53. Forman, *Black Manifesto*, 80–89.
54. "Black Panther Party: Platform," 159–64.

A King Called Caesar Out

To understand civil unrest, LBJ created the Commission on Civil Disorders which studied 23 cities in which race riots had erupted. It looked for a communist conspiracy, but found none. Instead, the *Kerner Report* found that the top three causes of the riots were: 1) police practices, 2) unemployment and underemployment, and, 3) inadequate housing. Other motivations for the violence included poor public education, disrespectful white attitudes, discriminatory applications of justice, discriminatory practices in consumer and credit practices, and inadequate welfare programs.[55]

In the same year the *Kerner Report* was released, MLK spoke at Riverside Church in New York. By then, King was pressured to defend non-violence. Peaceful demonstrations and legislation had not quelled racism, nor eased the grip of poverty in which many minorities lived. People wanted to know why it was acceptable to demand that the victims of American racism and poverty remain peaceful while their government routinely used vicious and obscene militarism to resolve their problems in distant lands.

King lamented that America had made peaceful revolution impossible and so made violent revolution inevitable. He recognized that both the Vietnamese and the American poor were Isaacs set on Caesar's altar, and believed they were here for the same reason: to maintain Caesar's power and privilege at home. He called attention to the reality that the poor paid twice for the war. They were not only killed and maimed in battle, but resources needed to lift them out of poverty were being diverted to pay for war. In prophetic stride he declared, "A nation that continues year after year to spend more money on military defense than on programs for social uplift is approaching spiritual death."[56] King called attention to the hypocrisy of asking black soliders to die for a democracy that scorned them, and petitioned the nation to make a revolution of values. The nation's spirit was troubled and diseased, King asserted, because it was enthralled by privilege and profit. He appealed to the nation to stop being a thing-oriented society and to become a person-oriented society. Without such a transformation, the country would never overcome racism, militarism, and extreme materialism.[57]

King had called Caesar out. He exposed the arrogance and inhumanity that bound the fate of Vietnam to that of America's minorities and poor. For King, the treatment of people as objects was not a manifest destiny—an

---

55. National Advisory Commission on Civil Disorders, *Kerner Report*, 207–277.
56. King, "Beyond Vietnam," 87.
57. Ibid., 86.

inevitable human act—it was a choice. Exactly one year to the day of his Riverside speech, King was shot dead in Memphis.

LBJ was furious at King for vilifying the war Vietnam. To the hard-headed Texan, King's speech was nothing less that betrayal. Enraged, LBJ pressured his aids to find links between King and communists.[58] King had violated one of Caesar's commandments: "Thou shall keep holy the reciprocity owed in the exchange of political favors." LBJ had "given" blacks the Civil Rights and Voting Rights Acts, and from his perspective MLK owed him a patriot's stance on the war. King's speech was unpopular in many circles, but it signaled the reality that Caesar did not control all narratives about war and poverty.

Minnesota Nice

The hatred and cynicism that lingered after the Civil Rights Act was passed was due in part to the way people framed the problem of race relations. George Wallace saw the problem as the refusal of blacks to keep "in their place." LBJ initially saw it as a matter of which concessions might keep "the Nigras" quiet, then later as a necessary part of his re-election and legacy for the Great Society. MLK saw the problem as a failure of society's ability to see Jesus Christ in each other's eyes. Solutions are strongly influenced by how the problem is framed. Wallace supporters employed thuggery to suppress blacks and sustain state's rights. LBJ engineered campaigns and legislation. King gave society a prophetic voice and an example of peaceful dissent.

Race remains a dominant factor in the American experience. In 2011, over 25 percent of Native Americans, African Americans, and Hispanics lived in poverty, while 9.8 percent of whites were poor.[59] America has not found a way to heal its racial injustices. Between 1999 and 2013, blacks represented about 13 percent of the U.S. population, but roughly 26 percent of fatalities due to police shootings.[60]

American has yet to have what MLK called a "revolution of values." Public solidarity on matters of assistance for the poor, job opportunities, and the cost of living is brittle and easily cracked as people take sides on which minorities are the most victimized. Americans prefer reforms that leave Caesar's paradigm intact. We know that it is not nice, for example, to call someone a "Nigger," but it is perfectly acceptable to keep wages low, inflate the cost of health care, send children to deplorable public schools, and gamble with

---

58. Kotz, *Judgement Days*, 376.
59. Iceland, *Poverty in America*, 42.
60. Amnesty International, *Deadly Force*, 4.

mortgages because somebody, somewhere is going to profit from these things. We do not regard actions that keep people in poverty, ignorance, ill health, and hopelessness as just another way of calling someone a "Nigger;" but it is.

The Civil Rights Movement is unfinished business. We are still learning about the difference between love and tolerance; we still tread the tightrope between empathy for and fear of others. We still have anxieties about our neighbors. In my home state, the anxiety has a name. It is called "Minnesota Nice." Some see it as "passive-aggressiveness" or being helpful without being genuinely friendly. Some say it is friendly behavior that, although might not take one to the emotional depths of Lake Superior, makes things pleasant nonetheless.[61] At its worst, "Minnesota Nice" represents the universally human tension between wanting to be good and fearing that others will ask more from us than what we want to give.

Boomer's experiences with the Civil Rights Movement teaches us that political correctness is not a replacement for the difficult conversations we, as a society and as individuals, need to have about bigotry in all of its forms. Political correctness is often motivated by the fear of confrontation and so, is a form of denial. It is defensive in nature and it often appeases people without resolving the source of discord.

Patronage is the flip side of political correctness. Patronage in Caesar's world is the currency of power, and it is not love. It is about ingratiating oneself to those with authority and influence to advance one's ambitions. It is about doing just enough to quell criticism, but not enough to make vital and substantial changes. It is concerned with what can be curried by pleasantries and promises, and doing favors to get favors. Patronage is often extended with no real tender regard for our physical or spiritual wellness. Patronage and political correctness both distract us from the robust reforms that might leaven the Kingdom of God into our lives.

What is often remembered about the Civil Rights Movement are the ferocious riots and dynamic personalities. Although these are important, some of the most profound aspects of the movement are overlooked and even invisible. These are the quiet events that happened when individuals mindfully and faithfully confronted their consciences. These are the moments when people acknowledge their own personal demons: narrow-mindedness, obsession with power, arrogance, fear, cruelty, selfishness, and self-hatred. These were the moments in which individuals could apprehend their own prophetic potential. In these moments, people saw that pleasantries were not enough to heal broken lives and desecrated spirits.

---

61. Atkins, *Creating Minnesota*, 242–44.

8

Sex and the Kingdom

Of Beds and Boundaries

IN 1948, BIOLOGIST ALFRED Kinsey published *Sexual Behavior in the Human Male*, followed by *Sexual Behavior in the Human Female* in 1953. Kinsey's work shattered assumptions about "normal" sex. He observed that human sexuality existed along a continuum of heterosexuality and homosexuality, and documented the fact that lots of Americans behaved in ways that would never be portrayed in a Norman Rockwell painting. Kinsey's work laid bare what many already knew by way of experience. Lots of people had pre-marital sex, cheated on their spouses, and enjoyed same-sex intimacy. Many saw Kinsey's work as pornographic filth. Without reading Kinsey's books, some ministers condemned them and stated that they did not represent born-again Christians, while others claimed the research was flawed because only perverts would ever complete a survey on sex.[1]

For a long time Americans got to pretend that their private lives were pristine by keeping pornography out of sight, censoring news reports about prominent citizens' dalliances with prostitutes, and maintaining silence about child molestation. Relying on Sigmund Freud's theories about sexuality and literal interpretations of the Bible to explain the human condition, people believed that deviations from heterosexual sex within marriage was the mark of sin and mental illness. Kinsey's work did not ignite the sexual revolution, but it was instrumental in decriminalizing some acts of consensual sex between adults, and fostering objective inquiries about the nature of sex and intimacy.

The sexual revolution of the 1960s and 1970s consisted of many agendas. Under the spreading canopy of civil rights, one found women demanding

1. Bancroft, "Kinsey," 3.

oral contraception, abortion, and federal protection against harassment, discrimination, and domestic violence. Homosexuals mobilized themselves against police brutality and bigotry in all facets of life. Artists, writers, and film-makers confronted censorship. Educators sought greater freedom to teach students about sex and sexuality, and counselors in both secular and ecclesiastical settings extended compassion to those who in earlier generations would have been shamed.

The media played a vital role in the sexual revolution as it widened the scope of subject matter explored in TV shows and film. In 1960, it was inconceivable that June Clever would have an abortion or a child out of wedlock, but in 1972 Maude became the first character to openly reveal she had an abortion, and in 1992 Murphy Brown was a single mom. Hollywood's attitudes shifted and films became more sympathetic to gay, lesbian, bisexual and transgendered persons. Bans against nudity and explicit sex in film were gradually lifted in the 1960s, thanks in part to the Supreme Court's ruling in Miller v. California. The Court ruled that obscenity should be judged by whether materials were wholly prurient in interest, offensive according to "contemporary community standards" and whether the work as a whole lacked "serious literary, artistic, political, or scientific value."[2] With the exception of child pornography, the highly subjective criteria suggested obscenity was in the mind of the beholder.

I was in high school in 1972 when Helen Reddy's hit single, *I Am Woman* topped the pop music charts, and when the Minnesota Supreme Court ruled against Jack Baker and Michael McConnell, who had applied for a marriage license in Minneapolis in 1970.[3] I was aware of the fear that permeated the air when people talked about sex and sexuality. I saw men and women being ridiculed and called "dykes" and "faggots" when they spoke up for women's rights. As adolescents, my peers and I mirrored society's distain for gays. We joked that a man who had sex with a donkey had a better chance of getting into heaven than did a "faggot." At least the man and the donkey, we howled, made God laugh.

The sexual revolution broadened the public conversation about sex, yet it did not produce true equality between the sexes or free society from anxieties about sex. Women gained more control over reproductivity when the Food and Drug Administration approved the contraceptive pill in 1960, but it took two Supreme Court decisions to make it universally accessible.[4] Women also

2. Miller v. California, 413, U.S. 12 (1973).
3. Baker v. Nelson 291 Minn. 310, 191 N. W.2d 185 (1971).
4. Griswold v. Connecticut, 381 U.S. 479 (1965) denied the right of individual states to prohibit the pill's use for married women, and Eisenstadt v. Baird, 405 U.S. 438 (1972)

gained the right to abortions in 1973,[5] but these things did not prevent thousands of children from being consigned to foster care, nor did they guarantee that all parents truly loved and nurtured their offspring. Attitudes towards sex have changed, but we have not created a society free of rape, discrimination, and hate crimes. The sexual revolution brought America closer to the Kingdom of God only to the extent that it increased public and legal tolerance for certain sexual activity, but we are still struggling to replace tolerance with love.

No Girls Allowed

When I was a kid, I saw my soul as a translucent white disc inside my chest, close to my heart. This disc was not as dense as flesh. It was as light as meringue, but sturdy enough to hold God. I thought that my soul, like all souls, was without gender. I believed that every time I sinned, my soul got smudge marks on it that could be wiped clean only by penance and acts of contrition. I feared that some sins would stick to my soul like tar and permanently stain it. People with clean souls could serve God in special ways, and at age seven, I wanted to be a priest. I draped table clothes around my shoulders, and celebrated Mass with white bread pressed into wafers for communion. My mother was amused by such play and did not scold me. As I grew older, I learned that it was impossible for me to become a priest. The Catholic Church had, and still has, a monolithic policy on this matter; put bluntly: no penis, no priest.

My option to being a priest was to become a nun, but that brought mixed feelings. Being a nun was like a consolation prize for having the right spirit but the wrong plumbing. Being a nun was not a bad alternative, but it was not a good one either. As a nun, I might be assigned the duties of being the priest's laundress, cook, or housekeeper, and not the duties of blessing the dying, counseling the troubled, or leading study clubs. For me, the option was unjust. Why cook and scrub floors when I could administer the sacraments? By age ten, I was already a rebel against Catholic sexism.

As a kid, I was sensitive to and unsettled by sexuality. The Church's teachings were reinforced by social norms. The rules about sexual identity were implicit in jokes, the way teachers talked about students' potential, and in TV shows and advertising. My family's cultural artifacts included a copy of Johnny Carson's book, *Happiness is a Dry Martini*, which had a cartoon of a naked woman hoisting a martini on the cover, and lots cartoons featuring

---

made it legal for unmarried women to take the pill.

5. Roe v. Wade, 410 U.S. 113 (1973).

men fixated on women's anatomy.[6] Herb Albert's record, *Whipped Cream*, featured a naked woman slathered in whipped cream, looking seductively at viewers.[7] I understood at a tender age that men saw women as sex toys. The neighborhood boys who read stolen *Playboy* magazines reinforced the message with the delight they expressed for centerfolds. When I told the boys that I would report their behavior to their parents, I was threatened with bodily harm. Thus, at a tender age, I learned that men controlled the narrative about sex and what it meant to be a woman, and were prepared to assault women if they rejected it.

As a child, I looked to Jesus and the saints for solace as I struggled with sexism. The Gospels seemed so often to champion the underdog, and women were by definition underdogs. I sensed that gender did not matter to Jesus, but did not apprehend the theological profundity of this until I read the Gnostic Gospels. In *Thomas*, Jesus takes his disciples "through the looking glass," where gender is irrelevant. Like generations of Jews who had gone before them, the disciples held that the Kingdom of God discriminated based on gender. They were irritated by Jesus' tolerance of women in their midst. Peter even demanded that Jesus expel Mary from their circle, stating that "women are not worthy of Life." Jesus refused Peter, stating that he would lead Mary so that she too would be male and a living spirit, and that, "every woman who will make herself male will enter the Kingdom of Heaven."[8]

Modern Christianity still justifies the sexual caste system. Some get around Jesus' statement by arguing that since the *Thomas* is not found in the orthodox canon of the Bible, its teachings are not authentic. Others say that Jesus was speaking in metaphors that were irrelevant to earthly social relationships. Theologian Marvin Meyer states that *Thomas* uses sexual imagery to convey the proposition that there is no dualism in the Kingdom of God. He admits that Jesus's declaration that he will make Mary male sounds misogynist, but observed that, like the teachings of the Essenes, *Thomas* preaches a renouncement of the world and material constructs.[9] In *Thomas*, Jesus confronted the cultural construct of sexual identity and advocated severance with that construct so that the faithful may apprehend the unconditional love and presence of God. Cultural constructs remain intact in the Catholic Church despite evidence that women were priests and prophets in the early Christian

---

6. Carson, *Happiness*, 1–68.
7. Herb Alpert's Tijuana Brass, *Whipped Cream*, album jacket.
8. Pagels, *Gnostic Gospels*, 49.
9. Meyer, M. W. "Making Mary Male," 554–570.

Church.[10] The Catholic hierarchy still holds that women cannot be priests because, according to God's plan, Jesus chose only men to be his disciples.[11]

Mystique and Misogyny

The feminist landscape was laced with political land mines. Conservative feminism, such as that of the National Organization of Women (NOW), focused on eradicating sexual harassment and discrimination. Liberals wanted to legalize abortion and to teach women's studies in grade school. Radical feminists renounced claims that biology had consigned women to non-negotiable duties as mothers, homemakers, and obedient wives. Lesbian separatists denounced the family and men's participation in the Women's Movement. Women who rallied for equal pay were not necessarily supportive of women in combat. Women who called for day care were not necessarily in favor of lesbian rights. Jewish women felt the anti-Semitism of Christian women and black women felt the bigotry of white women.[12]

Betty Friedan, journalist and co-founder of NOW, launched what has been called the "second wave of feminism" with her book, *The Feminine Mystique*[13] It described the magical aura of womanhood and the promise that women would find deep personal fulfillment in motherhood and homemaking. Friedan penned that instead, women were bored with homemaking and felt bound by guilt to suffer in silence. Some said that Friedan was going "too far" by inviting women to find fulfillment in a career outside the home. Other women dreamed of giving up their jobs if only they had bread-winning husbands.

Friedan's book was followed by a cascade of feminist compositions, each with its unique understanding of sexism and its remedies. Kate Millett's *Sexual Politics* argued that male artists and writers distorted women's identities by projecting their own fantasies, and that patriarchal culture alienated women from themselves as they assimilated male standards of normalcy.[14] Shulamith Firestone's *The Dialectic of Sex* offered a Marxist analysis of women's status, in

---

10. Torjesen *When Women Were Priests*.12–13.

11. John Paul II, *Reserving Priestly Ordination*, lines 4–10.

12. Plaskow, "Feminist Anti-Judaism," 99–108.

13. The "first wave" of feminism generally refers to movements aimed at social reforms and women's suffrage of the nineteenth century, which culminated in women's right to vote in 1920. Hymowitz and Weissman *A History of Women in America* provides a survey of the various causes and leaders of the first wave.

14. Millett, *Sexual Politics*, xxix-xxx.

which women were locked in a power struggle with men.[15] She declared that women could only be liberated when freed from the role of breeder. Humanity, she insisted, had outgrown nature, and that technology should be tapped in the service of freeing women from the drudgery of reproduction. She envisioned a world of artificial wombs and void of nuclear families, monogamy, and capitalism. Germaine Greer's *The Female Eunuch* rejected the idea that feminism was all about women competing with and acquiring the same rights and opportunities as men. She argued that feminism's cause was the right to express oneself sexually as one saw fit, which was not the same as acquiescing to other's expectations and advances.[16]

Female theologians brought spirituality in to the feminist conversation. Mary Daly's *Beyond God the Father* asserted that theology is oppressive to women because their point of view is marginal in traditional studies of God, and because the very conceptualization of God is male and thus posits that feminine aspects of identity are inferior to masculine.[17] Rosemary Radford Reuther observed in *Sexism and God Talk* that, "When the word *Father* is taken literally to mean that God is male and not female, represented by males and not females, then the word becomes idolatrous."[18] The idolatry concerned the imposition of gender on a deity that was the source and essence of both male and female, and transcendent of all human categories.

Lots of women, including those in my own family, were too busy running households and raising kids to study the philosophical implications of gender. Long before Friedan was published, women in my mother's family worked outside the home and managed the family's financial affairs because they had to. Albertine, my great-grandmother, was orphaned as a child and was eventually adopted. She adopted my mother's mother, Harriet, who had also been abandoned by her parents when she was five years old. Albertine was widowed when she was in her late 40s, and went to work as a secretary. She raised Harriet on her own. My mother's other grandmother, Grace, was also widowed early in life, and took on millinery work to keep body and soul together. My father's mother, Catherine, whose alcoholic husband rarely had a job, raised three sons on a cook's income. My mother went to work in 1977 when inflation and college tuitions drove the need for a second family income.

Although it is amusing to think of my meek and tender great-grand-mothers as anarchistic bra-burners, the women in my family were not intent on destroying the family, or trying to prove that life is better without men.

15. Firestone, *Dialectic of Sex*, 3–8.
16. Greer, *Female Eunuch*, 10–11.
17. Daly, *Beyond God*, 4–6.
18. Ruether, *Sexism and God Talk*, 66.

They were like millions of other women whose decisions to enter the work force was not dictated by political ideologies, but by necessity. My parents encouraged all of their six kids, including four daughters, to learn a trade or earn a college degree. Their guidance was void of feminist rhetoric and based on the belief that self-sufficiency was a practical and a moral obligation.

Feminism's Foes

The Women's Movement provoked religious and secular controversy. Jerry Falwell bellowed that, feminists were all "failures" and that, "these women just need a man in the house."[19] Pat Robertson declared that feminism was "about a socialist, anti-family political movement that encouraged women to leave their husbands, kill their children, practice witchcraft, destroy capitalism, and become lesbians."[20] Billy Graham preached true womanhood was obtained by way of having children and being obedient to husbands.[21]

Some of the most acerbic denouncement of feminism came from women. Constitutional lawyer and mother of six, Phyllis Schlafly said that feminists were "a bunch of bitter women seeking a constitutional cure for their personal problems."[22] She led a movement against the Equal Rights Amendment (ERA) in 1972, arguing that it would free men from their obligation to support their families, encourage abortion, and give constitutional rights to gays.[23] Journalist Midge Decter argued that feminism was little more than a temper tantrum and a flight from adult responsibilities. "Women's Liberation," she wrote, "is merely the last avatar of an eternal complaint: life is too hard."[24] Women, she stated, already had the freedom to attend college and enter the professions. She opined that feminists who found sex with men oppressive were simply immature. Marabel Morgan advised women her best-selling book, *The Total Woman*, that fulfillment and happiness awaited women who mastered the art of obedience and submission to their husbands.[25] Novelist Joan Didion castigated feminism for its "victim mentality."[26] She snarled that what feminists

---

19. Archer, *Breaking Barriers*, 181.
20. Levit, *Gender Line*, 127.
21. Marshall, "A Matter of Pride," 87–88.
22. Douglas, *Where the Girls Are*, 221.
23. Durham, *Christian Right*, 35.
24. Decter, *New Chastity*, 174
25. Morgan, M. *Total Woman*, 96.
26. Didion, *White Album*, 118.

really wanted was an ideal world where they were swept up in a world of romance void of life's heavy lifting.

The argument that feminists were awash in juvenile and selfish expectations distracted lots of people from fact that men, women, and children were and are constant victims of sexual violence. Prior to the Women's Movement, sexual harassment and domestic violence were not well-understood, and as legal concepts, they were not yet fully developed.[27] Until relatively recently, men beat and murdered their wives and lovers with relative impunity. Phyllis Chesler's classic, *Women and Madness*, exposed the ways physicians and psychiatrists justified such conduct by maintaining that depressed and angry women sometimes needed to be slapped around for their own good.[28] Police officers, lawyers, and judges often agreed with the medical community, which essentially locked these professions into paradigm in which they could not see life from women's point of view. By the time boomers were born, all states recognized "wife beating" as a criminal offense, but few treated it as a serious crime. Slowly, by way of legislation and court enforcement, women acquired greater legal protection and resources that enabled them to escape battery and prosecute their assailants. Between 1975 and 1995, mandatory police arrest laws and restraining orders were introduced and fortified. In the mid-1970s, states began to classify rape between married persons as a crime.[29]

Decades after the sexual revolution, the Center for Disease Control reported that 19.3 percent of women and 1.7 percent of men have been raped in their lifetimes, and another 43.9 percent of women and 23.4 percent of men have been victims of other forms of sexual assault.[30] Rape on college campuses has become a national issue, as 19 percent of college women report that they have been the victim of an attempted or competed rape.[31] Sexual assault in the military has found its way to the spotlight. In 2014, 6,131 rape victims—the vast majority women—filed reports, while many did not disclose their assaults for fear of rupturing morale and being the target of retaliation.[32]

---

27. In 1980, the Equal Employment Opportunity Commission issued policies to end sexual harassment. The Supreme Court ruled in Meritor Savings Bank v. Vinson, 477 U.S. 57, (1986), that persistent and unwanted sexual advances, lewd remarks, and retaliatory behavior are abuses of power and create a hostile work environment; and, as such, violate the Civil Rights Act of 1964.

28. Chesler, *Women and Madness*, 110–137. Ehrenreich and English *For Her Own Good* augments Chesler work, and explores the mythologies and biases that tainted medical and legal thinking about women's mental and physical health for centuries.

29. Flowers, *Sex Crimes*, 21–25.

30. Breiding, *Prevalence and Characteristics*, lines 15–20.

31. Nicoletti, et. al. *Violence Goes to College*, 131.

32. Skaine, *Sexual Assault*, 60–66.

Despite the sexual revolution, many people do not report sexual assault. Historically, law enforcement ignored many reports of sexual assault because the victims were poor, people of color, or gay.[33] At present, rape victims continue to be badgered by police who want victims to recant their reports, and nearly 10 percent of complaints against police officers involve sexual assault.[34] Annually, over 250,000 people are victims of domestic violence in the U.S., and one in four women and one in seven men will experience domestic violence at least once in their lifetime.[35] In addition, roughly 199,000 children in the U.S. are victims of sex trafficking.[36] Despite claims that America is a Christian nation, Americans continue to rape and batter each other with the expectation that cultural norms excuse them from having to treat others as persons made in the image of God, as the Turner case so vividly reveals.

At the Dumpster

Legislation cannot mandate empathy. In 2015, Brock Turner, a Stanford University star athlete, sexually assaulted an unconscious woman. He and the victim had been drinking heavily at a party. The attack took place behind a dumpster near a fraternity house and was interrupted when two graduate students discovered Turner atop the victim. As Turner attempted to flee the scene, the students captured and held him.[37] Despite the bruises and dried blood on the woman's body, Turner maintained the victim consented. Charged with assault with intent to rape an intoxicated woman, sexually penetrating an unconscious person with a foreign object, and sexually penetrating an intoxicated person, Turner faced up to 14 years in prison. With consideration for Turner's youth, lack of prior criminal convictions, and assailant's remorse, Judge Aaron Persky sentenced Turner to six months in prison and mandated that Turner register as a sex offender for the rest of his life. USA Swimming banned Brock from events including Olympic trials, and Stanford University expelled him.

Persky's leniency drew national outrage, but Brock's dad, Dan, was mortified for different reasons. Dan lamented that the sentence caused his son depression. He felt it was unfair to punish a boy so severely for "20 minutes of action." Dan's letter to the court pleaded for mercy and did not even mention

33. Meloy and Miller, *Victimization of Women*, 7–8.
34. Pollack, J. M. *Ethical Dilemmas*, 195.
35. Columbia Law School, *Domestic Violence*, 1.
36. Belles, *In Our Backyard*, 23–24.
37. Styles and Coleman, "She was Unconscious," lines 1–11.

the victim. Instead, Dan described Brock as a humble, talented, and intelligent young man. He described the awe he felt when welcomed into Stanford's highly selective embrace. His son, he pleaded, was trying to "fit into Stanford and fell into a culture of alcohol consumption and partying."[38] His appeal was familiar. Brock's conduct was just one of those little lapses in judgment that attend rites of passage, such as boozy frat parties. Dan's letter offered no empathy for the victim, who awoke from her assault on a hospital gurney, battered, with dirt in her vagina, and with doctors directing her to get checked for AIDS. Instead, Dan protested the material consequences of Brock's sentence.

Dan's petition was logical, given the reality that we live in a culture in which the individual's wants are placed above all other needs, and in which taking responsibility for hurting others has been replaced by making excuses for savage behavior. I wonder, however, if Dan, Brock, and the rest of us have the guts to take a serious look at how we help to maintain such a culture. When viewed through spiritual eyes, the Turner case indicts us for reasons other than for our attitudes towards sex. The case bears witness to the idolatry of individualism and materialism. A father's desperate petition to salvage his son's earthly opportunities and privileges made the victim as invisible as did the son's violation of her. It also made the University's reputation, public safety, and the victim's family invisible. The Turner case reminds us that at the core of spirituality is the visibility of others, and the dignity that God gave them.

Pornography

While feminists argued the case for legal protection against violence and discrimination, the sexual revolution pushed the boundaries of free expression. Many of its adherents believed that complete freedom of expression enhanced human dignity as it championed the capacity of individuals to judge the morality of sexual conduct for themselves. Some also posited that free expression decreased everyone's vulnerability to abuse because a sexually satisfied population has no cause to victimize others. It was an argument that ignored the reality that sexual assault and treating people like objects is largely about power and not about a steady diet of orgasms.

The battle over pornography encapsulates our propensity to hold two opposing ideas with equal reverence. On one hand we believe that stories, jingles, and images have the power to sway our attitudes and behaviors. Televangelists, political candidates, and Madison Avenue advertising executives all rely on this belief for their success. Yet, on the other hand, when people

---

38. "Letter from Dan A. Turner," lines 81–90.

criticize pornography for its impact on values, attitudes, and behavior, all of a sudden Americans insisted that the camera is impotent.

The Supreme Court decision of *Miller v. California* helped to transform pornography from an illegal cottage industry that circulated photographs of nudes and stag films to underground audiences into a multi-billion dollar public enterprise. The transformation was assisted by the video technology of the 1970s, which enabled people to privately view the burgeoning number of pornographic films in distribution. In 2005, 13,588 hard core pornographic DVDs were released, and annual sales are estimate at least $ 10 billion in the U.S. alone.[39] The digital revolution did not leave pornography behind. The first pornographic website was launched in 1994, and by 1998, between 5 and 10 percent of all revenue spent online was for pornography.[40] By 2006, twenty-five percent of daily search engine requests were for pornography.[41] Globally, consumers annually spend nearly $1 billion on Internet images of child pornography. Viewers can be highly selective and spend hours on sites exclusively dedicated to rape scenarios.[42]

Lots of pornographic images suggest that women like and deserve to be humiliated and assaulted.[43] Hence, lots of research has been devoted to determining if pornography causes violence. Causation is very difficult to prove because behavior is the result of many variables and studies sometimes contradict each other. Researchers have found, however, that pornography does influence viewers' perceptions of and attitudes. A 2006 review of studies concerning Internet pornography found that it contributed to individuals' beliefs about marriage, monogamy, child-rearing, and, that it often increased the viewer's aggression and decreased their satisfaction with sex in their relationships.[44] A 2011 investigation of university fraternity members noted that men who viewed pornography are significantly less likely to intervene in possible rape situations, report feelings of intent to rape, and are more likely to believe rape myths than others who do not view pornography.[45] Studies found that viewing pornography may increase aggressive tendencies and reinforce compulsion in some people.[46] They have found that pornography not only

39. Jensen, *Gender, Sex, and Politics*, 109.
40. Lane, F. *Obscene Profits*, xiv-xv.
41. Young, "Internet Sex Addiction," 22.
42. Gossett and Byrne, "Click Here," 690–701
43. For more documentation and commentary, see: MacKinnon *Only Words*, Dworkin *Pornography*, and Kettrey "Reading Playboy."
44. Manning, J. C. "Impact," 142–146.
45. Foubert, et. al. "Pornography Viewing," 222–25.
46. Malamuth, et. al. "Pornography and Sexual Aggression," 78–80

stimulates aggression in some, but reduces their sensitivity and empathy for others.[47] Research also finds that sex offenders use pornography to coax others, especially children, into participating in their own victimization.[48] While it can be argued that most people who view pornography do not sexually assault others, it can also be argued that pornography influences the way people see others and can lead to compulsive behavior.[49]

In its 1970 report, the President's Commission on Obscenity and Pornography found that there was no evidence to support claims that pornography was injurious to anyone.[50] President Nixon objected to the report, stating that, if the "proliferation of filthy books and plays has no lasting harmful effect on man's character," then, "it must also be true that great books, great paintings, and great plays have no ennobling effect on man's conduct."[51] In 1986, The *Meese Report* contested the Commission, and asserted that pornography does have harmful effects.[52] It argued that pornography promoted immorality, violence against women, and the degradation of women. Critics of the report charged that the investigation was highly subjective and prudish.

Pornography offended people who did not consider themselves feminists. Evangelist James Dobson held that pornography destroyed the family and encouraged violence against women.[53] Jerry Falwell opined that pornography was filthy and perverse as it glorified casual rather than committed relationships.[54] Phyllis Schlafly enjoined that pornography was by definition the degradation of women as it depicts women in subordinate and degrading positions from which men take sadistic pleasure.[55] The Catholic Church declared that pornography equally hurts the individuals in the images and those who consume the material. As a "sin against human dignity," the Church stated, pornography offers a distorted view of a person, and in making the human

---

47. Donnerstein, *Pornography*, 53–81.

48. Cusack, *Pornography*, 101.

49. An excellent discussion on these points is found in Wilson's *Your Brain on Porn*.

50. The President's Commission on Obscenity and Pornography conducted its research prior to the development of digital technology that permits researchers to identify brain activity when stimulated and changes in the brain over time due to repeated stimulation.

51. Zurcher and Kirkpatrick, *Citizens for Decency*, 343.

52. The 960-page report exposed the relationship between pornography and organized crime, took testimony from porn stars, and studied the matter from the viewpoint of sexual assault victims. See McManus, *Final Report*.

53. Focus on the Family, *Focus on the Family*, 181–82.

54. Winters, *God's Right Hand*, 137–153.

55. Schlafly, *Power of the Positive Woman*, 158.

being an object for personal gratification, diminishes the viewer's respect for love and healthy relationships.[56]

Feminist author, Andrea Dworkin, saw pornography as a way of seeing, thinking, and valuing. She held that it socialized men to objectify women, and argued that as pornography frequently eroticizes murder and torture, it was a form of terrorism. Her insight cut through legal and religious rhetoric and got to the heart of the matter:

> I live in a country where if you film any act of humiliation or torture, and if the victim is a woman, the film is both entertainment and protected speech. Now that tells me something about what it means to be a woman citizen in this country, and the meaning of being second class. When your rape is entertainment, your worthlessness is absolute.[57]

In light of Dworkin's observation, Peter's words from *Thomas* are haunting: Send Mary away, "she is not worthy of life."

Bunny Boys

For entrepreneurs, the sexual revolution was smorgasbord of opportunities to market sex and get rich. Hugh Hefner began publishing *Playboy* magazine in 1953, and opened the first Playboy Club in 1960. He sold the fantasy that men could "have" many sexy, young playmates without entangling commitments and responsibility. The Playboy bunny's appeal radiated not only from her voluptuous figure, but from her anonymity. By the mid-sixties, mainstream America embraced the bunny empire and its philosophy that morality should be defined by what made people happy.[58]

Gloria Steinem, a graduate from Smith College with a degree journalism, became a Playboy bunny in 1962 to study the realm of bunny happiness. Her covert research uncovered Playboy's specious claims and misogyny. Want ads for Playboy promised bunnies an average salary of $200 a week and a potential of $10,000 annually—roughly $4,000 more than the average American family income.[59] After the cost of make-up, costumes, tip-sharing, and penalties for

---

56. United States Conference of Catholic Bishops, *Create in Me*, 5–7.

57. Dworkin, *Letters*, 279.

58. Hugh Hefner was the chief architect of the Playboy philosophy, which appeared in 25 installments in Playboy between 1962 and 1965. Watts' *Mr. Playboy* addresses the philosophical, political, and aesthetic aspects of Hefner's world view, and Hefner's own vitriol for Puritan morality.

59. Bureau of National Affairs, "Daily Labor Report," 205–06.,

breaking Playboy's rules, however, the average bunny's basket had more jelly beans than golden eggs.[60] Steinem described the bunny empire as a world that reduced women to caricatures of themselves to serve juvenile male fantasies. Later, as the editor of *Ms. Magazine*, Steinem explored the murky lines between playful erotic fantasy and pornography.

The Playboy icon was an odd addition to the panorama of masculine icons. The Playboy, was often depicted as a cocktail-drinking rabbit dressed in a smoking jacket and surrounded by artifacts designed to give the impression he was very sophisticated. The Playboy was revered for his indulgence. He had endless leisure and money, which of course, was spent in pursuit of playmates. The Playboy was not a heroic figure. He was not a soldier who risked his life for freedom, nor an innovator or pioneer. He was not the virtuous proletariat who diligently labored for the good of the community, and he was not the sturdy and faithful patriarch at the center of the nuclear family. Men liked the Playboy not for his mind or humanitarianism, but because he represented a materially successful man who could have all the sex he wanted without the hassle of marriage, monogamy, and children.

Theologian Harvey Cox observed in 1961 that Playboy had reduced sex to an accessory to life, and in so doing had become anti-sexual. The Playboy approach to sexual relationships kept the human encounter at a distance. Cox found that Playboy's philosophy was heretical because it removed from sexual relations the possibility of true intimacy, which violated God's intentions that people refrain from treating people like masturbatory objects.[61]

Ironically, Playboy was an early defender of gay rights. *Playboy's* articles included the occasional reference to homosexuality as a psychological disorder and as a factor in the decline of masculinity, but Hefner believed that society's abuse of gays drove them to therapy and that gay liberation shared with Playboy a strong valuing for sex that was freed from procreative responsibilities.[62] Hefner recognized that, "gender was not a natural state of being, but rather a self-conscious construction intimately tied to American notions of sexuality."[63] The argument that sexuality was a social construct rather than a divinely ordained mandate for heterosexual conduct in the context of marriage was at the center of conflicting ideologies. Prostitutes and pornographers took comfort from Hefner's philosophy. Feminists vilified holy matrimony as a form of prostitution, and Gays argued the divine mandate of heterosexual-

60. Steinem's two-part report, "A Bunny's Tale," appeared in the May and June 1963 issues of *Show Magazine*.
61. Cox, "*Playboy's Doctrine*, 56–58.
62. Pitzulo, *Bachelors and Bunnies*, 109–117.
63. Ibid, 111.

ity could not be reconciled with their deepest sense of identity. Like feminism, The Gay Liberation Movement was a mix of objectives. Some sought committed to social justice and others wanted to pursue their interests free from judgement. Both causes required legal protection.

Gay Liberation

In Boomer's lifetime, homosexuals were psychologically and physically battered with impunity. The extent to which gays, lesbians, bisexuals and transgendered persons were victims of hate crimes during boomer's lifetime is difficult to know, as police records generally did not track such crimes, victims often did not report crimes, and as victims were terrified of revealing their orientations.[64] Books and movies routinely depicted gay characters as pathetic creatures who deserved unhappiness, isolation, abuse, and death.[65] The law offered no shelter. Police raided bars, arrested couples in parks, allowed journalists to harass the incarcerated, and beat those even suspected of being "queer." Anti-sodomy laws were enforced in the U.S. until 2003.[66] Being gay could cost one a job, church membership, or military commission. Being gay left one open to blackmail and violations of privacy in which photographs of gay bar patrons arrested in a raid were published in local newspapers. Religious institutions told gays that their souls were in peril, and that only through celibacy and conversion could they be pleasing to God. Until 1974, the American Psychiatric Association classified homosexuality as a disorder, and prescribed aggressive behavior modification therapies to "correct" the individual. Stigmatized, many gays succumbed to substance abuse, depression, and suicide. Some got married and led double lives. Others retreated to the convent or seminary, hiding in plain sight, but inwardly tormented.

On June 28, 1969, New York City police raided the Stonewall Inn, a tavern frequented by gay patrons. Police in those days routinely harassed gay bar clientele and extorted bar owners for the right to keep the doors open. This time, patrons fought back, and set off a two-day fracas.[67] Rioters were not political organizers or academic strategists who planned the event, yet it

---

64. Faderman, *Gay Revolution*, 3–26.

65. Epstein and Friedman adapted Russo's *The Celluloid Closet* to film. It beautifully illustrates Hollywood's love-hate relationship with homosexuality.

66. In Lawrence v. Texas, 539 U.S. 558 (2003), the Supreme Court overturned Bowers v. Hardwick, 478 U.S. 186 91986), stating that the state has no right to impose religious taboos against homosexuality.

67. Faderman, *Gay Revolution*, 171–86.

was pivotal. Like other minorities seeking civil rights, they reached a breaking point where silence was no longer the acceptable response to hatred.

Gay liberation was a part of the sexual revolution, but it was unique in important ways. While straights contested censorship and unequal wages, gays fought for the right to exist. Long before the Stonewall riots, gay activists articulated an agenda for gay liberation that mirrored the Civil Rights Movement more closely than it did Playboy's philosophy. The 1951 mission statement of the Mattachine Society called for: the unity of homosexuals that isolation would end; the education of gay and straight people so that understanding might yield compassion; and, the cultivation of leadership so that political action towards rights might be effective.[68] The Daughters of Bilitis, a lesbian organization, issued a similar statement in 1955.[69]

Even in the circle of middle class intelligentsia, where one expected to find empathy for those who felt isolated and abused, gay liberation caused folks to panic. Midge Decter, who had castigated feminism, turned her guns on the gay liberation, which had slain her genteel "sissy" and replaced him with a self-destructive, exhibitionist, drug-addicted, sadomasochist. Decter's summers on Fire Island placed her in the company of pre-liberation gays, who if not acceptable to straight America, could at least be admired for their style, taste, and manners by the elite and sophisticated vacationers on Fire Island.[70]

Like many of her peers, Decter believed that people chose the gay "lifestyle." Many also felt that gays "mocked" heterosexuality, the burden of families, and the maturity required for maintaining them. The "us" and "them" dynamics of the resort community did not facilitate much talk about what it meant to be a victim of queer-bashing and discrimination. Decter's essay leaves readers with the impression that gays needed no liberation movement. After all, they had found "their" niches in society and earned decent salaries in "their" professions. As gay liberation gained steam, Decter abandoned Fire Island, owing to a tipped "balance between the homosexuals and the straights." She lamented:

> What has indeed happened to the homosexual community I used to know—they who only a few short years ago were characterized by nothing so much as tender, sweet, vain, pouting, girlish attention to the youth and beauty of their bodies? Whose obsession with adolescent play, and whose safety valve for that obsession was alcohol?

---

68. Katz, *Gay American History*, 412.
69. Gallo, *Different Daughters*, 13.
70. Decter's, "The Boys on the Beach," takes rather puritanical line of discourse, which was not so pronounced in her criticisms for Women's Liberation.

Whose primary pleasure was in the dress and decor and all things that covered their world with sparkling if ambiguous surface?[71]

Decter's sentimentality rings of a Southern belle who is trying to rebuild the plantation after the Civil War has ravaged the county while the slaves refused to take orders. Her world had stopped being pretty. The Village People had kidnapped Liberace and she wanted him back. I wonder whether she and her peers on Fire Island ever thought about the parallels between the strange new gay cosmos alit by drugs and "kinky sex," and the good old heterosexual universe where alcoholism, infidelities, and wife-beating were dirty little secrets.

Christian conservatives were quick to condemn gay liberation. In the 1970s, as cities passed ordinances outlawing discrimination against gays, and as openly gay candidates were being elected into public offices, conservative preachers proclaimed that "God hates fags."[72] Fortified with the belief that homosexuals were all child molesters and degenerates, former Miss Oklahoma, Anita Bryant launched the "Save the Children" crusade in 1977. She urged voters to overturn Dade County's gay rights ordinance in Florida and succeeded. Both sides of the issue were emboldened. Greater numbers of gays came out and confrontations ensued.

In 1978, Californians defeated Proposition 6, (the Briggs Initiative), which called for a prohibition of gay teachers and any school personnel who openly advocated for gay rights. Twenty-one days later, Dan White, a former city supervisor, shot Mayor George Moscone and Harvey Milk, San Francisco's first openly gay Board of Supervisors' member. White was sentenced to seven years and eight months for his crime. His lawyer had argued the "Twinkie Defense" and convinced the jury that, at the time of the murders, White's judgement was crippled by depression and binges of junk food. Protestors in San Francisco stormed City Hall, set fire to police cars, and attacked police. In the decade that followed, opponents of gay rights did not morn the hundreds of thousands who fell to AIDS. Instead, many celebrated the fatalities as God's punishment for same-sex intimacy and gay "militancy."[73]

---

71. Decter, "Boys on the Beach," paragraph 90.

72. One of the more shocking displays of religious-based hate took place during Matthew Shepard's funeral in 1998, when Reverend Fred Phelps led demonstrators in their chants, declaring that Matthew was in hell because he was gay. Shephard was attacked on October 6, 1998, and left to die while tied to a fence near Laramie, Wyoming. See Cobb *God Hates Fags*, 1–5.

73. Treadwell, *God's Judgement*, 12.

When AIDS Made Us Laugh

The AIDS epidemic claimed the lives of over 550,000 Americans and 2.8 million people globally by 2005.[74] Fatalities were high as myths and superstitions about the disease diminished compassion for its victims. AIDS appeared in the U.S. in 1981 during Ronald Reagan's first term, but Reagan did not speak publically about AIDS until 1987. By then, AIDS had killed at least 40,000 Americans.[75] Reagan was surrounded by conservatives who echoed the Christian fundamentalist opinion that AIDS was God's punishment of gays, and who discouraged the President from allowing Surgeon General C. Everett Koop from conducting an in-depth study with public health recommendations.[76]

In 1982, journalist Reverend Lester Kinsolving questioned Deputy Press Secretary Larry Speakes about AIDS. Speakes joked about the matter and insinuated that Kinsolving's interest in the subject was perverse. Members of the press corps snickered and tossed verbal barbs at Kinsolving.[77] The administration made it clear that gays and people with AIDS were the least of their brothers. Indifference to the suffering bore witness to society's willingness to sacrifice many Isaacs to atone for the "sins" of sexual liberation. Whether homosexuality was a genetically determined orientation or a "chosen lifestyle" was irrelevant to religious zealots who wanted gays to suffer and die. For many Christians, the idea that God would create gay people for a sacred purpose was far more preposterous than the idea that a man could walk on water or be risen from the dead. America took AIDS seriously only after it was known that white, heterosexual, non-drug addicts could get the disease.[78]

I lost friends to AIDS including Jim, a beautiful, gentle, and intelligent gay man. Jim was a counselor, poet, and an activist. He established the first gay, lesbian, bisexual, transgender resource center on a college campus in my mother's home town. He was joyful and courageous. Jim was an Episcopalian who believed that he was created in the image of God. Nothing Christian fundamentalists said ever derailed his certainty that he had been created for a sacred purpose. I believe that he chose the day of his passing to underscore his faith in the eternity of life and love. He died on Easter Sunday, 2000.

---

74. Tulchinsky and Varavikova, *New Public Health*, 168.
75. Murray, *Not In this Family*, 137.
76. Lindsay, *Faith in the Halls*, 63–64.
77. *When AIDS Was Funny*, directed by 2015, DVD.
78. An excellent chronological documentation of the nation's response to the AIDS crisis is found in Shilts' *And the Band Played On*.

When Father Knew Best

As AIDS ravaged the nation in the 1980s, reports that children were being molested by Catholic priests began to appear in newspapers. The first trickles of news aroused tittering and embarrassment. The idea that priests had sexual liaisons was not new. People already whispered about the private lives of local priests, and had read Father Andrew Greely's novels that graphically described clerics gone wild. Then came the deluge of stories following the *Boston Globe's* 2002 coverage of the crisis and the Church's response. The reality that priests could molest children, dodge criminal prosecution, and remain in the ministry transformed the snickering and embarrassment to outrage and loathing.

In 2004, the *John Jay Report* published its study of 10,667 abuse cases that were reported between 1950 and 2002. Of these cases, 80 percent of the victims were boys under the age of 18.[79] The study is not exhaustive as many assaults were never reported and as documents were lost or destroyed. Assaults occurred in cars, parks, rectories, churches, and homes.[80] Offenders sometimes plied their victims with pornography, alcohol, and money. Of the 4,392 priests in the study, only 384, less than 10 percent, were criminally charged.[81] In most instances offenders were transferred from parish to parish. Some received "treatment" at a Church facility and went back into circulation. The number of priests defrocked as the result of sexual abuse reached 848 by 2014.[82] By 2003, the archdiocese of Boston had settled claims costing $85 million.[83] In 2006, settlements in the Los Angeles archdiocese were reportedly $660 million, and between 1950 and 2010, the clergy's abuse of children cost the Catholic about $3 billion.[84] The full cost may never be known since many charges of abuse were settled behind closed doors.[85]

The fallout from priestly assaults was catastrophic. Victims became depressed, defiant, and withdrawn. They often felt guilty for their abuse, and many dropped out of school. It was difficult for victims to participate in the sacraments. They panicked in the presence of priests and were seized by terrifying mental images of bodily functions, fluids, and sensations they did not understand. As adults, they frequently abused substances and had serious

---

79. John Jay College of Criminal Justice, *The Nature and Scope*, 6.
80. Ibid., 7.
81. Ibid.
82. Krames, *Leading with Humility*, 91.
83. France, *Our Fathers*, 589..
84. Barkan and Bryjak, *Myths and Realities*, 72.
85. Whittier, *Politics of Child*, 125.

problems with relationships.[86] Scores of assailants and their victims committed suicide. Parishes became battle grounds. Parents of victims fought with each other over whether to confront bishops, file police reports, talk to the media, warn other parents, and pull their kids from Catholic schools. Some left the Catholic Church in disgust.

It took the force of headlines and litigation to move the Catholic hierarchy to mercy. Typically, bishops who received complaints were defensive. Some accused parents of being histrionic; some threatened to deny accusers access to the sacraments; some would not even talk to concerned parents; and, some lied about how problems were being solved.[87] As decades of clerical abuse and denial cascaded from the closet, bishops poured salt in open wounds by refusing to offer public apologies, refusing to meet with survivors, and by casting the Catholic Church as the victim in the ordeal.

In January, 2015, the Archdiocese of St. Paul-Minneapolis added 17 more priests to its list of assailants, bringing its total to fifty-five.[88] In the list, I saw a familiar name, and it hit me like a wrecking ball to the chest. Patrick William Coates, the monsignor who cheered my team at basketball games, and under whom my father had served as a deacon at Ascension, was credibly charged with abuse. Coates had been the embodiment of Ascension's parish. He had been a peace-maker, a community-builder, and a resource for the poor. I learned how to swim in Ascension's pool and my brothers were schooled in Ascension's classrooms. The tragedy is profound. A man I once placed on a pedestal had helped to transform the Roman collar from an icon of God's love and protection to a symbol of weakness and depravity.

I grieve for Coates' victims. I also grieve for Father Coates. I imagine that he knew the special hell on earth that comes when a person does battle with demons that must not be named. Few words can convey the sorrow and rage that follows a crisis such as this that could have been prevented if the Church would only have a more spiritually enlightened approach to sexuality.

In a way, the priestly abuse of children began with Peter's rebuke of Mary's presence in the circle of disciples. Peter wanted an exclusively male ministry, and despite Jesus' objection, he got it. The Caesars of the Catholic Church demonized sexuality so thoroughly that it bred neurosis, denial, and self-destruction. As waves of sexual revolution washed over society and

---

86. France *Our Fathers* is a most meticulous and powerful account of the crisis, as he traces it from the 1950's indoctrination of seminarians to the present, and uses testimony from clerics, victims, and their families.

87. In addition to France, see Frawley-O'Dea's *Perversion of Power*. Frawley-O'Dea consulted with nuns, priests, psychiatrists, and families impacted by the crisis. Both France and Frawley-O'Dea speak passionately about the faith that means so much to them.

88. Mohr, "More Twin Cities Clergy," lines 1–2.

popular culture, seminarians prayed for the strength to resist sexual urges, and harbored contempt for their own bodies. As the Catholic Church battened down the hatches to protect its doctrinal ship from taking on water, it lost an opportunity to cleanse itself of its own sexism.

In their training for the priesthood, Catholic bishops left many seminarians woefully ignorant of what the biological and social sciences had to say about sex, humanity, and wellness. The repressive approach contributed to the arrested development of many priests, who were instructed to intensify their prayers, rather than to reflect upon and understand their sexual feelings, in order to purge themselves of sinful urges.[89]

The confessions of assailants reveal the link between the Church's perception of sex and pathology. Father Robert Van Handel, who sexually abused 17 boys, described his coming of age in a strict Catholic home. When Van Handel was 13, he and his father read a sex education booklet they received from a local priest. Robert said that the book was "anti-sex" and terrified him. Wet dreams, it warned, were like poison candy that tasted sweet but killed the immortal soul. Robert prayed desperately each night to be spared wet dreams and that his penis would "remain small like a boy's."[90] When Van Handel entered the seminary in 1965, he joined the ranks of other men who, like himself had troubling ideas about sex and their own bodies.

Richard Sipe, former Benedictine priest and sociologist, asserts that the Church's attitudes towards sex contribute to child abuse. The mystique of celibacy, he observed, reflects the Church's demonization of women and near cultish obsession with purity. The celibate, he notes, is superior to other men because he has conquered women. Priests often find that rational thinking is insufficient to the task of neutralizing the agony produced by isolation and lack of physical and emotional intimacy.[91] The priest is in a bind. If he says he would be happier and healthier with a wife, he has offended the Church's sense of masculinity and power; if he says he would be happier and healthier without a wife, he risks loneliness and inauthenticity.

Troubled by the Vatican's teaching on sexuality and other issues, men and women abandoned religious life. Between 1968 and 1971, over 10,500 men left the priesthood.[92] In 1965, enrollment in American seminaries totaled

---

89. Sipe, a former Benedictine priest and sociologist from the Minneapolis area, carefully documents and analyzes the Church's formation of priests and its profound limitations in his work, *Sex, Priests, and Power*.

90. Van Handel's autobiographical essay, "Robert Van Handel's Sexual History," may be accessed via ABC News. See bibliography.

91. Sipe, *Sex, Priests and Power*, 46; 58–62; 167–68.

92. France, *Our Fathers*, 42.

about 49,000, and by 1988, there were around 7,000.[93] Nuns were vexed by their second-class status in the Catholic Church. In 1965, the U.S. was home to nearly 180,000 nuns, and by 1988, they numbered about 107,000.[94]

The Catholic prohibition of female priests is troubling. A religious institution that does not does ordain the numbers of clerics necessary to serve the community is risking physical death. A religious institution that refuses to ordain those who hear the call to ordination because those people are women already has one foot in the spiritual grave.

A Long Way, Baby

The Woman's Movement and sexual revolution tempered but did not terminate Caesar. In 1946, 11 women served in Congress (2 percent), and seventy years later, 104 women (20 percent) served in the 114th Congress.[95] Prior to 1980, no women served as a Justice on the Supreme Court, and as of 2010, there were four. In 1980, there were no women in the executive tiers of Fortune 500 companies, and by 2014, women represented over 14 percent of executive officers.[96] Of the 29,498 doctorates that were awarded in 1970, 86.5 percent went to men and 13.5 percent went to women. In 2000, men received 56.2 percent of all doctorates and women received 43.8 percent.[97] In 2015, white women earned 80 cents for every dollar men earned in comparable work, and women of color earn even less.[98]

Looking at the legacies of feminism and the sexual revolution is like looking into a kaleidoscope filled with emotional shrapnel and shards of broken psyches. For every material step forward, we seemed to take a spiritual step backwards. Women got greater control over their bodies and reproduction, and in the thirty years that followed *Roe V. Wade*, 56 million fetuses were aborted.[99] Society was given a broader definition of protected speech, and now we are free to watch "reality shows" in which men and women indulge their narcissism and hurl vulgarities at each other. The sexual revolution sanctioned the right to make objects of ourselves and others, and then we punctuated that right with the assertion that those who had moral objections

---

93. Carey, P. W. *Catholics in America*, 120.
94. Ibid.
95. Manning, J. E. and Brudnick, *Women in Congress*, 105–06.
96. Warner, *Women's Leadership Gap*, 2.
97. Hoffer, et. al., *Doctorate Recipients*, 10–11.
98. Institute for Women's Policy Research, "Employment, Education & Economic Change," lines 1–9.
99. Keane, *Single and Catholic*, 81.

were hyper-sensitive and politically incorrect. To spin Erich Segal's novel, *Love Story*, liberation, it seems, "means never having to say you're sorry."[100]

In many respects, men and women are two genders separated by a common ego. The ego keeps us fearful that we are not sexy enough, masculine enough, and feminine enough. It fights over who is the greater victim. It keeps cultural constructs of gender, rather than our spiritual essence, at the forefront of our identity, and makes us defensive when others attack our sexuality. We came a long way, baby, but we did not reach the Kingdom of God in our revolution. As long as sex is about power and self-gratification, we will never reach our full potential for intimacy, nor reach the Kingdom wherein there is no male nor female.

---

100. Segal's popular line appears in chapter 13 of *Love Story*, a romantic tale of boomers published in 1970.

9

The Dignity of Labor

The Barber's Kids

LIKE LOTS OF PARENTS who brought boomers into the world, my parents expected that their children would be at least as well off financially as they were, if not better. All indicators seemed to point to unlimited potential for prosperity. In the 1950s, the economy was strong and the U.S. was not a debtor nation. America was the land of opportunity that had given my father, a barber without a high school diploma, the chance to raise a family in relative comfort and financial security. My father encouraged his children to get college degrees. He did not want to see his kids impoverished in the event that they made a poor choice in marriage. "You kids should always have something to fall back on," he said. He understood poverty. He grew up in it.

Unlike my mother's family, my father's family was not financially secure. My father's father, Leonard, rarely worked, and spent his days drinking beer, smoking cigarettes, and listening to baseball games on the radio. He never spent time with his three sons doing things that dads do with their boys. There were no park excursions, no church services, and no movies—nothing. My grandmother, Catherine, lovingly known as "Hawkeye" (for her ability to spot mischief), worked in bars and cafeterias all her life, cooking, washing dishes, and stocking shelves. Dad's family had to move 17 times before my father was 12 years-old because his parents could not pay the rent. My father began working as a young boy, picking rags and working on truck farms. He dropped out of high school in 1951 and joined the Navy, just in time for the Korean War. He sent his paychecks home with hope that he would have a tidy savings waiting for him when he was discharged. Hawkeye spent every penny on food, bills, clothing, and shoes for my father's two younger brothers.

The G.I. Bill provided my father with money for a college education, and so he enrolled with hopes of becoming a social worker. In his English class, the professor inadvertently returned a graded essay he had written to the woman sitting behind him. She read it, tapped him on the shoulder and asked rather starry-eyed, "Were you in the Navy?" Neither one of my parents completed their degrees.

My mother's family was financially secure, as her father, Benjamin Donald, whom my siblings and I called "Pops," owned a construction company that built schools, churches, office buildings, motels, restaurants, and homes. Pops took his Catholicism seriously and attended Mass weekly. He was a quiet man who practiced the Gospel but did not much like to discuss it. Pops disliked labor unions because he believed they were corrupt. On one occasion, he chased a union representative off a construction site with a two-by-four in his hand. Pops made unions irrelevant. He was generous with other contractors, his clients, and his workers. Once while bidding for a contract to build a church, he learned that a competitor who was teetering on the edge of bankruptcy placed a bid that was far lower than his bid. Knowing that the job could not be done properly at the reduced price, he told the pastor to hire his competitor, but to give the competitor the price that Pops had submitted. He saved his competitor's business and so too the families his competitor supported. Pops often loaned his employees money in times of medical or family crises, and he never charged interest. Sometimes, he forgave the debt altogether.

My mother never had to move from the home her father built, and was able to finish high school run by Jesuit priests. She had decent winter coats, and nice dresses, and was encouraged to become a nurse. While my father was fulfilling his duties in the Navy, my mother went to school and spent much of her time caring for her two youngest brothers. Her mother, Harriet, preferred socializing at the country club to raising children. The Sisters of Notre Dame and Jesuits who taught my mother were highly educated and strict. She learned not to question authority and to seek perfection, sometimes to the point of maniacal compulsion. She was also taught that good Catholics were good workers, leaders, and self-sacrificing servants.

When my father asked for my mother's hand in marriage, my mother's parents objected. Though a Catholic, my father came from poverty and his family had only arrived from Poland and Italy less than 50 years earlier. My mother's family was middle class, and her Irish, German, and Norwegian ancestors had settled in the U.S. prior to the Civil War. Harriet, whom my siblings and I called, "Gramma Ham," (in keeping with her preference for holiday dinners), wanted her daughter to marry somebody who would not have to borrow a suit to join her at the country club. Ham's sister warned that

THE DIGNITY OF LABOR

if my mother wed my father, she would be "living in one cold-water flat after the other." Out of respect for Pops, my father delayed the wedding for a year to see how his business went. When Ham protested that the couple wait a second year, mom and dad declined the petition and booked a wedding date at Holy Rosary Church, which Pops built.

My parents raised six kids on a barber's income. My siblings and I all went to Catholic schools, got medical attention when we needed it, and always had enough to eat. My siblings and I learned to work early in life. Prior to our first high school jobs in fast-food restaurants, nursing homes, and summer camps, we shoveled snow, mowed lawns, and babysat. We also learned about charity. On his days off, my father cut hair for free at a home for low-income elders run by the Little Sisters of the Poor. I tagged along as a youngster, happy to be out "bummin," as my father called it. As kids, my siblings and I extended our charity to our neighbors. At first, we did chores for them as mom directed. That usually meant errands and bringing meals to someone's home. Later, we did things without being asked. We went grocery shopping, drove people to Mass, and cleaned houses. We refused payment from our neighbors out of compassion and out of pride for being helpful. I have no doubt that my parents had opinions about our neighbors—the unwed mothers, alcoholics, and unemployed, but they chastised us kids if we were judgmental, and reminded us that we did not know the circumstances that brought them to such conditions. Our duties were simple then: judge not, care a lot.

Childhood lessons about class and the dignity of labor included those that came by way of comparing my grandmothers. Ham lived on rural acreage in a big house that maids kept spotless. Hawkeye lived near downtown Minneapolis in rented apartments with worn linoleum and peeling paint. Ham had a walk-in closet packed with dresses, suits, shoes, hats, and mink coats. Hawkeye had a few dresses and shoes that she wore long past the time when her sons insisted that they buy her new things. Ham openly judged others, and Hawkeye was remarkably silent on the matter of other people's characters. After my mom was married, Ham became a director of volunteers at a hospital and earned many awards and state recognition. She retired on a pension and a stash of stock holdings. Hawkeye retired after a lifetime in the kitchen without public acclaim, and lived month to month on her Social Security check. Ham loved to rub elbows with the elite at the country club and drive her Cadillac. Hawkeye loved to dance the polka at local pubs and took the bus. Ham complained that my siblings and I ate too much and were too noisy. Hawkeye played cards with us and fed us homemade mostaccioli and fried bread until we were too stuffed to move.

Although I could not define the term "dignity" as a child, as I got older, it seemed to me that Hawkeye embodied it. The word "dignity" is often used to connote honor. Both grandmothers did things that were honorable, yet their moral characters were very different. Ham trained people to take care of the sick, but neglected her sons, who abused Pop's credit, drank heavily, and cheated on their wives. Hawkeye peeled a lot of potatoes and mopped a lot of floors, but she loved her boys and gave them all she had. Hawkeye's generosity to us six kids was magnified by her meager earnings, just as Ham's parsimony was magnified by her wealth. Even as kids, my siblings and I seemed to sense that what people did with their wages mattered just as much as how they earned them.

Hawkeye wanted very little from the material world. It was enough to survive. Her family reached Ellis Island from Italy around 1910. She was the 11th of 12 children, and on her 15th birthday, her father was killed in a trolley accident. She never finished high school, but aspired to own her own dress shop, where could design and make women's apparel. She never had the chance. At age 18, she became pregnant with my father and was compelled, like all Catholics of her generation, to get married. Ham wanted much from the world. When she and her two siblings were abandoned by their parents, Ham was separated from her brother and sister. She was placed in an orphanage in southern Minnesota, while her siblings remained up north near Duluth. Ham was adopted by a judge and his wife, who provided the comforts of a middle class lifestyle. Ham went to a private school, and socialized with the sons and daughters of Mankato's upper classes. Ham's wants seemed to shut us kids out, while Hawkeye's wants let us in.

It is a Sin

At the Benedictine college where I earned a BA in Religious Studies, the business office was staffed by nuns and students. One day I watched an elderly nun gather and distribute mail. She was a small woman, thin and crinkled. She wore rimless glasses so thick they seemed to double the size of her eyes. Her face was fixed in a permanent smile, mouth wide open, and jaw slack to one side. She worked slowly, often setting envelopes down, losing them, and finding them again. I asked another nun, "Sister Pete," whether it would be better to let students do the work, and suggested that the office might run more efficiently that way. Pete smiled, but firmly chastised me. "No," she stated, "she has her place, and it is very important here that everyone feels like they contribute to our work." She added quietly, "It is a sin to take away somebody's sense of value to the community."

The fusion of love and labor was foundational to my orientation towards work. I learned, and I still believe, that all work is a ministry. It is an opportunity to use one's talents for the well-being of others. As kids, my siblings and I speculated about what we might be when we grew up. Even then we had already absorbed cultural ideas about which jobs brought more social status than others. Yet, we had also learned that work was not about getting rich or being the boss, it was about being honest, responsible and fair. We knew that as we pursed our vocational interests, we were developing the person we believed we were on the inside, and in the context of Catholic education, that internal sense of self was deeply spiritual. We understood that our choice of work said something about our character and regard for others. The crisis of unemployment was never just about the inability to put food on the table, it was also a spiritual crisis whereby one is made obsolete because others say so.

In Caesar's world, it is not a sin to deprive someone of a sense of value nor a decent wage. It is not a sin to relocate one's company so that stockholders and executives can earn more profit. In Caesar's world, it is not a sin to downsize and ask workers to do the jobs of two or three people, nor to punish people who expose flaws in products or management. Morality, we glean from our experience with Caesar, is not good for the bottom line.

Boomers have witnessed significant changes in business practices in their lifetimes. When I started working in 1975, I earned $1.90 an hour, and by 2013 minimum wage reached $7.25. Full-time workers earning minimum wages in 2014 made just enough ($13,920 before taxes, assuming one worked 52 weeks a year) to hover above the poverty line for a single person, which was $11,690.[1] Corporate executives earned a salary equal to what 24 workers earned in 1965, 71 workers earned in 1989, and 298 workers earned in 2000.[2] Greed was on the move, but Caesar kept telling us that economic hardships associated with low wages was unrelated to excessive profiteering at the top. Caesar still tells us that increasing minimum wages will not alleviate poverty, and claims that tax cuts create jobs. Millions of Americans live in fear that if they ask for decent wages and benefits, they will lose what little they have. Caesar sees no sin in this.

---

1. U.S. Department of Health and Human Service, "2014 Poverty Guidelines," Table: 2104 Poverty Guidelines for the 48 Contiguous States and the District of Columbia.

2. Visser, "CSR 2.0," 233.

Undercover Waitress

In the film, *The American Ruling Class*, journalist Barbara Ehrenreich has a conversation with "Jack," a fictitious character who represents the upper class. Jack is recent graduate of Yale who contemplates a career in investment banking.[3] Ehrenreich is working as waitress to learn about how people who work for minimum wage survive. The year was 1998. The economy was expanding, the dot-coms flourished, and jobs were created. As Ehrenreich discovered, however, many wages were so pitiful that it left full-time employees impoverished. She found that workers lived in their cars or motels, lacked medical care, and skipped meals to pay for necessities. She learned that many workers were routinely cheated out of wages and were offered no pension plans.

Jack was cynical about Ehrenreich's description of the problems workers faced and scoffed, "I am just having a tough time because you just don't see this—you don't see things being as bad as you describe them." Ehrenreich replied, "*You* don't see it Jack, because you hang out at Goldman Sachs or wherever you want to work." Jack persisted, "But they have philanthropy, public service—a lot of those people devote millions and millions of dollars to building houses in poor communities." Ehrenreich countered, "Philanthropy! Don't tell me about philanthropy, Jack! The real philanthropists in our society are the people who work for less than they can actually live on, because they are giving of their time and their energy and their talents all the time so that people like you can be dressed well and fed cheaply, and so on—*they're giving to you.*"

Lots of Americans think like Jack. Many hold that welfare, food stamps, and subsidized housing for the poor are magnanimous and perhaps too generous. What Jack and others like him ignore is that a handout does not remediate society's failure to see that decent-paying jobs are abundant, and people have access to affordable housing, health care, and meaningful education.

Many Americans talk about the market as if it is a self-propelling invisible hand—something that just seems to "happen" organically as if the wheels of supply and demand turned in a vacuum void of moral decisions. The reality is that human beings make decisions about wages and the distribution of profit. They decide how to manipulate consumer trends and the cost of everything from peas to petroleum. They decide which industries get subsidized, and which get bailed out when bankruptcy looms. Real people determine minimum wages and make choices about whether to offer workers a health care plan or whether to give executives millions of dollars in bonuses. Like

---

3. *The American Ruling Class*, directed by John Kirby (2005; USA: The Alive Mind, 2007), DVD.

Pops building churches, real executives decide when to counsel the pastor to make a contract with a competitor out of concern for his well-being and when to strike like a shark and kill the competition.

The American Ruling Class calls attention to the reality that the American struggle for economic justice stumbles and stalls for three reasons. First, Americans do not want to admit that it has a ruling class. Second, we believe the myth that the market is democratic. Third,, those who admit to the existence of a ruling class often want so much to be part of it that they gladly pardon its sins.

All Hail the Market

Theologian Harvey Cox observed that we have bestowed the market with attributes once reserved for God.[4] The market, he opined, is often thought to be all powerful, all knowing, and jealous of competing gods such as command economies and socialism. As God, the market has its own eschatology, or teachings on the end of the world, which warn of grave consequences for not abiding by the wisdom of Wall Street. Further, argues Cox, the market has flipped the world of the sacred and profane by making commodities out of creation made in the image of God. Sacred ancestral resting places, forests, mountains, our own blood, DNA, and tissue are properties that can be bought and sold. The market as God assess the value of human life in terms of what an individual can produce and consume. In Caesar's world, the poor, undereducated, physically handicapped, elderly, and mentally impaired have little value.

Many Americans hold that poverty is relative to a person's character. In 2014 Speaker of the House, Paul Ryan (R-WI), asserted that poverty is a problem because people are lazy. He cited the work of Charles Murray of the American Enterprise Institute, which claims that women and racial minorities are disadvantaged because they are intellectually and morally inferior to white men.[5] Americans are far more likely than people in other counties to believe that success is generally determined by forces individuals can control.[6] These sentiments amplify the notion that the market is fair, objective, and designed to reward effort, resourcefulness, and intelligence. This assertion is betrayed by lived experiences of people who do not get hired because they are not the right age, gender, or ethnicity. It is betrayed by the fact that exemplary employees are often denied promotions and fairly rewarded because supervisors

---

4. Cox, "Market as God," 18–23.
5. Volsky, "Paul Ryan Blames," line 1–13.
6. Pew Research Center, "Emerging and Developing Economies," lines 87–95.

feel threatened by their competence, intimidated by their ideas, or are maneuvering to curry favor with the boss.

In Caesar's empire, many who are unemployed and living in poverty do not figure in official statistics. Officially, in 2014 the unemployment rate ranged from between 5.7 and 5 percent, yet official measurements of unemployment do not include those who are by definition in the labor force, but not seeking work because they are discouraged, nor those who were laid off with expectations that they would be returning to work.[7] In 2014, 15.5 percent of Americans lived below the poverty line.[8] Yet, depending on how one measures poverty, and which variables are factored, the numbers can shift by several percentage points.[9]

In Boomer's lifetime, workers have become more productive only to earn less. Between 1948 and 1979, productivity rose 108.1 percent and hourly wages increased in the private sector by 93.4 percent. Then, between 1979 and 2013, productivity rose by 64.9 percent and hourly wages increased by only 8.2 percent.[10] The secret to being more productive and less prosperous lies in the distribution of profit. In 1979, for instance, the lowest quintile by income after taxes earned 6.9 percent of all income, while the top quintile earned 42 percent.[11] By 2010, the lowest quintile earned 5.4 percent of income in the U.S. while the top quintile raked in 49.4 percent.[12] In that year, the top 1 percent of income-earners in the U.S. saw an increase of 76 percent, while folks at the bottom and in the middle quintiles all saw their incomes drop by 4 to 22 percent.

The term "working poor" reveals the reality that people can have full-time jobs and still live in poverty. Officially, as of 2013, "low wages" were defined as less than $342.87 per week, or $1,371.48 per month. The rate of the working poor jumped from 6.4 percent in 2007 to 7.7 percent in 2013, reaching a total of 10.5 million people classified as working poor.[13]

Media plays an important role in what we know and what we do not know about the poor and unemployed. One report found that nearly one half of local and regional news tends to be about crime, sports and weather, and

---

7. Hansen, *National Economy,* 29–30.

8. Anderson, H. M. *State Profiles,* 1.

9. Iceland, *Poverty in America,* 22–38. Also see: U.S. Department of Labor, "How the Government Measures Unemployment."

10. Seip and Harper, *Trickle Down Delusion,* 161.

11. Ibid., 166.

12. Ibid.

13. Bureau of Labor Statistics, "A Profile", 1–3.

just about 4 percent is about human rights and the needy.[14] The poor tend to get the most attention and sympathy around Thanksgiving and Christmas or in the wake of natural disasters. The sympathy, however, is short circuited. News media tends to ignore the poor and to frame them in ways that consistently blame them for their poverty, and entertainment media tends to portray the rich and middle class as the social norm.[15] This leaves us with little understanding of why people are poor, and who benefits from their poverty.

Cheap Underwear

Boomers have seen what one corporation can do to impact an entire economy. Incorporated in 1969, Wal-Mart became the world's largest retailer in the world with sales of $276 billion.[16] It promised shoppers the lowest prices on items from French fries to firearms, and it promised prosperity to the communities into which it moved. By 2004, Wal-Mart had 3,661 stores in the U.S., and it left a trail of mixed blessings wherever it went. In 2005, the average Wal-Mart worker's salary was around $9.68 per hour, which was 26 percent lower than workers in comparable jobs.[17] Wal-Mart had adverse effects not only on employees, but on the state, as its practice of paying workers poorly and denying benefits gave other businesses the incentive to keep their workers' compensations at a minimum. The effect of opening 50 new Wal-Marts in a state had the effect of reducing retail wages by 10 percent and reducing employer-sponsored health care benefits by 5 percent.[18]

The documentary film, *Wal-Mart: The High Cost of Low Price*, revealed that tax-payers subsidize Wal-Mart workers, as poorly paid employees are counseled by managers to apply for Medicare, food stamps and utilities' programs.[19] Wal-Mart employees described how managers cheated workers out of overtime pay and bullied employees who took time off due to illness. Many people endured the abuse because they were afraid of being unemployed. In another documentary, *Capitalism: a Love Story*, Michael Moore exposed Wal-Mart's practice of purchasing "dead peasant" insurance on its employees.[20]

14. Heider and Fuse, "Class and Local TV," 87–107.
15. Kendall, *Framing Class*, 10–11.
16. Quinn, *How Walmart is Destroying*, xvii.
17. Dube, et. al. *A Downward Push*, 2.
18. Ibid., 5.
19. *Wal-Mart: The High Cost of Low Price*. Directed by Robert Greenwald. 2005. USA: Disinformation Company, 2005. DVD.
20. *Capitalism: A Love Story*. Directed by Michael Moore. 2009. USA: Dog Eat Dog Films, 2009. DVD.

Dead peasant life insurance policies cover workers without the worker's knowledge, and they are a financial tool that allows employers to lower their tax liabilities.[21] Wal-Mart profited handsomely from the roughly 350,000 policies it held, and stopped the practice not because it was immoral, but because it generated bad public relations.[22] As Wal-Mart cashed in on their macabre investments, families who lost their loved ones fought expensive court battles to collect compensations.

Corporations the size of Wal-Mart have the capacity to drive family businesses that have existed for generations in to the ground. They have turned thriving towns into depressed economies. Government subsides of Wal-Mart expansion have given the mega-retailer advantages that mom and pop shops do not have, and thus caused many family businesses to close. Al Norman, founder of Sprawl Busters, said, "They [Wal-Mart] don't get it; when we start talking about quality of life they start talking about cheap underwear."[23]

In her book, *Nickel and Dimed* Barbara Ehrenreich describes the impact of Caesars' sweatshop on people's sense of identity and self-respect. In her "sabbatical" from her regular life to take on minimum wage jobs, she met maids, cooks, and waitresses, who were routinely belittled by their supervisors, subjected to "employment tests" designed to enforce obedience, and expected to perform feats of physical exertion with speed and efficiency that conjures images of Gilded Age factories. She describes a world in which people endure the weight of drudgery as well as verbal abuse for getting sick or being injured on the job. For entertainment one night, Ehrenreich, an atheist, attended a Christian revival meeting. She wrote:

> The preaching goes on, interrupted with dutiful "amens." It would be nice if someone would read this sad-eyed crowd the Sermon on the Mount, accompanied by a rousing commentary on income equality and the need for a hike in the minimum wage. But Jesus makes his appearance here only as a corpse; the living man, the wine-guzzling vagrant and precocious socialist, is never mentioned, nor anything he ever had to say. Christ crucified rules, and it may be that the true business of modern Christianity is to crucify him again and again so that he can never get a word out of his mouth.[24]

---

21. Baker, D. "End of Looser Liberalism," 119.
22. Hightower, *Thieves in High Places*, 190–91.
23. *Capitalism: A Love Story.*
24. Ehrenreich, *Nickel and Dimed*, 68–69.

Ehrenreich, was raised to revere reason and to be skeptical of authority.[25] Yet, she seems to hear Jesus with greater precision than that of many evangelists.

Caesar's Workshop

Greed assaults the dignity of labor. Corporations that steal from the public through price fixing, kick-backs, tax loops, and subsidies hurt us. The dignity of labor is also mocked when people fraudulently collect unemployment insurance and other public assistance. Identity theft, bogus claims of disability, and welfare abuse, costs taxpayers billions and abuse the good will of citizens who support public assistance programs. Lots of boomers who in their youth defended such programs have become bitter about our government's generosity, and know people who have cheated the system. We are spiritually wounded when people take our money under false pretenses or in excess of what they actually need, because those actions tempt our vengeance, diminish our empathy and trust, and serve as a dangerous role model to others.

The dignity of labor is also assaulted by toxic behavior in the workplace that is often rationalized as "part of the culture." Folks say, "Well, that's just how it is," as if our work places were under the spell of a sorcerer who cursed our shops and offices with chronic incivility, jealously, combativeness, and inequity. Many have learned to tolerate the nastiness because they have learned to separate their spiritual lives from their work lives. Peter's paradigm accommodates such compartmentalization because it emphasizes heavenly rewards rather than activating the Kingdom of God where we stand. The Kingdom of God as a lived phenomenon, however, dissolves the compartments.

One of the gifts of the Catholic education my peers and I received was the idea that, regardless of what vocations we pursued, we were all called to leaven the Gospel in our work. The faithful, we learned, integrated their spirituality into their work, family relationships, and civic life. As we moved into our adult lives, we learned that Caesar's world is one of literal *dis-integration*. Caesar rewards us for locking our spirituality in the closet and for not openly leveraging it in our work and professional relationships. We learned in Caesar's workshop that compassion, collaboration, and humility could derail one's ascent to the top. Even in workplaces whose mission statements radiate a commitment to social justice, democratic processes, and caring, exploitation and abuse are common.

In Caesar's world, we learn to define ourselves and our value as human beings by our jobs. We have learned that executive positions and white collar

---

25. Ehrenreich, *Living with a Wild God*, 3.

professions entitle one to status and special regard. We have learned to patronize subordinate positions and blue collar careers. We have learned to chase certain jobs not because we believed we had particular gifts to share, or felt called to a special ministry, but because we liked the status and money they offered. We have also learned to promote people not because they are particularly gifted and responsible, but because they represent no threat to the status quo or privileges certain individuals have secured for themselves. There are many temptations to parrot Caesar in this way of business. We may even be rewarded for being dishonest, duplicitous, or belligerent.

Most of our workplaces are political. This is because many people see them primarily as a platform for personal advancement and not as venue to minister to society's needs. From a spiritual perspective, all vocations are ministries. They make possible the prosperity of our families, and provide a venue in which our talents may be shared for the benefit of others.

In Caesar's workshop, there are many unwritten rules about how people relate to each other. These rules represent the company's or the institution's culture, and are often primarily concerned with how people access, use, and relate to power in the workplace. These rules teach us about who is important, whose egos must be flattered in order to obtain or achieve certain things, who must be avoided because of their controversial opinions, and who to charm because they are close to power. Little by little, the unwritten rules become tumors on our conscience and thus corrupt our moral reasoning.

Political work environments tend to be unkind, unforgiving, and inequitable. In some instances, bullies are tolerated because they bring in lots of money to the organization. In some instances, supervisors exploit technicalities to punish workers or block their promotions because they are jealous. In some instances, executives promote the least competent employee as to neutralize any potential threats to his or her authority. Such workplaces often lose sight of their mission and suck the life out of staff morale. They offend our spirituality by withholding respect and encouragement from workers. In Caesar's workshop, people take credit for work they did not do, lie about productivity, blame others for their mistakes, abuse people's opinions by creating adversarial alliances, and participate in gossip that ruins reputations and collaboration.

Caesar's workshop is frequently not a psychologically safe place. Approximately 37 percent of Americans—about 54 million—have at some point been bullied on the job, and 60 percent of the bullies are male and 57 percent of the targets are female.[26] Caesar's workshop is frequently not a safe place for the truth. Honesty is often sacrificed for the sake of special interests or politi-

---

26. Namie and Namie, *Bully at Work*, 4–6.

cal correctness. Schools that lie about students' academic achievements stay open and win grants. Industries that lie about pollution do not pay penalties. Utility companies that lie about safety records get contracts. Politicians who lie about their love of justice become advance guards for special interests.

When boomers fixed their vision on making the world a better place, lots of us imagined that we would do so through our professions. We saw our future workplaces as venues for healing a broken and corrupted world, and not the things that broke and corrupted us. The idea that schools, hospitals, industries, and banks could be corrupt was to my grade school peers as remote and ridiculous as the idea that a president would participate in a hotel burglary. I once thought that when things went wrong on the job, it was because an individual goofed up and not because the system was flawed. I had to adjust this belief when I learned that there are people who profit from having things broken and corrupted.

The Love of a Lousy Buck

Christianity has had little quarrel with capitalism. Historically, though the Catholic Church was disturbed by the miseries endured by working class and poor, it blamed personal greed, not private ownership of the means of production and distribution, for poverty and labor unrest. During the Gilded Age, Pope Leo XIII's *Rerum Novarum* (often called *On the Condition of the Working Class*) was a key step in the evolution of Catholic teachings on economics. It embodied some of the Vatican's first convictions regarding social justice as an institutional, rather than an individual's way of respecting the dignity of the human being. It announced that the endeavor to level all people into one class was against nature, and that suffering is part of the human condition that need not exacerbate hostilities.[27] Leo penned that the government is obligated to take special care of wage-earners, since, unlike the rich, they lacked the means of shielding themselves from a violation of rights.[28] The moral imperative to circumvent revolution, Leo held, lay in the employers commitment to pay fair wages, and the willingness of or workers to give employers an honest days' work.[29]

In boomer's lifetime, Pope John XXIII underscored the obligation of "every civil authority to takes pains to promote the common good of all,

---

27. Leo XII, *Rerum Novarum*, paragraphs 17–19.
28. Ibid., paragraph 37.
29. Ibid, paragraphs 43–47.

without preference for any single citizen or civic group."[30] He observed that human dignity was linked to self-sufficiency and one's capacity to contribute to the common welfare, and that governments should strive to maintain full employment. Pope Paul VI decried materialism, consumerism, unjust wages, and argued that for the sake of protecting human dignity, it was fitting to give workers a say in management.[31] The Catholic social teachings of the twentieth century are among the things that make me proud of my religious heritage. At least in rhetoric, the Church insisted that the law, private business, and labor work in concert to bring about social justice.[32]

Periodically, the Church's social teachings were reincarnated in cinema, and I especially liked Father Barry, the priest in the 1954 film, *On the Waterfront*.[33] The story depicts the real-life corruption in New York's docks in the 1950s. The protagonist, Terry Malloy, is a boxer whose brother Charley works for a mob boss who extorts workers for the right to work. The boss also forces Charley to have Terry throw his matches so mobsters can cash in on bets. Following the mob's murder of a worker who was about to testify before the crime commission, Father Barry delivers an impromptu sermon over the man's dead body. While mobsters hurl garbage at him, Barry trumpeted:

> Some people think the Crucifixion only took place on Calvary. They better wise up! . . . Dropping a sling on Kayo Dugan because he was ready to spill his guts tomorrow, that's a crucifixion. And every time the Mob puts the pressure on a good man, tries to stop him from doing his duty as a citizen, it's a crucifixion. And anybody who sits around and lets it happen, keeps silent about something he knows that happened, shares the guilt of it just as much as the Roman soldier who pierced the flesh of our Lord to see if he was dead . . . Boys, this is my church! And if you don't think Christ is down here on the waterfront, you've got another guess coming . . .
>
> . . . You want to know what's wrong with our waterfront? It's the love of a lousy buck. It's making the love of the lousy buck—the cushy job—more important than the love of man! It's forgettin' that every fellow down here is your brother in Christ! But remember,

---

30. John XXIII, *Pacem in Terris*, paragraph 56.

31. Curran, *Catholic Social Teaching*, 129–34. Also see Paul VI, *Populorum Progressio*.

32. The United States Catholic Conference of Bishops' *Economic Justice for All* articulates the Church's position, with commentary on the challenges of capitalism and the U.S. economy in the twenty-fist century.

33. *On the Waterfront*. Directed by Elia Kazan. 1954. Culver City, CA: Sony Pictures, 2001. DVD.

Christ is always with you . . . He's sayin' with all of you, if you do it to the least of mine, you do it to me![34]

Barry's speech could have been delivered today. It could have been directed to corporate farm owners who have no problem with undocumented immigrants because they like how they settle for low wages and zero benefits; or, to Wal-Mart executives who fatten themselves at the expense of tax-payers and small businesses; or to airline titans who charge customers $200.00 to correct a spelling error on a boarding pass; or, to people who fake injuries for the purpose of collecting public assistance; or, to politicians who accept huge speaking fees and donations to their foundations from foreign leaders, who then receive favorable business contracts regardless of how reprehensible their human rights record might be.

In 2013, Pope Francis criticized a world wherein the hungry and the homeless perish daily with less recognition than hiccups in the stock market, and people are numb to the dominion money has over their lives. He rejected "trickle down" economics and observed that capitalism has come to rule rather than serve society.[35] Boomers know what Francis is talking about. As the government reduced corporate taxes and deregulated industries during the 1970s and 1980s, they watched supply-side economics polarize the rich and poor. Conservatives insisted then and now that business interests are the cornerstone of American prosperity. In recent decades, lots of Americans felt like the quality of their lives were being held hostage by a corporate elite who constantly demanded more ransom. Events leading to the 2008 Recession reveals how, under the spell of the right mythology, even a man who says his prayers by night, may become a wolf when derivatives bloom and moon of sub-prime lending shines bright.

---

34. *On the Waterfront*.
35. Francis I, *Evangelii Gaudium*, paragraphs 53–60.

10

Banksters and Creditmeisters

Working Hard, Losing Ground

BOOMERS BELIEVED, AS BILLY Joel sang in his song, *Allentown,* "Every child had pretty good shot to get at least as far as their old man got . . . if we worked hard, if we behaved."[1] Boomers were raised in a culture with high expectations for upward mobility and material comfort. Our parents, who experienced the Great Depression and WWII, believed Americans had "paid their dues" and so earned the right to leisure and comfort. Americans believed their values had been vindicated in war, and so we deserved the best. In general, boomers had confidence in the formula that education plus hard work equals success. Accordingly, college enrollment steadily climbed as boomers grew up, from 2.3 million in 1950, to 3.6 million in 1960, to 8.5 million in 1970, and to 12 million by 1980.[2] Boomers grew up confident that college graduates would have their pick of jobs, and that even those without degrees could someday own their own shop or advance in the company if they were diligent.

Boomers were taught that the value of their labor and the cost of the goods and services were determined by the dynamics of supply and demand. The lessons seemed logical: a surplus of workers in the job market kept wages low, and a shortage of workers kept wages high; a surplus of goods in the market kept prices low, a shortage of goods kept prices high. Many learned the hard way that this is not always true. After all, shortages, surpluses, wages, and costs can be manipulated. Government programs for farmers, for example, keep the price of agricultural products high by paying farmers not to produce a surplus. In 2013, 50 billion dollars subsidized about 838,391 farms, with 75

---

1. Billy Joel, *Allentown,* Columbia, 45 rpm. 1982.
2. National Center for Educational Statistics, *120 years of American Education,* 7.

percent dished out to the top ten agribusinesses.[3] The idea that the economy is the product of the "invisible hand" of supply and demand suggests that the economy is rational and objective. In reality, the economy is also the product of human judgments that are not always impartial or examples of Christian charity.

Boomers believed that the fortunes of the nation were determined by the fortunes of industry and commerce, and so, we needed to keep expanding the economy and to stay competitive. We learned prosperity was greatest when the government took a laissez-faire, or "hands-off" approach to business. Regulations, taxes, and antitrust laws, we were told, crippled productivity and limited innovation and full employment. Corporate executives and politicians alike encouraged citizens to trust the high priests of Wall Street, assuring us that they would be good shepherds because of their own self-interests. Boomers eventually learned, however, that corporations, investment firms, and banks found little moral objection to amassing great fortunes by preying upon vulnerable consumers, abusing legal latitudes, and expecting taxpayers to clean up their messes.

Boomers not only witnessed the erosion of regulation and tax laws that enabled their parents and grandparents to weather financial storms and scarcity, they were often the engineers of economic crises that included the Recession of 2008. Since the 1970s, the healthy and robust middle class that existed in boomer's youth has taken a beating. As the middle and working classes lost wealth, the top 1 percent, who earn $350,000.00 or more a year, have made gains. People in the top 1 percent of the 1 percent, who earn a million or more annually, did especially well over the last 35 years. In 2012 the wealthiest 160,000 families in America possessed as much wealth as did the poorest 145 million families.[4] Real family income growth between 1947 and 1979 was very different from real income growth between 1979 and 2003. Between 1947 and 1979, the lowest four quintiles of family income in the U.S. increased by over 100 percent, the fifth quintile by 99 percent, and the top 1 percent increased by 86 percent. Between 1979 and 2003, the real income growth for the lowest quintile was *minus* 2 percent, while gains between 8 and 51 percent were achieved in the next four quintiles, and the top 1 percent increased by 75 percent.[5]

Wealth and income are different, but both are concentrated at the top percentiles. The richest command a greater share of wealth that is represented more by income from property and investments than by annual salaries. In

---

3. Barkley and Barkley *Depolarizing Food,* 115.
4. Matthews, "Wealth Inequality," lines 19–47.
5. Ingalls and Johnson, *United States,* 217.

2013, the top 3 percent drew 31 percent of all salaries earned in the U.S., while in the same year the top 3 percent owned 54 percent of the nation's wealth. Conversely, the bottom 90 percent earned 53 percent of all salaries in 2013, and owned 25 percent of the nation's wealth.[6] The rich get richer because they have capital to invest in new businesses and stock options, whereas the bottom 90 percent of Americans have far less for such ventures.

The pain that workers feel varies not only by income, but by location. In 2014, for example, customer service representatives earned an average of $33,890, which was $9,472 above the poverty line for a family of four.[7] In theory, the service worker had something to invest. Had that service worker lived in San Francisco in 2014, however, he or she would probably not feel like he or she lived above the poverty line, as the median cost to rent a one-bedroom apartment at that time was about $2,700.00 per month, a total of $32,400.00 for a single year.[8]

Folks like to say that the number of millionaires and billionaires a country produces is a good way to measure that country's prosperity, but that criteria ignores misery at the bottom of the economic pyramid. In 1998, there were over 102,500 millionaires in the U.S., which was an increase of 83,893 millionaires since 1983. Of all millionaires in 2004, 75 percent had $10 billion in assets or more—a 65 percent jump in billionaires from 1986.[9] Even as the after tax income of families rose between 1977 and 1989, 13 percent of added income went to the top 1 percent.[10] By 1998, the top 1 percent of income earners represented 16 percent of all income earners and held 38.1 percent of all wealth, while the bottom 90 percent of income earners represented 58.5 percent of all income earners and held 29 percent of all wealth.[11]

The proposition that "the poor will always be with us" (Matt 26:11) typically does not upset Americans. Many believe that by nature, wealth pools around those who work the hardest and have the most talent. Many understand that it is possible to tip the flow of wealth by giving advantages to some and not to others, and they tolerate an occasional tip as long as there is a chance that the tip is in their favor. Boomers were raised to believe that serious economic abuses were nearly impossible, because the government would keep economic villainy in check. Nonetheless, a slow but steady series of changes

6. Stone, C. et. al. "A Guide to Statistics," Section II.
7. United States Bureau of Labor Statistics, *Occupational Employment Statistics*, 41–0000.
8. Kuchar, "Are You Sitting Down?" full essay and figures.
9. Ciment, *Social Issues*, 1365.
10. Reynolds, *Income and Wealth*, 76.
11. Jacobs and Skocpol, "American Democracy," 3–5.

in tax laws, banking regulation, and government oversight of financial institutions occurred in boomer's lifetime. Somebody let the villains in.

Mr. Grinch goes to Washington

The villains of the economic story presented themselves as noble public servants who were just trying to help strengthen the American economy. They believed that what was good for business was good for America. Like the Grinch in Dr. Seuss' story, *How the Grinch Stole Christmas,* those who created an economic landscape in which highly skilled and educated Americans can work over 40 hours a week and still struggle to make ends meet, were able to stuff our compensation and financial security up the chimney because they made themselves appear harmless and benevolent.[12] Since not all elected officials are experts in economics, and since the experts and elected officials are sometimes corrupt or incompetent, they were easy targets for "Grinchy" bankers and politicians who peddled their self-serving legal reforms as holiday chocolates.

Some executives saw trouble coming. In capitalism, President Eisenhower saw the potential for private interest to sabotage the "corporate commonwealth" by way of "unbridled acquisitiveness" and "contentious party politics."[13] The interests of government, the general public, and private interests, he held, had to maintain harmony for the sake of national stability. During his presidency, the top individual income tax bracket topped 90 percent, yet, nobody called Eisenhower a Marxist.[14] Like most presidents, he was pressured to reduce taxes and industrial regulation for the sake of strengthening the private sector. In 1953, corporate taxes represented about 28.4 percent of all federal tax revenue, but during Ronald Reagan's administration, they bottomed out at 1.3 percent.[15]

In general, income tax decreased between 1980 and 2010, but the percentage of the reduction was greater for the top three groups that earned over $150,000 annually.[16] When translated in to actual revenue, the disparities are significant. A person who earned $25,000 in 2010, for instance, paid 19 percent of that income for federal, state, and local taxes, which amounted to

12. Theodore Seuss Geisel [pseud. Dr. Seuss] published *How the Grinch Stole Christmas* in 1957, and may have named his malcontented villain after the French word, *grincheaux*, which means "grumpy."
13. Griffith, Dwight "Eisenhower," 88.
14. Delton, *Rethinking the 1950s,* 133.
15. Auerbach and Aaron, "Corporate Taxes," 453.
16. Bostock, et. al. "How the Tax Burden Has Changed," multiple interactive graphs.

$4,750, while the person who earned $350,000 paid 42 percent of that income in taxes, which amounted to $147,000. The person who earned $350,000 got slammed, but the person who earned $25,000 got slammed even more. Here is how that happened: the person who earned $25,000 was left with $20,250 on which to live, while the one who earned $350,000 was left with $203,000 on which to live. Even if the person earning $350,000 was taxed at a rate of 84 percent—twice the 2010 rate, that person would still have had nearly three times the amount on which to live as the person who made $25,000.

At present, corporate profits are subject to a federal tax of 35 percent. Tax loopholes however, enable companies to keep more of their profit. In a study of 288 of fortune 500 companies, researchers found that 39 percent paid no federal taxes.[17] Between 2010 and 2015, tax revenue lost through loopholes and subsides cost the U.S. Treasury $628.6 billion.[18] The Government Accountability Office found that 55 percent of U.S. controlled corporations reported no tax liabilities at least once between 1998 and 2015, and that in 2010, large corporations paid federal income taxes of 12.6 percent, "well below the top statutory rate of 35 percent."[19]

By squirreling away profits in off-shore accounts, corporations can avoid millions of dollars in U.S. taxes. It is estimated that the U.S. lost about $70 *billion* in tax revenue this way in 2011, and that some of the companies that nested their profits in oversea's havens—such as Bank of America and Citigroup—were later the recipients of bailout money during the 2008 Recession.[20] The expectation that handsome profits would result in more jobs openings does not always pan out. Between 2003 and 2012, 449 companies in the S&P 500 used 54 percent of their profits to buy stocks it lost in the 2008 recession. They also used another 37 percent of their profits to pay stockholders. That left less than 10 percent for expansion.[21]

Conjuring Capital

Many hands created the 2008 recession. Real people with real beliefs about what is best for all Americans, and real agendas of their own made decisions about tax codes and government oversight of banking and investment practices. Senators, representatives, presidential advisors, lobbyists, the chairpersons

17. McIntyre, et. al., *Sorry State*, i.
18. Stodola, "They Wrote What Off," lines 6–8.
19. United States Government *Accountability Office, Corporate Income Tax*, 1; 14.
20. Dobratz, et. al. *Power, Politics and Society*, 129.
21. Salaman, "New Corporate Leadership," 60.

of the Federal Reserve, the Commodity Futures Trading Commission, and the US Securities and Exchange Commission helped create the crisis. These individuals contested high taxes and robust regulation, claiming that they were outdated and harmful to modern economic operations.

The cornerstone of "outdated" legislation was the Banking Act of 1933—widely known as the Glass-Steagall Act—which regulated banks, credit, and investment.[22] It limited interest rates that banks could offer, prohibited savings and loans banks from selling insurance and investing in securities, and established the Federal Deposit Insurance Corporation (FDIC). It was a prophylactic against the reckless, credit-fueled speculation that had triggered the Great Depression, but by 1970, that tragedy was ancient history. Consumers wanted new ways to invest and grow their money, and financial institutions chimed in with hopes of providing customers with what they wanted. Financial institutions themselves were often the "customers" that exploited new ways to invest and grow their money. Thus, financial products, which traditionally included checking accounts, bonds, stocks, and loans proliferated to include mutual funds and credit default swaps.

Step by step, with "good intentions," Democrats and Republicans paved the way to 2008's disaster. In 1978, the Supreme Court ruled that banks doing business with banks and credit agencies outside their home state could require out-of-state entities to apply credit policies identical to their own.[23] The ruling energized competition among banks nation-wide. In the same year, President Jimmy Carter signed a law that reduced capital gains taxes from 48 percent to 28 percent. Two years later, he signed the Depository Institutions Deregulation and Monetary Control Act, which increased banks' deposit insurance and eliminated interest rate ceilings. Carter trusted that these actions would stimulate the economy and that banks would not abuse new government insurance and gouge customers with high interest rates for loans.[24]

President Ronald Reagan signed the Economic Recovery Act of 1981 reduced taxes for the top income bracket from 70 percent to 50 percent.[25] He also signed the Tax Reform Act of 1986, which lowered income tax for the top bracket from 50 percent to 28 percent, and raised the lowest bracket from 11 to 15 percent.[26] He supported the Garn-St. Germain Act, 1982 which

22. *Banking Act of* 1933, Public law 73–66, U.S. Statues at Large 48 (1933) 162.

23. Marquette Bank of Minneapolis v. First Omaha Service Corp., 439 U.S. 299 (1978).

24. *Depository Institutions Deregulation and Monetary Control Act of* 1980, Public Law 96–221, Statutes at Large, 94 (1980) 132.

25. *Economic Recovery Tax Act of* 1981, Public Law 97–34, U.S. Statute at Large 95 (1981) 172.

26. *Tax Reform Act of* 1986, Public Law 99–514, U.S. Statute at Large 100 (1986) 2085

allowed savings and loans banks to loan money to corporations.[27] In 1987, he signed the Competitive Equity Banking Act that allowed for the creation of "bridge" banks to manage the liabilities and assets of federally insured banks that failed.[28] In addition, he singed the Food Security Act, 1985, which increased farm subsidies for large agribusinesses, leaving family farms unable to compete with them.[29] Over 400,000 family farms were lost between 1985 and 1989. The $7.3 billion spent on corporate farms in 1985 rose to $25.8 billion by 1989, helping to create monopolies on food production.[30]

President Bill Clinton, our first boomer president, supported laws and policies that widened opportunities for banks and hedge funds to gamble wildly in the financial market. In 1996, Clinton signed the National Securities Market Improvement Act, reducing the state's role in regulating hedge funds, and permitting hedge funds to sell to an unlimited number of buyers who met certain criteria.[31] Clinton iced the cake with the Financial Services Modernization Act, 1999, which killed Glass-Steagall.[32] It permitted affiliations between savings and loans banks and investment banks and allowed commercial banks to participate in high-risk investments. This meant that the local savings and loan bank could invest a family's modest savings in the same high-risk ventures as investment banks that invested the fortunes of millionaires.

Clinton also signed the Commodities Futures Modernization Act, 2000, which deregulated the buying and selling of financial products, called "derivatives" and "credit-default swaps."[33] Swaps are essentially monetized debt, and derivatives are essentially monetized potential profit, or expected gains from loans and investments. Investing with debt and potential profit is risky business. To off-set the risk, investors borrowed millions to purchase insurance on the loans they held. This is a treacherous new twist to capitalism. Potential profits and monetized debt exist only in the abstract, but insurance is hard currency. So, it is possible for speculators to lose millions by chasing potential

---

27. *Garn-St. Germain Depository Institutions Act*, Public Law 97–320, U.S. Statute at Large 96 (1982).1496.

28. *Competitive Equity Banking Act of* 1987, Public Law 100–86, U.S. Statute at Large 101 (1987) 650–652.

29. *Food Security Act of* 1985, Public Law 99–198, U. S. Statue at Large 99(1985) 1354.

30. Kleinknecht, *Man Who Sold*, 11.

31. *National Securities Markets Improvement Act of* 1996, Public Law 104–290, U.S. Statute at Large 3416 (1996).

32. *Gramm-Leach-Bliley Act*, Public law 106–102, U.S. Statute at Large 113 (1999) 1338.

33. *Commodities Futures Modernization Act of* 2000, Public Law 106–554, U.S. Statute 114 (2000) 2763.

profit and by spending money that does not exist, and still cash in on the insurance they bought for it.

In 2001, President George W. Bush signed the Economic Growth and Tax Relief Reconciliation Act.[34] It decreased inheritance and capital gains taxes, and increased the ceiling for individual contributions to pension plans. Placing a cherry atop Clinton's icing, Bush signed the Emergency Economic Stabilization Act in 2008, which created the Troubled Asset Relief Program.[35] It gave billions of federal dollars to rescue bankrupt banks and investment firms. This meant that Wall Street could gamble recklessly with the nation's wealth and be assured that tax payers would clean up the mess in the event of a crisis. The stage was thus set for a spectacular collapse and a colossal bailout.

Initial Tremors

New millionaires sprouted up and old millionaires became billionaires in the financial market at the turn of the twenty-first century. Profits were nearly surreal. It seemed as if alchemists had found a way to make gold from salt. In the face of such mesmerizing success, only a heretic would challenge Wall Street's orthodoxy and call attention to the dangers of exempting hedge funds from regulation and oversight. Brooksley Born, Chairperson of the Commodities Futures Trading Commission during Clinton's administration, was a heretic.

Alarmed by the reality that billions of dollars were in play in markets that Congress did not really understand nor regulate, Born sought to increase transparency and oversight of hedge funds and derivative trading. Federal Reserve Chairman, Alan Greenspan, Secretary of the Treasury Robert Rubin, Undersecretary of the Treasury Larry Summers, and Securities and Exchange Commissioner, Arthur Levitt were outraged, claiming that to do so would cause an economic crisis of epic proportions. In May 1998, Born released a concept paper calling for reforms. Greenspan argued there was no need for transparency and regulation because hedge funds and investment firms were self-regulating in their own interest.[36] Rubin and Levitt asked Congress to impose a moratorium on such regulation and oversight.[37] A month later, Born testified before James Leach (R-IA), Chair of the House Banking Committee,

---

34. *Economic Growth and Tax Relief Reconciliation Act of* 2001, Public Law 107–16, U. S. Statute 115 92001) 38.

35. *Emergency Economic Stabilization Act of* 2008, Public Law 110–343, U.S. Statute 110 (2008) 3765.

36. Mosey, 2030, *Coming Tumult*, 178–182.

37. Barak, *Theft of a Nation*, 52.

where she was accused of over-stepping her authority and failing to understand the world of finance.[38]

As Born presented her concerns, the mortgage-backed securities market trembled. In July, 1997, fractures appeared in the fortresses of investment and speculation as global markets were disrupted by the collapse of the Thai baht (dollar). In August 1998, the cracks widened as Russia defaulted on bond payments. Among those hit hard by events was Long-Term Capital Management (LTCM), a hedge fund firm with global investments. By September, LTCM had lost a billion dollars and was deeply in debt as it had borrowed heavily to make investments. The New York Federal Reserve came to the rescue, with a bailout package of $3.6 billion dollars secured from other institutions, including J. P Morgan, Bear Stearns, Lehman Brothers, Goldman Sachs, Chase Manhattan, and Merrill Lynch.[39] Brooksley Born was vindicated, but few cared. The bailout made the problem "go away," and so banksters and creditmeisters went on with business as usual.

Main Street Takes the Hit

At the core of the 2008 financial meltdown was the desire of non-depository institutions to make a fast dollar. A favorite operation was predatory home loans. Citigroup, an investment firm that was formed by merging Travelers Insurance with Citibank, was a major player. Rubin, Clinton's Secretary of the Treasury, joined the board of Citigroup in 1999, where he earned $115 million in ten years as his firm exploited vulnerable home-buyers.[40] Eager to amass profits, Citigroup went on a lending spree, flooding the housing market with subprime loan money, which extended billions in "warehouse" lines of credit to other lenders.[41]

By definition, subprime loans are those made to high risk individuals who have either poor credit ratings, no collateral, or both. To compensate for the risk of these loans, lenders charge high fees and interest rates. Predatory lending lured hundreds of thousands of families into homes that they could not afford. The money they brought to the housing market drove home and rental prices up to artificial heights. Subprime lenders targeted the poor and vulnerable. African American and Latino borrowers were thirty times more

---

38. *The Warning*, directed by Michael Kirk 2009; Frontline TV Series, PBS, 2010. DVD.

39. Prins, *It Take a Pillage*, 112.

40. Sheer, *Great American Stickup*, 141.

41. National Commission on the Causes of the Financial and Economic Crisis in the United States, *Financial Crisis*, 113.

likely to get expensive subprime loans as were whites. Between 2006 and 2008, African American and Hispanic families lost approximately $200 billion in assets due to foreclosures.[42] Many who kept their homes found that they owed more on them than what they were worth.

The increase in the demand for houses that resulted from the increase in the number of people who secured loans drove the price of houses skyward in many regions. As many loan recipients borrowed on terms that left them vulnerable to adjustable interest and high fees, many of loans that were then monetized by financial institutions were of questionable value because the borrowers were not always in a position to keep up with the mortgage payments. When coupled with the reality that many subprime borrowers bought houses at fantastically inflated prices, the potential for the value of these monetized debts to fall through the floor was significant.

By the end of 2007, most of the subprime lending institutions had failed or were acquired by larger financial institutions. By then it was too late to reverse damage caused by subprime loans. In the summer of 2008, lenders Fannie Mae and Freddie Mac were placed into a federal conservatorship, and the government bailed out American International Group (AIG), while investment banks Merrill Lynch, Goldman Sachs, and Morgan Stanley teetered on the edge of ruin. AIG thanked the public for rescuing them by giving themselves $165 million in bonuses.[43]

Between 2008 and 2010, household wealth in the U.S. declined by $17 *trillion* dollars.[44] This wealth disappeared as pension funds were wiped out in speculative trading, home values fell far below the price of purchase, and businesses were re-possessed. Industries that depended on the increased demand for housing felt a sudden decline in demand for their products. Communities that expected a surge in employment and tax revenue for schools and public services were also disappointed. Eight million foreclosures left at least four million families homeless.[45] Many homes were abandoned and left to decay, driving down the value of adjacent properties. State and local governments lost tax revenue, which meant layoffs, furloughs, and cut-backs in public schools, law enforcement, and social services. As more individuals suffered the effects of unemployment, more sought public assistance. This spurred increases in the federal deficit that rose from $459 billion in 2008 to $1.4 trillion in 2009.[46]

42. Reynolds, "Minorities fall Victim," lines 44–52.

43. Ferrell and Ferrell, "Examining Organizational Integrity," 194.

44. National Commission on the Causes of the Financial and Economic Crisis in the United States, *The Financial Crisis*, 391.

45. Ibid., 631.

46. Gruber, *Public Finance*, 94.

Thanks to the bailouts of financial institutions that crashed in 2007 and 2008, many high rollers in the credit and investment industry experienced the recession as little more than a bad bout with indigestion. Main Street America, however, experienced a virtual bowel resection. In 2008, 3.6 million jobs were lost and in the following year, another 4.7 million jobs followed.[47] The greatest injury and insult the recovery had to offer went to the middle and working classes. Not only were millions still unemployed and homeless years after the "recovery," but between 2010 and 2013 the median income fell in every bracket except the top 10 percent. Further, the share of income rose for the top 3 percent of American families from 2010 to 2013, while the bottom 90 percent saw their share of income fall.[48] The mortgage crisis was in part a transfer of wealth. In Oakland, California, 42 percent of foreclosed homes were purchased by corporate real estate investors. Their rental units often cost more per month than the mortgages families had previously paid, and were managed by landlords who neglected repairs and hazardous conditions. One such company, Colony Starwood Homes, boasted, "We recognized the opportunity created by the housing crisis and acted upon it in a bold way."[49]

In the wake of the crisis, Congress passed the Dodd-Frank Wall Street Reform and Consumer Protection Act, 2010. It consolidated regulatory agencies, increased oversight of derivative trading, established an agency to protect consumers of financial products, created protocols to manage bankruptcies of banks and investment firms, and improved oversight of credit-rating agencies. Wall Street's lobbyists sprang into action, and spent over $200 million in 2013 and 2014 to convince Congress that it would good for America if Dodd-Frank were relaxed.[50]

Mr. Corporation is a Real Person

How were the banksters and creditmeisters allowed to pillage the public's wellbeing? In part, they were able to convince lawmakers that deregulating financial products was in the public's best interest. This was accomplished with the help of lobbyists who spend billions of dollars to influence elected officials and their advisors. In 2014, there were 12,000 registered lobbyists in

---

47. National Commission on the Causes of the Financial and Economic Crisis in the United States, *The Financial Crisis*, 390.

48. Angresano, *Corporate Welfare Economy*, 37.

49. Stavely, "From Foreclosure," paragraphs 23-32. Colony Starwood's billionaire co-chairman, Thomas Barrack, raised $35 million for Donald Trump's presidential bid, and in May, 2017, was under investigation for tax evasion in Italy. (See Buncombe)

50. Weisman and Lipton, "In New Congress," lines 47–58.

Washington, or roughly 26 lobbyists per Congressman.[51] Many lobbyists are former representatives and senators who have gone to work for corporations. They understand how to write bills, move them through committees, and they have friends in high places.[52] In the 1970s, nearly 15 percent of congressional members became lobbyists immediately after leaving office, and by 2000, that figure had reached 52 percent.[53]

The power of Wall Street and corporations was enhanced by the 2010 Supreme Court ruling in Citizens United v. Federal Elections Commission (FEC).[54] The case concerned whether Citizens United had violated the law as it planned to air a documentary about Hilary Clinton during the 2008 election, and whether laws pertaining to airing such material was a violation of free speech. Those who opposed Citizens United argued that the FEC had an obligation to protect the public from propaganda generated by private entities who have the resources to create and distribute material that spins reality to suit the agenda, and thus, have an advantage over people who lack the resources to produce and disseminate information that is nonpartisan. The Supreme Court ruled in favor of Citizens United. Writing for the majority, Justice Anthony Kennedy reasoned that since free speech is essential in a democracy, "political speech must prevail against laws that would suppress it by design or inadvertence."[55] Thus came the high court's declaration that corporations are people too.

In his dissent, Justice John Paul Stevens called attention to the duty of government to protect people from corporate power, and warned the Court's decision would open the floodgates of corporate cash into the political process in such volumes that it would drown competing voices.[56] Only 18 percent of Americans supported the Court's decision.[57] Despite public and congressional opposition to the judgement, the Supreme Court went on in 2014 to confirm that financial contributions represent protected speech in McCutcheon v Federal Elections Commission.[58] The Court struck down limits imposed upon aggregate donations to political parties and their candidates. Chief Justice Roberts opined that legal restrictions on such contributions are aimed at money given with the expectation that they will secure political favors, and

51. Parker, F. *Cancer in American Democracy*, 4.
52. Sheer, *Great American Stickup*, 112.
53. Parker, G. R. *Capitol Investments*, 116.
54. Citizens United v. Federal Elections Commission 558 U.S. 310, (2010).
55. Potter and Penniman, *Nation on the Take*, 35.
56. Ibid., 36.
57. Ibid., 37.
58. Mc Cutcheon, et. al. v. Federal Elections Commission 572 U.S.—(2014).

that large donations in and of themselves did not automatically constitute the expectation of favors.[59]

As a result of these decisions, PACs have amassed their fortunes and influence, while pushing campaign costs to dizzying heights. In addition to the proliferation of Super PACs, there was an explosion of "social welfare organizations" between 2004 and 2016, which qualify for tax exemptions per status as a 501(c) (4). These entities, such as billionaire Koch brother's America for Prosperity, may anonymously contribute undisclosed amounts of money to campaigns and candidates. Contributions of this type jumped from about $5 million in 2006 to $300 million by 2012.[60]

One might argue that campaign contributions and lobbyists have nothing to do with our spirituality, but experience says otherwise. In 2015, 58 percent of Americans believed that most members of congress sell their votes for campaign contributions, and listen to dollar-wielding individuals far more than they listen to their own constituency.[61] In my experience, the loss of public confidence in their leaders' authentic caring about them has produced anger and cynicism. It drained people of hope, the will to follow the rules, and to give of themselves as volunteers. This is a spiritual crisis. When society's leaders continually and aggressively demonstrate a preference for an elite, it tempts those who follow to abandon their concern for the "least of their brothers and sisters," suspend their respect for the law, and to invest their minds and bodies not in the Kingdom of God, but in getting and keeping what they can before somebody takes it away.

The Road to Jericho

American Christians have been tough on the poor. During the 2012 presidential campaign, Newt Gingrich (R-GA), a Baptist, accused Obama of supporting the distribution of free food for doing nothing to earn it.[62] Gingrich once proposed that to alleviate poverty it was time to repeal "truly stupid" child labor laws and put children to work as janitors in schools.[63] Candidate Rick Santorum (R-PA), a Roman Catholic, declared "I don't want to make black people's lives better by giving them somebody else's money."[64] Santo-

---

59. Millhiser, *Injustices*, 229–30.
60. Potter and Penniman, *Nation on the Take*, 52–53.
61. Ibid., 40.
62. Caliendo, *Inequality in America*, 135.
63. Weissmann, "New Gingrich Thinks," lines 1–5.
64. Pierre, "Rick Santorum," lines 1–7.

rum also declared that single mothers were a serious threat to society because they "breed criminals."[65] It was a brassy poke given the recent grand theft of the public's wealth by well-educated, white bankers and their Congressional hirelings. In 2012, Paul Ryan (R-WI), Chairman of the House Budget Committee and a Catholic, proposed a budget calling for deep cuts in food stamps and public housing. Catholic bishops were divided in their opinion of his plans. Some said that Ryan had neglected his moral obligation to look after the poor, while others claimed that the budget need not address the needs of the poor, since Jesus charged individuals and not governments with caring for the needy.[66] What does that mean in a government for and of the people?

During the 2012 campaign, Governor Mitt Romney (R-MA), a minister in the Mormon Church, stated that the 47 percent of voters were poised to re-elect President Barack Obama were people who are, "dependent on government," see themselves as "victims," and who believe that it is the government's job to provide them with health care, food and housing.[67] He also stated it was not his job to worry about such people, because, they would never accept responsibility for their lives. Romney's assertions were cruel and uninformed. Millions of voters who supported Obama were highly educated, hard-working, law-abiding citizens who paid their bills and gave to charity—often without the expectation that they would get a tax break for doing so.

In the months leading up to the Democratic and Republic nominations for the presidential election of 2016, candidates continued to bash and stereotype the poor. Mike Huckabee (R-AR), former President of the Arkansas Baptist State Convention, charged that most single moms are under-educated and can't get a job.[68] While single mothers have exceptionally high poverty rates, Huckabee was not on the mark. Roughly 25 percent of single mothers have a college degree and about 66 percent have a job.[69] During the campaign, Republican businessman Donald Trump said that he would move 50 million Americans out of poverty by giving them motivations to work. "People don't' have an incentive," he charged, "They make more money sitting there doing nothing than they make if they have a job."[70] Conservative Catholic, Marc Rubio (R-FL) insisted that the cure for poverty is marriage, which is no magic elixir, as 55 percent of low-income families already include a married couple.[71]

65. Murphy and Kroll, "Santorum," lines 1–8.
66. Sullivan, "You Say Subsidiarity," lines 1–34.
67. Wallace, *America is Self-Destructing*, 98.
68. Harris-Perry, "Mike Huckabee," lines1–7.
69. Casey and Moldanado, "Worse Off," 3–8.
70. Herbert, "Get Ready for a War," lines 35–37.
71. Rosen, "Marriage Will Not Fix," lines

In September, 2015, Pope Francis traveled to the U.S. and delivered several speeches in which he criticized capitalism's negligence of the poor and preference for inequality.[72] Rubio politely rejected the Pontiff's ideas, arguing that free enterprise is the best way to meet the needs of the poor. He said that, "On moral issues, he [the Pope] speaks with incredible authority . . . He's done so consistently on the value of life, the sanctity of life, and on the importance of marriage and on the family. [But] On economic issues, the pope is a person."[73] Apparently, Rubio could not see that the economy is a moral issue. He seemed oblivious to the notion that to give an assailant the weapons, the opportunity, and a license to beat and rob the man on the road to Jericho makes one more like the assailant than the Good Samaritan.

In some respects, the poor are offended by the rich for the same reason that the rich are offended by the poor. Both believe that the other has a grandiose sense of entitlement. Both the grumble that the other is never satisfied with what they have. Both believe that the other is stealing from the public treasury. The rich fear that the poor will take too much of their income in taxation and regulation, and the poor fear the rich will deprive them of the assistance and fair wages they need to survive.

The scenario does not sound like something out of a playbook for a Christian nation. When the faithful claim that religious leaders speak with no moral authority on matters of economics or politics because those issues are not moral issues, we hear the sound of our spirituality being not-so-surgically removed from our way of life. It is the sound of setting the faithful against each other. It is a priestly chorus vindicating economic exploitation, and shouting over the prophetic voice who reminds us that our use of money has moral implications and consequences.

The Born Again Movement did little to remedy the situation. There were just enough Caesars at the pulpit to ensure that the Jesus who taught followers to see the Kingdom of God within oneself would stay nailed to the cross while the Jesus that preached war on terrorism, the right to automatic rifles, and the right to tax loopholes for the rich was free to move about the country.

---

72. Cassidy, "Pope Francis' Challenge," lines 48–64.

73. Atkin and Legum, "Catholic Presidential Candidate," lines 5–10.

11

Born-Again Caesar

Jesus Goes to Washington

AMERICAN BOOMERS LIVE IN a world that places religion at the center of political debate and national identity. The reference to God in the Pledge of Allegiance was added in 1954, and the motto, "In God we trust," was added to U.S. currency in 1957. Chaplains have served Congress since its inception. For services rendered to elected officials and their families in 2014, the House Chaplain earned $172,500.00 annually, while the Senate Chaplain earned $157,100.00.[1] The world into which boomers were born was coming to grips with the idea that six million people were slaughtered during WWII just because they were Jewish. In boomer's senior years, Americans are confounded by the idea that radical Islamists wanted to kill millions of Americans because they would not submit to Allah. The Christian Right calls for legislation based on the Bible. Religious zealots say that God is love, and the most radical use explosives to punctuate that love.

Boomers have witnessed two profound events where religion and politics are concerned. The first was the shattering of the stained glass ceiling that kept Catholics from the Oval Office. John F. Kennedy broke the Protestant monopoly on the White House, and in 2008, nine Catholic candidates ran for president.[2] In addition, as of 2015, six Catholics sat in the Supreme Court.[3]

---

1. Brudnick, *Congressional Salaries*, 9, 10.

2. The Catholic candidates were: Rudy Giuliani; Sam Brown; Alan Keyes; Tommy Thompson; Bill Richardson; Denis Kucinich; Joe Biden; Tommy Vilsack; and, Christopher Dodd.

3. The Catholic Justices were: John Roberts; Samuel Alito; Anthony Kennedy; Antonin Scalia; Sonia Sotomayor; and Clarence Thomas.

The second event regards the rise of the Christian Right in the 1970s. As America underwent a modern Great Awakening, piety was politicized and evangelical Christians sought to redeem a nation they believed was wallowing in sin. The Born-Again Movement signaled that Americans had hit a psychological wall with liberal experiments in social engineering, and were ready to nestle into the soft breast of familiar and stable traditions. Some were attracted to evangelism because they saw the liberation of the 1960s as a carnival of hedonism. The "Jesus Revolution," as some called it, saw droves of former "hippies" abandon the counter-culture and take up life as Christian evangelicals.[4]

Conservative Christians believed that Americans could jump-start their corroded moral batteries by hooking up cables between religion and the law. They worried that America was drifting away from its religious moorings, and was becoming too secular in its world view. The Supreme Court had ruled in 1962 that public schools could not force individuals to recite prayers.[5] In 1963 it declared that reading the Bible in public schools was unlawful.[6] Conservative Christian communities and school boards fought back. The Christian Right undertook a campaign against secular humanism in schools and demanded that certain books and the teaching of evolution be banned. Secular humanism, they argued, was a philosophical ideology that replaced faith in God with faith in science and reason, and was central to a conspiracy to promote licentious behavior and moral relativism.[7]

Conservative Christians also reacted to what they believed was immoral conduct on the part of elected officials. The Watergate debacle shattered both assumptions that government officials were law-abiding and morally decent people. Sex scandals aggravated the situation, as the press—a long-time keeper of the secret sex lives of Washington's personalities—began to expose the details. An intoxicated Representative Wilbur Mills (D-AR) made headlines in 1974 with a press conference delivered from the dressing room of his mistress, stripper Fanne Foxe, and a slew of indiscretions committed by other public servants peppered newspapers throughout the decade. From Senator Bob Packwood's marital infidelities to Anita Hill's testimony that Supreme Court nominee Clarence Thomas had sexually harassed her, to President Bill Clinton's impeachment pursuant to the lies he told about his extra-marital affairs, Americans have been fascinated by the sexual adventures of our leaders.

---

4. Eskridge, *God's Forever Family*, 260–61.
5. Engle v. Vitale 370 U.S. 421 (1962).
6. Abington v. Schempp 374 U.S. 203 (1963).
7. Berlet and Lyons, *Right-Wing Populism*, 199–211.

Fixed on the spectacle, lots of people do not pay attention to other serious matters related to economics, human rights, and abuses of power.[8]

Before the twentieth century came to an end, the Christian Right had acquired a vast media holdings with which to proselytize the nation. Between 1968 and 1985, the number of stations affiliated with the National Religious Broadcasters rose from 104 to 1,050.[9] In addition, conservative Christian foundations proliferated in the 1970s and 1980s, including: Paul Weyrich's Heritage Foundation; Timothy LaHaye's American Coalition for Traditional Values and Coalition for Religious Freedom; Pat Robertson's Christian Coalition; and, James Dobson's Family Research Council. The aim of these organizations was to promote family values through legislation, lobby for conservative causes, and to elect conservative Christians to office.

The evangelical revival of the 1970s had moments of jubilant idealism as depicted in the hit film *Godspell*, but it had a foreboding edge.[10] Hal Lindsay's book, *The Late Great Planet Earth* invited readers to "give God a chance" to present his plan, keeping in mind that biblical prophecies warn that there is not much time left to listen.[11] The Christian right also picked a fight with democracy and the U.S. Constitution. Reconstructionist Christians believe that America should be a theocracy governed by a Christian aristocracy who will enforce the literal codices and directives found in the Old and New Testament. Reconstructionist theologian Rousas Rushdoony argues that democracy coddles failures, cowards, criminals, sexual deviants, abortionists, and secular humanism. He holds that government should be limited, and wants to end public education, welfare programs, and taxes.[12]

In the extreme, preachers recruited individuals to partake in deadly utopian schemes. In Guyana, on November 18, 1978, over 900 members of the People's Temple of the Disciples of Christ committed suicide by drinking cyanide-laced Kool-Aid. In a state of "cult induced psychosis," they surrendered their will to the charismatic Jim Jones, who had isolated his congregation in a jungle far from their American homes, and convinced them that he alone knew God's will.[13] In 1993, the federal government raided the Branch Davidian compound in Waco, Texas, killing seventy people and their leader, David Koresh, who had convinced his followers that he was a messenger sent

---

8. Apostolidis and Williams, *Public Affairs*, 1–7.

9. Schultze, "Mythos," 247.

10. *Godspell*, directed by David Greene (1973; Culver City, CA: Sony Pictures Home Entertainment, 2000), DVD.

11. Lindsey, H. *Late Great*, 1–2.

12. McVicar, *Christian Reconstruction*, 202–203.

13. Chidester, *Salvation and Suicide*, 30–31.

to earth to establish the new Davidic kingdom in Jerusalem.[14] These dark episodes remind us that people are vulnerable to charismatic individuals who offer those with a fragile sense of self a magical way out of social, economic, and spiritual ailment. They are examples of how the extreme priestly approach to faith in any religion often ends in a violent rejection of life when the world does not conform to its priestly paradigm.

In less than 30 years after WWII ended, lots of Americans believed that the moral bedrock of America was crumbling and that Armageddon was not far behind. In the last quarter of the twentieth century, Americans searched for prophetic leadership. Jesus, many thought, should preside over all matters in the Oval Office. America's desire for a good shepherd, however, was conditional. They wanted someone who closely followed Caesar's script.

As Good as Humphrey

At St. Bridget School, each day began with prayer and the Pledge of Allegiance. My peers and I dutifully bowed our heads and placed our hands on our hearts. We were taught to respect the authority of adults, our clergy, and our government leaders. As first graders in the fall of 1964, we stood obediently in our starched plaid uniforms in a classroom that smelled of paste and pencil shavings. We did what we were told to do. We had no idea that by the time we left the eighth grade in the spring of 1972, our society would be less respectful of authority, and, in some circles, even firmly committed to overthrowing it. In 1964, children believed that only the best people got elected to office, and they did so in fair and square elections. For lots of boomers, that belief did not survive the twentieth century.

One chilly spring day, my fifth-grade classmates and I took a field trip to St. Paul, where we toured Minnesota's state capitol. The grandeur of the dome and its chambers overwhelmed small folks. I was intimidated, but fascinated. As I walked down the marbled corridors, past tall portraits framed in gold, I knew I was walking where some of my parent's heroes like Hubert Humphrey had tread. I told myself: "If I work hard enough and am good enough, I can work here someday." At that time, I did not know about the relationship between money and political favors, and had no understanding of how my gender was an obstacle to high office.

The nuns and lay teachers who taught us said that there was goodness in everyone and that everyone had a part to play in the betterment of the world. I liked those ideas, and I wanted to be as good as those my community

14. Bull and Lockhart, *Seeking a Sanctuary*, 201–15.

revered. I wanted to be as good as Humphrey. Hubert Humphrey was elected Mayor of Minneapolis in 1945, and then to the Senate in 1948. He was a friend of Progressives and New Dealers, and was a tireless advocate of farmers and small businesses. He gained national attention at the 1948 Democratic National Convention with a speech that denounced Dixicrats and segregation. He referred to segregation as a spiritual crisis, and called upon the Democratic Party to rise above passion for state's rights.[15] In 1948, such statements could cost politicians their careers and lives.

Humphrey's world view and ideals were profoundly influenced by the Social Gospel, which taught that people are morally obligated to work for the improvement of human condition and especially for the betterment of the poor.[16] It also taught that private wealth is the greatest threat to integrity, and that government must prevent private greed from ravaging the public's well-being. Like others of his generation, he had to make his way through the political thicket of Cold War militarism and nationalism. He yearned to be president and understood that the competition for high office was stacked with scions of well-established political families, banking magnates, and industrial titans. He knew that as the son of a Midwest pharmacist, power was not his birthright, and so, came to believe that his best chances were to ride the coattails of Lyndon Baines Johnson into the Oval Office.[17]

President Johnson's domestic vision appealed to Humphrey. Johnson sought to create the Great Society and embraced the principles of Roosevelt's New Deal. He sought relief for the poor and support for education. Humphrey seemed to have what Pope Francis would later call the "smell of sheep" about him, because he was a good shepherd who proudly walked among, and identified with his working class flock. Humphrey was the Democratic heir apparent in 1968, but he had to make a critical decision about the war in Vietnam: should he take the side of doves like Senator Bobby Kennedy and fellow Minnesotan Senator Eugene McCarthy, or follow in LBJ's footsteps as the Democratic Party's cold warrior?

Humphrey was a cold warrior who detested communism, and had voted in favor of the McCarran Act in 1950 and the Communist Control Act of 1954, which advocated loyalty oaths and the creation of detention camps for American citizens thought to be communists.[18] He had also traveled to Southeast Asia during the Vietnam War, had conflicting thoughts about the

---

15. Humphrey, "1948 Democratic National," lines 85–93.
16. Garrettson, *Humbert H. Humphrey*, 242.
17. Solberg, *Humbert Humphrey*, 239–56.
18. Ibid., 158.

war, and understood that his career hinged on LBJ's hawkish approval.[19] Humphrey wrote in his autobiography, that in 1968, he was asked to resign as LBJ's Vice-President, but refused. He wrote that he could "break with the president and be denounced as irresponsible," or endure the quagmire because he so badly wanted to be president.[20]

In the end, Humphrey was unable to offer voters an alternative to the war, and stood with LBJ. He was badly beaten in Electoral College votes by a margin of 301 to 191, but the popular vote was narrower, as he gathered 42.7 while Richard Nixon collected 43.4 percent.[21] Many believe that had he stood firmly against the war, he might have secured the presidency. His story is meaningful to me as an American trying to understand what happens to spirituality and moral judgment when good men and women take up the life of an elected official. Humphrey entered public service with noble aspirations to serve the average citizen and keep the peace, only to receive Caesar's ultimatum: Forsake either your principles or high office; you cannot have both.

The glory Nixon enjoyed as he entered the White House was relatively short-lived. The man who rode into the presidency on a "law and order" platform was hounded by antiwar demonstrations and shamed out of office because of his own unlawful conduct. The Watergate scandal aroused bi-partisan public distrust for politicians. Following Nixon's and Ford's administrations The Christian Right assumed a more proactive role in the political process. Ironically, in 1960, people feared that a Catholic would use religion to subvert the Constitution, and by 1976, people feared that secular humanists would use the Constitution to subvert religion.

Water under the Gate

Americans tend to remember the Watergate burglary and Nixon's cover-up as an episode void of deep roots, unrelated to other events, and disconnected from political agendas that span many generations. I recall the shock people felt as the details Watergate were disclosed. As one incredible story followed the other, many claimed that America was experiencing something new, something out of the ordinary. Many have since questioned that premise. The Watergate narrative that has survived censorship in mainstream news and textbooks portray the scandal as a crude attempt to secure information of strategic value. Revisionists argue that it was really about removing a man from

---

19. Ibid., 271–74.
20. Humphrey, *The Education*, vii.
21. Gallup, "Election Polls," table.

office while maintaining the illusion that our republic is truly democratic. Whereas a comprehensive disclosure of the details might have enlightened citizens as to the nature of Caesar and his agenda, the abbreviated version of events left people with the impression that Watergate is the story of one man's depravity rather than one system's moral turpitude.

In the popular film, *All the President's Men* the anonymous informant, "Deep Throat," feeds clues about the burglary to investigative reporter, Bob Woodward (played by Robert Redford) of the *Washington Post*, and becomes frustrated when Woodward cannot seem to connect the dots or see their implications.[22] Deep Throat complains, "You're missing the overall." Woodward at that point sees Watergate as a clumsy caper and does not perceive the incident in the larger context of how Washington operates. Deep Throat attempts to correct his vision, by telling Woodward that the Republicans wanted to run against McGovern, and engineered his nomination by bugging offices, planting false press leaks, passing fake letters, planting spies, stealing documents, and investigating the candidates' private lives. He insists that Woodward has only the tip of the iceberg, and that Watergate involves the FBI, CIA, and Justice Department. "Cover-up had little to do with Watergate," hisses Deep Throat, it was mainly to "protect the covert operations," and it led "everywhere." What Deep Throat wanted to expose got lost in the spectacle. It was eclipsed by the drama of Nixon's Greek tragedy—it is water under the gate. It is the "everywhere" of which Deep Throat spoke that is Caesar's covert world, the world in which power is gained and lost not by ballots, but by laundered money, propaganda campaigns, terrorism, and assassinations.

Scholars have produced mountains of research on Watergate. More than identifying who did what, they offer insights to how our own government officials work with the CIA to advance their political agendas, and what happens when people get too close to the truth or want to disclose it. Again, readers might ask, "What has this to do with spirituality?" Assuming that Americans have choices about who they will elect to govern them, and what policies they will support, it is to their advantage to know how Caesar operates. Those who do not understand how Caesar operates are at risk for being enticed to serve an agenda that ultimately violates the morals and spiritual teachings they value the most.

At the time of the Watergate burglary, Nixon was ahead of George McGovern in the polls by 19 percent.[23] He went on to win in one of the nation's largest landslides. What did Nixon and his campaign staff believe they could

---

22. *All the President's Men*, directed by Alan J. Pakula (1976; Burbank, CA: Warner Home video, 1997), DVD.

23. Gallup, "Gallup Presidential Election," 1972 Presidential Trial Heats table.

gain by breaking into the Democrat's headquarters? Allegedly, Nixon wanted to know what the Democrats knew about Nixon when he was Vice-President, and the role he may have played in the plot to assassinate Castro. Roger Stone, Republican political consultant and lobbyist for forty years, alleges that once CIA operatives were involved in the burglary, they schemed with others in Nixon's circle to deliberately botch the job in order to bring Nixon down.[24] Stone suggests that the CIA and hawkish conservatives disliked Nixon's plan to "Vietnamize" the war in Vietnam, and were nervous about Nixon's interest in curbing the power of the CIA. Others postulate that Watergate was a coup aimed at forming an authoritarian government that would make "policies agreeable to the increasingly urgent dictates of the Morgan-Rockefeller-Mellon-Harriman financier faction."[25]

Stone opines that Nixon's fatal mistake was to cover-up of the Watergate burglary. Knowing that criminal convictions and jail time were on the horizon, Nixon replaced Vice-President Spiro Agnew, (who resigned in October, 1973 following charges of tax fraud), with Congressman, Gerald Ford (R-MI). Stone contends that Nixon selected Ford because he believed he could leverage a pardon from him. Ford, the last surviving member of the Warren Commission, was instrumental in promoting the "magic bullet" theory that "proved" JFK was shot by a lone gunman. FBI agent, James Sibert claimed that Ford authorized changes in the Warren Report's description of where a bullet entered Kennedy's body, as to increase the plausibility that a single bullet entered Kennedy's back, exited his throat, entered Governor Connally's back, damaged four inches of his ribs, exited his chest, shattered his wrist, lodged into his thigh, and was then discovered in pristine condition on the gurney whereon he awaited treatment at Parkland Hospital in Dallas.[26] Without such plausibility, the Warren Commission would have to explain evidence pointing to an excess of three shots fired and multiple shooters in Dealey Plaza on November 22, 1963. Stone believes that Nixon and Ford came to an agreement whereby Nixon vowed to keep silent on what he knew about the Warren Commission and JFK's assassination in exchange for Ford's pardon.

Investigative journalist, Russ Baker, offers another perspective, arguing that Nixon's enemies schemed to destroy him long before the 1972 election, and seeded Nixon's staff with individuals with close ties to the CIA and wealthy, right-wing conservatives. Baker points to oil barons and bankers, who were miffed by Nixon's interest in decreasing the oil depletion allowance, which would increase taxes on mining, timber, and petroleum industries, and

24. Stone, R. *Nixon's Secrets*, 428–36.
25. Tarpley and Chaitkin, *George Bush*, 241.
26. Stone, R. *Nixon's Secrets*, 544–45.

Nixon's slowness in setting limits on imported oil.[27] According to Baker, right-wing operatives in the Republican Party, the CIA, and corporate titans maneuvered events to place one of their own in the White House. Baker contends that one operative was Texas oilman and former Congressman, George H. W. Bush. Bush's Zapata Oil, an international enterprise, has often been described as a front for CIA activity in Latin America and George H. W. a willing agent.[28]

At the onset of his presidency, Nixon requested the CIA's complete file on the Kennedy assassination, but never received them. This according to Baker, was another source of aggravation in the intelligence community as they did not want Nixon to have information about covert activities, especially those that pertained to dirty tricks in American politics.[29] Had the agency complied, it would have given Nixon the information he needed to expose the CIA and eviscerate its power, or to simply blackmail them for favors. In theory, then, managing the narrative about Watergate, was in part a means of controlling what the public knew about the CIA, its relationship with America's ruling families, and those holding public offices.

For lots of boomers, all political roads lead to conspiracy, and the granddaddy of all conspiracies is that regarding the death of John F. Kennedy. Boomers have learned, as Baker notes, to take seriously the fact that the security apparatus of the state may have incentives for removing certain officials from office. Boomers have had to face the unsettling prospect that the security apparatus does not necessarily serve the people, but instead may sell its services to the highest bidder, including industrialists, bankers, and oil barons who want to build empires at home and abroad. Admittedly, those who believe these things are often labeled "conspiracy nuts," but those "nuts" perform a sacred task. Their research frequently provides important, yet obscure details and facts to bear on our assessment of the truth.

A Prophet in the White House

Despite the reality that the truth about Watergate remains controversial, the scandal was enough to prompt Americans to withhold support for the Republican presidential candidate, Gerald Ford and to find an executive with high moral standards. In 1976, many Americans felt they had found a prophet in Governor Jimmy Carter (D-GA). Carter announced that he was a born-again Christian, prayed daily, and believed that leaders should strive to "establish

---

27. Baker, R. *Family of Secrets*, 191.
28. Ibid., 7–9.
29. Ibid., 180–81.

justice" in tax programs, international relations, and in the criminal justice system.[30] Early in the race, evangelicals were excited by Carter's faith-based approach to governance, but were later disillusioned. Carter did not take a hard line against abortion, and had given an interview to *Playboy*. He offended some people by admitting that he had committed "adultery in his heart," and by using the colloquial term, "screw," when referring to sex. Ministers charged that "screw" was "not a good Baptist word," and that Carter was a foul-mouthed "hypocrite."[31] Billy Graham opined, "I would rather have a man in office who is highly qualified to be President who didn't make much of a religious profession than to have a man who had no qualifications but who made a religious profession."[32]

The popular vote that put Carter into the White House merely sagged in his favor by about two percentage points. Evangelicals gave Ford 3.2 million more votes than they gave Carter.[33] My vote for Carter was reflexively liberal. Like so many voters, I did not study Carter or the issues. That meant I was ignorant of his interests, the complex problems the country faced, and of how power operates in Washington. Carter was admired by liberals who appreciated the courage it took for him to admit he was human like everyone else. Many agreed with his assertion that too many Americans "worship self-indulgence and consumption," and so have misplaced the locus of life's meaning.[34] In his inaugural speech, Carter quoted from the prophet Micah, calling on the nation to "do justly, and to love mercy, and to walk humbly with God."[35] Justice, mercy and humility, however, irritated the Caesars of the nation, who were still fighting communism, not ready to let go of their empire, and who held that Vietnam was a tragedy because the U.S. had too much mercy.

On the domestic front, Carter failed Christian conservatives by supporting women's rights, including that of abortion. He also inherited an economy battered by oil embargos, inflation, and an unemployment rate of 7.7 percent in 1976.[36] In his *Address to the Nation on Energy*, Carter delivered a woeful message to Americans, and said that we were wasting too much energy and ignoring the inevitable depletion of fossil fuel.[37] He said that the nation's response to the crisis was a test of character, and he called for massive cuts in en-

30. Balmer, *Redeemer*, 58–61.
31. Ibid., 70–72.
32. Ibid., 63.
33. Ibid., 72.
34. Swartz, *Moral Minority*, 168.
35. Carter, Jimmy, "Inaugural Address," lines 5–8.
36. "A Brief History of U.S. Unemployment," interactive graph.
37. Carter, Jimmy, "Address to the Nation," lines 19–25.

ergy use and for the creation of alternative sources of energy. He had faith that if people were given the plain facts and asked to make reasonable sacrifices for the common good, they would generally comply and be understanding. Americans set their thermostats lower and kept to a freeway speed limit of 55 MPH, but often did so with bitter resentment.

Many believe that Carter's greatest achievements were in foreign policy. The *Camp David Accords*, 1979 created peace between Egypt and Israel, and the *Strategic Arms Limitation Treaty* (SALT II), 1979, limited the proliferation of intercontinental ballistic missiles, but both achievements were marred by crisis. The *Camp David Accords* left Palestinians without a state, and after the Soviets signed SALT II, they invaded Afghanistan. To protest Soviet aggression, the U.S. boycotted the summer Olympics in Moscow and banned the export of grain to the Soviet Union. Carter's idealism thus enraged athletes who looked forward to flexing nationalistic muscles in the land of Marx and Lenin, and farmers who lost revenue from wheat sales grumbled loudly.

Carter based his foreign policy on respect for universal human rights, but in the end, Cold War pragmatism kept Carter's moral aspirations in check. As a cold warrior, Carter condemned human rights abuses behind the Iron Curtain while supporting murderous dictatorships in other part of the globe. He sent U.S. aid to Indonesia's President Suharto, who had seized power in 1965 with U.S. assistance, and then murdered at least a half a million people.[38] Suharto invaded East Timor on the pretext of stemming a communist threat. As human rights organizations protested, Suharto's militia murdered about 150,000 civilians between 1975 and 1979.[39] He supported the oppressive regimes of Iran's Shah Pahlavi and the Philippine's Ferdinand Marcos.[40] With intentions to pressure Latin American dictators into a retreat away from human rights abuses, Carter reduced aid to the region from $210 million in 1977 to $54 million by 1979.[41] Despite the reductions, Guatemala's Efrain Rios Montt, and Nicaragua's Anastasio Somoza continued to torture, rape, and slaughter their own people in vicious civil wars. In 1980, Carter asked Congress for $5.7 million to support a military junta in El Salvador against revolutionaries who had seized government, nationalized private companies, and threatened U.S. holdings.[42] Over 75,000 people died in El Salvador before its civil war ended in

---

38. Kiernan, *Specter*, 46.
39. Ibid., 47–48.
40. Dumbrell and Barrett, *Making of U.S. Foreign Policy*, 72.
41. Colby, J. M. "Chasm of Values," 561.
42. Zinn, "Carter-Reagan-Bush," 41–65.

1991. The vast majority of human rights' violations that occurred during the war were committed by agents of the state, and not the leftist revolutionaries.[43]

In 1979, the Islamic revolutionary Ayatollah Khomeini ousted the Shah of Iran. The ideology driving the coup asserted that Islam was the true liberator of developing nations and that the Islamic world had to purge Western contamination and imperialism from non-Western societies.[44] Khomeini was a messianic voice in a society that revered such voices, and had harbored Islamic theocratic yearnings for generations. Knowing the importance of oil in the game of politics, he launched an oil embargo. A gallon of gas that cost .36¢ in 1970, cost $1.20 by 1980.[45] In November, Iranians stormed the U.S. Embassy in Tehran, took over sixty American hostages, and held them for 444 days. The Soviets remained in Afghanistan and Israelis and Palestinians continued to fight. To many, Carter's idealism and moralizing seemed to be a bizarre alternative to aggressive confrontations of America's enemies.

Ultimately, the empire rejected its prophetic president. He did not bring enough Caesar to the table. Carter personified weakness and equivocation in a society that glorifies strength and certainty. Americans love captains of industry and warriors, but they only tolerate poets, intellectuals, and peacemakers. Carter made people feel badly about their consumption and waste, and many did not want to link their material way of life to religious faith if that faith required material sacrifices. Christian conservatives wanted a Cold War militant with a priestly religious outlook.

Reagan's Revival

Reverend Jerry Falwell, a Baptist radio personality and founder of the Moral Majority gained national attention in the wake of Carter's administration. Falwell demonstrated little of the intellectualism of theologians, such as Protestants Reinhold Niebuhr and Harvey Cox, and Catholics Charles Curran and John Courtney Murray. He was simple, paternal, and sentimental. He was part of the Christian Right that included James Dobson, Phyllis Schlafly, Paul Weyrich, Pat Robertson, and Gary Bauer, who rallied opposition to the ERA, sex education, abortion, gay rights, and pornography. The Christian Right bristled at restrictions on gun ownership and supported home-schooling. It favored

---

43. Wood, *Insurgent Collective*, 8.
44. Baxter and Akbarzadeh, *US Foreign Policy*, 80–81.
45. Choron and Choron, *Money*, 98.

unconditional support for Israel because it believed that Jewish statehood in Palestine was a prerequisite of Jesus' return to earth.[46]

The Christian Right's support for the Republican Party in 1980 catalyzed a major shift in national politics. White evangelicals abandoned the Democrats in droves. Republicans nominated former California Governor Ronald Reagan for president. Reagan's election staff helped him appreciate the Christian Right, and Reagan did more than tip his hat to evangelicals. In August, he spoke to 17,000 people gathered at a meeting of the Religious Roundtable, and told them, "I know this event is non-partisan, so you can't endorse me, but I want you to know I endorse you."[47] At an ecumenical prayer breakfast in Dallas, he honored the role of religion in America's historical development and lamented the legal assaults against the tax-exempt status of churches and prayer in school. Evangelicals backed Reagan, giving him 56 percent of their votes, while giving Carter just 34 percent.[48]

The Christian Right wanted Republicans to restore America to its "rightful" place as the dominant force in world affairs, and to revive the cold warrior whose prowess they felt had been anesthetized by peace-making and arms-reductions. It held that America's restoration relied on fueling the engines of capitalism, and so they lobbied vigorously for tax reductions and deregulation.[49] Some offer evidence that the Christian Right sabotaged humanitarian aid and human rights in their zeal to make the world in their own image.[50] The legacy of military interventions and regime changes that took place while born again presidents held office seems to confirm the assertions.

In 1984, the Christian Right was influential in re-electing Reagan. Evangelicals were especially kind to Reagan, giving him 80 percent of their ballots.[51] Just over one half of the boomer voters chose Reagan. Many supported him because they were very concerned about their financial security. In 1983, only 15 percent of boomer households earned incomes over $40 thousand a year, and over 66 percent earned less than $30 thousand.[52] Boomers had become homeowners and parents with pressing financial obligations. The garden of liberalism that had bloomed in the 1960s had shriveled in the heat of the 1980's economy and the anxiety it created.

46. Brog, *Standing with Israel*, 63–90.
47. Woodard, *America that Reagan Built*, 30.
48. Crouse, *Cross and Reaganomics*, 79.
49. Ashford, *Republican Takeover*, 100.
50. Marsden, *For God's Sake*, 113–46.
51. Layman and Hussey, *Matter of Faith*, 190.
52. Brownstein, "Playing Politics," lines 35–42.

Reagan practiced a form of civil religion. He framed his objectives as God's will. His language conveyed the notion that his policies were unquestionably moral. Reagan repeated a favorite American creed, that the U.S. was civilization's greatest hope. He stated that, "If you take away the belief in a greater future, you cannot explain America—that we're a people who believed in a promised land; we were a people who believed we were chosen by God to create a greater world."[53] A devout cold warrior, Reagan called the Soviet Union the "evil empire." Many Russians agreed that the Soviet Union had been evil, inasmuch as it repressed human rights.[54] However, by using the term "evil" to describe the violent and abusive actions of the Soviets while not using the term to describe the United States' violent and abusive actions in places such as Latin America and Southeast Asia, Reagan blessed the notion that American motives were so virtuous and pure, that they stood above moral judgement.

Reagan's administration took civil religion down treacherous paths in Latin America and the Middle East. The Cold War had gone hot, as the Soviets had invaded Afghanistan, shot down Korean Airline flight 007, and were providing weapons and support to the Marxist Sandinista rebels in Nicaragua. The U.S. supported the Mujahideen, Islamic militants who fought against Soviets in Pakistan and Afghanistan. The crusading House Representative, Charlie Wilson (D-TX) secured dramatic increases in U.S. support for the Mujahideen during Reagan's administration, which ultimately armed and trained future Taliban and al-Qaeda terrorists.[55]

Islamic terrorists struck multiple targets during Regan's first term. In 1983, the US embassy, its annex, and Beirut barracks, were bombed in Lebanon, and six foreign targets in Kuwait were attacked. In June, 1985, Hezbollah (Shi'a Islamists based in Lebanon) and Islamic Jihad hijacked TWA flight 847 and took hostages including many Americans. They demanded the release of Lebanese and Iraqi prisoners in Israeli jails and an international condemnation of Israel and the United States. With hostages in the hands of Islamic terrorists, Reagan seemed to be reliving Carter's nightmare. His advisors, however, saw a way to capitalize on the crisis, and devised a plan to free the hostages while advancing American interests. In August, with Reagan's blessing, Israel

53. Reagan, "Remarks," lines 29–33.

54. Busch, *Ronald Reagan*, 197.

55. Dreyfus, *Devil's Game*, 270–89. Since World War I, Islamic fundamentalists resented U.S. interference in the Middle East, and were angered by deals between the Saudis and U.S. oil companies. Sayyid Qutb, an Egyptian who saw Western "decadence" firsthand, (1948–1950), is seen as the father of modern Islamic fundamentalism. He believed that only a theocratic government could save Islamic nations from ruin brought about by the assimilation of Western culture and values. See Calvert, *Sayyid Qutb*.

was to ship weapons to Iran and be reimbursed by the U.S., while Iran was to work with Hezbollah to free the hostages.[56]

The success of the deal inspired a covert operation to violate the Boland Amendment (1982), which banned U.S. funding of Contras in Nicaragua. Arms would be sold directly to Iran at a huge price increase, and a portion of the profits would go directly to Contras. In November 1986, a Lebanese magazine, *Ash-Shiraa*, leaked news of the secret venture. The information came on the heels of another crisis. The Senate Subcommittee on Drugs, Law Enforcement, and Foreign Policy found evidence that the CIA and State Department had used government money derived from the sale of cocaine to fund the Contras.[57] Caesar's minions were unrepentant. When confronted by the tragedies associated with drug trafficking and Nicaragua's civil war, former head of CIA operations in Latin America, Duane Clarridge said, "We will intervene whenever we decide it is in our national security interest to intervene, and it you don't like it, lump it. Get used to it, world. We are not going to put up with nonsense."[58] This was our civil religion.

George, Anointed with Oil

Reagan's successor, George Herbert Walker Bush, was also a fan of civil religion. He was sure that once nations were freed from dictatorships and state-run economics, prosperity would bubble abundantly from dormant wells. Bush took office with the majority of the evangelical ballot.[59] His inaugural speech was laced with prayer:

> Heavenly Father, we bow our heads and thank You for Your love . . . Make us strong to do Your work, will to heed and hear Your will, and write on our hearts these words: "Use power to help people." For we are given power not to advance our own purposes, nor to make a great show in the world, nor a name. There is but one just use of power, and it is to serve people. Help us remember, Lord. Amen.[60]

Like a pastor before his congregation, he sermonized:

---

56. Gardner, *Long Road to Baghdad*, 67–68.
57. Scott and Marshall, *Cocaine Politics*, 8–10.
58. Weil, "Duane Dewey Clarridge," lines 41–47.
59. Smidt and Kellstedt, "Evangelicals in the Post-Reagan," 335–36.
60. Bush, G. H. W., "Inaugural Address," 15–20.

My friends, we are not the sum of our possessions. They are not the measure of our lives. In our hearts we know what matters. We cannot hope only to leave our children a bigger car, a bigger bank account. We must hope to give them a sense of what it means to be a loyal friend; a loving parent; a citizen who leaves his home, his neighborhood, and town a little better than he found it. And what do we want the men and women who work with us to say when we're no longer there? That we were more driven to succeed than anyone around us? Or that we stopped to ask if a sick child had gotten better and stayed a moment there to trade a word of friendship?[61]

Placed against U.S. conduct during Bush's administration, these tender words ultimately left people wondering about what George H. W. meant by "God's work."

Bush's speech writer, Curt Smith, characterized George H. W. as an old fashioned Yankee, hard-working, competitive, generous to the defeated, and humble.[62] Smith's portrait of Bush as a dedicated family man and fiercely loyal patriot settles on the senses like the sights and sounds of little league baseball on Saturday, the warm glow of a fireplace on Christmas Eve, and the reminiscing of grandfathers who recall the stubborn romanticism of their courtships. It stands in contrast to the blunter, more scathing images of Bush as an American Caesar.

George of the Ruling Class

George H. W. Bush, or "Poppy" as he was known, was the offspring of powerful banking families. His father, Prescott worked for Brown Brothers Harriman, a Wall Street investment bank that created industrial empires at home and abroad and had ties to the intelligence community.[63] His maternal grandfather, George Herbert Walker, made fortunes in investments and money laundering as president of his own company and as an executive in J. P Morgan & Company, Guaranty Trust Company, W. H. Harriman & Company, and Union Banking Corporation. As a member of Yale's class of 1948, Poppy was a member of the Skull and Bones Society, an elite association that strengthens ties among the wealthiest and most powerful families in America. Bush worked for E. H. Harriman's Dresser Industries, which developed technology for ef-

---

61. Ibid., lines 43–48.
62. Smith, C. *George H. W. Bush*, vi–xv.
63. Baker, R. *Family of Secrets*, 7–18.

ficient oil extraction. Prior to WWII, Dresser acquired several companies that produced military equipment. It did business with the Soviet Union and other European nations, and it was a CIA front.[64]

In 1953 Poppy established Zapata Petroleum. His ventures took him offshore and in some very interesting directions. Zapata eventually had operations in the Gulf of Mexico, the Caribbean, Japan, Australia, Western Europe, Persian Gulf, and throughout South and Central America. As a favor to his dad's friend, CIA Director Allen Dulles, Poppy used his position as an international oilman to identify potential recruits to the CIA.[65] Poppy's link to the CIA prior to his appointment to be its director in 1975 was widely unknown until 1988. As journalist Joseph McBride was investigating JFK's assassination, he discovered an FBI memo regarding J. Edgar Hoover's November 23rd briefing of "Mr. George Bush of the Central Intelligence Agency."[66] The memo concerned the reaction of Cuban exiles in Miami to JFK's death. McBride notes that White House spokespersons and CIA personnel denied that the man in the memo was the same George Bush who was then the Vice-President, and so the truth remains ambiguous.

The familial coziness that the intelligence community, bankers, industrialists, and politicians enjoy is perfectly logical when viewed through Caesar's lens. All these entities share an interest in amassing wealth and power, and in imposing their sense of stability onto an unstable world. These goals require them to control the resources and the people who can help them achieve their objectives, and to work together. Banks and industries have always had an incentive to spy on the competition and discretely probe the opportunities and obstacles for business transactions at home and abroad. Since the state benefits from the success of banks and industry, it has an incentive to provide them with intelligence and military support. All of these entities stand to profit from illegal activities that generate billions of dollars—enough to operate secret empires within the empire. More than any other recent president, George H. W. Bush revealed the theology at the core of such activity.

Bush's orientation to the world was very different from my own and that of my peers. Ensconced in material wealth, his character was formed alongside the scions of the American aristocracy. His family traced their roots back to the Mayflower.[67] His parents and grandparents personified the American aristocratic lifestyle and ethic. Hard work, self-discipline, and the ability to work through pain and failure without complaint prepared one for the tough terrain of banking and corporate management. As a young Episcopalian, Bush

64. Carrier, *Hard Right Turn*, 170.
65. Trento, *Prelude to Terror*, 13–20
66. McBride, "Man who Wasn't There," 41–42.
67. Meacham, *Destiny and Power*, 4.

learned Bible verses from his parents and was taught that he was obligated to serve the world at large. Biblical mantras included the assertion that those who have been given much are required to give much in return, and those who have been given trust must prove worthy of it.[68]

Bush was raised in an environment wherein affluent Christians believed that they were called to bring order to the world, and would naturally be rewarded handsomely for doing a splendid job. He was schooled at Philips Academy Andover in Massachusetts, a college preparatory school for boys that served the sons of industrial and financial titans. Andover was similar to other boarding schools for the elite inasmuch as it prepared students to meet their obligations to the state, their peers, and the public as defined by the ruling class.[69] Within the walls of elite boarding schools, young men assimilated the prejudices of their social class regarding race, religion, and privilege.

In many respects, Bush's theology blended the tenets of Andrew Carnegie's "The Gospel of Wealth" and Woodrow Wilson's vision and principles for a new world order.[70] The steel baron assured the rich that there was no sin in amassing a fortune, and that it was virtuous if one sought fortune in order to spend money on public improvement. Carnegie preached that surplus fortune ought to be used for philanthropic projects, such as building libraries and schools. From Wilson, Bush took the notion that United States was destined to lead the New World Order.[71] From the perspective of American's aristocracy, nations, like social classes, had their proper place in the world, and global peace and prosperity depended on the way nations refrained from rebelling against "their betters." To the American aristocracy, underdeveloped nations that did not follow the lead of industrial, democratic, and Christian nations, were needlessly hurting themselves. To many Americans, the ruling class's outlook smacked of Machiavelli and social Darwinism.[72] To the indigenous populations of underdeveloped nations, the U.S. seemed to be leading people to Isaac's altar, as American-backed tyrants prospered while the poor stayed poor.

---

68. Ibid., 27.

69. Ibid., 33–34.

70. See Carnegie, *Gospel of Wealth* and Burnidge, *Peaceful Conquest*. Both reveal a world in which God's blessings are seen as rewards for material success, and in which many believed the perfectibility of the human society was within reach, not by way of conquest and genocide, but by way of industrial growth and cooperation.

71. Joseph, R. *New World Order*, 93–95.

72. Niccolo Machiavelli's *Prince*, (1532) argued that in society's best interest, monarchs must resort to any and all means of keeping public order, including terror and deception. Social Darwinism applies the concept of "survival of the fittest" to human societies, and asserts that for the sake of human progress and prosperity, some must be allowed to perish. See Hofstadter, *Social Darwinism in American Thought*.

Disposable Despots

To protect Caesar's agenda for the world, American patricians have installed and toppled dictators who do their bidding. For decades, Latin American narcotics found their way to the U.S. via Panama. Its banks did business with drug dealers and arms smugglers, and with U.S. financial institutions that helped launder the money that funded CIA covert activities.[73] In December 1989, the U.S. invaded Panama to extricate its leader, Manuel Noriega, claiming that he was a "narco-terrorist." After years of service to the CIA and U.S. interests in Latin America, Noriega had become disposable. The Soviets were in decline and he had played both sides of the Cold War. The U.S. invaded to apprehend its former ally. It bombed ghettos, torched homes, and took the lives of between 1,000 and 4,000 Panamanians.[74] Noriega was captured and prosecuted in the U.S. for drug trafficking, in France for money laundering, and in Panama for human rights violations. Bush had executed a regime change and faced no criminal charges. The United Nations deplored the invasion saying it violated international law, but its opinion was inconsequential.[75]

Saddam Hussein, a Cold War ally since 1979, rose to power in a nation festering with chaos and violence. He built himself palaces, brutally repressed his opponents, censored the press, and used chemical gases to kill 30,000 Kurds during the Iran-Iraq War, 1980–1988.[76] The U.S. supplied arms to Hussein during the war, and was slow to condemn the genocide. It had tolerated Hussein's poor record on human rights abuses as it used Hussein to halt the spread of Islamic revolution.[77] After the war, and as the Soviet Union was in decline, Hussein became more daring. He threatened to use chemical weapons against Israel and to acquire nuclear weapons. He invaded Kuwait in 1991, hoping to seize oil reserves that might help ease debts from the war with Iran. Saudis saw the move as a threat to their country and its oil reserves.

Bush was in some ways obligated to intervene in order to protect Saudi Arabia, a vital U.S. ally. During Nixon's administration, the U.S. Treasury and the Saudi Arabian Monetary Agency worked out the means of cycling Saudi profits from oil sales back into the U.S. via Saudi investments and purchases of T-bills.[78] The Saudis were enticed by America's promise to sell them arms, ex-

---

73. Chomsky, *How the World Works*, 39–43.
74. Independent Commission of Inquiry on the U.S. Invasion of Panama, *U.S. Invasion*, 1.
75. Lewis, "After Noriega," 1–13.
76. Angell and Gunaratna, *Terrorist Rehabilitation*, 12.
77. Bakhash, "Troubled Relationship," 21–23.
78. Spiro, *Hidden Hand*, 74–75.

change intelligence, and defend Saudi royals and their property.[79] In addition, the Saudi Binladin Group, a multi-billion dollar construction company, invested with Goldman Sachs, Merrill Lynch, and other American corporations.[80] They were business associates of Bush as investors in the Carlyle Group, an investment firm that is a "major component of the U.S. defense industry."[81] Bush was not just defending Kuwait, but a valuable friend in the oil business.

When I read about Bush's prayer life, compassion, sense of fairness, discipline, loyalty, and commitment to human progress, I feel a measure of admiration and humility. I think about the security and comfort that comes from reflexively following a leader who exudes confidence about the future and the right path to take. I imagine the life of well-ordered privilege that formed the world views of American paternal warriors. I imagine sturdy New England mansions and sprawling vacation homes, dressed in antique rugs and solid wood furniture that maids clean daily. I think of steaming platters of expensive meat and seafood, and of chowders and stews that never come out of a can. I think of ski trips to Europe and chauffeurs retrieving children from boarding school for Thanksgiving.

When I think about the world our millionaire senators, representatives, and law-makers occupy, I do not think about my home town of Minneapolis, and the crumbling working class homes of the Near North, Powderhorn, and Phillips neighborhoods. I do not envision elders huddled into cinder block high rises worried about whether to spend their tiny monthly allowance on heat, food, or medicine; nor do I imagine smell of poverty in alleys where the homeless cluster to get out of the rain and snow. I also do not envision families in Latin America living in shelters made from scraps of wood and sheet metal, nor children picking through the local dump for something to eat or wear.

When I focus my attention on the bloodshed and misery various populations have endured for the sake of "progress," and building a "new world order," the warm, cozy, and opulent Cape Cod mansion suddenly becomes a crime scene. I am distressed. I know that the American Caesar is not the source of all hunger, tyranny, and ignorance in the world. Yet, he has so often siphoned the cream of global resources into his pocket on terms that have deprived others of the comfort and security he takes for granted. I know that I am supposed to crave this "American dream" and embrace it as my individual right to happiness. Secular and religious leaders often tell us that the American dream and the spiritual journey can be reconciled, yet, I struggle. It seems that the pursuit of wealth and power so often makes excuses for environmental

---

79. Baker, R. *Family of Secrets*, 289–90.
80. Unger, *House of Bush*, 4–5.
81. Rupert, *Crossing the Rubicon*, 129–33.

destruction and deprivations endured by the poor and vulnerable. It seems busy with severing the connective tissue between the physical and the spiritual, and between ourselves and the rest of creation.

A voice in my head demands answers that I may never get. Did we have to let racism and urban neglect destroy our own neighbors? Did we have to devastate Vietnam to save the world? Was supporting juntas in Latin America really the best way to advance democracy? Did the CIA really have to run drugs to do God's will? Did we ever temper our messianic impulses long enough to seriously consider other people's points of view? Did we ever walk long enough in Isaac's shoes before our military interventions sent him to his death? Before we legislated so many advantages for the rich, did we behold the vulnerable Isaacs and think to ourselves, "How does this bring the love of God to them?" How much longer can we say that we are a "Christian nation" and pretend that our sense of individualism and entitlement has no effect on our love of neighbor? Have we lost the ability to tell the difference between Jesus and every Caesar who announces that he is a faith-based leader?

12

A View from Distant Shores

Isaac South of the Border

I REMEMBER HEARING ABOUT the rape and murder of the Maryknoll Sisters, Ita Ford, Maura Clark, the Ursuline Sister, Dorothy Kazel, and their lay associate, Jean Donovan. The women were missionaries in El Salvador who served the poor and ran refugee camps for those displaced by a civil war that lasted from 1979 to 1992. They were among the nearly 1,000 priests, nuns and bishops who were imprisoned, exiled or killed by Latin American governments between 1968 and 1982.[1] Several waves of rage went through me when I learned about what happened to these women.

The first wave was visceral and sickening. I knew women who had survived rape and was aware that sexual assault is often used to punish women who "step out of line." I understood that El Salvador was predominately Catholic, and so imagined that the assailants had perhaps been altar boys in their youth, or maybe even gone to Mass the Sunday before they committed these crimes. The whole thing deepened my resentment for machismo that normalizes sexual sadism and is especially titillated by the humiliation of women.

The second wave of rage was towards my own government's role in the tragedy. American taxes and the CIA had supported El Salvador's military junta that by 1992 had taken 80,000 lives in civil war.[2] It was a scenario played out in many other countries in the region as the "Christian" big brother to the north stamped out Marxism south of the border. The women died when Carter was president. He had wanted to make human rights the cornerstone of his foreign policy, but capitulated to pressure to counter leftist insurrec-

---

1. Peterson, *Martyrdom and the Politics*, 63.
2. De Rouen, *Civil Wars*, 345.

tions in Latin America. Over the objections of Archbishop Oscar Romero and other humanitarians, Carter had supported right-wing butchers that ruled El Salvador.

It would take years before I understood enough about Latin American history to feel the next wave of anger, which came as the result of learning that in all my years in formal education, I learned so little about history from the victim's point of view, and of the price people paid for America's obsession with making the world in its own image. I had learned little about how power operates behind closed doors, and about how a tiny percent of people in the U.S. control so much of the national agenda and democratic processes. American schools and universities do not require students to know how international banks, intelligence agencies, multinational corporations, news agencies, and mercenaries operate in the real world. So, we grow up ignorant, but confident that we are the greatest nation of all. My ignorance has often made me feel like my spiritual capital is fool's gold because my moral judgments have sometimes been based on a flawed understanding of the world.

Tinhorn Dictators

In many ways, Latin American history is a story of how the Gospel may be used for good or evil. For centuries, under the auspices of winning souls for Christ, Christian missions had helped European nations to colonize Latin America.[3] The Rockefellers and other American families sponsored missions and evangelical operations in Latin America as part of their efforts to bring order to regions in which they built empires of oil, cattle, rubber, sugar, coffee, tin, iron, and all the infrastructures and utilities required to manage them.[4] Missionaries consistently directed peasants to accept deplorable poverty and horrible working conditions, because God would reward their earthly suffering with an eternity in heaven. At the other end of the spectrum were clerics, nuns, and lay volunteers who rigorously and openly advocated for social justice.

As in so many wars of decolonization, the U.S. used anti-communist rhetoric to prevent reforms that threatened U.S. investments. Coffee barons controlled El Salvador's presidency until the Great Depression, during which leftists and Marxists launched reform movements. Prior to the Bay of Pigs invasion in 1961, JFK created the Alliance for Progress. It aimed to neutralize Latin American interest in socialism by encouraging land and tax reforms,

---

3. A comprehensive history can be found in Dussel, *A History of the Church in Latin America*.
4. See Colby, G., *Thy Will be Done*, an extensive history on the topic.

and called for the U.S. to aid Latin Americans with economic development. Kennedy, confided to his assistant, Richard Goodwin:

> We can't just embrace every little tinhorn dictator who tells us he's anticommunist while he's sitting on the necks of his own people. And the United States government is not the representative of private business. Do you know in Chile the American copper companies control eighty percent of all foreign exchange? We wouldn't stand for that here. And there's no reason they should stand for it.[5]

Kennedy's support for land reform drew accusations from Latin America's ruling class that he was a communist.[6] Nelson Rockefeller objected to the idea that the U.S. should invest in factories and smelting plants that would give Latin Americans greater autonomy in their industrial development.[7] To protect their interests, America's bankers and industrialists supported military dictators that crushed peasant uprisings, attacked unions, and spied on charitable organizations working on the poor's behalf.[8] The U.S. allied with dictators throughout Latin America, and the CIA undertook propaganda campaigns, tampered with elections, and orchestrated coups.[9]

By the mid-1970s, about 14 families controlled over 90 percent of El Salvador's arable land and lived in fabulous wealth while the malnourished masses lived in hovels that lacked safe drinking water and sanitation.[10] Civil war erupted in 1979 following a coup against the fraudulently elected President Carlos Romero. Romero had promised reforms, but they were not substantial. In addition, his bloody suppression of dissent caused Catholic clerics to protest his presidency. In 1979, José Duarte of the Christian Democratic Party led a coup against Romero. The Farabundo Martí Liberation Front (FMLF), a leftist revolutionary group with communist affiliations, contested Duarte and initiated a 12-year civil war. The U.S. supported Duarte despite his regime's use of torture, terrorism, kidnapping, rape, and murder to secure itself.[11] Over the course of the civil war, the U.S. spent approximately $6 billion on military and civil aid to El Salvador.[12]

---

5. Goodwin, *Remembering America*, 147.
6. Barry and Preusch, *El Salvador*, 39. Also see Goodwin, 160.
7. Goodwin, *Remembering America*, 176.
8. Lernoux, *Cry of the People*, 159–60.
9. Rabe, *Killing Zone* presents a concise history of Cold War operations in Latin America
10. Castellano, *Civil War Interventions*, 68.
11. Ehrman and Flamm, *Debating the Reagan Presidency*, 135.
12. Blum, *Killing Hope*, 357.

In addition to funding Duarte's regime, the U.S. trained soldiers who were members of death squads across Latin America. The School of the Americas (SOA), was established in Panama in 1946 for the purpose of training Latin American soldiers to counter Marxism. American tax dollars were thus used to teach foreign militia about how to use propaganda, surveillance, kidnapping, torture, assassination, and other acts of terrorism.[13] In 1984, the SOA was relocated to Fort Benning in Georgia, and later renamed the Western Hemisphere Institute for Security Cooperation (WHISC).

Ford, Clark, Kazel and Donovan were just four of the tens of thousands who were slaughtered in El Salvador, and whose butchered bodies were left along the streets, tossed into rivers, and laid out in local dumps as warnings to those who opposed Duarte. Reagan's administration showed marginal sympathy for the missionaries. Jeanne Kirkpatrick, one of Reagan's foreign policy advisors, stated that, "The nuns were not just nuns, they were political activists," and Secretary of State, Alexander Haig speculated that the women had run through a roadblock or that there had been "an exchange of fire."[14] The families of the diseased missionaries expected the U.S. government would do all it could to bring the killers to justice, but instead found it was blaming the victims.

Reagan placed little pressure on Duarte to investigate the incident. Weeks after the murders, Haig, fired Robert White, ambassador to El Salvador, because he asserted that Reagan's administration aided the murders by way of political policy.[15] Pressure to identify and prosecute the killers came from attorney William Ford, Ita Ford's brother. In 1984, five low-level soldiers were found guilty of rape and murder, but Ford was not satisfied. He wanted the U.S. to prosecute those who ordered, then covered up the murders. In 1989, following the assassinations of six Jesuit priests, their housekeeper and her daughter, public outrage led to the U.N. Truth Commission study that revealed Generals José Garcia and Carlos Vides Casanova had orchestrated the murders and their cover-up.[16] Garcia and Casanova had been allowed to retire in Florida and lived there comfortably until the U.S. passed the Intelligence Reform and Terrorism Prevention Act in 2004, which led to efforts to deport them.[17]

---

13. Gill, L. *School of the Americas* is a disturbing look at the SOA and other U.S. entities that train personnel around the world in the "arts" of espionage, repression, and terror.

14. Bonner, "Bringing El Salvador Nun Killers," Lines 47–52.

15. LeoGrande, "Remembering Robert White," lines 65–80.

16. United Nations Commission on the Truth for El Salvador, *From Madness to Hope*, 62–63.

17. *Intelligence Reform and Terrorism Prevention Act,* Public Law 108–458, U. S.

President Reagan defended Latin American dictators, calling them "the moral equivalent of the Founding Fathers."[18] When asked about events in Latin America, a U.S. Defense Department official said, "When your house is on fire you don't call an interior decorator."[19] The message was as eerie as it was clear: Human rights are luxuries afforded people only when Caesar has secured his interests.

Members of the Christian Right and liberal Christians both donated time and resources to help the victims of El Salvador's civil war. They did not, however, share a common moral outlook. One group was no threat to Caesar, and the other group was. The Christian Right disliked Catholic missionaries' advocacy for social justice. They supported U.S. aid to the dictators as they believed that the U.S. was on the right side of a cosmological war against evil. Paralife Ministries of Texas sent clerics to El Salvador to encourage Duarte's soldiers, telling them that killing was "necessary to fight against an anti-Christ system,"[20] Jerry Falwell asserted that Congressmen who did not support Reagan's support for Duarte were destroying a covenant with God.[21] Pat Robertson lobbied Congress to provide military aid to Duarte, and his Christian Broadcast Network dedicated lots of time to reports about El Salvador and instruction on how viewers could petition elected officials to fight harder against the FMLF.[22]

Among the casualties of the war in El Salvador was Archbishop Oscar Romero. On March 24, 1980, he was assassinated while celebrating the Eucharist. Romero was among the highest-ranking Catholics in the world who openly challenged the West to embrace the liberation of the poor from systematic economic and political injustice. In a homily broadcast on international radio the day before he was murdered, he appealed directly to El Salvador's National Guardsmen to stop the repression and to "obey your consciences rather than the orders of sin."[23] Romero acknowledged that the Church's mission was primarily spiritual, but argued that the mission prompted the faithful to structure and serve the community in ways becoming of "divine law."[24] Romero's teachings were central to liberation theology, which challenges some of the ideas found in religious fundamentalism and Peter's paradigm.

Statute 118 (2004) 3638.
18. Stone, O. and Kuznick, *The Untold History*, 431–432.
19. Carothers, *In the Name of Democracy*, 23.
20. Diamond, *Spiritual Warfare*, 177.
21. Apple, "Perfected Drama," 35.
22. Heilbrunn, *They Knew*, 177–78.
23. Will, *Archbishop Oscar Romero*, 181.
24. Romero, "Church's Mission," 4.

Liberation Theology

Liberation theology evolved during the 1950s and 60s in the jungles and on the plantations of Latin America. It took shape in the hearts and minds of clerics and religious volunteers who saw the Catholic Church's social teachings of Vatican II through the eyes of the destitute. Liberation theology, begins with the premise that poverty in a world of plenty is by definition a scandal and an injustice created by the denial of human rights.[25]

Liberation theology is perhaps best articulated in the work of Gustavo Gutiérrez, a Dominican priest whose work with the Peruvian poor led him to contemplate the sins of materialism. He asserted that liberation theology seeks to free people from all forms of servitude as it is oppressive.[26] Gutierrez held that efforts to relieve the poor of their burden by way social reform was consistent with the Church's teaching that the Gospel be brought to bear in anthropological dimensions.[27]

Although liberation theology does not call for a communist revolution, some who embraced it were socialists. In addition, liberation theology shares with Marxism the belief that capitalism exploits the poor and working class.[28] That made liberation theology an easy target for its critics. Nonetheless, over the objections of their bishops, many clerics spoke openly against death squads and unjust governance. Some priests were former operatives of the CIA who changed their minds about serving their imperial masters.[29] Clerics and nuns who openly embraced liberation theology risked criticism, imprisonment, torture, and death. Liberation theology was provocative, and Christians took sides.

Pope John Paul II validated liberation theology's commitment to seek justice for the poor, but rejected its tendency to base the conversation about justice and humanity on social and economic situations rather than on God's divine plan for humanity. The revolutionary aspect of Jesus, he held, concerned revolutions of values.[30] As prefect of the Sacred Congregation of for the Doctrine of the Faith, Cardinal Joseph Ratzinger, who later became Pope Benedict XVI, oversaw the composition of *Instruction on Certain Aspects of the "Theology*

---

25. Boff, and Boff, *Introducing Liberation*, 2–3.
26. Gutierrez, *A Theology*, xliv.
27. Ibid., 5–6.
28. Long, *Divine Economy*, 93.
29. The Vatican and the CIA began their relationship during WWII when Pope Pius XII collaborated with the Office of Strategic Services (the CIA's predecessor) to gather vital intelligence on enemy operations. See Lee, "Their Will Be Done," lines 24–47.
30. Hebbletwaite, "Liberation Theology," 182–83.

of Liberation." It acknowledged that, while liberation theology showed an authentic concern for human dignity and the poor, any theology that posits that class warfare is at the heart of the human experience, and that equates political revolution with moral transformation are erroneous.[31] Ratzinger's remarks beg the question of how to reform an economic system without addressing the political mechanisms that keep the system intact.

Some evangelicals saw truth and hope in liberation theology. Reverend Jim Wallis, of the evangelical left, wrote that, "At the deepest level, our global economy is not fulfilling the role that economics is meant to fulfill," and instead of creating happiness, stability, fairness, and sustainability, it has created the opposite.[32] The economy, argues Wallis, is not a moral agent because it defines the highest activity of mankind in material terms, rewards greed, and exploits human beings and the environment. Jimmy Carter, another member of the evangelical left, argued that in matters of economics, human rights, not theological doctrine, should be at the center of policy-making, and yet, when Archbishop Romero begged him to stop sending money to El Salvador's junta, he rejected his plea.[33] Liberation theologians were cynical towards Carter's human rights' rhetoric, as U.S. support for deadly dictators was unyielding.[34]

The Christian Right has generally disliked liberation theology. When theologian Harvey Cox visited Pat Robertson's Regent University he observed Regent's rhetoric had something in common with liberation theology. Both, he noted, see the Gospel as more than an invitation for personal conversion, and want the Gospel to transform society through institutional change. The rhetoric differed, however, on the matter of corporate behavior and the morality of the rich. "Why," asked Cox, "does so much evangelical social theology slide so easily over Jesus' harsh warnings to the rich and powerful, so that one rarely hears any criticisms of corporations that close their factories to help the bottom line, or congressmen who pour more money into the military than what the Pentagon asks for?"[35] He found that whereas liberation theology embraces a preference for the poor and identifies with the powerless, Christian conservatives tend to prefer and identify with the rich and powerful.

Secular opposition to liberation theology tended to echo conservative faith in free market capitalism. Nelson Rockefeller, whose family investments in Latin American oil, minerals, agriculture, cattle, railroads, and banks

---

31. See Congregation for the Doctrine of the Faith, *Instruction on Certain Aspects*, sections VII and VII.
32. Wallis, *On God's Side*, 208.
33. Tombs, *Latin American*, 164.
34. Engler, "Towards Rights," 206.
35. Cox, "Warring Visions," 68–69.

represent an empire from Mexico to Argentina, toured Central America in 1969 and filed a report on what he found. Several Latin American leaders concluded from the report that it was time to silence those who preached liberation theology.[36] The *Rockefeller Report on the Americas* noted in 1969 that while the Catholic Church had traditionally been "a conservative force resistant to change," it had recently experienced changes that had aroused idealism, produced an interest in revolution, and left people "vulnerable to subversive penetration."[37] Rockefeller's report left little doubt that private business interests did not necessarily see the primary function of the Church as a ministry in the business of saving souls, but rather saw its purpose as an agent that cultivated public docility and the status quo.

Following Reagan's ascent to the White House, his advisors, the "Committee of Santa Fe," met to discuss Marxist threats in Latin American. They issued a report, *A New Inter-American Policy for the Eighties* that criticized Carter's administration for not doing enough to meet the communist threat in the Western Hemisphere. It targeted Cuba for boycotts and propaganda campaigns, as it laid the blame for Marxist uprisings in Central America at Castro's feet, rather than the lived experience of poverty and colonialism.[38] The report also called for increased efforts to repress liberation theology.[39]

Grace

I was introduced to liberation theology in college. It spoke to the part of me that was always interested in defending the underdog. Determined to change the world, I pursued a degree in Religious Studies. Before I undertook college studies, however, I took a detour at age sixteen, and began my short career as a "born again" Christian. For me, the experience was highly egotistical. It offered my sense of self-esteem the special kind of boost that one gets when one believes that one possesses very special and esoteric knowledge, and so are superior to others.

For a short time, I attended Campus Church of Minneapolis, located near the University of Minnesota, and heard the preaching of Reverend Ernest O'Neill. His sermons rolled along in melodic Irish brogue as he quoted scripture and sprinkled his homilies with stories. O'Neill often preached against the "cheap grace" of salvation, which is to accept redemption without changing

---

36. Ryan, "Option," 222.
37. Rockefeller, *Rockefeller Report*, 31–32.
38. Haney and Vanderbush, *Cuban Embargo*, 55.
39. Boff and Boff, *Introducing Liberation*, 86.

our lives. O'Neill did not address social justice or corporate obligations to the poor and vulnerable. He focused on the cross as the means of dying to our sinful selves. His lectures gave the impression that the political and economic world was rather incidental to one's faith.

O'Neill's priestly view of God came through in a sermon he delivered years after I stopped attending his services. He said that the Holocaust happened because God "withdrew his protecting sword" from the Jews as a consequence of their "iniquity" and treachery.[40] His remarks were not unlike those uttered by other evangelicals of the era. Billy Graham blamed the Jews for monopolizing the media and proliferating pornography.[41] Pat Robertson warned readers of Jewish conspiracies and told them that Jews who have not converted to Christianity were incomplete.[42]

Eventually, I saw the assertion that Jews brought the Holocaust upon themselves as a form of blasphemy, a kind of cheap theology characterized by the smug judgment of those who profess to know the mind of God because they have read the Bible. Cheap theology requires no understanding of the historical contexts or hermeneutics from which emerge religious traditions, doctrines, and canons of scripture. It is not open to the notion that God's revelation to humanity is constant and on-going in human history. It tends to reject the assertion that God may be revealed through the teachings of people outside the faith. Cheap theology is also the idea that only literal interpretations of the Bible can be true, and that, while Jesus used symbols in his parables, he never graduated to metaphors.

The orthodox proposition declares that Jesus was God's last revelation—the last call—take it or leave it. Ultimately, that proposition did not resonate with my experience. Formal studies and life taught me that my need for certainty and absolutism could kill the most profound aspects of my own spirituality, and also cause me to deprive others of hope and grace. I became a heretic for the sake of embracing a Jesus that lots of Christians do not like. I could not accept that non-Christians were damned for eternity, nor that God punishes sinners by causing disease and natural disasters.

My dissent has a price. An acquaintance once snapped, "Don't you read the Bible? Jesus clearly said in John that 'I am the way the truth and the life; no one comes to the Father but through me'—you can't be a Christian and go to heaven if you don't' believe that!" I have no doubt that Jesus revealed God in his statement, but *what* about God and the individual's relationship to God did he reveal? Here the literal confronts the mystical. My insistent acquaintance

40. "Anti-Semitic Sermons," lines 32–39.
41. Pollack, J. C. Billy *Graham Story*, 128.
42. Goldberg, "Are You," 40.

believed that "the way" is the literal sacrifice of Jesus on the cross, which is the only price God accepts for personal salvation. Mystically, however, Jesus may be "the way" in the sense that he lived and died as though his person were already one with God, and no ego stood between.

Recently, I had the wonderful occasion to be reunited with one of my high school English teachers—a beautiful woman who encouraged me to love life, the world of ideas and principles, and writing. When I was her student, I babysat her sons. That was a big deal. I was honored by the reality that she trusted me with her babies. As my teacher and I reminisced, she reminded me that when I was in my "born-again" phase, she asked me if I thought she would go to hell because she was not a Christian. I shuttered, dreading my imminent mortification. She said that I had indeed told her that she would be lost if she did not accept Jesus as her personal savior. A wave of shame washed over me. I squirmed in my chair and folded forward. With my head in my hands, I vainly trying to deflect profound embarrassment. I apologized and assured my dear teacher that my statement was not something that came from my Catholic upbringing, but from the fundamentalism that had mesmerized me at age sixteen. She was kind and said she took the statement as a part of normal, youthful idealism. Her understanding was the grace of God incarnate.

My own reaction to words I had uttered decades earlier to a teacher whom I deeply admire and respect was telling to me. In the decades since our last meeting, I had grown to revile the judgment I so capriciously dispatched as an adolescent. The answer I had given my teacher was that of Caesar, and not that of a sister whose love transcends creeds, ethnicity, gender, class, and culture. They were the sentiments of somebody whose theological box is too small for God. There were other things that led me to the same conclusion, including my trips to Russia, a land I was not supposed to love.

Twilight in Moscow

Eventually, the Cold War—the thing that provided the rationale for the sacrifices we were asked to make and the wars we were asked to fight—came to an end. Given the way we had endowed the conflict with theological significance, one would think Americans celebrated in the streets with parades and champagne when it ended. That is what happened in Europe, but it did not happen in the United States. On December 25, 1991, when the Soviet flag was lowered for the final time over the Kremlin, and the tri-colors of the Republic were hoisted, Americans seemed to yawn as if the event were as routine as a sneeze. The absence of fanfare, however, did not mean the absence of grand-standing.

Pundits were quick to credit Ronald Reagan with "winning" the Cold War. They argued that Reagan brought down the Soviet Union by undermining its economy and pursuing the Strategic Defense Initiative (SDI).[43] President George H. W. Bush announced in 1992 that, "By the grace of God, America won the Cold War."[44] He said, "We never would have got there if we'd gone for the nuclear-freeze crowd."[45] The conservative narrative resonated with familiar jingoism, and gave a nod to America's faith in the use of force to resolve conflict. Bush's rhapsody offered little praise for what others had done to end the Cold War.

George Kennan, the U.S. diplomat to Moscow, who's "Long Telegram" of February 1946, was the cornerstone of containment, opined that Bush's claim was "intrinsically silly."[46] Perhaps more than anyone who advised presidents during the first years of the Cold War, Kennan deeply understood Russia. He had studied its history, spoke its language, and lived in the Soviet Union for long periods.[47] He knew that U.S. claims to glory diluted the truth and complexity of the historical record. Kennan noted that by the 1950s, the Soviets felt the need to liberalize its policies, but found it difficult to pursue this course because both American and Soviet military extremists dominated the process of crafting foreign policy. Soviet historian, Vladislav Zubok, confirms Kennan's assertions, and stated that the "Soviet political and intellectual elites" lost their will to defend an ideology that not only risked nuclear war, but that offered no prosperity.[48]

The whole world was involved in the Cold War and so it also participated in its end. One cannot ignore the sacrifices of thousands of dissidents who from 1945 to 1989 were incarcerated, tortured, and murdered in prisons and gulags across Eastern Europe and Siberia. Their work—including that of Andrei Sakharov, the dissident nuclear physicist who argued for arms reduction, and Alexander Solzhenitsyn, who documented the injustices and horror of Soviet oppression in his book, *Gulag Archipelago*, kept an international spotlight on the inhumanity of the Soviet system.[49]

---

43. Schweizer, *Victory* 282.
44. Bush, G. H. W. "State of the Union," lines 17–18.
45. Bush, G. H. W. "Presidential Debate," lines 193–98.
46. Kennan, "G.O.P Won," lines 1–3.
47. Isaacson and Thomas *Wise Men* documents Kennan's career, his profound empathy for Russia, and the ways in which his peers, including John McCloy, Dean Acheson, and Averell Harriman shaped foreign policy during the Cold War.
48. Zubok, *Failed Empire*, 342–44.
49. See Drell and Schultz, *Andrei Sakharov* and Pearce, *Solzhenitsyn*.

East Europeans deserve much credit for their role in shaking the Kremlin off the world's back. The protest against Moscow that began behind the Iron Curtain in the 1940s was energized by disillusioned communists who risked their lives for reform. For decades, people in the Soviet Bloc chipped away at their own oppression through espionage, secret gatherings, and illegal publications.

East Germans workers launched strikes against the Sovietization of their economy in 1953.[50] In 1956, 15,000 Hungarians took up arms in their quest for reforms, and were met with Soviet tanks and bullets.[51] Czechoslovakia's "Prague Spring," 1968, also called for democratic reforms and a retreat from the Warsaw Pact, and was summarily crushed by a Soviet military intervention.[52] In 1980, Polish workers formed the Solidarity Movement and held strikes and demonstrations. They demanded that Moscow make good on its promises of socialist abundance, pay increases, and better living conditions.[53] Dissidents negotiated with the Polish government, and won reforms and an election in 1989, in which 99 percent of the new parliament's seats went to non-communists. The "Velvet Revolution" in Czechoslovakia, saw thousands of people took to the streets demanding that human the government honor human rights and the release of hundreds of dissidents.[54] Intellectuals practiced "samizdat," a form of dissent in which protesters reproduced and distributed forbidden and censored essays, and documents. In 1989, the Hungarian government cut the barbed wire fences along the Austrian border, and turned a blind eye to the numbers escaping to the West.[55]

Pope John Paul II played a vital role in the collapse of the Soviet Union, and he had no army and no nuclear stockpile. Some credit him with instigating the public process that led to the collapse of Soviet communism.[56] In December, 1989 he met with Soviet Premier Mikhail Gorbachev in Rome. John Paul was open to dialogue with his adversaries, and offered a comprehensive critique of both the East and the West. He acknowledged that Western and Soviet economic systems were both detrimental to progress and human dignity.[57] Gorbachev was listening.

50. Harrison, H. M. *"Berlin and the Cold War,"* 57–60.
51. Gati, *Failed Illusions*, 3; 16–17.
52. Latysh, *Czechoslovak Crisis*, 1–18.
53. Ost, *Defeat of Solidarity*, 75–76.
54. Wheaton and Kavan, *Velvet Revolution*, 24–28.
55. Meyer, M. *Year that Changed*, 67.
56. Renehan, *Pope John Paul II*, 60–62.
57. Hehir, "Papal Foreign Policy," 38–39.

Caesar Meets Perestroika

Without Gorbachev's leadership, the Cold War may have ended very differently. He took risks that other Caesars were not willing to take. Gorbachev took office in 1985, inherited a war in Afghanistan, dissent movements in the Eastern Bloc, and ethnic conflicts in the Soviet republics. The black market and worn infrastructures left the Soviet economy in ruins. Modern technology brought images of the West into Soviet living rooms and excited viewers' appetites for goods and a way of life communism failed to produce. Gorbachev's vision for reform made him a target of Soviet militants and ordinary citizens whose patience and resilience in the face of economic strife were fading fast.

Gorbachev did not believe the Soviet Union was set to collapse. Instead, he believed that communism was on the brink of reforms that would align Russia with the modern world.[58] He undertook *perestroika*, (restructuring) and *glasnost* (openness and transparency), and was poised to integrate capitalism, expand democratic rights, and reduce his stash of nuclear weapons. Rather than maintaining the status quo, he refused to mobilize forces against reform movements that erupted in the Eastern Bloc.

In addition to crises at home, Gorbachev confronted America's resolve to destroy communism on its own terms. Reagan called for the Soviets to withdraw troop from Afghanistan and developing nations in Africa without commensurate U.S. withdrawals of forces in Latin America.[59] Reagan called for massive military spending, including millions for SDI, which would develop satellites capable of destroying intercontinental ballistic missiles from space. At a 1986 summit with Gorbachev in Reykjavik, Iceland, Reagan's refusal to abandon SDI soured hope for a substantial retreat from the arms race. Hardliners in the Kremlin saw SDI as proof of America's hostile intentions, which hardened their resistance to Gorbachev's reforms.[60]

In July, 1989, Gorbachev dissolved the Warsaw Pact and within months, Poland, Hungary, East Germany, and Czechoslovakia established non-communist governments. Four months later, the Berlin Wall fell and made possible the reunification of Germany. In December, Gorbachev met with President George H. W. Bush in Malta where the two addressed the possibility of Russia's membership in the General Agreement on Tariffs and Trade (GATT). At the summit, Gorbachev promised not to send troops to repress independence movements in the Baltic States, and Bush promised not to send support to these movements.

58. Gorbachev, *On My Country*, 67–68. Also see Gorbachev, *Perestroika*, 17–25.
59. Cronin, *Global Rules*, 161.
60. D'Agostino, *Gorbachev's Revolution*, 98–99.

In the spring of 1990, the Soviet Union adopted a multi-party system and the Communist Party was dissolved. Republics in the Baltic, Central Asia, and Caucus Mountains region demanded independence. Gorbachev then proposed a treaty to allow former Soviet republics greater autonomy while remaining part of the union. By then, several republics had already declared independence and made it clear that they wanted nothing to do with Moscow. The crisis peaked in January 1991 as Soviet forces attacked Latvia's Ministry of the Interior. The world held its breath fearing civil war. Gorbachev denied responsibility for the assault, and kept his pledge not to use force to hold independence-seeking ethnic groups to the Soviet Union.[61]

Gorbachev welcomed Bush to Moscow as the two met in July 1991 to discuss arms treaties and other avenues of cooperation. Kremlin hardliners feared that Gorbachev was going to give the U.S. too many concessions and resented his plans to ask the West for financial assistance that would ease the Soviet transition to capitalism and democracy. Gorbachev had indeed crafted a daring proposal. He was prepared to give the West access to elite Soviet defense pants and research institutions in exchange for billions of dollars in aid that would convert defense industries to factories that produced consumer goods. The idea shocked Soviet officers who jealously guarded their nation's arsenal.[62] In August, extremists launched a coup against Gorbachev. The hardliners who occupied the Kremlin after Gorbachev was ambushed did not last long. Reformers led by Boris Yeltsin, who had left the Communist Party a year earlier and been elected President of the Russian Republic, gave the communist militants no quarter. With mass military and public support, Yeltsin thwarted the coup and saved Gorbachev's life.[63] Gorbachev returned to an unfamiliar Kremlin, as the Central Committee voted to dissolve itself, and Belarus and Ukraine were poised for independence.

As the Soviet economy continued to deteriorate, fuel and food shortages became acute. In October, Gorbachev pursued full membership in the International Monetary Fund (IMF), so that he could secure badly needed loans to help his country in its economic transition. Taking its lead from the U.S., the IMF refused to give the Soviet Union full membership, but made it an associate. With only an associate status, the Soviet Union did not qualify for IMF loans. Secretary of State James Baker and others thought that perhaps the U.S. could help Gorbachev with a Soviet Marshall Plan. Devout cold warriors rejected the idea as they felt it would prolong the Soviet's collapse.[64] In the

61. Karklins, *Ethnopolitics*, 106–07.
62. Coleman, *Decline and Fall*, 339.
63. Volkogonov, *Autopsy*, 515.
64. Anderson, P. J. *Global Politics*, 48.

end, there was only humanitarian and technical aid, but no Marshall Plan. The mortally wounded communist juggernaut was allowed to die.

In the Land of Lenin

The notion that the U.S. should get sole credit for the collapse of the Soviet Union fits neatly into the myth that the U.S. prevailed because of its moral superiority. History, however, is not so clean. Having been to Russia four times, twice when it was communist (1989 and 1991) and twice when it was a republic (1992 and 1993), I had the opportunity to see that the "evil empire" was not categorically Satanic. When I saw the condition of life in Soviet villages and cities, I saw a world in want. The assertions that the Soviets were always poised to put the world under Moscow's heel made no sense. Surely, the Soviets could have blasted the planet to pieces, but it is doubtful that they could have occupied it. The Cold War had imposed a terrible burden on Russians who had not yet recovered from the excruciating hardships of Stalinism and WWII.

During my first two trips, I travelled as a tourist, making my way with friends to Nakhodka, Irkutsk, Novosibirsk, Moscow, Novgorod, Leningrad, Donetsk, Kharkov, and Lugansk. I am still overwhelmed by the beauty of Siberia, the hospitality of my hosts, and Russia's historical splendor. My companions and I visited museums, monuments, and wandered through market places and neighborhoods of interest. We met people who wanted desperately for us to help their families immigrate to the United States. We met people who cautiously initiated conversation, and, in broken English told us how wonderful it was to meet Americans. They gave us gifts on the spot—whatever they happened to have in their bags—a piece of fruit, a book of poetry. We also met people who made an industry of following tour buses and preying on distracted travelers by stealing their wallets and other valuables. We met "entrepreneurs" who wanted us to buy them American alcohol and cigarettes from special state stores, the *beryoshka*, so they could resell their treasures on the street for grossly inflated prices.

On my second trip to the Soviet Union, I befriended a translator who wanted to organize an exchange. She would teach where I taught for six months and I would teach for six months at the University of Rostov. Thus, in the spring of 1992 Lyudmila taught in California, and in the fall, I taught in Rostov-on-Don. In the summer of 1993, I returned to Rostov to visit friends. By that time, Russia had been radically transformed by capitalism and mafia activity. The state economy had collapsed suddenly, leaving strong men and those with access to rubles and hard currency to legally and illegally monopolize shops and industries.

The Russia in which I traveled in 1989 and 1991 was a military powerhouse, but it was a nation that was shedding old skins. There was already a McDonalds and Pizza Hut in Moscow, and tourism from the West was a growing industry. Many of the people I met were card-carrying communists out of necessity to obtain certain jobs. I rarely met people with the slavish devotion to communist ideology that I was taught drove Russian mentality.

The vast majority of people I met were not interested in exporting Marxist revolutions. They had doubts about Moscow's quest for empire. Their interests were the interests of my own friends and family. They wanted to work in their fields, earn decent wages, enjoy life, and care for their families. Russian boomers impressed me with their knowledge of history, literature, and language. They often made a point to say that they rejected the propaganda that all Americans were monsters, and they readily compared their war with Afghanistan with the U.S. war against Vietnam. On a few occasions, when the vodka flowed freely, my travel mates and our Russian hosts resolved that the people of the United States and the Soviet Union had no quarrel with each other. We agreed that American Caesars in the Pentagon and Russian Czars in the Politburo created more conflict than was reasonable. We agreed that life was about love, cooperation, and mutual respect.

Very few Russians I met were dazzled by Gorbachev. Decades of deprivations had propaganda made them cynical and hopeless. Opinions about Gorbachev boiled down to economic security. Glasnost and perestroika had terrific consequences for countries in the Eastern Bloc, but they failed to produce the goods and services Soviets so badly needed. At times, water was shut off for hours, even days. At times buses did not run and car parts were not available for months. Orphanages were over-crowded and shops were chronically short of foodstuffs and household items. Hospitals re-used needles and were often in disrepair.

Russian streets told the story of change between 1989 and 1993. During my first trip, I walked streets that were daily swept clean, and rode subways through stations adorned with chandeliers, stained glass, polished marble, murals, and everywhere the face of the Bolshevik hero, Vladimir Lenin. The cities were void of commercial advertising. Instead, billboards and the sides of buildings featured artwork proclaiming the glory communism and hope for world peace. If there were homeless, they were not visible in public. The only beggars I encountered were elderly men and women who stood outside churches, praying and begging for kopecks (pennies). They were often blind or missing limbs. They were the generation that fought the Nazis.

By 1993, the scenario had changed. There were homeless people in the subway and rail stations. Women and children begged for food on the streets.

Crime soared and the police were overwhelmed. The official crime rate per capita had more than doubled since 1989, with homicides rising from 6.3 per one thousand inhabitants in 1987 to 21.8 in 1993.[65] In the summer of 1993, I encountered one of those statistics. The train my friend and I were traveling from Rostov to Moscow was delayed near a river crossing. The police were clearing up the remains of a woman who had been tossed, naked, from the proceeding train. The *provodnik* (conductor) told us that the police said the woman was probably a prostitute or a rape victim. Passengers exchanged their thoughts only in hushed tones. My friend cautioned me that open discussion was risky as trains were always full of mafia who preferred, and were ready to enforce, the silence of witnesses.

In 1993, gangsters brazenly fought for control over newly created businesses and banks, while government officials helped themselves to wealth through corruption.[66] The mafia controlled everything from heating fuel to heroin. The streets were not so clean. People lucky enough to own a car frequently left their jobs to taxi people in what was a lucrative, unregulated private business. While not driving, car owners routinely hired people to guard their cars against theft. In the wake of the state's collapse, professionals, including teachers, doctors, and engineers, set up "shop" on the street. There, they would sell jeans, shoes, watches, candy, perfume, and cigarettes ostensibly legally imported. The billboards that once sanctified Lenin were replaced by ads for Marlboro, Coca-Cola, and Gucci. Casinos and prostitution proliferated.

Life that was once cheapened by political repression and chronic mismanagement of resources became cheapened by capitalism and violent competition for scarce or novel resources. Few in the new republic were prepared for the shock wave of privatization that hit Russia in the 1990s. The "classless" society all of a sudden had a very visible poor and a very visible rich.

I tried at times to image that Russia was going to invade the U.S. and rule the world, but it was too bizarre. In 1993, bullet holes from WWII still pocked buildings, people still relied on horse drawn carts in small towns where roads were unpaved, and the earth still yielded human bones and war debris left in battle fields all along the Eastern Front. The Soviets suffered far greater losses than the U.S., and so recovery was far more monumental. At the peak of German occupation, the Nazi army controlled territory roughly the size of the U.S. from the Atlantic coast to Chicago. While about 350,000 Americans died in the war, an estimated 26.6 million Soviets died.[67]

---

65. Gilinskiy, "Crime," 262.
66. Handelman, *Comrade Criminal*, 3.
67. Zubok, *Failed Empire*, 1. Also see Ellman and Maksudov, "Soviet Deaths," 671–80.

Americans like to think that the Soviet Union collapsed because communism is an untenable economic system. However, any economic system that was as burdened by the scale of recovery from war as was Russia, would have staggered, not sprinted towards prosperity. In addition, any economic system that is required to sustain an empire consisting of populations that do not want to be controlled will ultimately fail to provide for its own people. The Soviets spent a fortune on defending, policing, and subsidizing the Eastern Bloc for 45 years. Resources that could have been spent on infrastructure, the production of food and necessities, education, and health care were diverted away from the country with disastrous consequences for both those who sincerely believed in a socialist utopia and those who did not.

The Spiritual Atheist

As a good communist, Gorbachev was not expected speak in spiritual terms about the world, but he did. His statements about the opportunities to create a more cooperative and humane world order in the wake of the Soviet collapse convey a belief in God, and a matured spirituality. A decade after he was driven from office, he intoned as would a prophet against the world's hypocritical concerns about a crisis of values. He observed the world and assessed its progress since the collapse of Soviet communism. The collapse was supposed to usher in a new era of international cooperation and virtue, but that was not forthcoming. He asserted that, "Many so-called new values are more life justifications for egoism and self-serving behavior, for pride and ambition, for money-grubbing and unrestrained consumption," and added that this degenerated humanity, "God's highest creation."[68]

These words echo the critiques of both capitalism and communism that spiritual leaders offered throughout the Cold War. They are not the words of an evil emperor. They confirm that God speaks through the most unexpected prophets, including "the other," our "enemy."

Gorbachev stated that, his reforms "started precisely with a reexamination of moral values and the need for everything to be ruled by criteria common to all humanity."[69] He revealed that the quest for the core principals of human equality drove many Marxists and atheists to reread the Sermon on the Mount.[70] Gorbachev found that Marxism was compatible with the Gospel and Buddhism inasmuch as they all criticized the accumulation of earthly

68. Gorbachev, *My Country*, 268–69.
69. Gorbachev and Ikeda, *Moral Lessons*, 65–66.
70. Matt. 5–7.

treasures and invited people to share their resources and to treat others as equals. He found religious intolerance barbaric, and yearned for a world order based on mutual reverence for universal principles such as good will and respect for human dignity. Individualism and materialism, he held, created a moral crisis In Western civilization. "Western bourgeois civilization," he stated, "cannot necessarily provide spiritual guidelines for the future," because, of its obsession with wealth, hedonism, and indifference to others' needs.[71]

The spiritual and philosophical aspects of Gorbachev's agenda were not widely publicized during the twilight of the Soviet empire. Media coverage of Gorbachev's reforms marginalized Gorbachev's prophetic aspect. The dominant American narrative told us that Gorbachev's reforms were purely pragmatic. By stripping the prophetic essence from his reforms, Americans could view the Soviets as pathetic losers in the Cold War, and also leave the question of their own moral conduct during the Cold War in the margins of history. Despite lingering cynicism about the former Soviet Premier, I believe that Gorbachev was sincere when he wrote:

> Considering past history and events which have unfolded quite recently, it can be said that the Soviet Union was willing to find a way to arrive at genuinely democratic and peaceful international relations. In the West, particularly in the United States, no such willingness existed. In the Soviet Union the new thinking and the foreign policy based on it had already put the new approaches into actual, material practice and had already applied the corresponding methods for resolving problems. In contrast, when the United States spoke about the new world order it essentially meant a continuation of its previous policy with some corrections in methodology. The United States viewed the end of the Cold War as the removal of many substantial obstacles on the road to obtaining long-standing goals of American policy.[72]

I was in the audience at the Masonic Auditorium in San Francisco on October 1, 1995 listening to former President George H. W. Bush, former British Prime Minister, Margaret Thatcher, and Mikhail Gorbachev discuss global affairs. In discussion at the State of the World Forum, the three addressed global changes and how to best manage international affairs. At various points in the conversation, it seemed as though Gorbachev was the odd man out. Thatcher was sometimes dismissive of his remarks, and Bush offered little insight to what leaders of the twenty-fist century should be thinking about, claiming difficulty with "the vision thing." Bush and Thatcher were polite on the whole,

71. Ibid.
72. Gorbachev, *On My Country*, 210.

but their condescension towards Gorbachev's advocacy of a larger role of the United Nations in peace-keeping and creating conditions wherein peace is likely to prevail was apparent. Thatcher argued that the United Nations should not replace the Anglo-American dominance in world affairs because the U.S. and Great Britain tend to bear the largest burden for defense and aid to struggling nations. She stated:

> Do not use the United Nations for something for which it was not founded. You have 170 nations. They don't all agree that democracy is the best way to conduct affairs. They don't all have the same view of human rights as we have. You can't put executive decisions into their hands about war and peace. What you can use them for—and they're excellent at—is for famine relief, for help to peoples who need it. And they're marvelous at that and they've done wonderful work in Africa, and we should enhance their capability of doing that . . . [73]

Gorbachev saw the United Nations as a facilitator of international collaboration in economic and political problem-solving, not just as an agency for disaster relief, but the Anglo-American Caesar did not agree. Thus, with the Cold War behind us, we live with the paradox that for the U.S. to lead the world towards democracy, it must limit what others have to say about it.

Boomer's Cold War experiences reveal that it is possible to be a very religious nation, yet not a very spiritual one. They teach us that religion and moral principles can be co-opted by the state. They teach us that we can look a prophet in the face and see a demon, and look a demon in the face and see a prophet. Those who currently wage war on terrorism have appropriated God for their cause. Like the cold warriors, they bid us to decide whether Caesar's religion enriches our spirituality and love of neighbor, or simply enriches Caesar.

---

73. Thatcher, "Margaret Thatcher Highlights." video.

13

Post-Cold War Caesar

Cultural War

IN 1991, THE PATH to an American-led new world order had been cleared of Soviet landmines. The communist beast had perished, leaving Americans with the critical decision of whether the U.S. would help to create a world that would be truly democratic in its distribution of sovereignty and resources, or, instead, augment empires, enrich the fortunes of the few, and fortify the authority of an elite. Throughout boomer's lifetime, Americans spent enormous fortunes on defense and rationalized exceptions to civil rights because the world is a dangerous place. Americans consistently saw themselves as the remedy and not the cause of the danger.

At the turn of the twenty-first century, we elected our first baby boomer presidents. Neither one retreated from the charge to advance Caesar's empire, nor did they relax the religious rhetoric that had brought so many to high office. The 1992 race for the White House was the first post-Cold War presidential election and was exuberant in religious tones. "Never before," wrote columnist William Safire, "has the name of God been so thoroughly invoked, and never has this or any other nation been so thoroughly and systematically blessed, as in the 1992 campaign."[1] Family values and prayer in school figured in public debate as readily as taxes and defense spending. At the Republican National Convention, Pat Buchanan said that there was a "religious war going on in this country" that was being waged "for the soul of America."[2] Denouncing abortion, militant homosexuals, and feminists, Buchanan called for voters to restore America's place as the world's champion of Judeo-Christian values and beliefs.

---

1. Safire, "God Bless," A23.
2. Buchanan, "Cultural War," 39.

After the Republican National Convention, Bush attended a "National Affairs Briefing" in Dallas at which Jerry Falwell, Pat Buchanan, Phyllis Schlafly, and Christian conservatives gathered to instruct preachers on the issues and how to get congregants to vote for Bush. Reverend Donald Wildmon, President of the American Family Association, declared that, "If Bill Clinton goes to the White House, he'll take all his friends, the homosexuals, the abortionists, and the pornographers," and Buchanan cried that the removal of prayer from public schools led to urban barbarity.[3] Voters were leery of Clinton's character, as he had "dodged the draft" during the Vietnam War and cheated on his wife.

Despite their touting of religious credentials to prove their fitness for high office, neither Bush, Clinton, nor Ross Perot offered explicit scriptural exegesis when they took positions on militarism, debt, deregulation, and trade. Politicians and pundits reserved the harshest moral judgment for personal matters such as sexual conduct rather than for matters of state.

In the end, Bush got 60 percent of the evangelical vote, but only 38 percent of the popular vote, giving Clinton the White House.[4] In the subsequent five presidential elections, evangelical voters continued to give roughly 75 percent of their votes to Republican candidates, while Jews gave Democrats about 73 percent of the votes, and Catholics were evenly divided in party allegiance.[5] The outcome showed a gradual list to the right, whereby evangelicals and Catholics who were once mostly Democratic in 1960 had by 2004 became more Republican.

Brother Boomer Bill

Clinton's 1992 campaign message was largely about the economy. He sounded the alarm that something was wrong in Washington, because, "1 percent of America's people at the top of the totem pole now have more wealth than the bottom 90 percent," and that, "For the first time in a decade personal income in our country as a whole fell last year."[6] Clinton criticized Bush for reducing taxes as a way to stimulate businesses, arguing that "trickle down" economics did not work. To keep jobs in the U.S. and to keep American industries competitive in the global market, Clinton proposed government subsidies

---

3. Suro, "1992 Campaign," lines 75–77; 90–96.
4. Wilcox, C. "Premillennialists," 27.
5. Pew Research Center, "How the Faithful Voted," table.
6. Ifil, "1992 Campaign," lines 20–28.

for industrial modernization and worker training, and that subsidies should come from new taxes on the rich.

In his acceptance speech, Clinton announced a "New Covenant, a solemn agreement between the people and their government based not simply on what each of us can take but what all of us must give to our Nation."[7] He mocked Bush's fumbling of "the vision thing," and quoted the Bible stating, "Where there is no vision, the people perish."[8] His vision, "a place called hope," was an America that paid decent wages to the working class, gave everyone medical care and outstanding public education, reduced middle-class taxes, and ended discrimination of all kinds.

Christian conservatives were irritated by Clinton's remarks. With stunning hypocrisy, Jerry Falwell said that Clinton was "manipulating the Holy Scripture for political purposes."[9] Pat Robertson declared that Clinton's New Covenant was "pseudo-Christianity," that bordered blasphemy.[10] Clinton, a self-declared born-again Christian, wrote that his theological views were profoundly influenced by Jesuit instructors at Georgetown, who taught respect for the world's religions, and by historian Carroll Quigley, who imparted a sturdy appreciation for the advantages that pluralism offered civilization.[11] As Arkansas' Attorney General, Clinton thwarted the Christian Right's agenda by withholding support for legislation that would outlaw pornography, homosexual acts, and impose a $1,500.00 tax on couples who cohabitated outside the sacrament of marriage.[12] The Christian Right never forgot these things.

Clinton's liberalism on social matters offended the Christian Right. He prohibited the military from probing into individuals' sex lives to determine whether they were gay, and supported the right to abortion. He did not, however, disappoint Caesar on the economic front. Remember, Clinton signed legislation that repealed the Glass-Steagall Act, thus allowing investment banks, commercial banks, and insurance companies to merge, and he did so after Wall Street spent about $1.2 billion dollars on lobbying and campaign contributions after Clinton took office.[13] After telling voters that he would be

---

7. Clinton, "Address Accepting," lines 65–66.

8. Prov. 29:18. Clinton quoted the King James Version of Proverbs. The RSV states, "Where there is no prophecy, the people cast off restraint." That people perish for lack of restraint in want and temper seems to be a reoccurring theme in boomer's lifetime.

9. Menendez, *Evangelicals*, 158.

10. Domke and Cole, *God Strategy*, 5.

11. Clinton, *My Life*, 69–81.

12. Ibid., 246.

13. Sanders, *Our Revolution*, 201.

the Robin Hood to right the wrongs of pecuniary poaching, he gave a nod and a wink to Caesar's monetary marauders.

Wheelin' and Dealin'

Clinton supported the North American Free Trade Agreement (NAFTA), which reduced trade barriers and tariffs between the U.S., Mexico, and Canada. In 1993, he signed the agreement that created the World Trade Organization (WTO). Members of the WTO include former communist nations into its ranks, who helped create trade agreements and resolved disputes. The WTO embraces principles of fair trade, including justice, sustainability, and the dignity of workers are core values.[14] The charter of the WTO reads like a a Catholic epistle on social justice. It is globalism with a happy face. It is not, however, the Kingdom of God. The WTO has been criticized by many of its member nations of exploiting developing regions and for being dominated by the interests of developed nations.[15]

One of the most important policy changes Clinton undertook concerned U.S. relations with communist China. After trading with China since 1971, the U.S. imposed sanctions in 1989, following the Chinese government's massacre of hundreds of pro-democracy demonstrators in Tiananmen Square. Some believed that if China were given financial incentives, it would swiftly embrace human rights and democracy.[16] In Executive Order 12850, Clinton established seven human rights conditions for grating China most favored nation status. Subsequent haggling over these conditions wore down the U.S. will to wait for China to meet the conditions before the U.S. granted it most favored nation status.[17] In 1995, China joined the WTO.

Some Americans perceived China's new status as a threat to national security and domestic employment. The road to trade with China was not always silky, but many saw windfalls on the horizon of trade. McDonnell Douglas, producer of U.S. fighter jets, sold machinery to China, but discovered in 1995 that its materials were being used at a cruise missile plant. A federal grand jury indicted McDonnell Douglas for violating export laws.[18] Despite complaints about Chinese manipulation of their currency, lack of human rights, and use

---

14. World Trade Organization, "A Charter," 6–8.
15. Hopewell, *Breaking the WTO*, 4–6.
16. Rice, "Promoting the National," 55.
17. Harrison, J. *Human Rights Impact*, 104.
18. McGregor, *One Billion Customers*, 180.

of toxins in their products, U.S. trade with China remained brisk well in to the twenty-fist century.

The American-Chinese romance was tainted in 1995 when details regarding Chinese espionage in the 1980s came to light. China had stolen nuclear secrets from the weapons lab in Los Alamos, New Mexico, which were used to put China's development of miniature nuclear weapons on par with the U.S.[19] China also transferred nuclear technology to developing nations in the 1980s. Hoping to counter balance the West's possession of weapons and keep its enemy India in check, China supported the development of nuclear weapons in Pakistan, North Korea, and Iran.[20] Given the history of Arab resentment towards U.S. conduct in the Middle East, political experts found the distribution of nuclear weapons to Islamic states especially troubling.

Clinton had spoken for campaign finance reform during his first term. Nonetheless, Clinton took hundreds of thousands of dollars from corporate entities. Goldman Sachs gave Clinton $375,000 and the U.S. backed their purchase of $2 million in Mexican bonds, and Archer, Daniels, Midland donated $271,000 while Congress maintained an annual subsidy of $500 million for the company to produce ethanol.[21] In the wake of Clinton's re-election, Congress investigated allegations that the Democratic National Committee had accepted $3 million dollars in contributions from Chinese sources.[22] Republicans were poised for litigation over the matter, but retreated in their own interest. At that time, the Senate was investigating the Coalition for Our Children's Future (CCF), which spent about $700,000 on ads that attacked Democratic candidates. The CCF had links to Triad Management Services, a front organization of billionaires David and Charles Koch, who supported right-wing candidates. An investigation of Triad would have exposed the tainted financial operations of all campaign spending, and so, Republicans offered a deal: Democrats would back off the CCF and Triad investigation, and Republicans would back off of Clinton.[23]

Globalism and the Poor

Globalism is not inherently evil, but those who control its treaties, contracts, and loans have an economic advantage which may or may not be exploited.

19. Gup, *Nation of Secrets*, 142.
20. Kan, S. *China and Proliferation*, 3–18.
21. Kobrak, *Cozy Politics*, 162.
22. Heineman, *God is a Conservative*, 242.
23. Palast, Greg. *Best Democracy*, 113.

Caesar has already hinted that globalization is not about equity. When Clinton signed the North American Free Trade Agreement (NAFTA), in 1994, he indicated that it represented a commitment to help other nations grow and to lift workers up.[24] The stories of Mexico and China suggest that globalization actually does improve the lives of people living in developing nations, but that the bounty wrought by trade agreements does not always find its way into the hands of the poor.

NAFTA brought jobs and consumer good to Mexico, as foreign investors increased their pre-NAFTA investments from $4 billion to $13 billion after the deal.[25] Yet, NAFTA has not achieved what it promised in the way of decreased emigration, increased wages, and rapid economic growth. Instead, the poverty rate in 2013 was the same as it was in 1994, and the economy grew at a rate of just 1.3 percent while other Latin American countries grew at a much greater rate.[26] While creating an increase of jobs in car manufacturing in Mexico from 120,000 to 550,000, NAFTA has resulted in the loss of about 350,000 auto manufacturing jobs in the United States.[27] In addition, NAFTA has not displaced Mexico's drug cartels, which operate in over 1,000 cities in the United States.[28] Drug trafficking between the U.S. and Mexico yields between $18 and $39 billion annually, which is far more than the $11 billion Mexico earns yearly in its tourist industry.[29] Drug cartels not only murder their rivals and law enforcement, they terrorize witnesses to their crimes, judges, and news reporters on both sides of the border.

Globalism has had a similar impact on China. As American retailers sought consumer goods manufactured cheaply in China workers, nearly 3 million workers in the U.S. lost jobs between 2001 and 2003.[30] By 2010, China was the second largest economy in the world, and in 2010, the U.S. national debt was roughly $14 trillion, including nearly $1 trillion owed to China.[31] China's membership in the international market lifted many out of poverty, but the distribution of wealth has favored those—largely communist Party officials—who own property and stocks. Between 2002 and 2007, the poorest 10 percent saw an income increase of 46 percent while the richest 10 percent saw

24. Clinton, *Public Papers*, 337.
25. Edmonds-Poli and Shirk, *Contemporary Mexican*, 308.
26. McBride and Sergie, "NAFTA's Economic Impact," Lines 130–37.
27. Ibid., lines 75–81.
28. Longmire, *Border Insecurity*, 131.
29. Kan, P. R. *Drug Trafficking*, 54.
30. Turkson, *Save American*, 155.
31. Uradnik, et. al., *Battleground*, 389.

an increase of 94 percent.[32] Ten years after China joined the WTO in 2002, the poverty rate declined. Yet, as of 2010, there were 150 million Chinese living on less than $1.90 per day, and nearly 360 million living on less than $3.10 per day.[33]

Globalization has brought work to many around the world while not necessarily delivering justice. Critics of globalization have argued that U.S. industries abroad exploit workers by forcing them to work in filthy and hazardous environments, extorting sexual favors, prohibiting unions, mandating overtime, and paying low wages.[34] Proponents of globalization argue that work in an American sweatshop is better than being unemployed. However, doubling the amount of crumbs distributed to the working poor is not the same thing as giving them a loaf of bread.

Lots of boomers thought Clinton was a good president because during his administration, job growth was 30 million, while the median income increased by 17 percent.[35] We learned, however, that in Caesar's empire modest gains by the masses must be paid for by spectacular gains for the very rich. During Clinton's administration, the richest 1 percent grew by about one third, reaching the equivalent of 21 percent of all income in the U.S.[36] The real impact of his policies, including the repeal of the Glass-Steagall Act, decreased taxes on capital gains, and other deregulations would not hit us until years after brother Bill's presidency was over.

Genocide

Some folks felt the consequences of Clinton's policies in immediate and savage ways. In 1993, a civil war ended in Rwanda without reconciling warring factions of Hutus, who controlled the government, and Tutsis, a minority who resented Hutu dominance. In the wake of the war, Hutu leaders called for the death of Tutsis. By that time, United Nations troops were already in Rwanda and reports of atrocities were gripping world attention. The world looked to the U.S. to act, but in the spring of 1994, Clinton wavered, saying that the killing was a lingering effect of the war and random acts rather than a calculated

---

32. Li and Sicular, "Distribution of Household," 9–12.
33. Shapiro, J. "China is Still Really Poor," lines 20–29.
34. See Ross, *Slaves to Fashion*, which exposes the dehumanizing and exploitative practices in modern factories, and tells the story from a Jewish perspective with tenderness and compassion for human dignity.
35. Noah, "Can Bill Clinton Defend," lines 37–42.
36. Ibid., lines 67–73.

genocide.[37] In meetings of the United Nation's Security Council, the U.S. had expressed its belief that security forces should be withdrawn as it seemed they were unable to do their job and be properly protected. The Pentagon also opposed both military and humanitarian intervention.[38]

During his campaign, Clinton declared support for interventions to protect people in times of civil war. Then, in May, 1994, he issued the Presidential Decision Directive 25, which said that such interventions would depend on certain conditions, including proof that American interests would be advanced by the intervention.[39] America's reluctance to intervene caused other nations to hesitate, and suggested the U.S. placed self-interest above humanitarianism.

In the end over 800,000 people died.[40] When Clinton finally acted in 1994, he asked Congress for $320 million in aid, and sent 4,000 troops to assist in the distribution of humanitarian aid to assist refugees, but not to keep the peace. Congress approved only $170 million in aid, and critics argue that if Clinton had ordered troops earlier to assist the United Nations in keeping the peace, the cost would have been just $30 million.[41]

As corpses piled up in Rwanda, another genocide was under way in the Balkan Peninsula. Ethnic tensions between Serbian Christians and Muslim populations in Bosnia and Kosovo erupted in mayhem in April, 1992. By the summer of 1993, most Americans were aware that Serbia was engaged in ethnic cleansing, and about one half of Americans wanted the U.S. to intervene.[42] Again, the Clinton administration waffled on sending forces. In the debate over intervention, Clinton often invoked images of the Holocaust, and lauded those who had defeated the Nazis.[43] Sentiment, however, is not action. The U.S. ultimately deployed its military and sent humanitarian aid in 1995, only after considerable international duress. The Serbian war against Muslims left over 200,000 dead and created two million refugees.[44] The war was especially vicious for women, as Serbians created rape camps where 50,000 women and girls were tortured and sexually enslaved.[45]

In 1998, Clinton went to Kigali, Rwanda and gave a speech in which he offered an apology. He acknowledged the evil of the genocide in which

37. Burkhalter, "Question of Genocide," 46–47.
38. Ibid., 47.
39. Ibid., 48.
40. Troy, *Age of Clinton*, 127.
41. Power, *Problem from Hell*, 364–85.
42. Sobel, "Trends," 251–52.
43. Steinweis, "Auschwitz Analogy," 282.
44. Shay, *Islamic Terror*, 25.
45. Kennedy-Pipe, *Kosovo Tragedy*, 73.

executioners working with machetes and clubs did their work faster than Nazi gas chambers. He announced that he was present to "pay the respects of my nation to all who suffered and all who perished in the Rwandan genocide."[46] He regretted that, "We did not immediately call these crimes by their rightful name: genocide," and vowed to "increase our vigilance and strengthen our stand against those who would commit such atrocities in the future here or elsewhere."[47] Clinton's solemn notes on the Holocaust and "confessions" rang with political correctness, but they did not expunge the possibility that U.S. tolerance of crimes against humanity is linked to the material value of intervention.

During the Cold War, the U.S. vowed it would intercede when peril faced vulnerable populations. Some think that U.S. interventions around the world will be more selective because there are no countries that present a serious threat to the United States.[48] Many believe that Islamic terrorism replaced the Soviet menace. There are other threats to peace and global brotherhood, however, as some Caesars are willing to sell their own country for personal gain.

In 2001, Bill and Hillary Clinton created the Clinton Foundation, to "unlock human potential through the power of creative collaboration."[49] The non-profit organization dispenses charitable donations from individuals, governments, and corporations to fight hunger and disease around the world. Its philanthropic motives however, have been challenged. According to Peter Schweitzer, journalist and co-founder of the Government Accountability Institute, the Clinton Foundation peddles access to U.S. law-makers and political favors to foreign businesses.

Schweitzer points to a pattern of gift-giving which seems to coincide with major business deals that arouse concern for national security. In 2009, for example, the Russian mining company, Rosatom, acquired 17 percent of the Canadian mining company Uranium One, which mined uranium from Texas to North Dakota, and which wanted to expand its U.S. operations. Expansion required approval of the Senate Committee on Foreign Investment in the United States, and many on the committee did not trust that a company with Russian stockholders could be trusted to respect American nuclear interests.[50] As the committee debated the matter, Russia acquired 52 percent of Uranium One, and its chairman, Ian Tefler, quietly channeled $2.3 million to the Clinton Foundation. In 2010, the Canadian charitable foundation, Salida Capital,

46. Clinton, "Text of Clinton's Rwanda," lines 11–12.
47. Ibid., lines 45–53.
48. Carey, H. F. "U.S. Domestic," 72–82.
49. Clinton Foundation, "About Us," line 1.
50. Schweitzer, *Clinton Cash*, 40–49.

received an anonymous donation of $3.3 million and gave about 25 percent of it to Clintons' Foundation; then, Bill made $500,000 for a speech he delivered in Moscow.[51] A year later, Salida Capital appeared in Rosatom's annual report as a subsidiary of the Russian state nuclear agency. Many suspected it was the same organization in Canada that gifted the Clintons.[52] Secretary of State, Hillary Clinton, initially gave Uranium One's interest in mining U.S. soil a frosty reception, but by October, she had warmed and helped to secure Senate approval. By 2013, Russia owned all of Uranium One.

The Clinton Foundation assisted Haiti's recovery from the 2010 earthquake and has provided resources to fight AIDS in Africa. The Foundation radiates zeal for making the world a better place. Schweitzer observed, however, that the beneficiaries of the Clintons' statecraft are often oligarchs in developing nations who pocket vast sums of foreign aid while oppressing their own people, and the corporations that win the right to extract resources in the oligarch's impoverished country. It is difficult to understand why nations, such as India, that have such an appalling amount of poverty would donate to an entity, such as the Clinton Foundation, when they could directly invest the capital in their own hospitals, food distribution, and sanitation projects.[53]

Christianity is deeply concerned with how the faithful identify with others, and it seems that at dazzling heights of political power, people stop identifying with the common masses who offer them their trust, and start to identify more with the world's rich and powerful who offer them their favors. At this altitude, fellow countrymen and national borders fade from view, and all that remains are the interests of global aristocracy who no longer identifies with those who are condemned to struggle for a decent human existence, because Caesar does not believe they are worth a revolution in values. Like Clinton, George W. Bush wooed voters with his born-again Christian faith, but left the nation no closer to the Kingdom of God in the post-Cold War world than did brother boomer Bill.

---

51. Becker and McIntire, "Cash Flowed," lines 35–38.

52. Schweitzer, *Clinton Cash*, 50–52.

53. Ibid., 59–78. Schweitzer traces the flow of cash from Indian sources to the Clintons during the debate over whether the U.S. should lift restrictions on nuclear trade with India. As Senator of New York in 2006, Hillary allegedly leveraged a favorable outcome for India. One of India's "vehicles" of "donations" was Sant Chatwal, who pleaded guilty in 2014 to illegal campaign contributions. See Clifford and Buettner, "Clinton Backer," lines 19–30.

Brother Boomer George

In his book, *A Charge to Keep*, George W. Bush spoke about his about how being a born-again Christian changed his life. He stated, "I could not be governor if I did not believe in a divine plan that supersedes all human plans," and explained how his faith freed him to "put the problems of the moment in proper perspective."[54] Bush said that he believed God wanted him to be president, and many of his supporters felt like he had been chosen for a divine cause.[55]

In 2000, G. W. Bush made his way to the Oval Office via a Supreme Court decision. As Florida's votes were too close to call, Al Gore (D-TN) requested a manual recount of ballots. Bush sued to block the recount, and Florida Secretary of State, Kathrine Harris, declared Bush the winner. Gore appealed, and the Florida Supreme Court ordered a manual recount. Bush then went to the Supreme Court, which gave him his victory.[56] Some hold that if the ballots had been recounted, Bush would have won. Others believe that the balloting itself was tainted by way of preventing minorities form voting in Florida.[57] Bush's re-election in 2004 brought additional charges of fraud.[58] In Ohio's Democratic precincts voting machines were insufficient in number. In some counties, votes for Bush miraculously appeared after all the precincts finished their reports, and in one county, 4,258 votes were cast in a precinct that had only 800 registered voters.[59]

As Governor of Texas from 1994 to 2000, G. W. Bush gave the world his version of God's divine plan, and it was not pretty. He presided over an economy flush with the fortunes of oil, cattle, and defense industries. During his tenure, Texas had the fifth highest poverty rate and the highest levels of air and water pollution in the country.[60] Bush entered the governor's office with a $7.5 billion dollar surplus in Austin's treasury and left a deficit of nearly $12 billion left six years later.[61] Under his watch a record-breaking 152 prisoners were executed.[62] In 1998, 27.5 percent of Texans aged 19–65 and 39.1 percent

---

54. Bush, G. W. *Charge to Keep* 6.
55. Smith, G. S. *Faith and the Presidency*, 406.
56. Green, A. *Understanding*, 121. Also see Bush v. Gore 531 U.S. 98 (2000).
57. Joseph, A. L. *Dynamics*, x.
58. Miller, *Fooled Again*, 19–20.
59. Fitrakis, et. al. *What Happened* documents voting fraud in Ohio and speaks to its implications.
60. Redd, *Blood on Their Hands*, 24.
61. Ivins, *Shrub*, xxvii.
62. Prejean, *Death of Innocents*, 241.

poor children were without health insurance. Texas State Commissioner of Health, Dr. William Archer, III claimed that 589,000 children were eligible for Medicaid, but were not enrolled because politicians did not want to "rock the boat" of a balanced budget.[63]

Bush took pride in the "Texas miracle," which saw a 20 percent increase in the passing rate of high school students who took the Texas Assessment of Academic Skills test (TAAS), and accountability numbers nearly doubled between 1994 and 1998. The massive improvement in reading, writing, and math, however, turned out to be smoke and mirrors.[64] Test data had been manipulated by omitting scores from certain segments of the student population. In spite of the schoolhouse shenanigans, Bush appointed the man credited with the "miracle," Ron Paige, his Secretary of Education.

The words that leap to my mind when reading George W. Bush's books, *A Charge to Keep* and *Decision Points* is "certainty."[65] George W. is a boomer who had terrific confidence in himself, his faith, and his instincts. He gives the impression that truths are rather self-evident, and that exploring the details with expert analysts is often unnecessary. He conveys the idea that once his mind is set, there is no anxiety and no need to reconsider. The source of Bush's certainty appears to be his rock-solid faith in God—a faith he declares "frees" him:

> My faith frees me. Frees me to put the problem of the moment in proper perspective. Frees me to make decisions that others might not like. Frees me to do the right thing even though it may not poll well. Frees me to enjoy life and not worry about what comes next . . . I live in the moment, seize opportunities, and try to make the most of them.[66]

Bush's response to the 9/11 attacks and Hurricane Katrina seem to indicate that he spoke truly about decisions others might not like. Whether his responses to crises were merely expedient can be argued. Whether his responses were those of a deeply spiritual man, and whether they brought us any closer to the Kingdom of God is perhaps best left to the confessional.

---

63. Clymer, "Bush and Texas," lines 72–78.
64. Bovard, Bush Betrayal, 71–73.
65. *Decision Points* is a memoir in which G. W. Bush recalls pivotal events that shaped his character and approach to the world and its problems.
66. Bush, G. W. *Charge to Keep*, 6.

September 11, 2001

My experience of 9/11 was colored by the fact when it happened, I was living in San Francisco, had many Arab friends, and worked at a very liberal Catholic high school. At work, everyone was stunned by what they saw unfolding on television. "Those kids are going to remember where they were when those towers were hit," said teachers, "just like we remember where we were when Kennedy was shot." I agreed, but something was missing. America collectively and literally wept for days when JFK was murdered, but I saw very, very few tears on 9/11. At the time I wondered if society had become so desensitized and cynical about of war and terror that we were now incapable of the searing sadness that accompanies tragedy. I wondered too if, at some subconscious level, we understood that the attacks represented a day of reckoning for American imperialism.

The faculty organized an evening "teach-in" in which parents, students, and guests explored the history of and political tensions in the Middle East. It was well attended and appreciated. One of the most striking things about the experience was that everyone wanted to see the assault from all perspectives. We all felt the attack was outrageous, but we all wanted to understand it. We agreed that Americans had an obligation to grasp the source of the world's animosity towards the United States.

On 9/11, the priests at the school led prayers for our leaders, enemies and victims. These prayers were in sharp contrast to the vitriol in the press. Former Judge Jeanine Pirro, exclaimed that it was time to stop being politically correct and shed some blood. "We need to kill them," she said, "It's time for this to be over and stop sending American dollars to any Arab country that does not support this mission."[67] Media celebrity Ann Coulter wrote that the U.S. should invade the terrorists' countries, kill their leaders and force their people into Christianity.[68] *Time* magazine's Lance Murrow offered a shocking editorial, which called upon Americans to forget about healing and embrace rage and hatred. He thundered: "Anyone who does not loathe the people who did these things, and the people who cheer them on, is too philosophical for decent company."[69] By Murrow's standards Jesus would be "too philosophical for decent company." After all, Jesus did ask us to pray for our enemies and bless those who curse us.[70]

---

67. Nelson, C. C. "Fox News Host," lines 5–6; 19–21.
68. Little, *Us versus Them*, 224.
69. Murrow, "Case for Rage," 50.
70. Matt. 5:43–48.

America's reaction to 9/11 revealed a nation struggling to overcome its own mythologies. For generations, Americans have extoled the messianic quality of capitalism and the American way of life. Our leaders told us that we are hope of the world—the nation that all others look to for its gold standard of virtue. It was at the time, and still is to some extent, nearly impossible for Americans to believe that 9/11 was anything less than a summative rejection of America's identity. Despite their country's sins against decency and humanity at home and abroad, Americans were unable and unwilling to link the attacks to the nation's conduct abroad.

Following 9/11, the media steered us away from introspection that might have given us some understanding of the link between U.S. conduct abroad and what happened. Many Americans reflexively believed, as Bush told the nation, that the U.S. was targeted by people who hate American freedom and democracy.[71] It was a statement easily swallowed by millions of Americans who had never studied Middle Eastern history, Islam, or Arab culture and the West's impact on it. In his letter to America, Osama bin Laden, mastermind of the attack, ranted against American decadence and called the U.S. to forsake gambling, alcohol, and sexual promiscuity, and to submit to Allah. He also made clear that the 9/11 attacks were not just about freedom and democracy, but were in retaliation for U.S-supported oppression of Palestine, the presence of U.S. military bases in Saudi Arabia, and the U.S. sanctions against Iraq.[72]

The attack and the president's steady mantra for a war against terrorism diverted attention away from Caesar's assaults against public wellness. Receding into the background were Bush's whopping May, 2001 tax cut for the rich and the Enron scandal. Chaired by Ken Lay, a major donor to Bush's campaigns, the Houston-based Enron became outlandishly rich by manipulating electricity supplies in California, dishonest stock appraisals, shady trading in derivatives, and tax evasion. When Enron filed for bankruptcy in December, 2001, it held assets of $63.4 billion dollars.[73] Lay "earned" $100 million in the year Enron crashed, while its 5,000 employees lost their jobs and $800 million in Enron stock that they (unlike Enron executives) were forbidden to sell.[74]

---

71. Jackson, R. *Writing the War*, 54.

72. Bin Laden's, letter appeared in November, 2002. Ironically, it criticizes America for the same reasons that Americans criticize America, including its violations of human rights, its contamination of the environment, and its corruption of governance by way of lobbying and campaign contributions. See Bin Laden "Full Text."

73. Prins, *Other People's Money*, 162.

74. Corn, *Lies of George Bush*, 175–80. Enron and Bush were business allies in 1986, thought George W. denied he met "Kenny Boy" before 1994, and Enron shredded evidence of their malfeasance prior to a Congressional inquiry. Lay was found guilty of securities fraud, but died before sentencing. Also see Phillips, *American Dynasty*, 164–70 and

The consequences of 9/11 were immediate. In October, 2001, Bush sent troops to Afghanistan—a sovereign nation that had not declared war on the U.S.—because he believed that was where bin Laden was hiding. In the war that lasted until 2014, U.S. and NATO forces fought to purge Afghanistan of the Taliban, a political movement that sought to establish a fundamentalist Islamic state. At the time, I wondered whether Bush would kill bin Laden. The Bush and bin Laden families were friends and had a long legacy of business partnerships.[75] Like others, I found it odd that 140 Saudi nationals were flown out of the U.S. on 9/11, making their exit before the identities of the 19 hijackers, including 15 Saudi nationals, were made public, and while all commercial flights were grounded.[76] By the end of 2001, the mission to Afghanistan had become regime change.

As the twisted wreckage of the WTC was cleared, Bush, the Supreme Court, and Congress hastened to improve national security. On October 23, the House of Representative introduced the Patriot Act, and Bush signed it three days later.[77] In just six weeks following 9/11, Congress developed the bill, and passed it with 98 percent of Senate and 83 percent of House support.[78] It called for enhanced border security, increased surveillance, the removal of legal barriers to accessing personal records, and aggressive action against money-laundering. It vastly expanded the government's right to tap phones, intercept e-mails, and track Internet use. Many Americans embraced it without flinching, as they placed national security above their rights.

In the fall of 2002, the Bush administration released *The National Security Strategy of the United States of America, September* 2002 (NSS-02). It articulated the Bush Doctrine, identified the rationale for new national security policies, identified those strategies, and confirmed the Bush administration's belief that the U.S. should remain the preeminent world power. The new strategy was based on "nonnegotiable demands of human dignity," which included the rule of law, limited state authority, freedom of speech and worship, and respect for private property.[79] NSS-02 represents a grand plan for global stabilization that relies on the U.S. to foster the expansion of democracy around the

---

Robinson and Murphy, *Greed is Good*, 120. Incidentally, $63 billion dollars in 2001 was more than the individual Gross Domestic Product of 142 nations.

75. Kellner, *From 9/11 to Terror*, 119. Also see Unger *House of Bush House of Saud*, which gives this considerable attention to the details of this alliance.

76. Graham and Nussbaum, *Intelligence Matters*, 106.

77. The Patriot Act is also the *Uniting and Strengthening America by Providing Appropriate Tools Required to Intercept and Obstruct Terrorism Act of* 2001, Public Law 107–56, U. S. Statute 115 (2001) 272.

78. Final Vote Results for Roll Call 398, H.R. 3162, October 24, 2001.

79. Bush, G. W., *National Security Strategy*, 3.

world, and to meet the challenges of new threats, including terrorism.[80] The Bush Doctrine, justifies the use of preemptive strikes against nations who pose a threat to national security, and marginalizes the consent and participation of U.S. allies.[81]

Prior to NSS-02, on September 20, 2011, Bush announced, "Every nation, in every region, now has a decision to make: Either you are with us, or you are with the terrorists."[82] Bush's assertions about taking sides and the American right to launch preemptive strikes sent a clear message to the world that the U.S. would not wait for the assistance of other nations to resolve—let alone define the parameters and meaning of—international conflicts. The Bush Doctrine foreshadowed Bush's next move, which may have startled even the devil himself.

Just 72 days after 9/11, Bush met with Secretary of Defense, Donald Rumsfeld and inquired about existing plans to invade Iraq. Bush urged swift and drastic measures because terrorists were on the loose. In 2002, he asked Congress to double the budget for Homeland Security, because Iraq intended to use its "stockpiles" of weapons of mass destruction against the U.S. and its allies.[83] He said that Hussein was going to give biochemical toxins to terrorists. In his speech announcing his intent to invade Iraq, Bush made clear that the U.S. going to remove Hussein from office."[84] It was a blatant assault against national sovereignty, and a violation of Just War principles.

Evangelical Christians rallied around the President. Pat Robertson of the Christian Coalition labeled Islam "a bloody, brutal type of religion," while Billy Graham's son, Franklin, puffed that Islam "is an evil and wicked religion," and Jerry Falwell declared that Muhammed was a terrorist.[85] Deputy Undersecretary for Defense Intelligence, General William Boykin, said that, "The battle this nation is in is a spiritual battle, it is a battle for the soul . . . the enemy is a guy called Satan," who wanted to "destroy us as a Christian army."[86] The rhetoric conjured images of medieval Crusades. Pope John Paul II urged Bush to restore Iraq's sovereignty and to join other nations in negotiations for peace.[87] Among Christians, evangelicals were among the most enthusiastic supporters

---

80. Dunmire, *Projecting the Future*, 20–22.
81. Rupp, *NATO After 9/11*, 100–12.
82. Bush, G. W. "Address before a Joint Session," September 20, 2001, lines 96–97.
83. Bush, G. W. "Address before a Joint Session," January 28, 2003, lines 222–65.
84. Bush, G. W. "Address to the Nation on Iraq," lines 56–60.
85. Baumgartner, et. al., "A Clash," 173.
86. Froese and Mencken, "US Holy War," 103.
87. John Paul II, *Address of Pope John Paul II*, 4.

of the war with 87 percent backing the U.S invasion.[88] Protestant, Orthodox Christian, and Jewish religious leaders wrote dozens of statements criticizing the war for its reliance on violence as an instrument of foreign policy and for its disregard for what the global community thought about how to respond to Saddam Hussein.[89]

Bush held that God wanted him to fight terrorism and tyranny in Afghanistan and Iraq.[90] When pressed to explain the certainty of his holy war, he baffled seasoned advisors telling them that he was operating on instincts.[91] The mission got dark real fast. During the war, U.S. forces found no weapons of mass destruction and public support waned. By December 2008, nearly 90,000 Iraqi civilians had perished in the war and more than two million were displaced. In addition, 117 British troops had been killed along with 4,209 Americans and another 167 U.S. soldiers had committed suicide.[92] The loss of resources and good will was significant, as was the torture of prisoners and war-profiteering. Indifference to the horror was staggering.

Nice Rug

One hundred days following 9/11, Bush and his wife Laura invited reporters into the Oval Office to see the room-sized rug they had specially-made for the President. They chatted gleefully about how its design featured the Texas Lone Star. Bush quipped, "all in all, it's been a fabulous year for Laura and me . . . It's a joy to walk in here every morning, realizing that I'm the President of the greatest country on the face of the Earth."[93] A year after the U.S. invasion of Iraq, Bush narrated a slide show of his first term at a formal event for journalists. He clowned, peeking under furniture and chirping, "Those weapons of mass destruction have to be around here somewhere . . . Nope, no weapons over there . . . "[94] Lots of wounded veterans and families of those killed in the war did not see humor.

Bush's mother, Barbara Bush, apparently shared her son's lack of empathy. In an interview on *Good Morning America* aired on March 18, 2003, the former first lady said that media coverage of the war should censor the

---

88. Marsh, *Wayward Christian*, 5.
89. Pew Research Center, "Religious Groups Issue," sample of 30 statements.
90. MacAskill, "George Bush: God Told Me," lines 7–13.
91. Cashman and Robinson, *Introduction to the Causes*, 336.
92. Robben, "Mimesis in a War," 151.
93. Bush, G. W. "Remarks on the New Oval Office," lines 1–5; 48–50.
94. Rountree, *Chameleon President*, 30.

carnage. "Why should we hear about body bags and death . . . Its not relevant," she whined; "So why should I waste my beautiful mind on something like that?"[95] In October, 2013, Rupert Merdoch, Donald Rumsfeld, and Joe Lieberman, and other Washington insiders gathered at the New York Plaza Hotel to honor and roast Dick Cheney. The jovial crowd joked about torture, waterboarding, and war crimes.[96] The comic relief offered the nation's enemies one more example of America's Christian reverence for life.

The cost of waging war in Iraq and Afghanistan topped $3 trillion dollars, which accounts for enhanced security in foreign embassies, troops, weapons, supplies, and foreign assistance, but does not account for rebuilding or long-ranged veteran care.[97] For a few, the war was a jackpot: Halliburton (former employer of Vice-President Dick Cheney) gained $17.2 billion in a no-bid contract; DynCorp netted 1.4 billion for security training; Washington Group International made $931 million from maintaining oil rigs; Environmental Chemical got $878 million for its clean up services; International American Products collected $759 million for providing electricity; Perini Corporation (led by Senator Diane Feinstein's husband, Richard Blum), earned $650 million for its clean-up efforts; and, URS Corporation (another Blum entity), collected $792 million.[98] War delivered $6.6 billion to the Carlyle Group, an investment firm, in which the Bush family did business.[99] Carlyle's investors included the bin Laden family, friends of the Bush family, who sank millions into funds tied to aerospace and defense.[100] The Carlyle Group severed ties with the bin Ladens as the prospect that they would benefit handsomely from U.S. military campaigns against terrorism created a potential public relations disaster.[101] The Saudi defense minister had allegedly given $6 million dollars to charities that funded Osama bin Laden and al Qaeda, which meant that if the Saudis were to make a pile of money on the wars and interventions sure to follow 9/11, it would appear that Osama had done his family a great favor by attacking the United States.[102]

95. Rich, *Greatest Story*, 76.
96. Keneally, "Dick Cheney Roasted," lines 1–15.
97. Stiglitz and Blimes, *Three Trillion*, 9.
98. "25 Most Vicious," slides 2–27. Also see Chatterjee, *Iraq, Inc.* for a look at how private companies have made fortunes by doing what soldiers once did for themselves, and by inflating the cost of their services.
99. Baker, R. *Family of Secrets*, 475.
100. Ruppert, *Crossing the Rubicon*, 127–33.
101. Bernardo and Weiss, *Citizen in Chief*, 70.
102. Marrs, *Terror Conspiracy*, 249–50. *Inside Job* (Marrs), argues that Bush and his associates had incentives to cooperate with assailants, including: creating a rational for regime changes, increasing control over global oil supplies, and reducing civil rights.

War is terribly expensive, and tax breaks to the wealthy meant less money for military ventures. The government had to cut corners. Armored vehicles were in short supply, leaving soldiers exposed to enemy fire.[103] A Pentagon study found that 80% of the deaths resulting from injuries to soldiers' torsos could have been prevented by Kevlar vests that were "too expensive" to adequately distribute.[104] In 2003, the Pentagon petitioned Congress to end the soldiers' bonus pay of $75.00 per month for combat duty, and the $150.00 per month pay for families separated by troop assignments.[105] The pay reductions were rejected, but the Pentagon found other ways to reduce military expenses, including the closure of commissaries and the reduction of transportation funds for soldiers on leave.

Adding shame and obscenity to the war, U.S. soldiers engaged in depraved acts against humanity in their treatment of prisoners at Abu Ghraib. They posted images of their victims on the Internet. They showed naked men smeared with feces, hooded prisoners attached to electrodes, and nude prisoners piled in pyramids. Prisoners were deprived of sleep, put in stress positions for hours, raped, and forced to masturbate in front of others.[106] Like images from Vietnam and Latin American wars, the pictures told the story of the soldiers' obsession with sex and torture, but this time around, things were different.

Atrocities at Abu Ghraib were committed while women were on watch. Condoleezza Rice was our National Security Advisor, the Director of Abu Ghraib was Brigadier General Janis Karpinski, and one of the assailants was Private Lynndie England. The photos mocked feminist claims that the world would be a kinder and gentler place with women in charge. Abu Ghraib also confirmed that America's claim to be the world's champion of human dignity and decency—a thousand points of Christian light to all nations—was vain and vulgar.

Griffin, *New Pearl Harbor*, presents disturbing evidence of conspiracy such as the delayed response of defense jets, collapse patterns of the WTO, Building 7, and the Pentagon. Rich, *Greatest Story Ever Sold*, reveals how FBI agents with incriminating information were prevented from pursuing suspects prior to the 9/11 attacks.

103. Bugliosi, *Prosecution of George Bush*, 39.
104. Moss, G. D. "Pentagon Study", lines 1–6.
105. "Pentagon Seeks Cut," lines 1–10.
106. Danner, *Torture and Truth*, 1–9.

Perfect Storm

In his second term, Bush was given a huge opportunity to demonstrate his compassion and Christian charity. On August 25, 2005, Hurricane Katrina slammed in to Gulf Coast. The storm claimed over 1,800 lives, left $108 billion in damages in its wake, and displaced over one million people. In New Orleans, where 67 percent of the population was African American and 38 percent lived in poverty, Katrina was especially brutal.[107] As the hurricane advanced, Bush was vacationing in the Southwest. Bumbling rescue efforts and his delayed presence in the city was seen as evidence that the born-again executive cared little for the least of his brothers and sisters.

At the urging of the Federal Emergency Management Agency (FEMA), Mayor Ray Nagin of New Orleans called for the voluntary evacuation of New Orleans on Saturday, August 27th. The following day, after speaking with Bush and Louisiana Governor Kathleen Blanco, he issued a mandatory evacuation notice. Roughly 80 percent of New Orleans' residents left the city, but hundreds of thousands stayed behind. Many did not own a car.[108] Survivors lived for days atop roofs and in the Superdome without adequate food, medicine, and sanitation.

At the helm of FEMA, which had been absorbed by the Department of Homeland Security after 9/11, was Michael Brown. He was a friend of the Bush family with limited credentials for directing national emergency relief. He had been an inspector of Arabian race horses, a lawyer, a public relations assistant, and had worked in the Washington office of Dresser Industries.[109] Brown got his job when his friend, Joseph Allbaugh left the position. Allbaugh also knew little about emergency management, but got the job as a token of Bush's appreciation for his performance as Bush's campaign manager.[110] The cronyism produced fatal outcomes.

On Monday, August 29th, Bush declared emergency disasters in Louisiana, Mississippi, and Alabama, then called the Secretary of Homeland Security, Michael Chertoff, not to discuss the storm, but to discuss immigration.[111] As winds of over 140 mph ravaged New Orleans and massive flooding was underway, Bush delivered a speech in Arizona about Medicare reform. The following day, fires erupted in New Orleans as the water rose. Communication, electricity, and plumbing systems were still down. Hospitals and clinics

---

107. Levitt and Whittaker, "Truth Crushed," 1–21.
108. Brinkley, *Great Deluge*, 626–67.
109. Baker, R. *Family of Secrets*, 487.
110. Ibid., 478–79.
111. Brinkley, *Great Deluge*, 629.

were overwhelmed. Over 100,000 people were crowded into shelters and other facilities above water. Bush visited San Diego to give a speech on August 30th. On Wednesday, August 31st, he surveyed New Orleans by plane. "It's devastating," he said, "It's got to be doubly devastating on the ground."[112] Bush found his way to the ground on Friday, September 2nd. By then 6,500 National Guard troops were in New Orleans, and victims were still stranded. The city festered with toxic air and flood waters that smelled of chemicals, mildew, rotten vegetation, excrement, and decomposing corpses.

In the storm's aftermath, people pointed fingers. Nagin and Blanco were criticized for not forcing evacuation sooner. The the Army Corps of Engineers derided politicians for not maintaining New Orleans' levees. Government officials said they were not warned of the storm's potential severity and meteorologists spat objections in reply. Brown blamed state and local personnel for their slow response, and, Chertoff blamed Brown. A Senate hearing on New Orleans' response to Katrina revealed that the city did not have adequate evacuation plans and that evacuation and relief were muddled by unclear protocols and chains of command.[113] Some even blamed the victims. Senator Rick Santorum (R-PA) suggested that people who do not evacuate when told to so should face penalties.[114]

Michael Brown stated that at the heart of the crisis there was no heart. He holds that Katrina was an example of how the public's well-being is routinely ignored by officials who care more about budgets, political favors, and business deals than people, and who allow their biases against certain socioeconomic groups to guide their thinking.[115] In the case of Katrina, indifference meant pretending to be prepared for disaster, and pretending to care when it struck.

At the onset of this book, I noted that I was inspired to write because many of my boomer peers had become cynical about life. Things did not turn out the way they thought things should turn out, and they are distraught. "Why bother to care or to be good," boomers grumbled, "when everybody else, including your own government and your own church, doesn't seem to give a damn?" Some have reached the conclusion that only nitwits and misguided idealists believe that spirituality has any real currency and meaning in the material world. Indeed, the term "faith-based" has been used so frequently

---

112. Ibid., 406.

113. See: Senate Committee on Homeland Security and Governmental Affairs, *Hurricane Katrina: Managing the Crisis and Evacuating New Orleans* 119the Cong., 2nd sess., February 1, 2006.

114. Gotham and Greenberg, *Crisis Cities*, 70.

115. Brown and Schwartz, *Deadly Indifference*, 13–14.

in tandem with the priestly view of God, that what was revolutionary about the rabbi Jesus of Nazareth seems locked away in a tomb near Calvary.

Jewish theologian William Herberg wrote that, "By every realistic criterion, the American Way of Life is the operative religion of the American people."[116] He observed that Puritanism had given the nation its sense of righteous judgment and that religious revivalism had given it a sense of urgency to act upon the world for its own good. Herberg's observations ring true, but they leave readers to contemplate what makes judgement "righteous," and what it means to act upon the world for "its own good." It is possible, after all, that both may be undertaken with something other than the Kingdom of God in mind.

Lots of Americans like to say that the U.S. is a Christian nation. Yet, many resist the heavy work of bringing the Kingdom of God to bear in their world, and then mock those who at least try to do so. In boomer's lifetime, America has fortified its standing as an empire at the expense the poor, the vulnerable, and perhaps even national sovereignty. Our nation's morality has become suspect in the eyes of world because we are willing to slay so many Isaacs for the sake of amassing power and wealth, and because we are so smug in our claim that we alone know what is best for the world. America, it seems, "knows" how to "save" the world, but not so much how to love it. The restoration of hope and spirituality will not come about because we have built a new church, enrolled our children in parochial academies, or given more money to charities. It will arrive when we have learned to be still, and when we happily spend time with the eternity that is already within us.

---

116. Herberg, "America's Civil Religion," 227.

14

In Excelsis Deo

Frog Soup

IT IS SAID THAT when a frog is placed in a pot of boiling water, it will panic and desperately try to escape death; but, when placed in a pot of cold water that is slowly heated to fatal degrees, the frog remains calm and unconcerned until the frog's nerves and muscles are too cooked to save it. Baby boomers were raised in a pot of cold water, which has been warming up since 1946. Boomers believed that the future was bright. We had confidence in our government as a fair and just arbitrator of rights, and as a public defender against the abuses of corporate power. We believed government would be transparent and honest. Things change. In 1958, 77 percent of Americans said that they trusted the government most of the time or always, and by 2015, just 19 percent felt the same way.[1]

As most of us swam in the cool waters of comfort and opportunity, Caesar snuck into the kitchen and raised the temperature. A regime change here, a Wall Street pillage there, made it difficult for the faithful to deny that we were asked to serve two masters, one spiritual and compassionate, the other materialistic and belligerent. It was also difficult to deny that democracy itself was losing ground, and not by accident.

In one of the most explicit, yet not widely known disclosures concerning liberty and citizenship that appeared in boomer's lifetime was *The Crisis of Democracy, A Report on the Governability of Democracies*. The report was written by political and social scientists who submitted their work to the Trilateral Commission (TC), an organization formed in 1973 by David Rockefeller that pursues globalization dominated by corporate interests. The report observed

---

1. Pew Research Center, "Beyond Distrust," graph: "Americans Overall."

that in the 1960s, democracy had expanded as civil rights were enhanced and as publically-funded resources and services were increased.

The report lamented that these changes threatened democracy, as they imposed additional burdens on the public treasury and disrupted international trade.[2] In addition, these changes heightened the public's expectation that they could tell authorities what to do, which led to chaos in public agencies, including the military and higher education.[3] The authors were distressed as the rejection of government authority could neutralize the will of the people to fight wars. They asserted that, "A government which lacks authority and which has committed to substantial domestic programs will have little ability, short of cataclysmic crisis, to impose on its people the sacrifices which may be necessary to deal with foreign policy problems and defense."[4]

The report concluded that, in order to save democracy, the government had to moderate it, and to restore the authority of law-makers and experts who knew more than the general public knew about the right way to run a country. Caesar was listening and ready to impose sacrifices necessary to deal with foreign policy and other problems. After the Vietnam War, the military increased its control over news media's access to information.[5] In the 1970s and 1980s, Caesar increased the attention he gave to private interests at the expense of public concerns as he opened the door to an ever-increasing number of corporate lobbyists.[6] Subsequent to 9/11, Americas found their civil liberties, such as privacy and free speech, in jeopardy.[7]

Democracy might not survive the twenty-first century, but that is not the faithful's chief concern. The greater question is whether spirituality and the love of neighbor will survive. Ultimately, all forms of government compel their citizens to live in tension between what is owed the state and what individuals may reserve for themselves. The faithful have historically managed to keep their spirituality alive in the Roman Empire, the Soviet Union, feudal monarchies, colonial states, and in modern fascist regimes. It is possible that the faithful will someday lose the democracy they were once told was God's right hand. That loss may trigger new understandings of faith itself.

2. Crozier, et. al., *Crisis of Democracy*, 102–05.
3. Ibid., 113–15.
4. Ibid., 105.
5. Oates, *Introduction to Media*, 130..
6. Drutman, *Business of America*, 8–11.
7. Cassel, *War on Civil Liberties*, xii-xviii. Leone and Anrig, *War on Our Freedoms* also offers several insightful essays by lawyers, journalists and scholars concerning civil liberties and the lack of public discourse about how the war on terrorism has impacted them.

Like all manmade governments, democracy is an artifact of civilization that is destined to be only as righteous and just as are those who steer its course. The undoing of American democracy might disturb some people who associate their faith with their nation's agenda, and that is understandable. Yet, it is important to remember that the Kingdom of God is not the property of the state. The deterioration of democracy and all the privileges that go with it are difficult to bear for those who believed that God would bless America with prosperity and power if we were industrious, pious, and patriotic. Yet, the faithful are not called to be rich and to lord over the world, they are called to love and serve it.

When disillusioned about democracy and upward economic mobility, we boomers sometimes shook our fist at God. We did so because we diligently fought the "good fight" for civil rights, peace, and social justice and did not achieve the outcome for which we hoped. Instead, Caesar continued to wage imperious wars, hate crimes proliferated, and Wall Street ransacked the economy. For some, faith seemed to be an embarrassing mistake. Spirituality seemed puny and ridiculous in a world of mighty Caesars with their big science, big money, and big guns. In the world of reason, realism, and neurological explanations for the religious experience, spirituality seemed to be a waste of time and intelligence.

To be fair, Caesar cannot take full responsibility for the spiritual deficits in our world. We, the faithful, did our share of damage. Sometimes, we were the ones cranking the temperature under our own frog pot. We sometimes gave up on public discourse about faith out of fear that others would perceive us as fanatics. Sometimes we projected our own limitations on God, and expected others to gladly accept it. Sometimes we gave up on spirituality because, like kids disappointed by Santa Claus, we did not get the things for which we prayed. Some gave up on spirituality because they had the feeling that making the world a better place was a futile endeavor, or because they were frustrated by the thought that they were only ones who were trying to leaven the Kingdom of God into our world. These feelings are what I call "messianic fatigue," and it is a sign that we may have expected spirituality to do things in our world that it was never intended to do.

Messianic Fatigue

Lots of boomers suffer from messianic fatigue, or the exhaustion that comes from trying to be the world's savior. This malady of spirit is characterized by anger and despair over the fact that, no matter what we give to charity, how many degrees we earn in college, and how hard we work, things don't change;

our lives are still hard and the world is not fair. Victims of messianic fatigue are often cynical. They complain that regardless of what they do, the poor stay poor, the warmongers make war, corporations and banks get away with economic murder, and politicians still pee on our legs and tell us it is raining.

It is logical that boomers experience messianic fatigue. After all, we were told that we could and should save the world. We expected that when we worked hard and made sacrifices, we would see results. We expected that reason and the force of intellect would stimulate goodness. We expected our charity, mercy, and actions on behalf of peace and justice would yield dividends. It is possible that our messianic fatigue is due to erroneous presumptions and expectations about spirituality. Maybe our deepest spiritual lesson is to take solace and blessing in the fact that we are in the process of becoming the Kingdom of God and realizing our spiritual identities one day at a time. That is hard to do in a culture that fixates on measurable outcomes and finished products. Maybe the highest expression of spirituality is to keep on loving, keep on learning, and keep on improving ourselves knowing that we will never be perfect, and being content with the idea that we may do some good for others nonetheless.

It is possible that the faithful who have lost hope and inspiration feel this way because they have set their sights on a Kingdom of God that is too high to reach. As a child, my prayers were filled with petitions for the big stuff. A simple blessing on my parents was not enough. I wanted Johnson to end the war and UNICEF to end starvation.[8] We ascended the mountain tops with eyes on the clouds where the Kingdom of God might be, and so we could not see it God in the valleys. If we had we approached spirituality at a more humble elevation—that of family or local community plateaus—we might have more easily seen the presence of God. Big ambitions often cause people to look for God only in the spectacular. It begs the questions: Was Jesus' quiet forgiveness of the adulteress made trivial by his feeding of the multitudes with only a few loaves and a couple of fish? Is the act of giving a homeless man a coat diminished by the fact that one cannot personally house every homeless family in America?

Messianic fatigue takes many forms, but its principle feature is hopelessness. The weary have given up not only on the "good fight" on the national or global level, but at home as well. Messianic fatigue is expressed when parents

---

8. UNICEF stands for the United Nations International Children's Emergency Fund. My grade school classmates and I collected money for UNICEF on Halloween after our teachers gave us little orange UNICEF boxes for money. My peers and I could tell which kids came from wealthier families and neighborhoods by the amount of money somebody collected. I still remember the faces of kids who were ashamed by their small contributions.

allow their children to do whatever they want to do because they are too tired to fight their child's objections. It is expressed in our schools and universities each time teachers inflate grades and lower standards, because they are tired of wrongfully being accused of discrimination, or don't care about students that seem not to try very hard to learn. Messianic fatigue is manifest in every workplace where nurses, mechanics, drivers, accountants, technicians, and workers at all levels are silent in the face of incompetence and bullying, not because they think these things are acceptable, but because they are debilitated by the eternal mantra: "ya can't fight city hall."

Americans feel entitled to happiness, which we often see as feelings of joy and high energy. The faithful, however, should expect to feel exhausted in Caesar's world. Being exhausted is not the same as being spiritually depleted, but it seems the difference eludes us. Spirituality is hard work. It invites the faithful to *be* the love of God not in the abstract, but in the way our families, businesses, and public institutions need in order for them to become people-oriented instead of thing-oriented. Spirituality is not for wimps. It takes grit and guts to deny Caesar control over our hearts and minds. Living and working in a way that brings the Kingdom of God to bear in our world requires the resiliency to maintain our integrity in the face of social and institutional inhumanity, and relies on a loving community of mutual support.

Our Crummy Little Town

In Frank Capra's classic film, *It's a Wonderful Life*, the protagonist, George Bailey has big dreams.[9] He wants to shake the dust of his "crummy little town," Bedford Falls, from his feet and see the world. He doesn't want to work in his dad's bank, Bailey's Building and Loan. He wants to "build skyscrapers a hundred stories high" and "bridges a mile long." As he embarks on his honeymoon, he is met with a serious crisis. Uncle Billy misplaced $8,000.00 dollars that is owed to the state examiner. George cancels his plans and is devoured by stress, anger, and exhaustion as he tries to save the bank. The mean and miserly Mr. Potter, another banker, who wants to own everything in Bedford Falls, finds the money in a newspaper that Uncle Billy absent-mindedly left on his desk. He does not return the cash to its rightful owner. Baily's bank and family are headed for ruin. In despair, George wishes he had never been born, and contemplates suicide. He is rescued by Clarence, an angel, who escorts him through his past and shows him what life would be like for others had

---

9. *It's a Wonderful Life*, directed by Frank Capra (1947; Los Angeles, CA: Paramount Pictures, 2006), DVD.

he never been born. George's friends ultimately collect the needed cash, and Baily's bank is salvaged. The story ends, however, with no mention of Potter's culpability and thus, no restorative justice.

Every time I watch the film, my heart leaps for the goodness of George's family and friends, but I am miffed about the reality that justice was not done. For all viewers know, Mr. Potter got to keep the $8,000.00, which was more than twice the average American's income in 1947, the year the film was released. It just wasn't fair! George was rescued by charity, but the evil that threatened him and the community's well-being lived to strike another day. Capra's tale leaves us with the nagging paradox that even when justice is not achieved, it is still possible for goodness to prevail.

George Baily was blessed when his friends and family gathered the funds he needed, but his redemption—his renewed faith in the sanctity of life—was not achieved by the money. It came from realizing that life for others would have been very different had he never been born, and from realizing that life is about loving and being loved. It came from understanding that no man is an island and that spirituality draws us to community. George learns that there is something life-giving in the simple but virtuous choices he made. Potter lived another day to cannibalize his own community, but George Baily lived another day to love and care for it.

The Caesars and Potters of the world often prevail because they are exceptional at five tasks. First, they make business and political alliances with like-minded individuals, and purge from their ranks those whose views stray from their interests. Second, they know how to spin the truth, control the narratives that tell us what is real and meaningful, and discredit those who dissent. Third, they have no moral objection to dirty tricks and destroying their enemies by any means necessary. Fourth, they accumulate favors by distributing plum appointments, political favors, money, and business deals. Finally, they remain steadfast in their objectives regardless of the Isaacs that must be sacrificed.

The faithful often prevail because they are very good at five different tasks. First, they welcome and respect the perspectives of all stakeholders in matters, and collaborate in addressing their needs and concerns. Second, they value and seek the truth. Third, they work with their adversaries to find common ground and see that everyone has an honorable way out of conflict. Fourth, they demonstrate gratitude to others and extend charity without expectations. Fifth, they remain steadfast in their objectives regardless of whether their egos are bruised and their reputations are mangled by public opinion and the judgment of authority.

In my own spiritual journey as a boomer in the American empire, two lessons about spirituality and bringing the love of God to bear on earth seem especially poignant, and both involve dissent. The first lesson is that spirituality is not the same as doctrine or sentimentality. The second is that, in order to restore and invigorate spirituality, it is essential for the faithful to get off Caesar's treadmill as often as possible.

Doctrine and Sentiment

Though doctrines may be inspired by spirituality, they are not the same. Doctrines articulate the official beliefs and rules that are foundational to an institution. They are the material manifestations of Peter's paradigm. Their functions are to maintain consistency in institutional beliefs and practices, and preserve the hierarchy that operationalizes the institution. Doctrines represent how institutions interpret the truth. They establish the boundaries between those whose thinking is aligned with the institution's truth and those whose thinking is "heretical." Spirituality sometimes requires dissent from doctrine because institutional rules can be insufficient to the task of love. While doctrines may prohibit women from administering the sacraments, for example, spirituality demands that regardless of our gender or sexuality, we offer blessings to the sick, reconciliation to the offender, and confirm the presence of God in everyone.

Spirituality is also not the same thing as sentimentality. Sentimentality is emotional and nostalgic. It is easily manipulated and exploited. Sentimentality has played a large role in the American religious experience. The Great Awakenings and evangelical revivals pleaded with society to return to the "faith of their fathers." The yearning for those "simpler times" when folks were certain about right and wrong drove believers to preachers who had easy answers to tough questions. Many preachers have offered melodramatic and charismatic sermons that necessitated very little thinking. Magic is a close cousin of sentimentality, and some preachers have made fortunes by coaxing folks to send them money with more than a little hint that God will then heal or especially bless them because they did so.

The doctrinal approach to spirituality troubles the way of the heart, and the sentimental approach troubles the way of the mind. Strict adherence to doctrines might anesthetize our sensitivity to the contradiction between our espoused values and our own actions. Our ignorance warns us that we might miss the most profound spiritual experiences because we have made assumptions about others and will not let the facts of his or her life's journey inform our judgments.

The absence of scholarship in my "born-again" days killed the mysticism of faith and replaced it with tidy formulas. When I think of tidy formulas, I think of Donna Reed in a ruffled, pastel apron making cake from a box of ingredients. I do not think of the Lord of Creation who endowed human beings with just enough intelligence to wrestle with moral judgment, but not enough to fully comprehend the mind of God. With a cake mix that only required eggs, milk, and an oven set at 350 degrees, Donna was sure to bake a near perfect dessert. The Kingdom of God, however, is not a box of doctrines to which the faithful add compliance. It is love that makes a mess by forgiving those who persecute us, welcoming women to the ministry, embracing people we are not supposed to embrace, and tossing the money-changing tables into the air with righteous indignation. Had Jesus taken the cake mix approach to spirituality, he might have hurled a few stones at the adulteress and banished Mary as Peter requested. He did not.

My excursion into Christian fundamentalism taught me that religious sentimentality is often accompanied by arrogance. Emotionally charged prayer meetings left my brain awash in celestial serotonin and the happy hormones that are released when one is in a state of certainty and security. The rush of pleasure had a price. "Being right with God" often meant that I was right with peers who held certain beliefs about God, and that left me unable to see God wherever my peers did not see God. To sustain my credentials as a "born-again" Christian, I had to narrow God's access to me. It was not acceptable to welcome the spiritual wisdom of Native Americans, Jews, Buddhists, or atheists. God was treated like the exclusive property of Christian evangelicals, and that in itself makes God an idol, not God.

Off the Treadmill

Reclaiming and invigorating our spirituality requires us to get off Caesar's treadmill as often as possible. Caesar's treadmill represents the rituals and routines of life driven by material concerns and the anxieties of our own egos. It is sometimes compulsive activity done without thought or care. On the treadmill, we consume a steady diet of propaganda about our world and what we should value without necessarily taking time to assess the credibility and implications of what we are being told. The treadmill is also a psychological state that is characterized by a reflexive fear of others and the belief that we must maintain an aggressive posture in order to get what we need. As we keep pace with the machine, we consume things we do not need, waste things others need, and have little sense of what we need most of all. On the treadmill we keep pace with popular trends and opinions, and often lose sight of our own spiritual story.

It is important to get off the grid and take time to be still, quiet, and contemplative. This literally means shutting off the television, the Intent, mobile phones, and retreating from the din of neighborhoods, work, and family activity. In going off the grid, we grant ourselves permission to hear what our own sacred voices have to say about our well-being, our values, our actions, and our judgements. It is a time to be intuitive and introspective. In making ourselves absent to the world, we make ourselves present to ourselves.

Spirituality requires time and space away from the treadmill and off the grid. It is in the quiet that we may undertake honest inventories of ourselves. Sincere self-examination allows us to see how we have assimilated Caesar and what we expect to get from that. It allows us to identify why we do what we do and think what we think. It is a moment to re-calibrate our attitudes and values. The spiritual retreat, prayer, meditation, and counseling are tools for maintaining our sense of wholeness and integrity. These activities have the potential to recharge our spiritual batteries, and to clarify our personal relationship to the Kingdom of God.

Spiritual reflection invites us to think objectively about who we are, who we want to be, and what keeps us from being who we want to be. Objectivity is essential to cultivating spirituality. In his wonderful book of Toltec wisdom, *The Four Agreements*, Don Miguel Ruiz reminds readers that that our spirituality is often paralyzed because we take everything personally and believe that our assumptions about others are always true.[10] By not taking things personally and not making assumptions, the faithful give themselves permission to see the work of God in unexpected and even unorthodox ways. By releasing ourselves from taking things personally and making assumptions, we free ourselves from the tyranny of other people's judgments about ourselves, and from our own constant judgment of others.

Getting off the treadmill is a way to unpack the assumptions we make about the meaning of our lives and what we treasure most. Fearless personal reflection allows us to recognize the Isaacs in our own lives. It sheds light on why we readily sacrifice certain people while protecting others. It also illuminates the ways in which we allow others to make us the Isaacs in their lives. In our reflection, we might ask tough questions of ourselves: Do we contribute to the ruin of another's reputation? Do we use our positions to serve others or only our own interests? Are we fair to and patient with those who depend on us? Do we resent being asked to help or to conserve? If we had to describe our

---

10. Ruiz, *Four Agreements*, 30–49.

spirituality as prophetic or priestly, which would we be? What evidence would we offer to support our claims?

Going off the grid is no small matter. We regularly do not know that we are out of touch with our inner selves. This is true in part because we are distracted, in part because we are in denial of our own spiritual pain, and in part because we are driven to get things done and have lots of ways of compensating for fatigue, depression, and pain. We are often unaware of our own stress and unhappiness, and move mindlessly through our daily chores. People who are glued to the grid have often stopped listening to inner voices. Some are afraid that if they get off the grid, they will not know how to deal with pain and anxiety. This places them at risk for becoming reactionary and reckless without even knowing it. It also makes them vulnerable to living a life that is far from authentic because they have allowed others to write their life's script. Mindless of our place on the grid, we sometimes forget that we have choices, and that there are serious consequences to what may seem like a not so serious decisions.

To overcome the obstacles between ourselves and our spirituality, we sometimes need assistance. This is where spiritual directors, pastors, rabbis, study groups, and teachers may enrich our growth. As family members and friends, can nourish each other by explicitly creating a safe place to open our hearts and talk about our lives and what matters most to us.

Since we are creatures of story, it should be no surprise that we use them to not only explain our lives, but to find the way back to wholeness and love when we have lost the way. We learn about who we are and the world around us by listening to and telling stories. These stories concern our experiences, our struggles with life, feelings, beliefs, and relationships. The authenticity of our spiritual lives is in danger when we are not permitted to tell our stories and when Caesar imposes his narrative on our lives.

Telling stories is not always about finding answers to difficult questions. Sometimes it is about closing the emotional distance between people. Sometimes it is a way to collect new perspectives and ideas. Sometimes it is about clarifying common memories. Stories told between siblings and parents can be especially healing because, even though we may have grown up in the same family, we may have experienced things very differently. Those differences can unnecessarily alienate us from each other. Beautiful discussions and reflection happen because we have the courage to create a safe spaces where this can happen, and because we take the time and effort to tell our stories and listen to each other tell their stories.

One of the most challenging aspects of cultivating a spiritual family is that of letting go of one's ego. Building a spiritual family means taking risks in personal disclosures. It means learning to be humble about one's mistakes, weaknesses, and need for love. In a culture that glorifies extreme individualism—where men don't cry and where the strong devour the weak—it is not easy to choose vulnerability. Moreover, extreme individualism teaches us to pay more attention to the things that *set us apart* from others more than we pay attention to the things that *we have in common*. At times, I have felt tempted to mock the idea that I am very similar to others and that are very similar to me. I grew up in a culture that prized the things that set people apart from each other, even though most of those differences were superficial. Ego tells us that we must distinguish ourselves from others, yet spirituality invites us to find ourselves and to cultivate ourselves for very different reasons than to stand apart from the crowd.

Getting off Caesar's treadmill can take many forms. Book clubs that discuss multiple sources on a single issue or topic, and seminars facilitated by local spiritual teachers, civic leaders, and scholars can help folks improve their sense of what is going on in the world, and refresh their moral direction. Film clubs that study documentaries and feature films for insights to the human condition, and how our world is being impacted by human activity offer another venue of inquiry and conversation. These can easily be hosted in a church basement, community center, or someone's home. Starting study clubs at the local school where children and adults can gather to discuss what they encounter on television, the Internet, and news media can not only benefit participants, but can inspire changes in curricula that could be integrated into the classroom and religious sermons. Community service can be a way to get off the treadmill. Serving the poor at a soup kitchen or shelter places one in the presence of those who need us, and also in proximity to those who share our vision. Prayer circles and religious retreats are also places of spiritual respite, reflection, and stories.

We are accustomed to the treadmill, and so to jump off of it might seem a terrifying thing to do. The treadmill is safe and familiar. Lots of friends are there. Getting off the treadmill, however, can be a scared act of dissent. It is a sacrament we can administer to ourselves.

Bang, Bang, Jesus

Dissent from popular culture is seldom easy. As Christmas approached in 2015, I was reminded that dissent and moral boundary-making take lots of courage. On December 2, Syed Rizwan Farook and Tashfeen Malik shot and killed 14 people and wounded 22 others in San Bernadino, California. The assault was an act of terrorism, part of the assailants' commitment to Islamic jihad.[11] As the nation expressed outrage, many condemned religious teachings that glorify murder in the name of God. Some were more vitriolic, demanding that Muslims should never be allowed into the United States. Others snarled that some cultures should be destroyed because they breed violence through religion. I thought about the many festive holiday packages that were sitting beneath Christmas trees. I wondered how many contained toy guns and violent video games, ready to be enjoyed by children and adults celebrating the birth of Jesus.

I tried to reconcile the Christmas narrative with guns for presents, but I could not. I saw images of war, terrorism, gang violence, and assault rifles in the hands of depressed, angry, and alienated adolescent boys who punish innocents at places like Columbine, Colorado, and Newtown, Connecticut.[12] A most cynical image popped into my mind. At the manger where Jesus was born, the three wise men show up with their gifts of automatic rifles, stinger missiles, and napalm. Fighting Satan requires some serious fireworks. Mary is mortified. Joseph is confused, and the oxen and lamb run for their lives.

I mentioned my thoughts to others and was surprised by the reactions of people who said that it was unfair to compare a child's use of toy guns to a terrorist's use of real guns. I have trouble with the notion that there is absolutely no relationship between the way we play and the way we see the world. First, because studies tell us that violent video games increases aggression in children and diminishes their empathy for others.[13] Secondly, because the time invested in virtual terrorism and war games could be spent in social activities that build and enhance empathy, literacy, charity, artistic skills, physical fitness, and problem-solving abilities.

Some chided my disgust for the idea that violent toys make great Christmas gifts because I did not appreciate the conflict that follows when children do not get what they want from Santa Claus. This comment hit a nerve. How many children, I wonder, never learn moral restraint or even delayed gratification because their parents are afraid to say "no" to their children? Indeed, how many parents have surrendered their moral authority to their children because they cannot cope with conflict? How many have allowed their children to extort their indulgence in exchange for the child's compliance or affection? Lots of children grow up in families where this dynamic is called "love."

---

11. "San Bernadino Shooting," lines 1–14.

12. In, 1999, Dylan Klebold, age 17, and Eric Harris, age 18, killed 15 people and wounded 24 others at Columbine High School in Colorado. In 2012, 20-year-old Adam Lanza shot and killed 20 students and six adults at Sandy Hook Elementary in Newtown, Connecticut. See Follman, et. al., "A Guide" for data on mass shootings.

13. Anderson, C. et. al. *Violent Video*, 12.

The holiday hassle over guns reminds me of the cleft we have placed between our spirituality and the lives we lead. It reminds me that human beings are capable of rationalizing any combination of the sacred and the profane, and any contradiction. We are still a society fiercely committed to the idea that exposure to violent toys and entertainment does not socialize our children. If we *really* believed that, then there would be no outraged fathers across the land on Christmas morning when their sons opened gifts of baby dolls and tea sets. Toys, after all, don't have anything to do with our sense of self, right?

Caring about Caring

Lots of my boomer friends and I have spent hours trying to understand what the hell happened to our world and our lives. We wonder how the professions we chose became corrupted by a lack of integrity and senseless with greed. We wonder why our government, the people's guardian, has permitted private industry to cripple our wellness and economic stability. We wonder why public assistance failed to liberate people from poverty. We wonder when entitlement became the national religion for rich and poor alike. One friend, a former Peace Corps volunteer, lamented, "At some point we decided that we wanted to do something other than make the world a better place; we stopped caring about caring."

The question of what a person who cares can do in a world that seems to have lost its sense of caring is on the minds of believers and atheists alike. It is an enduring and universal problem in the human condition. There will always be Caesars who pirate the public treasury and rally their armies to fight for empire. For every Caesar who falls, there are legions behind him waiting to take his place. What is a person who cares supposed to do when Caesar is inevitable? The short answer to the question is: "Don't be a Caesar."

The longer version of the answer is to do the heavy lifting of spirituality. Get off the grid, think about who we are, get busy with leaning more about the choices we have, and endorse revolutions of values. Caring about the world requires nourishment, so we might need to change our circle of friends, move away from those who drag our spirits down, and move towards those who lift us up. Like George Baily, we never know how much of a lifeline we are to others. We never know which campfire chat or embrace will be the one to walk somebody back from the abyss of hopelessness and self-destruction. We never know which act in the workplace will be the one that triggers reform, or which vote will determine whether justice will prevail. Spirituality is an ecosystem of love and empathy that is maintained by the willingness to be the person our egos would never let us be.

Mrs. Timmerman's Dream

In May, 1999, I had a remarkable dream, the kind that stays with one for years and is just as vivid in recall as it was in the original dreaming. In this dream, I found myself at Patrick Henry High School in Minneapolis, from which I graduated in 1976. I entered the school, hoping to find familiar faces and to explore the changes that had inevitably occurred since I left. The school was dark and seemed vacant and hollow. Security cameras and metal detectors stood watch in the doorways. I made my way past the pitch black classrooms and stairwells, groping, walking cautiously, then came upon an illuminated room on the Morgan Avenue side of the building near an entrance.

I entered what appeared to be a greenhouse, a glass classroom with ornate frosted windows and filigree in the ceiling. Outside, the limbs of maple and elm trees quivered against the gray November sky. The room was filled with shelves and tables, heaped with books, drafting tools, paint, brushes, and art supplies. Students dressed in t-shirts, bell-bottoms, and jean jackets busied themselves. I recognized some of the students, my former classmates. My memories were judgmental as I noted the pot-smokers, the drop-outs, and girls who got pregnant before they graduated. They talked, laughed, and directed each other as they drew and constructed things. The activity was frenetic and clamorous. At first, I saw no teacher. Then, I saw Mrs. Timmerman, one of my former English teachers, bending over projects and chatting cheerfully with students.

Mrs. Timmerman, or "Timmy" as my pals and I affectionately called her, was perhaps five feet tall in heels. She was a gracious woman and ever-joyful. She encouraged students routinely and was quick to praise even the smallest of efforts. I was so happy to see her. We spoke about my work as a teacher as students buzzed from one table to the next and the air crackled with conversation. I said to her, "This school has become so dark, so cold, like a prison! With all these kids in disarray—all this chaos—how can you be so patient and give these students so much love?"

Mrs. Timmerman grinned broadly and her eyes twinkled, "Oh, I don't have to produce all the love, I just have to be a conduit of it."

Struck dumb by her insight, I stood speechless.

Snow had begun to fall during class. As the first powder of the season covered the grass and lined the branches of the trees with white ribbons, the students began singing Christmas carols. They sang "Angels We Have Heard on High." Mrs. Timmerman and I joined in the harmonies. We smiled at each other as we loudly sang "Gloria in excelsis Deo."[14] As I sang, I began to cry. I sobbed and shook.

---

14. "Gloria in excelsis Deo" is Latin for "Glory to God in the highest."

When I woke from the dream, my throat was tight and aching, like I had been holding back a great sorrow. My eyes were full of tears. I went through the next several days seized by the dream.

A theological reading of the dream might say that Mrs. Timmerman was calling upon me to be open to the love of God or higher power, which is given as a gift and ever available. Such a reading might be an invitation to always remain open to a higher power and to imitate the patience, charity, and caring that are modeled in the Gospels and sacred teachings. A theological interpretation might suggest that the Kingdom of God is already part of who I am, and to activate it, I need only allow love to flow through me without interference from my judgements, fears, and assumptions.

A secular interpretation of the dream suggests that in order to love and bring goodness to others, we need to suspend our egos. In the dream, Timmy felt safe enough to let the students work independently. She was confident that she had given them what they needed to create something that evidenced their skills, and did not need to dictate what that would be. The students also felt safe and confident. They behaved as do teenagers who, given the opportunity to collaborate and be creative, are boisterous, yet, they did not abuse their autonomy and were quite productive. The lesson was not so much about the finished product. The constant cycle of innovations and critiques at each table were themselves learning outcomes. The lesson was about the value of process. It was about incremental progress guided by a leader who loved rather than feared, and who valued her students' capacity to experience and discover more than their ability to parrot.

America in boomer's lifetime has exemplified the best and worst of humanity. We have put men on the moon, conquered diseases, revolutionized communication, and sent millions of volunteers to all corners of the world to help victims of poverty and natural disasters. We have also contaminated our natural habitat, brought nuclear terror to the world, cultivated violence as a way of life, made sexual commodities of our bodies, and allowed the caliber of public dialogue to slip into mediocrity and vulgarity in our classrooms and mass media.

We are a society in which political correctness clouds our vision in one direction, and vanity and greed clouds it in the other. We are a generous nation whose charity has been a poor substitute for badly needed changes in our economic paradigm. We are in so many ways no different from other empires who rose and fell throughout the ages. We are a nation populated by people who believe in God, who are sometimes uneasy about the prospect that God loves people we don't love.

In the end, Florence Timmerman, who appeared in my dream to comfort a troubled teacher, had an important message for those struggling with faith and spirituality. All of creation, every ecosystem, plant, animal, individual, family, community, and nation will live or die according to how we respond to the message. We are called to be, and we have the honor of being, a conduit of the Kingdom of God, a conduit of love, no more, and no less.

Bibliography

"A Brief History of U.S. Unemployment." *The Washington Post*. http://www.washingtonpost.com/wp-srv/special/business/us-unemployment-rate-history/. Accessed March 7, 2017.
A Patch of Blue, directed by Guy Green (1965, Burbank, CA: Warner Bros., 2003), DVD.
Adams, Michael C. C. *The Best War Ever: America and World War II*. Baltimore: Johns Hopkins University Press, 1994.
All the President's Men. Directed by Alan Pakula. (1976. Burbank, CA: Warner Home Video, 1997), DVD.
Allison, William Thomas. *My Lai: An American Atrocity in the Vietnam War*. Baltimore: Johns Hopkins University Press, 2012.
Alperhovitz, Gar. *The Decision to Use the Atomic Bomb*. New York: Vintage, 1995.
Amnesty International. *Deadly Force: Police Use of Lethal Force in the United States Executive Summary*. New York: Amnesty International USA, 2015.
Anderson, Craig, Douglas A. Gentile, and Kathrine Buckley. *Violent Video Game Effects on Children and Adolescents: Theory and Research*. New York: Oxford University Press, 2007.
Anderson, Hannah M. ed. *State Profiles: the Population and Economy of Each U.S. State*, 8th ed. Lanham: Bernan, 2016.
Anderson, Paul. A. "Decision Making by Objection and the Cuban Missile Crisis." *Administrative Science Quarterly*, 28, (1983) 201–222.
Anderson, Peter J. *The Global Politics of Power, Justice and Death: An Introduction to International Relations*. New York: Routledge, 2005.
Angell, Ami and Rohan Gunaratna. *Terrorist Rehabilitation: The U.S. Experience in Iraq*. Boca Raton: CRC, 2012.
Angresano, James. *A Corporate Welfare Economy*. New York: Routledge, 2016.
"Anti-Semitic Sermons Evoke Shock. Anger from Jews and Christians." *Jewish Telegraph Archive*, March 28, 1980. http://www.jta.org/1980/03/28/archive/anti-semitic-sermons-evoke-shock-anger-from-jews-and-christians.
Apostolidis, Paul and Juliet Williams. *Public Affairs: Politics in the Age of Sex Scandals*. Durham: Duke University Press, 2004.
Appel, Edward. C. "The Perfected Drama of Reverend Jerry Falwell." *Communication Quarterly*, 35, no. 1 (1987) 26–38.

Appy, Christian G. *American Reckoning: The Vietnam War and Our National Identity*. New York: Penguin, 2015.
———. *Patriots: The Vietnam War Remembered from All Sides*. New York: Penguin, 2004.
Archer, Jules. *Breaking Barriers: the Feminist Revolution from Susan B. Anthony to Margaret Saner to Betty Friedan*. New York: Penguin, 1996.
Ashford, Nigel. "The Republican's Policy Agenda and Conservative Movement," In *The Republican Takeover of Congress*, edited by Dean McSweeney and John E. Owens, 96–116. New York: St. Martin's, 1998.
Atkin, Emily and Judd Legum. "Catholic Presidential Candidate Explains Why He Won't Listen to Pope Francis." *Think Progress*, September 24, 2015. http://thinkprogress.org/politics/2015/09/24/3704841/marco-rubio-pope-francis/.
Atkins, Annette. *Creating Minnesota: A History from the Inside Out*. St. Paul: Minnesota Historical Society, 2007.
Auerbach, Alan. J., Henry J. Aaron, and Robert E. Hall. "Corporate Taxes in the United States." *Brookings Papers on Economic Activity*, no. 2, 1983.
Bagdikian, Ben. *The New Media Monopoly*. Boston, MA: Beacon, 2004.
Baker, Dean. *The End of Looser Liberalism: Making Markets Progressive*. Washington, D.C.: Center for Economic and Policy Research, 2011.
Baker, Russ. *Family of Secrets: The Bush Dynasty, the Powerful Forces that put it in the White House, and What Their Influence Means for America*. New York: Bloomsbury, 2009.
Bakhash, Shaul. "The Troubled Relationship: Iran and Iraq, 1930–80. In *Iran, Iraq, and the Legacies of War*, edited by Lawrence G. Potter and Gary G. Slick, 11–28. New York: Palgrave Macmillan, 2004.
Balmer, Randall. *Redeemer: The Life of Jimmy Carter*. New York: Basic, 2014.
Bancroft, John. "Alfred C. Kinsey and the Politics of Sex Research." *Annual Review of Sex Research*, 15, no. 1 (2004) 1–39.
Barak, Gregg. *Theft of a Nation: Wall Street Looting and Federal Regulatory Colluding*. Lanham: Rowman & Littlefield, 2012.
Barkan, Steven E and George J. Bryjak. *Myths and Realities of Crime and Justice: What Every American Should Know*, 2nd ed. Burlington: Jones and Bartlett Learning, 2014.
Barkley Andrew and Paul W. Barkley. *Depolarizing Food and Agriculture: An Economic Approach*. New York: Routledge, 2015.
Barnes, John. *John F. Kennedy on Leadership: The Lessons and Legacy of a President*. New York: American Management Association, 2007.
Barry McGuire. *Eve of Destruction*. Dunhill D-50003. 331/3 rpm. Originally Released 1965.
Barry, Tom and Deb Preusch. *El Salvador, the Other War*. Madison: Resource Center, 1986.
Baumgartner, Jody. C., Peter L. Francia, and Jonathan S. Morris. "A Clash of Civilizations? The Influence of Religion on Public Opinion of US Foreign Policy in the Middle East." *Political Research Quarterly*, 61, no. 2 (2008) 171–79.
Baxter, Kylie and Shahram Akbarzadeh. *US Foreign Policy in the Middle East: The Roots of Anti-Americanism*. New York: Routledge, 2008.
Beavis, Mary. A. "The Kingdom of God, Utopia, and Theocracy." *Journal for the Study of the Historical Jesus*, 2, no. 1 (2004) 91–106.
Becker, Jo and Mike McIntire. "Cash Flowed to Foundation Amid Russian Uranium Deal." *New York Times*, April 23, 2015. https://www.nytimes.com/2015/04/24/us/

cash-flowed-to-clinton-foundation-as-russians-pressed-for-control-of-uranium-company.html?_r=0.

Beckwith, Francis and Todd E. Jones (Eds). *Affirmative Action: Social Justice or Reverse Discrimination?* Amherst, NY: Prometheus, 1997.

Belles, Nita. *In Our Backyard: Human Trafficking in America*. Grand Rapids: Baker, 2015.

Berg, Herbert. *Elijah Muhammed and Islam*. New York: New York University Press, 2009.

Berger, Albert I. *Life and Times of the Atomic Bomb: Nuclear Weapons and the Transformation of Warfare*. New York: Routledge, 2016.

Berlet, Chip and Matthew N. Lyons. *Right-Wing Populism in America: Too Close for Comfort*. New York: Gilford, 2000.

Bernardo, Leonard and Jennifer Weiss. *Citizen in Chief: The Second Lives of American Presidents*. New York: HarperCollins, 2009.

Billy Joel. *Allentown*. New York: Columbia 45 rpm. 1982.

Bilton, Michael and Kevin Sim. *Four Hours in My Lai*. New York: Penguin, 1992.

Bin Laden, Osama. "Full Text: Bin Laden's 'Letter to America.'" *The Guardian*, November 24, 2002. http://www.theguardian.com/world/2002/nov/24/theobserver. Accessed March 10, 2017.

Bird, Kai and Martin J. Sherwin. *American Prometheus: The Triumph and Tragedy of J. Robert Oppenheimer*. New York: Alfred A. Knopf, 2005.

Black, Edwin. *Nazi Nexus: America's Corporate Connections to Hitler's Holocaust*. Washington, DC: Dialog, 2009.

"Black Panther Party: Platform and Programs" in *The Sixties Papers*, edited by Judith Clavir Albert and Stewart Edward Albert, 159–64. New York: Praeger, 1984.

Blight, James. G. and Janet M. Lang. *The Armageddon Letters: Kennedy/Khrushchev/Castro in the Cuban Missile Crisis*. Lanham: Rowman & Littlefield, 2012.

———. and Janet M. Lang. *The Fog of War: Lessons from the Life of Robert S. McNamara*. Lanham: Rowman & Littlefield Publishers, 2005.

Bliss, Edward Jr. *Now the News: The Story of Broadcast Journalism*. New York: Columbia University Press, 1991.

Blodget, Henry, "The Truth about Taxes: Here's how High Today's Rates Really Are." *Business Insider*, July 12, 2011. http://www.businessinsider.com/history-of-tax-rates.

Blum, William. *Killing Hope: U.S. and CIA Interventions since World War II*. Monroe: Common Courage, 2004.

Boehm, Omri. "Child Sacrifice, Ethical Responsibility and the Existence of the People of Israel." *Vetus Testamentum*, 54, no.2 (2004) 145–156.

Boff, Leonardo and Clodovis Boff. *Introducing Liberation Theology*. Translated by Paul Burns. Maryknoll: Orbis, 2000. First published in translation in Great Britain by Burns & Oates/Search Press, Ltd., 1987.

Bohi, Douglas R. "Profit Performance in the defense industry." *The Journal of Political Economy*, 81, no. 3 (1973) 721–728.

Bonner, Raymond. "Bringing El Salvador Nun Killers to Justice." *The Daily Beast*, November 9, 2014. http://www.thedailybeast.com/articles/2014/11/09/bringing-el-salvador-nun-killers-to-justice.html.

Bork, Robert. *Slouching towards Gomorrah*. New York: Harper and Collins, 1996.

Bossie, David N. *The Many Faces of John Kerry: Why This Massachusetts Liberal is Wrong for America*. Nashville: WND, 2003

Bostock, Mike, Matthew Ericson, and Robert Gebeloff. "How the Tax Burden Has Changed." *New York Times*, November 29, 2012. http://www.nytimes.com/interactive/2012/11/30/us/tax-burden.html.

Bothwell, Cecil. *The Prince of War: Billy Graham's Crusade for a Wholly Christian Empire*. Ashville: Brave Ulysses Books, 2007.

Bovard, James. *The Bush Betrayal*. New York: Palgrave Macmillan, 2004.

Bowersock, Glen. W. *Martyrdom & Rome*. Cambridge: Cambridge University Press, 1995.

Boyer, Paul. *By the Bomb's Early Light. American Thought and Culture at the Dawn of the Atomic Age*. Chapel Hill: University of North Carolina Press. 1985.

Braden, Waldo W. *The Oral Tradition in the South*. Baton Rouge: Louisiana State University Press, 1983.

Brader, Ted. *Campaigning for Hearts and Minds: How Emotional Appeals in Political Ads Work*. Chicago: University of Chicago Press, 2006.

Brandes, Stuart. D. *Warhogs: A History of War Profits in America*. Lexington: The University Press of Kentucky, 1997.

Breiding, Matthew. *Characteristics and Prevalence of Sexual violence, Stalking, and Intimate Partner violence Victimization—National Intimate Partner and Sexual violence survey, United States,* 2011, Center for Disease Control. September 5, 2014. https://www.cdc.gov/mmwr/preview/mmwrhtml/ss6308a1.htm?s_cid=ss6308a1_e.

Bridges, Linda and John R. Coyne Jr. *Strictly Right: William F. Buckley, Jr. and the American Conservative Movement*. Hoboken: John Wiley & Sons, 2007.

Brinkley, Douglas. *The Great Deluge: Katrina, New Orleans, and the Mississippi Gulf Coast*. New York: Harper Perennial, 2007.

Brody, David. "Obama to CBN News: We're no Longer Just a Christian Nation." *CBN News*, July 30, 2007. http://www.cbn.com/CBNnews/204016.aspx.

Brog, David. *Standing with Israel: Why Christians support the Jewish State*. Mary Lake: FrontLine, 2006.

Bronski, Michael. *A Queer History of the United States*. Boston: Beacon, 2011.

Brown, Dee. *Bury My Heart at Wounded Knee: An Indian History of the American West*. New York: Owl, 1970.

Brown, Michael and Ted T. Schwartz. *Deadly Indifference: The Perfect (Political) Storm Hurricane Katrina, the Bush Administration, and Beyond*. Lanham: Taylor Trade, 2011.

Brown, Robert McAfee. "Dissent in an Age of Conformity." *The Princeton Seminary Bulletin* 65, no 1 (1972) 13–19.

Brown, William R. "Television and the Democratic National Convention." *Quarterly Journal of Speech*, 55, no. 3 (1969) 237–246.

Brownstein, Ronald. "Playing Politics for Baby Boomers." *Los Angeles Times*, January 4, 1987. http://articles.latimes.com/1987-01-04/opinion/op-1902_1_baby-boomers.

Brudnick, Ida. A. *Congressional Salaries and Allowances: In Brief*, 2004. Congressional Research Service. https://www.senate.gov/CRSReports/crs-publish.cfm?pid=%270E%2C*PL[%3D%23P%20%20%0A.

Buchanan, Pat. "Cultural War Speech: Address to the Republican National Convention." August 17, 1992. Voices of Democracy. http://voicesofdemocracy.umd.edu/buchanan-culture-war-speech-speech-text/.

Bugliosi, Vincent. *Prosecution of George W. Bush for Murder*. Cambridge: Vanguard, 2009.

Bull, Malcom and Keith Lockhart. *Seeking Sanctuary: Seventh-Day Adventism and the American Dream*. Indianapolis: Indiana University Press, 2007. Originally published in 1989 by Harper & Row.

Bump, Philip. "The New Congress is 80% White, 80% Male, and 92 Percent Christian," *The Washington Post*, January 5, 2015. http://www.wasbumphingtonpost.com/blogs/the-fix/wp/2015/01/05/the-new-congress-is-80-percent-white-80-percent-male-and-92-percent-christian/.

Buncombe, Andrew. "Donald Trump's Friend and Fundraiser 'Investigated for alleged Tax Evasion in Italy.'" *Independent*, May 30, 2017. http://www.independent.co.uk/news/world/americas/us-politics/donald-trump-thomas-barrack-fundraiser-friend-tax-evasion-italy-probe-latest-a7761936.html.

Bureau of Labor Statistics. "A Profile of the Working Poor," 2013, July 2015. http://www.bls.gov/opub/reports/cps/a-profile-of-the-working-poor-2013.pdf.

Bureau of National Affairs. *Daily Labor Report, Issues* 214–231. Arlington: Author, 1963.

Burkhalter, Holly J. "The Question of Genocide: The Clinton Administration and Rwanda." *World Policy Journal*, 11, no. 4 (1994/1995) 44–54.

Burnidge, Cara Lea. *A Peaceful Conquest: Woodrow Wilson, Religion and the New World Order*. Chicago: The University of Chicago Press, 2016.

Burns, Jeffrey. M. "No Longer Emerging: *Ramparts* Magazine and the Catholic Laity, 1962–1968." *Catholic Historian*, 9, no. 3 (1990) 321–333.

Busch, Andrew. *Ronald Reagan and the Politics of Freedom*. Lanham: Rowman & Littlefield, 2001.

Bush, George H. W. "Address to the Nation Announcing Allied Military Action in the Persian Gulf," January 16, 1991. American Presidency Project. http://www.presidency.ucsb.edu/ws/?pid=19222.

———. "Inaugural Address," January 20, 1989. American Presidency Project. http://www.presidency.ucsb.edu/ws/?pid=16610.

———. "Presidential Debate in St. Louis," October 11, 1992. October 11, 1992, American Presidency Project. http://www.presidency.ucsb.edu/ws/?pid=21605.

———. "State of the Union Address," January 29, 1992. America Presidency Project. http://www.presidency.ucsb.edu/ws/?pid=20544.

Bush, George W. *A Charge to Keep*. New York: William Murrow, 1999.

———. "Address before a Joint Session of the Congress of the United States Response to the Terrorist Attacks of September 11." September 20, 2001. American Presidency Project. http://www.presidency.ucsb.edu/ws/index.php?pid=64731.

———. "Address before a Joint Session of Congress on the State of the Union." January 28, 2003. American Presidency Project. http://www.presidency.ucsb.edu/ws/index.php?pid=29645.

———. "Address before a Joint Session of Congress on the State of the Union." January 29, 2002. American Presidency Project. http://www.presidency.ucsb.edu/ws/index.php?pid=29644.

———. "Address to the Nation on Iraq." March 17, 2003. American Presidency Project. http://presidency.proxied.lsit.ucsb.edu/ws/index.php?pid=63713&st=&st1=.

———. *Decision Points*. New York: Random House, 2010.

———. *National Security Strategy of the United States of America*, September, 2002. https://www.state.gov/documents/organization/63562.pdf.

———. "Remarks on the New Oval Office Carpet and an Exchange with Reporters." December 21, 2001. American Presidency Project. http://www.presidency.ucsb.edu/ws/index.php?pid=63340.

Butler, Jerry. P. "God, Preachers, and Segregation." Presented at the Annual Meeting of the Southern Speech and Communication Association, Austin TX, April 7–10, 1981.

Buzzanco, Robert. *Masters of War: Military Dissent & Politics in the Vietnam Era.* New York: Cambridge University Press, 1996.

Cagin, Seth and Philip Dray. *We Are Not Afraid: The Story of Goodman, Schwerner, and Chaney, and the Civil rights Campaign for Mississippi.* New York: Nation, 2006.

Caliendo, Stephen M. *Inequality in America: Race, Poverty, and Fulfilling Democracy's Promise.* Boulder: Westview. 2015.

Calvert, John. *Sayyid Qutb and the Origins of Radical Islamism.* New York: Oxford University Press, 2013.

Campbell, Joseph. *The Hero's Journey: Joseph Campbell on His Life and Work.* Novato: New World Library, 1990.

Capitalism: A Love Story, directed by Michael Moore (2009; USA: Dog Eat Dog Films, 2009) DVD.

Carey, Henry F. "U.S. Domestic Policies and the Emerging Humanitarian Intervention Policy: Haiti, Bosnia and Kosovo." *World Affairs,* 164, no. 2: (2001) 72–82.

Carey, Patrick W. *Catholics in America: A History.* Westport: Praeger, 2004.

Carmichael, Stokely. "What We Want," In *The Sixties Papers,* edited by Judith Clavir Albert and Stewart Edward Albert, 137–44. New York: Praeger, 1984.

Carnegie, Andrew. *The "Gospel of Wealth" Essay and Other Writings.* Selected and introduced by David Nasaw. New York: Penguin, 2006.

Caro, Robert. A. *Master of the Senate: The Years of Lyndon Johnson.* New York: Vintage, 2002.

———. *Means of Ascent: The Years of Lyndon Johnson.* New York: Vintage, 1990.

Carothers, Thomas. *In the Name of Democracy: U.S. Policy toward Latin America in the Reagan Years.* Berkeley: University of California Press, 1991.

Carrier, Jerry. *Hard Right Turn: Assassination of the American Left-A History.* New York: Algora, 2015.

Carson, Johnny. *Happiness is a Dry Martini.* New York: Doubleday, 1965.

Carter, Dan T. *The Politics of Rage: George Wallace, the Origins of the New Conservatism, and the Transformation of American Politics.* 2nd ed. Baton Rouge: Louisiana State University Press, 2000.

Carter, James. M. War Profiteering from Vietnam to Iraq. *Counterpunch,* December 11, 2003. http://www.counterpunch.org/2003/12/11/war-profiteering-from-vietnam-to-iraq/.

Carter, Jimmy. "Address to the Nation on Energy," April 18, 1977. American Presidency Project. http://www.presidency.ucsb.edu/ws/index.php?pid=7369.

———. "Inaugural Address," January 20, 1977. American Presidency Project. http://www.presidency.ucsb.edu/ws/index.php?pid=6575.

Carty, Thomas J. "Secular Icon or Catholic Hero?: Religion and the Presidency of John F. Kennedy." In *The Evolving American presidency: Religion and the American Presidency,* edited by Mark J. Rozell and Cleaves Whitney, 131–55. New York: Palgrave Macmillan.

Casey, Timothy and Laurie Maldonado. "Worst Off—Single-Parent Families in the United States." *Legal Momentum*, December 2012. http://www.legalmomentum.org/resources/report-worst-%E2%80%93-single-parent-families-united-states.

Cashman, Greg and Leonard C. Robinson. *An Introduction to the Causes of War: Patterns of Interstate Conflict from World War I to Iraq*. Lanham: Rowman & Littlefield, 2007.

Cassel, Elaine. *The War on Civil Liberties: How Bush and Ashcroft Have Dismantled the Bill of Rights*. Chicago: Lawrence Hill, 2004.

Cassidy, J. "Pope Francis' Challenge to Global Capitalism." *The New Yorker*, December 3, 2013. http://www.newyorker.com/news/john-cassidy/pope-franciss-challenge-to-global-capitalism.

Castellano, Isaac M. *Civil War Interventions and Their Benefits: Unequal Return*. Lanham: Lexington, 2015.

Chan, Sue. "U.S. Admits Bio-Weapons Tests." CBS News, October 8, 2002. Retrieved from http://www.cbsnews.com/news/us-admits-bio-weapons-tests/.

Chapuis, Oscar. *A History of Vietnam: From Hong Bang to Tu Duc*. Westport: Greenwood, 1995.

Chatterjee, Pratap. *Haliburton's Army: How a Well-Connected Texas Oil Company Revolutionized the Way America Makes War*. New York: Nation, 2009.

———. *Iraq, Inc. A Profitable Occupation*. Open Media Book, series editor Greg Ruggiero. New York: Seven Stories, 2004.

Chesler, Phyllis. *Women and Madness*. New York: Four Walls Eight Windows, 1972.

Chidester, David. *Salvation and Suicide: Jim Jones the People's Temple, and Jonestown*. Indianapolis: Indiana University Press, 1988.

Chomsky, Noam. *How the World Works*. The Real Story Series, edited by Arthur Naiman. Berkeley: Soft Skull, 2011.

———. *Media Control: The Spectacular Achievements of Propaganda*. 2nd ed. Open Media Book, 2002.

———. *Rethinking Camelot: JFK, the Vietnam War, and U.S. Political culture*. Chicago: Haymarket, 2015.

Choron, Sandra and Harry Choron. *Money: Everything You Never Knew about Your Favorite Thing to Find, Save, Spend & Covet*. San Francisco: Chronicle, 2011.

Ciment, James. *Social Issues in America: an Encyclopedia*. New York: Routledge, 2015. First published in 2006 by M. E. Sharpe.

Clifford, Stephanie and Russ Buettner. "Clinton Backer Pleads guilty in a Straw Donor Scheme." *New York Times*, April 17, 2014. https://www.nytimes.com/2014/04/18/nyregion/clinton-backer-pleads-guilty-in-a-straw-donor-scheme.html.

Clinton, Bill. "Address Accepting the Presidential Nomination at the Democratic National Convention in New York," July 16, 1992. American Presidency Project. http://www.presidency.ucsb.edu/ws/?pid=25958.

———. *My Life*. New York: Alfred A. Knopf, 2004.

———. *Public Papers of the Presidents of the United States: William J. Clinton*. Washington, D.C: Office of the Federal Registrar, 1999.

———. "Text of Clinton's Rwanda Speech." *CBS News*, March 25, 1998. http://www.cbsnews.com/news/text-of-clintons-rwanda-speech/.

Clinton Foundation. "About Us." https://www.clintonfoundation.org/about. Accessed March 30, 2017.

Clymer, Adam. "Bush and Texas Have Not Set High Priority on Health Care." *The New York Times*, April 11, 2000. http://www.nytimes.com/2000/04/11/us/bush-and-texas-have-not-set-high-priority-on-health-care.html?pagewanted=all.

Coats, George. W. "Abraham's Sacrifice of Faith." In *The Sacrifice of Isaac Studies in the Development of a Literary Tradition*, edited by Eli Yassif, 389–400, Jerusalem: Makor 1973.

Cobb. Michael. *God Hates Fags: The Rhetorics of Religious Violence*. New York: New York University Press, 2006.

Coffey, Thomas M. *Iron Eagle: The Turbulent Life of General Curtis LeMay*. New York: Crown, 1986.

Cohrs, Patrick. O. "Towards a New Deal for the world? Lyndon Johnson's Aspirations to Renew the Twentieth Century's Pax Americana." In *Beyond the Cold War: Lyndon Johnson and the New Global Challenges for the 1960s*, edited by Francis J. Gavin and Mark Atwood Lawrence, 44–75. New York: Oxford University Press, 2014.

Colby, Gerard. *Thy Will Be Done: The Conquest of the Amazon: Nelson Rockefeller and Evangelism in the Age of Oil*. New York, Harpercollins, 1996.

Colby, Jason. M. "'A Chasm of Values and Outlook:'" The Carter Administration's Human Rights Policy in Guatemala." *Peace & Change*, 35, no. 4 (2010) 561–593.

Cole, Leonard. A. *Clouds of Secrecy: The Army's Germ Warfare Tests over Populated Areas*. Lanham: Rowman & Littlefield, 1988.

———. A. *The Eleventh Plague: the Politics of Biological and Chemical Warfare*. New York, NY: Macmillan, 1996.

Coleman, Fred. *The Decline and Fall of the Soviet Empire: Forty Years that Shook the World, from Stalin to Yeltsin*. New York: St, Martin's Griffin, 1996.

Collins, John J. *Lives of Great Religious Books: The Dead Sea Scrolls*. Princeton: Princeton University Press, 2012.

Columbia Law School. *Domestic Violence & Sexual Assault in the United States: A Human Rights Based Approach & Practice Guide*, August, 2014. http://www.law.columbia.edu/sites/default/files/microsites/human-rights-institute/files/dv_sa_hr_guide_reduce.pdf.

Commission on Obscenity and Pornography. *The Report of the Commission on Obscenity and Pornography*. New York: Bantam, 1970.

Congregation for the Doctrine of the Faith. *Instruction on Certain Aspects of "Theology of Liberation,"* 1984. http://www.vatican.va/roman_curia/congregations/cfaith/documents/rc_con_cfaith_doc_19840806_theology-liberation_en.html. Accessed March 8, 2017.

Cooney, John. *The American Pope: The Life and Times of Cardinal Spellman*. New York: Times, 1984.

Corn, David. *The Lies of George W. Bush: Mastering the Politics of Deception*. New York: Three Rivers, 2003.

Coven. *One Tin Soldier*. Warner Bros. Records 7509. 45 rpm. Originally released 1971.

Cox, Harvey. "Playboy's Doctrine of Male." *Christianity and Crisis* 21, no. 6: (1961) 56–58.

———. "The Market as God." *The Atlantic Monthly*, 283, no. 3 (1999) 18–23. http://www.theatlantic.com/past/issues/99mar/marketgod.htm.

———. *The Secular City: Secularization and Urbanization in Theological Perspective*. New York: Collier Books, 1965.

———. "The Warring Visions of the Religious Right." *The Atlantic Monthly*, November, 1995, http://www.theatlantic.com/magazine/archive/1995/11/the-warring-visions-of-the-religious-right/376472.

Craighill, Payton. M. "Poll: 62 Percent Believe Broader Plot Killed Kennedy," *Washington Post*, November 20, 2013. http://www.washingtonpost.com/blogs/post-politics/wp/2013/11/20/poll-62-percent-believe-broader-plot-killed-kennedy/.

Crenshaw, Charles. A. *Conspiracy of Silence*. New York: Signet, 1992.

Cronin, James E. *Global Rules: America, Britain and a Disordered World*. New Haven: Yale University Press.

Crouse, Eric R. *The Cross and Reaganomics: Conservative Christians Defending Ronald Reagan*. Lanham: Lexington Books, 2013. New York: St. Martin's. First published in Great Britain by Macmillan 1998.

Crozier, Michael J., Samuel P. Huntington, and Joji Watanuki, J. *The Crisis of Democracy: Report on the Governability of Democracies to the Trilateral Commission*. New York: New York University Press, 1975. http://trilateral.org/download/doc/crisis_of_democracy.pdf. Accessed March 14, 2017.

Cunningham, Sean P. *Cowboy Conservatism: Texas and the Rise of the Modern Right*. Lexington: University of Kentucky Press, 2010.

Cuordileone, K. A. " 'Politics in an Age of Anxiety': Cold War Political Culture and the Crisis in American Masculinity, 1949–1960." *Journal of American History*, 87, no. 2 (2000) 515–545.

Curran, Charles. *Catholic Social Teaching, 1891-Present: A Historical, Theological, and Ethical Analysis*. Washington, D.C.: Georgetown University Press, 2002.

Current Population Reports. "Labor Force," U.S. Department of Commerce, Bureau of the Census. Series P-50, No. 74. April 1957. https://books.google.com/books?id=NlPy9aLaDxAC&pg=RA1-PA10&dq=1958+recession+unemployed&hl=en&sa=X&ved=0ahUKEwjN4 iHktnSAhWJmpQKHWkBAAMQ6AEIKDAD#v=onepage&q=1958%20recession%20unemployed&f=false.

Curry, George, ed. *The Affirmative Action Debate*. New York: Basic, 1996.

Curtis, Richard. *Hubris and the Presidency: The Abuse of Power by Johnson and Nixon*. New York Rutledge, 2000.

Cusack, Carmen M. *Pornography and the Criminal Justice System*. Boca Raton: CRC, 2015.

D'Agostino, Anthony. *Gorbachev's Revolution, 1985–91*. London: Macmillan, 1998.

Daly, Mary. *Beyond God the Father: Toward a Philosophy of Women's Liberation*. Boston: Beacon, 1985. Originally published 1973.

Dallek, Robert. *An Unfinished Life: John F. Kennedy, 1917–1963*. Boston: Little, Brown, 2003.

———. *Flawed Giant: Lyndon Johnson and His times, 1963–1973*. New York: Oxford University Press, 1998.

———. *Lyndon B. Johnson: Portrait of a President*. New York: Oxford University Press, 2004.

Danner, Mark. *Torture and Truth: America, Abu Ghraib, and the War on Terror*. New York: New York Review, 2004.

Darby, Phillip. *Three Faces of Imperialism: British and American Approaches to Asia and Africa*. New Haven Yale University Press, 1987.

Davidson, Osha Gray. "My Lai Massacre Leader Speaks." *Mother Jones*, August, 23, 2009. http://www.motherjones.com/mojo/2009/08/my-lai-massacre-leader-speaks.

Davies, Kenneth. C. "America's True History of Religious Tolerance." *Smithsonian*, October 2010. http://www.smithsonianmag.com/history/americas-true-history-of-religious-tolerance-61312684/?no-ist.

Davies, Steven. "The Christology and Protology of the Gospel of Thomas." *Journal of Biblical Literature*, 111, no. 4 (1962) 663–682.

Davis, Townsend. *Weary Feet, Rested Souls: A Guided History of the Civil Rights Movement*. New York: W. W. Norton & Company, 1998.

Dean, Robert D. *Imperial Brotherhood: Gender and the Making of Cold War Foreign Policy*. Amherst: University of Massachusetts Press, 2001.

DeBenedetti, Charles. *An American Ordeal: The Antiwar Movement of the Vietnam Era*. Syracuse: Syracuse University Press, 1990.

Decter, Midge. "The Boys on the Beach." *Commentary Magazine*, September 1, 1980. https://www.commentarymagazine.com/articles/the-boys-on-the-beach/.

———. *The New Chastity and Other Arguments against Women's Liberation*. New York: Coward, McCaan, & Geohegan, 1972.

Delton, Jennifer A. *Rethinking the 1950s: How Communism and the Cold War made America Liberal*. Cambridge: Cambridge University Press, 2013.

DeNavas-Walt, Carmen and Bernadette D. Proctor "Income and Poverty in the United States: 2014," *Current Population Reports*, P60-252, United States Census, U.S. Department of Commerce, Washington, D. C., 2015. https://www.census.gov/content/dam/Census/library/publications/2015/demo/p60-252.pdf.

De Rouen, Karl. And Uk Heo, eds. *Civil Wars of the World: Major Conflicts Since World War II*. Vol. I. Santa Barbara: ABC CLIO, 2007.

Diamond, Sara. *Spiritual Warfare: The Politics of the Christian Right*. Boston: South End, 1989.

Dickerson, James. *Dixie's Dirty Secret: The True Story of How the Government, the Media, and the Mob Conspired to Combat Integration and the Vietnam Antiwar Movement*. Armonk: M. E. Sharpe, 1998.

Dickey, C. R. *The Bible and Segregation*. Merrimac: Destiny, 1958.

Didion, Joan. *The White Album*. New York: Simon & Schuster, 1979.

Dobratz, Betty, Lisa K. Waldner, and Timothy Buzzell. Power, *Politics, and Society: An Introduction to Political Sociology*. New York: Routledge, 2012.

Domke, David and Kevin Coe. *The God Strategy: How Religion became a Political Weapon in America*. Updated ed. New York: Oxford University Press, 2010.

Donaldson, Robert H. *Liberalism's Last Hurrah: The Presidential Campaign of 1964*. New York: Routledge, 2003.

Donnerstein, Edward. "Pornography: Its Effect on Violence against Women." In *Pornography and Sexual Aggression*, edited by Neil M. Malamuth and Edward Donnerstein, 53–81. Orlando: Academic, 1984.

Douglas, Susan J. *Where the Girls Are: Growing up Female with the Mass Media*. New York: New York Times, 1994.

Douglass, James. W. *JFK and the Unspeakable. Why He Died and Why it Matters*. Maryknoll: Orbis, 2008.

Dr. Seuss [pseud. Theodore Geisel]. *How the Grinch Stole Christmas*. New York: Random House Children's Books, 1957.

Drell, Sidney D. and George P. Schultz, eds. *Andrei Sakharov: The Conscience of Humanity*. Publication no. 663. Stanford: Hoover Institution, 2015.

Dreyfus, Robert. *Devil's Game: How the United States Helped Unleash Islamic Fundamentalism*. New York: Owl, 2005.

Drutman, Lee. *The Business of America is Lobbying: How Corporations Became Politicized and Politics Became More Corporate*. New York: Oxford University Press, 2015.

Dube, Arindrajit, T. William Lester, and Barry Eidlin. *A Downward Push: The Impact of Wal-Mart Stores on Retail Wages and Benefits*. The Berkeley Center for Labor Research and Education, December 2007. http://laborcenter.berkeley.edu/pdf/2007/walmart_downward_push07.pdf.

Dumbrell, John and David M. Barrett. *The Making of U.S. Foreign Policy*, 2nd ed. Manchester: Manchester University Press, 1977. First published by Manchester University Press, 1990.

Dunmire, Patricia L. *Projecting the Future through Political Discourse: The Case of the Bush Doctrine*. Discourse Approach to Politics, Society and Culture (DAPSAC), series editors Ruth Wodak and Greg Myers. Amsterdam: John Benjamins, 2011.

Durham, Martin. *The Christian Right, the Far Right and the Boundaries of American Conservatism*. Manchester: Manchester University Press, 2000.

Dussel, Enrique. *A History of the Church in Latin America: Colonialism to Liberation*. Grand Rapids: Wm. B. Eerdmans, 1981.

Dworkin, Andrea. *Letters from a War Zone*. Brooklyn: Lawrence Hill, 1993.

———. *Pornography: Men Possessing Women*. London: Women's Press, 1981.

Edmonds-Poli, Emily and David A Shirk. *Contemporary Mexican Politics*. 2nd ed. Lanham: Rowman & Littlefield, 2012.

Edwin. Starr. *War and Peace*. Gordy GS948. 331/3 rpm. Originally released in 1970.

Ehler, Sidney Z and Morrall, John B. *The Church and State throughout the Centuries*. Cheshire: Biblo & Tannen Booksellers, 1988.

Ehrenreich, Barbara. *Living with a Wild God: A Nonbeliever's Search for the Truth about Everything*. New York: Twelve, 2014.

———. *Nickel and Dimed: On (Not) Getting by in America*. New York: Holt, 2001.

———. and Deidre English. *For Her Own Good: Two Centuries of the Experts Advice to Women*. Revised edition. New York: Anchor, 2005.

Ehrman, John and Michael W. Flamm. *Debating the Reagan Presidency*. Lanham: Rowman & Littlefield, 2009.

Ellis, E. Earle. "Segregation and the Kingdom of God." *Christianity Today*, 18 (1957). 6–9.

Eisenhower, Dwight D. "Farewell Address," January 17, 1961." Avalon Law. http://avalon.law.yale.edu/20th_century/eisenhower001.asp.

———. "The chance for Peace," April 16, 1953. Avalon Law http://avalon.law.yale.edu/20th_century/eisenhower001.asp.

Ellman, Michael and S. Maksudov. "Soviet Deaths in the Great Patriotic War: A Note." *Europe Asia Studies*, 46, no. 4 (1994) 671–680.

Ellsberg, Daniel. *Secrets: A Memoir of Vietnam and the Pentagon Papers*. New York: Penguin, 2002.

Enelow, Hyman Gerson. *A Jewish View of Jesus*. New York: Macmillan, 1920.

Engler, Mark. "Towards the Rights of the Poor: Human Rights in Liberation Theology." In *Liberating Faith: Religious Voices for Justice, Peace, and Ecological Wisdom*, edited by Roger Gottlieb, 203–21.Lanham: Rowman & Littlefield, 2003.

Eric Burdon and the Animals. *The Twain Shall Meet*. MGM Records SE 4537. 331/3 rpm. Originally released 1967.

BIBLIOGRAPHY

Eshel, Hanan. *The Dead Sea Scrolls and the Hasmonean State.* Grand Rapids: Eerdmans, 2008.

Eskridge, Larry. *God's Forever Family: The Jesus people Movement in America.* New York: Oxford University Press, 2013.

Eynon, Bret. "Community in Motion: The Free Speech Movement, Civil Rights, and the Roots of the New Left." *The Oral History Review,* 17, no. 1 (1989): 39–69.

Faderman, Lillian. *The Gay Revolution: the Story of the Struggle.* New York: Simon & Schuster, 2015.

Ferrell, James J. *The Spirit of the Sixties: The Making of Postwar Radicalism.* New York: Routledge, 1997.

Ferrell, Linda and O. C. Ferrell. "Examining Organizational Integrity Failures." In *Business and Corporate Integrity: Sustaining Organizational Compliance,* Vol. I, *Perspectives,* edited by Robert C. Chandler, 181–204. Santa Barbara: Praeger, 2014.

Ferriss, Susan and Ricardo Sandoval. *The Fight in the Fields: Cesar Chavez and the Farmworkers Movement.* Orlando: Paradigm, 1997.

"Final Vote Results for Roll Call 398." H.R. 3162, October 24, 2001. http://clerk.house.gov/evs/2001/roll398.xml. Accessed March 13, 2017.

Firestone, Shulamith. *The Dialectic of Sex.* New York: Farrar, Straus, and Giroux, 1970.

Fitrakis, Robert, Steven Rosenfeld, and Harvey Wasserman. *What Happened in Ohio: A Documentary Record of theft and Fraud in the 2004 Election.* New York: New Press, 2006.

Flint, Peter W. *The Dead Sea Scrolls.* Core Biblical Studies. Nashville: Abingdon, 2013.

Flowers, Ronald Barri. *Sex Crimes: Perpetrators, Predators, Prostitutes, and Victims.* 2nd ed. Springfield: Charles C. Thomas, 2006.

Flusser, David. *Judaism of the Second Temple Period: Sages and Literature,* Vol 2. Translated by Azzan Yadin. Grand Rapids: William B. Eerdmans, 2009.

Focus on the Family. *Focus on the Family Celebrating Twenty-five Years of God's Faithfulness.* San Diego: Tehabi, 2002.

Foerstel, Herbert N. *From Watergate to Monicagate: Ten Controversies in Modern Journalism and Media.* Westport: Greenwood, 2001.

Follman, Mark, Gavin Aronsen, and Deanna Pan. "A Guide to Mass shootings in America." *Mother Jones,* January 8, 2017. http://www.motherjones.com/politics/2012/07/mass-shootings-map.

Forman, James. "The Black Manifesto." In *Black Theology: A Document History,* 1966–1979, edited by Gayraud S. Wilmore and James Cone, 80–89. Maryknoll: Orbis, 1979.

Foubert, John. D., Matthew W. Brosi, and Sean Bannon. "Pornography Viewing and Men: Effects on Bystander Intervention, Rape Myth Acceptance, and Behavioral Intent to Commit Rape." *Sexual Addiction & Compulsivity,* 18, no. 4, (2011) 212–231.

France, David. *Our Fathers: The Secret Life of the Catholic Church in an Age of Scandal.* New York: Random House, 2004.

Francis. I. "Evangelii Gaudium," (Joy of the Gospel), 2013. Papal Encyclicals. http://w2.vatican.va/content/francesco/en/apost_exhortations/documents/papa-francesco_esortazione-ap_20131124_evangelii-gaudium.html#No_to_the_new_idolatry_of_money.

Frawley-O'Dea, Mary Gail. *Perversion of Power: Sex Abuse in the Catholic Church.* Nashville: Vanderbilt University Press, 2007.

Fredriksen, Paula. *From Jesus to Christ: The Origin of the New Testament Images of Jesus.* New Haven: Yale University Press, 2008.

Fridell, Ron. *Prisoners of War.* Tarrytown: Marshall Cavendish Benchmark, 2008.

Friedan, Betty. *The Feminine Mystique.* New York: W. W. Norton, 1997.

Friedman, Max Paul. "Anti-Americanism and U.S. Foreign Policy Relations." *Diplomatic History*, 32, no. 4 (2008) 497–514.

Friis, Robert H. *Essentials of Environmental Health.* Sudbury: Jones and Bartlett Learning, 2012.

Froese, Paul and F. Carson Mencken. "A US Holy War? The Effects of Religion on Iraq War Policy Attitude." *Social Science Quarterly*, 90, no. 1 (2009) 103–116.

Fry, Joseph. A. *Debating Vietnam: Fulbright, Stennis, and their Senate Hearings.* Lanham: Rowman & Littlefield, 2008.

Fursenko, Aleksandr and Timothy Naftali. *Khrushchev's Cold War: The Inside Story of an American Adversary.* New York: W. W. Norton, 2006.

———. and Timothy Naftali. *"One Hell of a Gamble:" Khrushchev, Castro, and Kennedy, 1958–1964.* New York: W. W. Norton, 1997.

Gable, Richard W. "The Politics and Economics of the 1957–1958 Recession." *The Western Political Quarterly*, 12, no. 2 (1959) 557–559.

Galbraith, John Kenneth. *The Affluent Society.* New York: Houghton Mifflin, 1958.

Gallo, Marcia, M. *Different Daughters: A History of the Daughters of Bilitis and the Rise of the Lesbian Rights Movement.* Emeryville: Seal, 2007.

Gallup Poll. "Election Polls—Vote by Groups, 1968–1972." http://www.gallup.com/poll/9457/election-polls-vote-groups-19681972.aspx. Accessed March 6, 2017.

———. "Presidential Election Trial-Heat Trends, 1936–2008." 1972 Presidential Trial Heats, Based on Registered voters. http://www.gallup.com/poll/110548/gallup-presidential-election-trialheat-trends-19362004.aspx#4. Accessed March 6, 2017.

———. "Religion." http://www.gallup.com/poll/1690/religion.aspx.

Galvão-Sobrinho, Carlos R. *Doctrine and Power. Theological Controversy and Christian Leadership in the Later Roman Empire.* Berkeley: University of California Press, 2013.

Gamble, Richard, M. *In Search of the City on a Hill: The Making and Unmaking of an American Myth.* New York: Continuum International, 2012.

Gardner, Lloyd. *The Long Road to Baghdad: A History of U.S Foreign Policy from the 1970s to the Present.* New York: W. W. Norton, 2008.

Garrettson, Charles. Lloyd. III. *Hubert Humphrey: The Politics of Joy.* New Brunswick: Transaction, 1993.

Garrison, Jim. *On the Trail of Assassins: One Man's Quest to Solve the Murder of President Kennedy.* New York: Sheridan Square, 1988.

Gati, Charles. *Failed Illusions: Moscow, Washington, and Budapest, and the 1956 Hungarian Revolt.* Washington, D. C.: Woodrow Wilson Center, 2006.

Gentleman's Agreement, directed by Elia Kazan (1947; Century City, CA: Century Fox, 2003), DVD.

Germillion, Joseph. *The Gospel of Peace and Justice: Catholic Social Teaching since Pope John.* Maryknoll: Orbis, 1976.

Gilinskiy, Yakov. "Crime in Contemporary Russia." *European Journal of Criminology*, 3, no. 3 (2006) 259–292.

Gill, Jill. K. "Religious Communities and the Vietnam War." In *The Vietnam War Era: People and Perspectives*, edited by Mitchell K. Hall, 97–115. Santa Barbara: ABC-CLIO, 2009.

Gill, Lesley. *The School of the Americas: Military Training and Political Violence in the Americas*. Durham: Duke University Press, 2004.

Gillespie, Alex. "Dialogical Dynamics of Trust and Distrust in the Cuban Missile Crisis." In *Trust and Conflict: Representation, Culture, and Dialogue*, edited by Ivana Markova and Alex Gillespie, 139–156. New York: Routledge, 2012.

Gitlin, Todd. *The Sixties: Years of Hope, Days of Rage*. New York: Bantam, 1987.

———. *The Whole World is Watching: Mass Media and the Unmaking of the New Left*. Berkeley: University of California Press, 2003.

Godspell. Directed by David Greene (1973. Culver City, CA; Sony Pictures Home Entertainment, 2000). DVD.

Godden, Richard and Richard Maidment. "Anger, Language and Politics: John F. Kennedy and the Steel Crisis." *Presidential Studies Quarterly*, 10, no. 3 (1980) 317–331.

Goldberg, Jeffrey. "Are You a Completed Jew?" *New York Magazine*, October 2 (1995) 40–41.

Goodwin, Richard. *Remembering America: A Voice from the Sixties*. Boston: Little Brown, 1988.

Gorbachev, Mikhail. *On My Country and the World*. New York: Columbia University Press, 2000.

———. *Perestroika: New Thinking for Our Country and the World*. New York: Harper & Row, 1987.

——— and Daisaku Ikeda, D. *Moral Lessons of the Twentieth Century: Gorbachev and Ikeda on Buddhism and Communism*. New York: I. B. Tauris, 2005.

Gordon, Max. "A Case History of U.S. Subversion: Guatemala, 1954." *Science & Society*, 35, no. 2 (1971) 129–55.

Gossett, Jennifer Lynn and Sarah Byrne, S. "'Click Here'" A Content Analysis of Internet Rape Sites." *Gender & Society*, 16, no. 5 (2002) 689–709.

Gotham, Kevin Fox and Miriam Greenberg. *Crisis Cities: Disaster and Redevelopment in New York and New Orleans*. New York: Oxford University Press, 2014.

Graham, Bob with Jeff Nussbaum. *Intelligence Matters: The CIA, the FBI, Saudi Arabia, and the Failure of America's War on Terror*. New York: Random House, 2004.

Green, Abner. *Understanding the 2000 Election: A Guide to the Legal Battles that Decided the Presidency*. New York: New York University Press, 2001.

Green, Ronald M. "Abraham, Isaac, and the Jewish Tradition: an Ethical Reappraisal." *The Journal of Religious Ethics*, 10, no. 1 (1982) 1–21.

Greer, Germaine, *The Female Eunuch*. New York, Harpercollins, 1970.

Griffin, David Ray. *The New Pearl Harbor Revisited: The 9/11 Cover-Up, and the Exposé*. Northampton: Olive Branch, 2008.

Griffith, Robert. "Dwight D. Eisenhower and the Corporate Commonwealth." *The American Historical Review*, 87, no. 1 (1982) 87–122.

Gruber, Jonathan. *Public Finance and Public Policy*, 4th ed. New York: Worth, 2013

Guess Who's Coming to Dinner, directed by Stanley Kramer (1967; Culver City, CA: Sony Pictures Home Entertainment, 2004), DVD.

Gup, Ted. *Nation of Secrets: The Threat to Democracy and the American Way of Life*. New York: Anchor, 2008.

Gutiérrez, Gustavo. *A Theology of Liberation*. Translated. by Matthew J. O'Connell. Maryknoll: Orbis, 1973. Originally published as Teologica de la liberación, Lima: Perspectivas, 1971.

Hagar, Tom. *Linus Pauling: and the Chemistry of Life*. Oxford Portraits in Science. New York: Oxford University Press, 1998.

Haines, Herbert H. *Black Radicals and the Civil Rights Mainstream, 1954-1970*. Knoxville: The University of Tennessee, 1988.

Hall, Mitchell. K. *Because of their Faith: CALCAV and Religious Opposition to the Vietnam War*. New York: Columbia University Press, 1990.

Handelman, Stephen. *Comrade Criminal: Russia's New Mafiya*. New Haven: Yale University Press, 1997.

Haney, Patrick J. and Walt Vanderbush. *The Cuban Embargo: The Domestic Politics of an American Foreign Policy*. Pittsburgh: University of Pittsburgh Press, 2005.

Hanhimaki, Jussi M. *The Flawed Architect: Henry Kissinger and American Foreign Policy*. New York: Oxford University Press, 2004.

Hansen, Bradley A. *The National Economy*. Greenwood Guides to Business and Economics, Wesley B Truitt, series editor. Westport: Greenwood, 2006.

Hanson, Eric. O. *The Catholic Church in World Politics*. Princeton: Princeton University Press, 1987.

Hanson, Richard Patrick Crosland. *The Search for the Christian Doctrine of God: The Arian Controversy 318-381 AD*, Grand Rapids: Baker Academic, 2005.

Harrington, Michael. *The Other America: Poverty in the United States*. New York: Macmillan, 1962.

Harris-Perry, Melissa. "Mike Huckabee: Wrong on Single Moms." *The Nation*, March 6, 2011. https://www.thenation.com/article/mike-huckabee-wrong-single-moms/.

Harrison, Hope M. "Berlin and the Cold War Struggle over Germany." In *The Routledge Handbook of the Cold War*, edited by Artemy M. Kalinovsky and Craig Daigle, 56–73. New York: Routledge, 2014.

Harrison, James. *The Human Rights Impact of the World Trae Organization*. Oxford: Hart Publishing, 2007.

Harvey, Paul. *Freedom's Coming: Religious Culture and the Shaping of the South from the Civil War to the Civil Rights Movement*. Chapel Hill: University of North Carolina Press, 2005.

Hayden, Tom. "The Port Huron Statement of the Students for a Democratic Society," 1962. http://coursesa.matrix.msu.edu/~hst306/documents/huron.html. Accessed March 10, 2017.

Hebbletwaite, Peter. "Liberation Theology and the Roman Catholic Church." In *The Cambridge Companion to Liberation Theology*, edited by Christopher Rowland. Cambridge: Cambridge University Press, 2001. First published in 1999.

Hedges, Chris. *War is a Force That Gives Us Meaning*. New York: Public Affairs, 2002.

———. *What Every Person Should Know about War*. New York: Free Press, 2003.

Hehir, J. Bryan. "Papal Foreign Policy." *Foreign Policy*, 78, (Spring, 1990) 26–48.

Heider, Don and Koji Fuse. "Class and Local TV News." In *Class and News*, edited by Don Heider, 87–107. Lanham: Rowman & Littlefield, 2004.

Heilbrunn, Jacob. *They Knew they Were Right: The Rise of the Neocons*. New York: Anchor Books, 2009.

Heineman, Kenneth J. *God is a Conservative: Religion, Politics, and Morality in Contemporary America*. New York: New York University Press, 1998.

Helen. Reddy. *I Am Woman*. Capitol Records ST-11068. 33 1/3 rpm. Originally released 1972.

Henkin, Louis. "Judaism and Human Rights. *Judaism*, 25, no. 4 (1976) 435–447.

Herb Alpert's Tijuana Brass. *Whipped Cream & Other Delights*. A & M Records LP-110. 33 1/3 rpm. Originally released 1965.

Herberg, William. "America's Civil Religion: What it is and Whence it Comes." *Modern Age A Quarterly Review*, 17, no. 3 (1973) 226–233.

Herbert, Bob. "Get Ready for a War on the Poor." *The Nation*, November 22, 2016. https://www.thenation.com/article/get-ready-for-a-war-on-the-poor.

Herring, George. C. "'Peoples Quite Apart'": Americans, South Vietnamese and the War in Vietnam." *Diplomatic Policy*, 14, no. (1990) 1–23.

———. *The Pentagon Papers*. Abridged edition. New York: McGraw-Hill, 1993.

Hersh, Seymour M. *The Dark Side of Camelot*. Boston: Little, Brown, 1997.

———. *The Price of Power: Kissinger in the Nixon White House*. New York: Simon & Schuster, 1983.

Hershman, D. Jablow. *Power beyond Reason: The Mental Collapse of Lyndon Johnson*. Fort Lee: Barricade, 2002.

Herzog, Jonathan. P. *The Spiritual-Industrial Complex: America's Religious Battle against Communism in the Early Cold War*. New York: Oxford University Press, 2011.

Hightower, Jim. *Thieves in High Places: They've Stolen Our Country—and Its Time to Take It Back*. New York: Plume, 2003.

Hirschman, Charles, Samuel Preston, and Vu Manh Loi. "Vietnamese Casualties during the American War: A New Estimate." *Population and Development Review* (1995): 783–812.

Hoff, Joan. *Nixon Reconsidered*. New York: Basic, 1994.

Hoffer, Thomas B. et. al. *Doctorate Recipients from United States Universities: Summary Report*, 2000. Chicago: National Opinion Research Center, 2001.

Hoffman, David E. *The Oligarchs. Wealth and Power in the New Russia*. Cambridge: Perseus, 2011. First published in 2002.

Hofstadter, Richard. *Social Darwinism in American Thought*. Boston: Beacon, 1992. Originally published in 1944 by University of Pennsylvania Press.

Hopewell, Kristen. *Breaking the WTO: How Emerging Powers Disrupted the Neoliberal Project*. Stanford: Stanford University Press, 2016.

Horwitz, Helen Lefkowitz. "The 1960s and the Transformation of Campus Cultures." *History of Education Quarterly*, 26, no. 1 (1986) 1–38.

Humphrey, Hubert. H. "1948 National Democratic Convention Address," July 14, 1948 *American Rhetoric*. http://www.americanrhetoric.com/speeches/huberthumphey1948dnc.html

———. *The Education of a Public Man. My Life in Politics*. Minneapolis: The University of Minnesota Regents, 1976

Hunt, Andrew. E. *The Turning: A History of Vietnam Veterans against the War*. New York: New York University Press, 1999.

Hunter, Jay. "Wealth of Congress Jumps $150 Million," *Roll Call*, October 22, 2014. http://www.rollcall.com/hill-blotter/wealth-of-congress-jumps-150-million-50-richest/.

Hymowitz, Carol. And Michael Weissman. *A History of Women in America*. New York: Bantam, 1978.

Iceland, John. *Poverty in America: A Handbook*. Berkeley: University of California Press, 2003

Ifil, Gwen. "The 1992 Campaign; Clinton's Standard Campaign Speech: A Call for Responsibility." *International New York Times*, April 26, 1992. http://www.nytimes.

com/1992/04/26/us/the-1992-campaign-clinton-s-standard-campaign-speech-a-call-for-responsibility.html?pagewanted=all.
Independent Commission of Inquiry on the U.S. Invasion of Panama. *The U.S. Invasion of Panama: The Truth behind Operation 'Just Cause'.* Boston: South End, 1991.
Ingalls, Robert. P. and David K. Johnson. *The United States since 1945: A Documentary Reader.* Malden: Blackwell, 2009
Institute for Women's Policy Research. "Employment, Education & Economic Change," 2017. https://iwpr.org/issue/employment-education-economic-change/pay-equity-discrimination/.
In the Heat of the Night, directed by Norman Jewison (1967; Beverly Hills, CA: MGM, 2008), DVD.
Isaacson, W. and Evan Thomas. *The Wise Men: Six Friends and the World They Made.* New York, NY: Touchstone, 1986.
It's a Wonderful Life, directed by Frank Capra (1947. Los Angeles, CA: Paramount Pictures, 2006). DVD.
Ivins, Molly and Lou Dubose. *Shrub: The Short but Happy Political Life of George W. Bush.* New York: Vintage, 2002.
Jackson, Hugh. "The Resurrection Belief of the Earliest Church: A Response to Failure of Prophecy?" *The Journal of Religion*, 55, no. 4 (1975) 415–425.
Jackson, Richard. *Writing the War on Terrorism: Language, Politics and Counter-Terrorism.* Manchester: Manchester University Press, 2005.
Jacobs, Lawrence and Theda Skocpol. *Inequality in American Democracy: What We Need to Know and What We Need to Lean.* New York: Russell Sage Foundation, 2005.
Jacobsen, Annie. *Operation Paperclip: The Secret Intelligence Program that brought Nazi Scientists to America.* New York: Little, Brown, 2014.
Jamison, Kathleen Hall. *Packing the Presidency: A History and Criticism of Presidential Campaign Advertising*, 2nd ed., New York: Oxford University Press, 1996.
Jensen, Robert. "Just a John? Pornography and Men's Choices" In *Gender, Sex, and Politics: In the Streets and between the Sheets in the 21st Century*, edited by Shira Tarrant, 107–12. New York: Routledge, 2016.
Jerome, Fred. *The Einstein File: J. Edgar Hoover's Secret War against the World's Most Famous Scientist.* New York: St. Martin's, 2002.
Joesten, Joachim. *The Dark Side of Lyndon Baines Johnson.* Ketchum: Inconoclassic, 2013.
John XXIII. "Pacem in Terris," 1963. Papal Encyclicals Online. http://www.papalencyclicals.net/John23/j23pacem.htm. Accessed March 10, 2017.
John Jay College of Criminal Justice. *The Nature and Scope of Sexual Abuse of Minors by Catholic Priests and Deacons in the United States 1950–2002*, 2004. Washington, D.C. United States Catholic Conference of Bishops. http://www.usccb.org/issues-and-action/child-and-youth-protection/upload/The-Nature-and-Scope-of-Sexual-Abuse-of-Minors-by-Catholic-Priests-and-Deacons-in-the-United-States-1950–2002.pdf. Accessed March 2, 2017.
John Paul II. "Address of Pope John Paul II to the Honorable George W. Bush, President of the United States of America." June 4, 2004. Vatican Library. http://w2.vatican.va/content/john-paul-ii/en/speeches/2004/june/documents/hf_jp-ii_spe_20040604_president-usa.html.
———. "On Reserving Priestly Ordination." 1994. Vatican Library. http://w2.vatican.va/content/john-paul-ii/en/apost_letters/1994/documents/hf_jp-ii_apl_22051994_ordinatio-sacerdotalis.html.

Johnson, Lyndon B. "Address at Johns Hopkins University," April 7, 1965. http://www.presidency.ucsb.edu/ws/index.php?pid=26877.

———. "Remarks to Delegates to the National Farmers Union Convention in Minneapolis," March 18, 1968, Lyndon B. Johnson. American Presidency Project. http://www.presidency.ucsb.edu/ws/index.php?pid=28741.

Joseph, Antoine L. *The Dynamics of Racial Progress: Economic Inequality and Race Relations since Reconstruction*. New York: Routledge, 2015. Originally published by M. E. Sharpe in 2005.

Joseph, Roy. "The New World Order: President Bush and the Post-Cold War Era." In *The Rhetorical Presidency of George H. W. Bush*, edited by Martin J. Medhurst, 81–101. College Station: Texas A & M University Press, 2006.

Judis, John. B. *William F. Buckley, Jr.: Patron Saint of the Conservatives*. New York: Simon & Schuster, 2001.

Kan, Paul Rexton. *Drug Trafficking and International Security*. Lanham: Rowman & Littlefield, 2016.

Kan, Shirley A. *China and Proliferation of Weapons of Mass Destruction and Missiles: Policy Issues*. Congressional Research Service, RL31555, December 23, 2009.

Karklins, Rasma. *Ethnopolitics and the Transition to Democracy: The Collapse of the USSR and Latvia*. Baltimore: Johns Hopkins University Press, 1994.

Katz, Jonathan. *Gay American History*. New York: Thomas Y. Crowell, 1976.

Kean, Judy. *Single and Catholic*. Manchester: Sophia Institutes, 2016.

Kellner, Douglas. *From 9/11 to Terror War: The Dangers of the Bush Legacy*. Lanham: Rowman & Littlefield, 2003.

Kendall, Diana. *Framing Class: Media Representations of Wealth and Poverty in America*. Lanham: Rowman & Littlefield, 2011.

Keneally, Meghan. "Dick Cheney Roasted with Jokes about WATERBOARDING at a Conservative Dinner in His Honor." *Daily Mail*, October 9, 2013. http://www.dailymail.co.uk/news/article-2451052/Cheney-roast-jokes-waterboarding.html. Accessed March 13, 2017.

Kennan, George. F. "The G.O.P. Won the Cold War? Ridiculous." *New York Times*, October 28, 1992. http://www.nytimes.com/1992/10/28/opinion/the-gop-won-the-cold-war-ridiculous.html.

Kennedy, John. F. "A Democrat Looks at Foreign Policy." *Foreign Affairs*, 36, no. 1, (1957) 44–59.

———. "Address and Question and Answer Period at the Economic Club of New York," December 14, 1962. American Presidency Project. http://www.presidency.ucsb.edu/ws/index.php?pid=9057&st=&st1.

———. "Civil Rights Address," June 11, 1963. American Rhetoric. http://www.americanrhetoric.com/speeches/jfkcivilrights.htm.

———. "Commencement Address at American University in Washington." June 10, 1963. American Presidency Project. http://www.presidency.ucsb.edu/ws/index.php?pid=9266&st=&st1=.

———. "Inaugural Address," January 20, 1961. Presidency Project http://www.presidency.ucsb.edu/ws/?pid=8032

———"Letter from President Kennedy to Chairman Khrushchev," April 18, 1961. Department of State Office of Historian. https://history.state.gov/historicaldocuments/frus1961–63v06/d10.

BIBLIOGRAPHY

———. "News Conference," April 11, 1962. John F. Kennedy Library. http://www.jfklibrary.org/Research/Research-Aids/Ready-Reference/Press-Conferences/News-Conference-30.aspx.

———. "Telegram from the Department of State to the Embassy in the Soviet Union." October 25, 1962. Department of State. Office of the Historian. https://history.state.gov/historicaldocuments/frus1961-63v06/d64.

Kennedy, Robert F. *Thirteen Days: A Memoir of the Cuban Missile Crisis*. New York: W. W. Norton, 1968.

Kennedy-Pipe, Caroline and Alex J. Bellamy. "Rape in War: Lessons of the Balkan Conflicts in the 1990s." In *The Kosovo Tragedy: The Human Rights Dimension*, edited by Ken Booth, 67–86. London: Frank Cass, 2001.

Kettrey, Heather Hensman. "Reading Playboy for the Articles: The Greying of Rape Myths in Black and White, 1953–2003." *Violence Against Women*, 19, no.8 (2013) 968–994.

Khrushchev, Nikita. "Letter from Chairman Khrushchev to President Kennedy," April 22, 1961. Department of State Office of Historian. https://history.state.gov/historicaldocuments/frus1961-63v06/d11

———. "Letter from Chairman Khrushchev to President Kennedy," September 29, 1962. Department of State Office of Historian. https://history.state.gov/historicaldocuments/frus1961-63v06/d21.

———. "Letter from Chairman Khrushchev to President Kennedy." October 24, 1962. Department of State office of Historian. https://history.state.gov/historicaldocuments/frus1961-63v06/d63.

———. "Telegram from the Embassy in the Soviet Union to the Department of State," April 18, 1961. Department of State Office of Historian. https://history.state.gov/historicaldocuments/frus1961-63v06/d9.

———. "Telegram from the Embassy in the Soviet Union to the Department of State." October 26, 1962. U.S. Department of State. Office of the Historian. Retrieved from: https://history.state.gov/historicaldocuments/frus1961-63v06/d65.

Kiernan, Ben. "Twentieth Century Genocides: Underlying Ideological Themes from Armenia to East Timor." In *The Specter of Genocide: Mass Murder in Historical Perspective*, edited by Robert Gellately, and Ben Kiernan, 29–52. Cambridge, UK: Cambridge University Press, 2003.

Kimmel, Michael S. *Manhood in America: A Cultural History*. New York: Oxford University Press, 2006.

King, Martin Luther Jr. "Beyond Vietnam—A Time to Break the Silence," April 4, 1967. American Rhetoric. http://www.americanrhetoric.com/speeches/mlkatimetobreaksilence.htm.

———. "Letter from a Birmingham Jail," May 3, 1963. The King Center. http://thekingcenter.rog/archive/document/letter-birmingham-city-jail-0#.

———. "Why am I Opposed to the War in Vietnam?" April 30, 1967. The King Center. http://www.thekingcenter.org/archive/document/mlk-sermon-why-i-am-opposed-war-vietnam.

Kinsey, Alfred C., Wardell B. Pomeroy, and Clyde E. Martin. *Sexual Behavior in the Human Male*. Bloomington: Indiana University Press, 1975.

———. Wardell B. Pomeroy, Clyde E. Martin, and Paul Gebhard. *Sexual Behavior in the Human Female*. Bloomington: Indiana University Press, 1998.

Kissinger, Henry. *Nuclear Weapons and Foreign Policy*. New York: W. W. Norton, 1957.

Kleinknecht, William. *The Man Who Sold the World: Ronald Reagan and the Betrayal of Main Street America*. New York, NY: Nation, 2009.

Klinghoffer, Judith A. *Vietnam, Jews, and the Middle East*. New York: St. Martins, 1999.

Kobrak, Peter. *Cozy Politics: Campaign Finance, and Compromised Governance*. Boulder: Lynne Rienner, 2002.

Koester, Helmut. *Introduction to the New Testament, Vol. 2: History and Literature of Early Christianity*, 2nd ed. Berlin: Walter de Gruyter, 2000.

Kotz, Nick. *Judgement Days: Lyndon Baines Johnson and Martin Luther King, Jr., and the Laws that Changed America*. Boston: Houghton Mifflin, 2005.

Krames, Jeffrey A. *Lead with Humility: 12 Leadership Lessons from Pope Francis*. New York: AMACOM, 2014.

Kristensen, Hans M. "How Presidents Arms and Disarm," October 15, 2014. Federation of American Scientists. https://fas.org/blogs/security/2014/10/stockpilereductions/.

Kuchar, Sally. "Are You Sitting Down? Median Rent Rate is 3,200/Month." *Curbed*. April 14, 2014. http://sf.curbed.com/archives/2014/04/14/are_you_sitting_down_sfs_median_rent_rate_is_3200month.php.

Kulikowski, Michael. *Rome's Gothic Wars*. New York: Oxford University Press, 2007.

Ladd, George, E. "The Kingdom of God in the Jewish Apocryphal Literature: Part II." *Bibliotheca Sacra*, 109, (1952) 164–174.

Lane, Frederick S. *Obscene Profits: Entrepreneurs of Pornography in the Cyber Age*. New York, Routledge, 2001.

Lane Mark. *Rush to Judgment*. Charlottesville: Lane Group, 1966.

Langguth, A. J. *Our Vietnam: the War, 1954–1975*. New York: Touchstone, 2000.

Latysh, Mikhail, V. "The Czecholslovak Crisis of 1968." In *Prague Spring and the Warsaw Pact Invasion of Czechoslovakia, 1968*, edited by M. Mark Stolarik, pp. 1-18. Mundelein, IL: Bolchazy-Carducci, 2010.

Layman, Geoffrey and Laura S. Hussey. "George W. Bush and the Evangelicals: Religious Commitment and Partisan Change among Evangelical Protestants, 1960–2004." In *A Matter of Faith: Religion in the 2004 Presidential Election*, edited by David E. Campbell, 180–198. Washington, DC: Brookings Institution, 2007.

Ledbetter, James. *The Unwarranted Influence: Dwight D. Eisenhower and the Military Industrial Complex*. New Haven: Yale University Press, 2011.

Lee, Martin A. "Their Will be Done." *Mother Jones*, July/August, 1983. http://www.motherjones.com/politics/1983/07/their-will-be-done.

Lemann, Nicholas. *The Promised Land: The Great Black Migration and How it Changed America*. New York: Vintage, 1992.

Leo XIII. "Rerum Novarum" (Revolutionary Change), 1891.Papal Encyclicals. http://www.papalencyclicals.net/Leo13/l13rerum.htm.

LeoGrande, William M. "Remembering Robert White." *The Nation*, January 22, 2015. http://www.thenation.com/article/195801/remembering-robert-white.

Leonard Mark and Rob Blachurst. "I Don't Think Anybody Thought Much about Whether Agent Orange was Against the Rules of War." *The Guardian*, May 18, 2002. http://www.guardian.co.uk/world/2002/may/10/theobserver.

Leone, Richard C. and Gregory Anrig. eds. *The War on Our Freedoms: Civil Liberties in an Age of Terrorism*. New York: The Century Foundation, 2003.

Lernoux, Penny. *Cry of the People: The Struggle for Human Rights in Latin America—the Catholic Church in Conflict with U.S. Policy*. New York: Penguin, 1980.

BIBLIOGRAPHY

"Letter from Dan A. Turner to Judge Aaron Persky." Document Cloud March 1, 2017. https://www.documentcloud.org/documents/2852614-Letter-from-Brock-Turners-Father.html. Accessed March 20, 2017.

Levit, Nancy. *The Gender Line: Men, Women, and the Law*. New York: New York University Press, 1998.

Levitt, Jeremy and Matthew C. Whitaker. "'Truth Crushed to Earth Will Rise Again:' Katrina and its Aftermath." In *Hurricane Katrina: America's Unnatural Disaster*, edited by Jeremy I Levitt and Matthew C. Whitaker, 1–21. Lincoln: University of Nebraska Press, 2009.

Lewis, Paul. "After Noriega: United Nations; Deal is Reached at U.N. on Panama Seat as Invasion is Condemned." *The New York Times*, December 30, 1989. http://www.nytimes.com/1989/12/30/world/after-noriega-united-nations-deal-reached-un-panama-seat-invasion-condemned.html.

Li, Shi and Terry Sicular. "The Distribution of Household Income in China: Inequality, Poverty and Policies." *The China Quarterly*, 217, no. 1 (2014) 1–41.

Lichtblau, Eric. *The Nazis Next Door*. Boston: Houghton Mifflin Harcourt, 2014

Lifton, David. S. *The Best Evidence: Disguise and Deception in the Assassination of John F. Kennedy*. New York: Macmillan, 1980.

Lindsay, D. Michael. *Faith in the Halls of Power: How Evangelicals Joined the American Elite*. New York: Oxford University Press, 2007.

Lindsey, Hal. *The Late Great Planet Earth*. Grand Rapids: Zondervan, 1970.

Little Douglas. *Us versus Them: the United States, Radical Islam, and the Rise of the Green Threat*. Chapel Hill: The University of North Carolina Press, 2016.

Long, D. Stephen. *Divine Economy: Theology of the Market*. New York: Routledge, 2000.

Longmire, Sylvia. *Border Insecurity: Why Big Money, Fences, and Drones aren't Making Us Safer*, New York: St. Martin's. First published by Palgrave Macmillan, 2014.

Lundestad, Geir. *East, West, North, South: Development in International Politics since 1945*. Revised Sixth ed. Los Angeles: Sage, 2010.

Lytle, Mark Hamilton. *America's Uncivil Wars: the Sixties Era from Elvis to the Fall of Richard Nixon*. New York: Oxford University Press.

Machiavelli, Niccolo. *The Prince*. Trans. By Tim Parks. New York: Penguin Classics, 2009.

MacKinnon, Catherine. *Only Words*. Cambridge: Harvard University Press, 1993.

Malamuth, Neil. M., Tamara Addison, and Mary Koss. "Pornography and Sexual Aggression: Are There Reliable Effects and Can We Understand Them?" *Annual Review of Sex Research*, 11, no. 1 (2000) 26–91.

Mann, Robert. *Wartime Dissent: A History and Anthology*. New York: Palgrave Macmillan, 2010.

Manning, Jennifer E. and Ida A. Brudnick. *Women in Congress, 1917–2015: Biographical and Committee Assignment, Information, and Listing by State and Congress*. Washington, D.C.: Congressional Research Service, 7–5700., November 7, 2015.

Manning, Jill. C. "The Impact of Internet Pornography on Marriage and the Family: A Review of the Research." *Sexual Addition & Compulsivity*, 13 (2006) 131–165.

Maraniss, David. *They Marched into Sunlight: War and Peace Vietnam and America October 1967*. New York: Simon & Schuster, 2003.

Marrs, Jim. *Crossfire: The Plot that Killed Kennedy*. New York: Carroll & Graff, 1989.

———. *Inside Job: Unmasking the 9/11 Conspiracies*. San Rafael: Origin, 2004.

———. *The Terror Conspiracy: Deception, 9/11 and the Loss of Liberty*. Disinformation Company, 2006.

Marsden, Lee. *For God's Sake: The Christian Rights and US Foreign Policy.* New York: Palgrave Macmillan, 2008. First published by Zed Books, 2008.

Marsh, Charles. *Wayward Christian Soldiers: Freeing the Gospel from Political Captivity.* New York: Oxford University Press, 2007.

Marshall, Ellen Ott. "A Matter of Pride." In *The Legacy of Billy Graham: Critical Reflections on America's Greatest Evangelist,* edited by Michael G. Long, 79–92. Louisville: Westminster John Knox, 2008.

Martin, William. *With God on Our Side: The Rise of the Religious Right in America.* New York: Broadway, 1996.

Matthews, Chris. "Wealth Inequality in America: It's Worse than You Think." *Fortune,* October 31, 2014. http://fortune.com/2014/10/31/inequality-wealth-income-us/.

Mattox, John Mark. *St. Augustine and the Theory of Just War.* New York, NY: Continuum, 2006.

Mazlish, Bruce. *In Search of Nixon: A Psychohistorical Inquiry.* New Brunswick: Transaction, 2016.

McAdam, Doug. *Freedom Summer.* New York: Oxford University Press, 1988.

MacAskill, E. "George Bush: 'God Told me to End the Tyranny in Iraq.'" *The Guardian,* October 7, 2005. http://www.theguardian.com/world/2005/oct/07/iraq.usa.

McBride, James and Mohammed Aly Sergie. Sergie. "NAFTA's Economic Impact. CFR Backgrounders. Council on Foreign Relations," January 24, 2017. http://www.cfr.org/trade/naftas-economic-impact/p15790 Accessed March 10, 2017.

McBride, Joseph. "The Man Who Wasn't There: 'George Bush' CIA Operative." *The Nation,* July 16–23 (1988) 1; 41–42.

McCarthy, Dennis J. "The Symbolism of Blood and Sacrifice." *Journal of Biblical Literature,* 88, no. 2 (1969) 166–176.

McCarthy, Eugene. "Senator Eugene McCarthy Crystalizes Dissent by Denouncing the War in Vietnam in *Lend Me Your Ears: Great Speeches in History,* edited by. William Safire, 147–150. New York: Norton & Norton, 1997.

McCormick, Patrick T. and Russell B. Connors. *Facing Ethical Issues: Dimensions of Character, Choices, & Community.* New York: Paulist, 2002.

McDonald, Lee Martin. *The Biblical Canon: Its Origins, Transmission, and Authority.* Grand Rapids: Baker Academic, 2007.

McGreevy, John T. "Racial Justice and the People of God: the Second Vatican Council and the Civil Rights Movement." *Religion and American Culture,* 4, no.2 (1994) 221–254.

McGregor, James. *One Billion Customers: Lessons from the Front Lines of Doing Business in China.* New York: Free Press, 2005.

McIntyre, Robert. S., Matthew Gardner, and Richard Phillips. *The Sorry State of Corporate Taxes: What Fortune 500 Firms Pay (or Don't Pay) in the USA and What They Pay Abroad*—2008–2012, February, 2014. Citizens for Tax Justice. http://www.ctj.org/corporatetaxdodgers/sorrystateofcorptaxes.pdf.

McMahon, Eileen M. *What Parish are You From?: A Chicago Irish Community and Race Relations.* Lexington: The University of Kentucky Press, 1995.

McManus, Michael J. and the United States Attorney General's Commission on Pornography. *Final Report of the Attorney General's Commission on Pornography.* New York: Rutledge Hill, 1986.

McMaster, Herbert Raymond. *Dereliction of Duty: Johnson, McNamara, the Joint Chiefs of Staff, and the Lies that Led to Vietnam.* New York: HarperCollins, 1997.

McNamara, Robert S. *In Retrospect.* New York: Vintage, 1995.

McVicar, Michael. *Christian Reconstruction: R. J. Rushdoony and American Religious Conservatism*. Chapel Hill: University of North Carolina Press, 2015.

Meacham, Jon, *Destiny and Power: The American Odyssey of George Herbert Walker Bush*. New York: Random House, 2015.

Meir, August and Elliot E. Rudwick, E. *CORE: A Study in the Civil Rights Movement 1942–1968*. New York: Oxford University Press, 1973.

Meloy, Michelle, L. and Susan L. Miller. *The Victimization of Women: Law Policies, and Politics*. New York: Oxford University Press, 2011.

Menendez, Albert J. *Evangelicals at the Ballot Box*. New York: Prometheus, 1996.

Merton, Thomas. "Passion for Peace," in *The Social Essays of Thomas Merton* edited by. William H. Shannon, 327–328. New York: Crossroad, 1995.

———. "The Black Revolution." *Ramparts*, Christmas, (1963) 4–23.

———. "The Roots of War are Fear" in *The Power of Non-Violence: Writings by Advocates of Peace*, edited by. Howard Zinn, 96–104. Boston: Beacon, 2002.

Meyer, Marvin. W. "Making Mary Male: The Categories 'Male' and 'Female' in the Gospel of Thomas." *New Testament Studies*, 31 (1985) 554–570.

———. "The Gospel of Thomas." In *The Secret Teachings of Jesus*, 19–38. Translated by Marvin Meyer. New York: Random House, 1984.

———. "The Secret Book of James." In *The Secret Teachings of Jesus*, 3–15. Translated by Marvin Meyer. New York: Random House, 1984.

Meyer, Michael. *The Year That Changed the World: The Untold Story Behind the Fall of the Berlin Wall*. New York: Scribner, 2009.

Miller, Mark Crispin. *Fooled Again: How the Right Stole the 2004 Election & Why They'll Steal the Next One Too (Unless We Stop Them)*. New York: Basic, 2005.

Millett, Kate. *Sexual Politics*. New York: Doubleday, 1970.

Millhiser, Ian. *Injustices: The Supreme Court's History of Comforting the Comfortable and Afflicting the Afflicted*. New York. Nation, 2015.

Minh, Ho Chi. "Vietnamese Declaration of Independence (1945)." In *Selected Works of Ho Chi Minh*, 85–88. New York: Prism Key, 2011.

Mirza, Rocky M. *The Rise and Fall of the American Empire: A Reinterpretation of History*. Victoria: Trafford, 2007.

Mohr, Elizabeth. "More Twin Cities Clergy Accused of Sexual Abuse." *Pioneer Press*, February 11, 2015. http://www.twincities.com/2015/02/10/more-twin-cities-clergy-accused-of-sexual-abuse/.

Moreno, Jonathan. D. *Undue Risk: Secret State Experiments on Humans*. New York: Routledge, 2001.

Morgan, Joseph G. "A Change of Course: American Catholics, Anticommunism, and the Vietnam War." *U.S. Catholic Historian*, 22, no. 4 (2004) 117–130.

Morgan, Marabel. *The Total Woman*. Old Tappan: Fleming H. Revell, 1973.

Morris, Aldon. D. *The Origins of the Civil Rights Movement*. New York: Free Press, 1984.

Morrow, John Andrew. "Malcolm X: Message to Humanity." In *Malcolm X: From Political Eschatology to Religious Revolutionary*, edited by Dustin J. Byrd and Sayed Javad Miri, 211–230. Leiden: Brill, 2016.

Moser, Richard. *The New Winter Soldiers. GI and Veteran Dissent during the Vietnam Era*. New Brunswick: Rutgers University Press, 1996.

Mosey, Richard. M. *2030: The Coming Tumult-Unlimited Growth on a Finite Planet*. USA: Algora, 2009.

Moss, George Donelson. *Vietnam: An American Ordeal*. New York: 2016.

Moss, Michael. "Pentagon Study Links Fatalities to Body Armor." *New York Times*, January 7, 2006. http://www.nytimes.com/2006/01/07/politics/07armor.html?pagewanted=all.

Moss, Michael. *Salt Sugar Fat: How the Food Giants Hooked Us*. Toronto: McClelland & Stewart, 2014.

Murphy, Tim and Andy Kroll. "Santorum: Single Moms Are 'Breeding More Criminals.'" *Mother Jones*, March 6, 2012. http://www.motherjones.com/politics/2012/03/santorum-single-mothers-are-breeding-more-criminals.

Murray, Heather. *Not In this Family: Gays and the Meaning of Kinship in Postwar North America*. Politics and Culture in Modern America, series editors Glenda Gilmore, Michael Kazin and Thomas Sugrue. Philadelphia: University of Pennsylvania Press, 2010.

Murrow, Lance. "The Case for Rage and Retribution." *Time*, September 14, 2001.

Muste, Abraham J. "Getting Rid of War," in *The Power of Non-Violence: Writings by Advocates of Peace*, edited by. Howard Zinn, 83–91. Boston: Beacon, 2002.

Namie, Gary and Ruth Namie. *The Bully at Work: What You Can do to Stop the Hurt and Reclaim Your Dignity*. Naperville: Sourcebooks, 2009.

National Advisory Commission on Civil Disorders. *The Kerner Report*. James Madison Library in American Politics. Princeton: Princeton University Press, 1967.

National Center for Education Statistics. *120 Years of American Education: A Statistical Report*. Washington, D.C. U.S. Department of Education, 1987. http://nces.ed.gov/pubs93/93442.pdf.

National Commission on the Causes of the Financial and Economic Crisis in the United States. *The Financial Crisis Inquiry Report*, February 25, 2011. https://www.gpo.gov/fdsys/pkg/GPO-FCIC/pdf/GPO-FCIC.pdf.

National Conference of Catholic Bishops. "The Challenge of Peace: God's Promise and Our Response." http://www.usccb.org/upload/challenge-peace-gods-promise-our-response-1983.pdf.

National Security Action Memorandum 263, October 11, 1963. John F. Kennedy Presidential Library and Museum. Retrieved from: http://www.jfklibrary.org/Asset-Viewer/w6LJoSnW4UehkaH9Ip5IAA.aspx.

National Security Action Memorandum 273. LBJ Library, University of Texas. Retrieved from: http://www.lbjlib.utexas.edu/johnson/archives.hom/NSAMs/nsam273.asp.

Nelson, Cara C. "Fox News Host Jeanine Pirro: Muslims 'Need to Kill All Radical Islamists.'" *The Huffington Post*, January 13, 2015. http://www.huffingtonpost.co.uk/2015/01/13/fox-news-host-jeanine-pirro-islamic-terror-rant-we-need-to-kill-them_n_6461328.html.

Nelson, Deborah. *The War behind Me: Vietnam Veterans Confront the Truth about U.S. War Crimes*. New York: Basic, 2008.

Nelson-Pallmeyer, Jack. *School of Assassins. A Case for Closing the School of the Americas and for Fundamentally Changing U.S. Policy*. Maryknoll: Orbis, 1999.

Nelson, Phillip F. *LBJ: From Mastermind to "The Colossus."* New York: Skyhorse, 2014.

Nepstad, Sharon Erickson. "Disruptive Action and the Prophetic Tradition: War Resistance in the Plowshares Movement." *U.S. Catholic Historian*, 27, no. 2 (2009) 97–113.

New Oxford Annotated Bible: With the Apocrypha, Revised Standard Version. Herbert G. May and Bruce M. Metzger, editors. New York: Oxford University Press, 1962.

Newman, John M. *JFK and Vietnam: Deception, Intrigue, and the Struggle for Power*. New York: Warner Books, 1992.

Nichter, Luke. *Lyndon B. Johnson: Pursuit of Populism, Paradox of Power.* New York: Nova Science, 2013.

Nickelsburg, George, W. *Resurrection, Immortality, and Eternal Life in Intertestamental Judaism.* Cambridge: Harvard University Press, 1972.

Nicoletti, John, Sally Spencer-Thomas and Christopher Bollinger. *Violence goes to College: The Authoritative Guide to Prevention and Intervention*, 2nd ed. Springfield: Charles C. Thomas, 2010.

Niebuhr, Reinhold. *The Irony of American History.* Chicago: University of Chicago Press, 1952.

Nixon, Richard M. *The Memoirs of Richard Nixon.* New York: Touchstone, 1978.

Noah, Timothy. "Can Bill Clinton Defend his Record on Inequality?" *MSNBC.* May 2, 2104. http://www.msnbc.com/msnbc/bill-clinton-defends-his-record. Accessed March 10, 2017

Oates, Sarah. *Introduction to Media and Politics.* Thousand Oaks: SAGE, 2008.

O'Brian, Michael. *John F. Kennedy: A Biography.* New York: Thomas Dunne, 2005.

O'Malley, John W. *What Happened at Vatican II.* Cambridge: Harvard University Press, 2010.

O'Neill, J. C. "The Kingdom of God." *Novum Testamentum*, 35, no. 2, (1993) 130–141.

On the Waterfront, directed by Elia Kazan (1954 Culver City, CA; Sony Pictures, 2001) DVD.

Ost, David. *The Defeat of Solidarity: Anger and Politics in Postcommunist Europe.* Ithaca: Cornell University Press.

Overy, Richard. *Russia's War: A History of the Soviet War Effort, 1941–1945.* New York: Penguin, 1998.

Packard, Vance. *The Hidden Persuaders.* New York: David McKay, 1957.

Pagels, Elaine. *Beyond belief. The Secret Gospel of Thomas.* New York: Random House, 2003.

———. *The Gnostic Gospels.* New York, NY: Vintage, 1981.

Palast, Greg. *The Best Democracy Money Can Buy: The Truth about Corporate Cons, Globalization, and High Finance Fraudsters.* New York: Penguin, 2004.

Parker, Frederick. *Cancer in American Democracy!: The Causes and the Cures.* Indianapolis: Dog Ear, 2016.

Parker, Glen R. *Capitol Investments: The Marketability of Political Skills. Economics, Cognition, and Society.* Ann Arbor: The University of Michigan Press, 2008.

Patterson, Thomas. G. *Kennedy's Quest for Victory: American Foreign Policy, 1961–1963.* New York: Oxford University Press, 1989.

Patton, John H. "Rhetoric at Cantonsville." *Today's Speech*, 23 (1975) 3–12.

Paul VI. "Pastoral Constitution on the Church in the Modern World," December 7, 1965. Vatican Archives. http://www.vatican.va/archive/hist_councils/ii_vatican_council/documents/vat-ii_cons_19651207_gaudium-et-spes_en.html.

———. "Populorum Progressio (On the Development of Peoples), 1967. Papal Encyclicals. http://www.papalencyclicals.net/Paulo6/p6develo.htm.

Pauling, Linus. *Linus Pauling in his Own Words: Selections from His Writings, Speeches, and Interviews.* New York: Touchstone, 1995.

Payne, Charles. "Ella Baker and Models of Social Change." *Signs*, 14, no. 4 (1989) 885–899.

Pearce, Joseph. *Solzhenitsyn: A Soul in Exile.* New York, HarperCollins, 1999.

"Pentagon Seeks Cut in Danger Pay in Iraq". *Washington Times*, August 14, 2003. http://www.washingtontimes.com/news/2003/aug/14/20030814-110411-2389r/?page=all.

Perkins, John. *The New Confessions of an Economic Hit Man*. Oakland: Barrett-Koehler, 2016.

Perlstein, Rick. *Nixonland: The Rise of a President and the Fracturing of America*. New York: Simon & Schuster, 2010.

Perrin, Norman. *Jesus and the Language of the Kingdom*. Philadelphia: Fortress, 1976.

Pete Seeger. *Rainbow Race*. CBS 64445. 33 1/3 rpm. Originally released 1973.

Peterson, Anna Lisa. *Martyrdom and the Politics of Religion: Progressive Catholicism in El Salvador's Civil War*. Albany: State University of New York Press, 1997.

Pew Research Center. "Beyond Distrust: How Americans View their Government," November 23, 2015. http://www.people-press.org/2015/11/23/beyond-distrust-how-americans-view-their-government/. Accessed March 14, 2017.

———. "Emerging and Developing Economies Much More Optimistic Than Rich Countries about the Future." October 9, 2014. http://www.pewglobal.org/2014/10/09/emerging-and-developing-economies-much-more-optimistic-than-rich-countries-about-the-future/.

———. "How the Faithful Voted: 2012 Preliminary Analysis." November 7, 2012. http://www.pewforum.org/2012/11/07/how-the-faithful-voted-2012-preliminary-exit-poll-analysis/.

———. "Religious Groups Issue Statements on War with Iraq," March 19, 2003. http://www.pewforum.org/2003/03/19/publicationpage-aspxid616/.

Phil Ochs. *I Ain't Marching Anymore*. Electra 7287. 33 1/3 rpm. Originally released 1964.

Phillips, Kevin. *American Dynasty: Aristocracy, Fortune, and the Politics of Deceit in the House of Bush*. Lanham, MD: Rowman & Littlefield, 2004.

Pierre, Robert. E. "Rick Santorum Singles Out Black People at Iowa Event." *The Washington Post*, January 3, 2012. http://www.washingtonpost.com/blogs/therootdc/post/rick-santorum-singles-out-black-people-at-iowa-event/2012/01/03/gIQAAn1JYP_blog.html.

Pious, Richard M. "Cuban Missile Crisis and the Limits of Crisis Management." *Political Science Quarterly*, 116, no. 1 (2001) 81–108.

Pitzulo, Carrie. *Bachelors and Bunnies: The Sexual Politics of Playboy*. Chicago: The University of Chicago Press, 2011.

Plaskow, Judith. "Feminist Anti-Judaism and the Christian God." *Journal of Feminist Studies in Religion*, 7, no. 2 (1991) 99–108.

Pollack, John Charles. *The Billy Graham Story: Revised and Updated Edition to All Nations*. Grand Rapides: Zondervan, 2003.

Pollack, Joycelyn M. *Ethical Dilemmas and Decisions in Criminal Justice*. Boston: Cengage Learning, 2014.

"Poster Artist Peter Max is Making His Mark Just About Everywhere." *Life*, September 5, 1969, 34–39.

Potak, Chaim. *The Chosen*. New York: Ballantine, 1982. First published in 1967.

Potter, Wendell and Nick Penniman. *Nation on the Take: How Big Money Corrupts Democracy and What We Can do about It*. New York: Bloomsbury, 2016.

Power, Samantha. *"A Problem from Hell:" America and the Age of Genocide*. New York: Basic. 2013. First published by HarperCollins in 2003.

Prejean, Helen. *The Death of Innocents: An Eyewitness Account of Wrongful Execution*. Norwich: Canterbury, 2006.

Pringle, Peter. *Food, Inc. From Mendel to Monsanto*. New York: Simon & Schuster, 2003.

Prins, Naomi. *It Takes a Pillage*. Hoboken: John Wiley, 2009.

———. *Other People's Money: The Corporate Mugging of America*. New York: The New Press, 2004.

Prouty, Lee Fletcher. F. *JFK: The CIA, Vietnam, and the Plot to Assassinate John F. Kennedy*. New York: Skyhorse, 2009.

Quinley, Harold, E. "The Protestant Clergy and the War in Vietnam." *Public Opinion Quarterly*, 34, no. 1 (1970) 43–52.

Quinn, Bill. *How Wal-Mart is Destroying America (and the World): And what You Can do About It*. Berkeley: Ten Speed, 2005.

Rabe, Stephen G. *The Killing Zone: The United States Wages cold War in Latin America*. New York: Oxford University Press, 2011

Ramsey, Paul. "The Just War According to St. Augustine." In *Just War Theory*, edited by Jean Bethke Elshtain, 8–22. New York University Press, 1992.

Rasor, Dina and Robert Bauman. *Betraying Our Troops: The Destructive Results of Privatizing War*. New York: Palgrave Macmillan, 2007.

Rauschenbusch, Walter. *A Theology for the Social Gospel*. New York: Macmillan, 1917.

Reagan, Ronald. "Remarks at the Annual Conservative Political Action Conference Dinner," March 2, 1984. American Presidency Project. http://www.presidency.ucsb.edu/ws/?pid=39591

———. "Remarks During a White House Briefing on the Program for Economic Recovery," February 24, 1981. American Presidency Project. http://www.presidency.ucsb.edu/ws/index.php?pid=43450.

Redd, Forrest P. *Blood on Their Hands: How Callous Conservatives Capitalize on the Clueless Constituents*. Lanham: University Press of America, 2009.

Reich, Robert. *Supercapitalism. The Transformation of Business, Democracy and Everyday Life*. New York: Vintage, 2016.

"Religion." *Online Etymological Dictionary*, 2001–2014. http://www.etymonline.com/index.php?term=religion.

Renehan, Edward. Jr. *Pope John Paul II*. New York: Chelsea House, 2006.

Reynolds, Alan. *Income and Wealth*. Greenwood Guides to Business and Economics, edited by Wesley B. Truit. Westport: Greenwood, 2006.

Reynolds, Barbara. "Minorities Fall Victim to Predatory Loaners." *The Washington Post*, July 16, 2012. http://www.washingtonpost.com/blogs/therootdc/post/minorities-fall-victim-to-predatory-lenders/2012/07/16/gJQAraMYpW_blog.html.

Rhodes, Richard, *The Making of the Atomic Bomb*. New York: Simon & Schuster, 1986.

Rice, Condoleezza. "Promoting the National Interest." *Foreign Affairs*, 79, no. 1 (2000) 45–62.

Rich, Frank Kelly. *The Greatest Story Ever Sold: The Decline and Fall of Truth from 9/11 to Katrina*. New York: Penguin, 2004.

Richardson, Peter. *A Bomb in Every Issue: How the Short, Unruly, Life of Ramparts Magazine Changed America*. New York: New Press, 2009.

Ritter, Scott. *Dangerous Ground: America's Failed Arms Control Policy from FDR to Obama*. New York: Nation, 2010.

Robben, Antonius C. G. "Mimesis in a War among the People: What Argentina's Dirty War Reveals about Counterinsurgency in Iraq." In *Iraq at a Distance: What*

BIBLIOGRAPHY

Anthropologists Can Teach Us about the War, edited by Antonius C. G. Robben, 133–158. Philadelphia: University of Pennsylvania, 2010.
"Robert Van Handel's Sexual History." Document Cloud. https://www.documentcloud.org/documents/555084-father-robert-van-handel-sexual-autobiography.html. Accessed March 21, 2017.
Roberts, Nancy. L. *Dorothy Day and the Catholic Worker.* Albany, NY: State University of New York Press, 1984.
Robinson, James M, ed. *The Nag Hammadi Library.* San Francisco: Harper and Row, 1988.
Robinson, Matthew and Daniel Murphy. *Greed Is Good: Maximization and Elite Deviance in America.* Lanham, MD: Rowman & Littlefield, 2009.
Rockefeller, Nelson A. *The Rockefeller Report on the Americas.* Chicago: Quadrangle, 1969.
Romero, Oscar. "The Church's Mission amid the National Crisis," August 6, 1979. http://www.romerotrust.org.uk/sites/default/files/fourth%20pastoral%20letter.pdf. Accessed March 8, 2017.
Rosen, Rebecca J. "Marriage Will Not fix Poverty." *The Atlantic.* March 11, 2016. https://www.theatlantic.com/business/archive/2016/03/marriage-poverty/473019/.
Ross, Robert J. S. *Slaves to Fashion: Poverty and Abuse in the New Sweatshops.* Ann Arbor: University of Michigan Press, 2004.
Roukema, Riemer. *Jesus, Gnosis and Dogma.* New York, NY: T & T Clark International, 2010.
Rountree, Clarke. *The Chameleon President: The Curious Case of George W. Bush.* Santa Barbara: Praeger, 2011.
Rubenstein, Richard. E. *When Jesus became God: The Struggle to Define Christianity in the Last Days of Rome.* Orlando: Harcourt, 1999.
Ruether, Mary Radford. *Sexism and God Talk: Toward Feminist Theology.* Boston: Beacon, 1983.
Ruiz, Don Miguel. *The Four Agreements.* San Rafael: Amber-Allen, 1997.
Rupp, Richard E. *NATO after 9/11: An Alliance in Continuing Decline.* New York: Palgrave Macmillan, 2006.
Ruppert, Michael C. *Crossing the Rubicon: The Decline of the American Empire at the End of the Age of Oil.* Gabriola Island, Canada: New Society, 2004.
"Russell-Einstein Manifesto," 1955. http://scarc.library.oregonstate.edu/coll/pauling/peace/papers/peace6.007.5.html. Accessed march 30, 2017.
Russo, Vito. *The Celluloid Closet: Homosexuality in the Movies.* New York, NY: Harper & Row, 1987.
Ryan, David. "Option for the Poor: Liberation Theology and Anti-Americanization." In *Anti-Americanism in Latin America and the Caribbean,* edited by Alan McPherson, 215–238. New York: Berghahn, 2006.
Rychlak, Ronald J. "A War Prevented: Pope John XXIII and the Cuban Missile Crisis." November 11, 2011. http://www.crisismagazine.com/2011/preventing-war-pope-john-xxiii-and-the-cuban-missile-crisis
Sachs, Dana. *The Life We were Given: Operation Babylift, International Adoption, and the Children of War in Vietnam.* Boston: Beacon, 2010.
Safire, William. "God Bless Us." *New York Times,* August 27, 1992.
Salaman, Graeme. "The New Corporate Leadership." In *Leadership in Organizations: Current Issues and Key Trends,* edited by John Story, 54–69. New York: Routledge, 2016.

"San Bernadino Shooting: Who were the Attackers?" BBC News. December 11, 2015. http://www.bbc.com/news/world-us-canada-35004024. Accessed March 15, 2017.

Sanders, Bernie. *Our Revolution: A Future to Believe In*. New York: Thomas Dunne, 2016.

Sayonara, directed by Joshua Logan (1957; Beverly Hills, CA: MGM Home Entertainment, 2001), DVD.

Schlafly, Phyllis. *The Power of the Positive Woman*. New York: Jove/HBJ, 1978.

Schlesinger, Arthur. *A Thousand Days*. New York: Mariner, 2002. First published by Houghton Mifflin, 1962.

Schlesinger, Stephen and Stephen Kinzer. *Bitter Fruit: The Story of the American Coup in Guatemala*. Cambridge: Harvard University Press, 1982.

Schlosser, Eric. *Fast Food Nation: The Dark Side of the All-American Meal*. Boston: Houghton Mifflin, 2001.

Schmidt, Donald E. *The Folly of War: American Foreign Policy, 1898–2005*. New York: Algora Publishing, 2005.

Schmitz, David F. *Richard Nixon and the Vietnam War: The End of the American Century*. Lanham: Rowman & Littlefield, 2014.

Schneider, Gregory L. *Cadres for Conservatism: Young Americans for Freedom and the Rise of the Contemporary Right*. New York, NY: New York University Press, 1999.

Schultheis, Emily. "Joe Biden: 'We are America, Second to None, and We Own the Finish Line.'" CBS News. July 27, 2016. http://www.cbsnews.com/news/joe-biden-democratic-convention-we-are-america-second-to-none-and-we-own-the-finish-line/.

Schultze, Quentin. J. "The Mythos of the Electronic Church." *Critical Studies Mass Communication*, 4, (1987) 245–261.

Schweitzer, Peter. *Clinton Cash: The Untold Story of How and Why Foreign Governments and Businesses Helped make Bill and Hillary Rich*. New York: Harpers, 2015.

———. *Victory: The Reagan Administration's Secret Strategy that Hastened the Collapse of the Soviet Union*. New York: Atlantic Monthly, 1994.

Scott, Peter Dale. *Deep Politics and the Death of JFK*. Berkeley: University of California Press, 1993.

Scott, Peter Dale and Jonathan Marshall. *Cocaine Politics: Drugs, Armies, and the CIA in Central America*, updated edition. Berkeley, CA: University of California Press, 1998. First published 1991.

Segal, Eric. *Love Story*. New York: Harper & Row, 1970.

Seip, John and Dee Wood Harper. *The Trickle Down Delusion: How Republican Upward Redistribution of Economic and Political Power Undermines Our economy, Democracy, Institutions, and Health—and a Liberal Response*. Lanham: University Press of America, 2016.

Shapiro, Fred. C. *Race Riots, New York, 1964*. New York: Crowell, 1964.

Shapiro, Jacob. "China is Still Really Poor." *Real Clear World*, September 16, 2016. http://www.realclearworld.com/articles/2016/09/16/china_is_still_really_poor_112050.html. Accessed March 10, 2017.

Shay, Shaul. *Islamic Terror and the Balkans*. New Brunswick: Transaction, 2009. Originally published by the Interdisciplinary Center Herzilya, 2007.

Sheatsley, Paul. B. and Feldman, Jacob. J. "The Assassination of President Kennedy: A Preliminary Report on Public Reactions and Behavior." *Public Opinion Quarterly*, 28, no. 2 (1964) 189–215.

Sheehan, Thomas. *The First Coming. How the Kingdom of God became Christianity.* New York: Vintage, 1986.
Scheer, Robert. *The Great American Stickup.* New York: Nation, 2010.
Sheinkin, Steve. *Most Dangerous: Daniel Ellsberg and the Secret History of the Vietnam War.* New York: Roaring, 2015.
Sherry, Michael S. *In the Shadow of War: The United States since the 1930s.* New Haven: Yale University Press, 1995.
Shilts, Randy. *And the Band Played On: Politics, People, and the AIDS Epidemic.* New York: St. Martin's Griffin, 2007. Originally published 1987.
Shiva, Vandana. *Stolen Harvest: The Hijacking of the Global Food Supply.* Boston: South End, 2000.
Sidney, Hugh. "Daffy Datelines for a Critical Sermon." *Life*, November 24, 1967, 38 B.
———. "L.B.J.'s Ombudsman for the Cities," *Life Magazine*, October 6, 1967.
Siegel, Reva. B. "The Rule of Love": Wife Beating as Prerogative and Privacy." *The Yale Law Journal*, 105 no. 8 (1996) 2117–2207.
Silbergeld, Ellen K. *Chickenizing Farms and Food: How Industrial Meat Production Endangers Workers, Animals, and Consumers.* Baltimore: Johns Hopkins University Press, 2016.
Sipe, A. W. Richard. *Sex, Priests, and Power: Anatomy of a Crisis.* New York: Routledge, 1995.
Skaine, Rosemarie. *Sexual Assault in the U.S. Military: The Battle within America's Armed Forces.* Santa Barbara: ABC-CLIO, 2016,
Skipper, John. C. *Showdown at the 1964 Democratic Convention.* Jefferson: McFarland, 2012.
Small, Melvin. *Antiwarriors: The Vietnam War and the Battle for America's Hearts and Minds. Vietnam America in the War Years,* Vol I. Lanham: SR, 2002.
———. *Covering Dissent: The Media and the Anti-Vietnam War Movement.* New Brunswick: Rutgers University Press, 1994.
Smidt, Corwin and Paul Kellstedt. "Evangelicals in the Post-Reagan Era: An Analysis of Evangelical Voters in the 1988 Presidential Election." *Journal for the Scientific Study of Religion*, 31, no. 3 (1992) 330–338.
Smith, Curt. *George H. W. Bush: Character at the Core.* Lincoln: Potomac, 2005.
Smith, Gary Scott. *Faith and the Presidency from George Washington to George W. Bush.* New York: Oxford University Press, 2006.
Sobel, Richard. "Trends: United States Intervention in Bosnia." *The Public Opinion Quarterly*, 62, no. 2 (1998) 250–78.
Solberg, Carl. *Hubert Humphrey: A Biography.* New York: W. W. Norton, 1984.
Solomon, Norman. "Judaism and the Ethics of War." *International Review of the Red Cross*, 87, no. 858 (2005) 295–309.
Spalding, Elizabeth Edwards. *The First Cold Warrior: Harry Truman, Containment, and the Remaking of Liberal Internationalism.* Lexington: The University Press of Kentucky, 2006.
Spiro, David. E. *The Hidden Hand of American Hegemony: Petrodollar Recycling and International Markets.* Ithaca: Cornell University Press, 1999.
"Statistical Information about Casualties of the Vietnam War," National Archives. 2008. https://www.archives.gov/research/military/vietnam-war/casualty-statistics.html.
Staub, Michael. E. *Torn at the Roots: The Crisis of Jewish Liberalism in Postwar America.* New York: Columbia University, 2002.

Stavely, Zaidee. "From Foreclosure to Eviction: One Family's Struggle to Recover." KQED News, May 30, 2017. https://ww2.kqed.org/news/2017/05/30/from-foreclosure-to-eviction-one-familys-struggle-to-recover/.

"Steel: The Ides of April." *Fortune*, May, 1962, 97–98, 100.

Steinem, Gloria. "A Bunny's Tale: Part I." *Show Magazine*, May, 1963:90–93; 114–15.99–114.

———. "A Bunny's Tale: Part II." *Show Magazine*, June, 1963:66–69; 110–113.

Steinfels, Peter. "Roman Catholics and American Politics." In *Religion and American Politics: From the Colonial Period to the Present*, edited by Mark A. Noll and Luke E. Harlow, 345–66. New York: Oxford University Press, 1990.

Steinweis, Alan, E. "The Auschwitz Analogy: Holocaust Memory and American Debates over Intervention in Bosnia and Kosovo in the 1990s." *Holocaust and Genocide Studies*, 19, no. 2 (2005) 276–89.

Stern, Sheldon M. "The Inside Story of the Cuban Missile Crisis." *Boston Globe*, October 16, 2002. http://archive.boston.com/news/globe/magazine/articles/2002/10/06/the_inside_story_of_the_cuban_missile_crisis/.

———. *The Week the World Stood Still: Inside the Secrete Cuban Missile Crisis*. Stanford Nuclear Age Series. Stanford: Stanford University Press, 2005.

Stevens, Jason W. *God-Fearing and Free. A Spiritual History of America's Cold War*. Cambridge: Harvard University Press, 2010.

Stiglitz, Joseph E. and Linda J. Blimes. *The Three Trillion Dollar War: The True Cost of the Iraq Conflict*. New York: W. W. Norton, 2008.

Stodola, Sarah. "They Wrote Off What? $628.6 Billion in Corporate Tax Loopholes." *The Fiscal Times*, February 9, 2011. http://www.thefiscaltimes.com/Articles/2011/02/09/10-Big-Corporate-Tax-Breaks#page1.

Stoll, Ira. *JFK: Conservative*. Boston: Houghton Mifflin Harcourt, 2013.

Stone, Chad, et. al. "A Guide to Statistics on Historical Trends in Income Equality." Center on Budget Priorities. November 7, 2016. http://www.cbpp.org/cms/?fa=view&id=3629.

Stone, Oliver and Peter Kuznick. *The Untold History of the United States*. New York: Gallery, 2012.

Stone, Roger *The Man Who Killed Kennedy: The Case against LBJ*. New York: Skyhorse, 2014.

———. *Nixon's Secrets. The Rise Fall, and Untold Truth about the President, Watergate, and the Pardon*. New York: Skyhorse, 2014.

Styles, Ruth and Ashley Coleman. "She was Unconscious the Entire Time: Hero Tells How He Saved the Stanford Rape Victim as Fellow Swedish Graduate Revealed to have Wept after Pinning Attacker to the Ground." *Daily Mail*, June 7, 2016 http://www.dailymail.co.uk/news/article-3630103/Student-came-rescue-Stanford-rape-victim-speaks-judge-let-attacker-light-sentence.html.

Sullivan, Amy. "You Say Subsidiary, I Say Bullshit—Why Paul Ryan and His Bishop Defenders Are Wrong." *New Republic*, September 27, 2012. http://www.newrepublic.com/article/107826/why-paul-ryan-and-his-bishop-defenders-are-wrong.

Suri, Jeremi. *Henry Kissinger and the American Century*. Cambridge: Harvard University Press, 2009.

Suro, Robert. "The 1992 Campaign: The Religious Right; Bush Bets Full Support at Religious Gathering." *The New York Times*, August 23, 1992. http://www.nytimes.com/1992/08/23/us/1992-campaign-religious-right-bush-gets-full-support-religious-gathering.html.

Swartz, David R. *Moral Minority: The Evangelical Left in the Age of Conservatism.* Politics and American Culture, series eds. Margot Canaday, Glenda Gilmore, Michael Kazin and Thomas J. Sugrue. Philadelphia: University of Pennsylvania Press, 2012.

Swerdlow, Amy. *Women Strike for Peace: Traditional Motherhood and Radical Politics in the 1960s.* Chicago: The University of Chicago Press, 1993.

Tarpley, Webster and Anton Chaitkin, *George Bush. The Unauthorized Biography.* Joshua Tree: Progressive. Originally published by Executive Intelligence Review, 1992. 2004.

Taubman, Philip. *Secrete Empire. Eisenhower, the CIA, and the Hidden Story of America's Space Espionage.* New York: Simon and Schuster, 2003.

Taubman, William. *Khrushchev: The Man and his Era.* New York: W. W. Norton, 2003.

Taylor, Alan. "1964: Civil Rights Battles," *The Atlantic,* May 28, 2014, http://www.theatlantic.com/photo/2014/05/1964-civil-rights-battles/100744/.

Thatcher, Margaret. "Highlights with George Bush & Mikhail Gorbachev. State of the World Forum." San Francisco, California, October 1, 1995. https://www.youtube.com/watch?v=4_OWyroC-5s. Accessed March 10, 2017

"The 25 Most Vicious Iraq War Profiteers." *Business Pundit,* July 22, 2008. http://www.businesspundit.com/the-25-most-vicious-iraq-war-profiteers/2/. Accessed March 13, 2017.

The American Ruling Class, directed by John Kirby (2007, USA: Alive Mind Media, 2007), DVD.

The Association. *Greatest Hits.* Warner Bros. Seven Arts Records WS 1767. 33 1/3 rpm. Originally released 1967.

The Celluloid Closet, directed by Rob Epstein and Jeffrey Friedman (1995; Culver City, CA: Sony Pictures Classic, 1996), DVD.

The Fog of War, directed by Errol Morris (Culver City, CA: Sony Picture Classics, 2003), DVD.

The Warning. Directed by Michael Kirk. 2009. *Frontline* TV Series, PBS, 2010. DVD.

Thimmesch, Nick. "How Kissinger Fooled Us All." *New York Magazine,* 6, no. 23 (1973) 48–59.

Thomas, M. Ladd. "A Critical Appraisal of SEATO." *The Western Quarterly,* 10, no. 4 (1957) 926–936.

Thomas, Norman. *The Prerequisites for Peace.* New York: W. W. Norton, 1959.

To Kill a Mockingbird, directed by Robert Mulligan (1962, Hollywood, CA: Universal Studios Home Entertainment, 2012) DVD.

Tombs, David. *Latin American Liberation Theology. Religion in the Americas* Vol. I. Boston: Brill, 2003.

Torjesen, Karen J. *When Women were Priests: Women's Leadership in the Early Church & the Scandal of Their Subordination in the Rise of Christianity.* San Francisco: HarperCollins, 1995.

Treadwell, Perry. *God's Judgement? Syphilis and AIDS: Comparing the History of Prevention of Attempts of Two Epidemics.* San Jose: Writers Club, 2001.

Trento, Joseph J. *Prelude to Terror: Edwin P. Wilson and the Legacy of America's Private Intelligence Network.* New York: Carrol & Graf, 2005.

Troy, Gil. *The Age of Clinton: America in the 1990s.* New York: Thomas Dunne, 2015.

Truman, Harry S. "Address at the Cornerstone Laying of the New York Avenue Presbyterian Church. April 3, 1951." Truman Library. https://trumanlibrary.org/publicpapers/index.php?pid=280&st=new+york&st1=.

———. "Address in Spokane at Gonzaga University, May 11, 1950." Truman Library. https://trumanlibrary.org/publicpapers/index.php?pid=750&st=&st1.

———. "Address to the Washington Pilgrimage of American Churchman, September 28, 1951." Truman Library. http://www.trumanlibrary.org/publicpapers/index.php?pid=457&st=pilgrimage&st1=.

———. "Inaugural Address, January 20, 1949." Truman Library. http://www.trumanlibrary.org/whistlestop/50yr_archive/inagural20jan1949.htm.

Tulchinsky, Theodore H. and Elena Varavikova. *The New Public Health*, 2nd ed. Burlington: Elsevier, 2009.

Tuosto, Kylie. "The 'Grunt Truth' of Embedded Journalism: The New Media/Military Relationship." *Stanford Journal of International Relations*, 10, no. 1 (2008) 20–31.

Turkson, Abraham K. *Save American Jobs: New Business Ideas to Retain Jobs in America*. New York: iUniverse, 2005.

Turse, Nick. *Kill Anything that Moves: The Real American War in Vietnam*. New York: Picador, 2013.

Unger, Craig. *House of Bush, House of Saud: The Secret Relationship between the World's Two Most Powerful Dynasties*. New York: Scribner, 2004.

United Nations Commission on the Truth for El Salvador. *From Madness to Hope: The 12-Year War in El Salvador*.1993. United States Institute for Peace. http://www.usip.org/sites/default/files/file/ElSalvador-Report.pdf. Accessed March 30, 2017.

United States Accountability Office "Corporate Income Tax: Effective Tax Rates Can Differ Significantly From the Statutory Rate." GAO 13–520. 2013. http://gao.gov/assets/660/654957.pdf.

United States Bureau of Labor Statistics. "Occupational Employment and Wage Estimates," May, 2014. Retrieved from http://www.bls.gov/oes/current/oes_nat.htm#41-0000.

United States Census Bureau. "Table 24: Minnesota-Race and Hispanic Origin for Selected Cities and Other Places: Earliest Census to 1990." 1990. https://www.census.gov/population/www/documentation/twps0076/MNtab.pdf.

United States Commission on Civil Rights. *School Desegregation in Minneapolis, Minnesota*. May, 1977. https://www.law.umaryland.edu/marshall/usccr/documents/cr12d459.pdf.

United States Conference of Catholic Bishops. *Create in Me a Clean Heart*. Washington, D. C. United States Conference of Catholic Bishops, 2015. http://www.usccb.org/issues-and-action/human-life-and-dignity/pornography/upload/Create-in-Me-a-Clean-Heart-Statement-on-Pornography.pdf.

———. *Economic Justice for All: Pastoral letter on Catholic Social Teaching and the U.S. Economy*. Washington, D. C. United States Conference of Catholic Bishops, 2006. http://www.usccb.org/upload/economic_justice_for_all.pdf.

United States Department of Health and Human Service. "2014 Poverty Guidelines." 2014. https://aspe.hhs.gov/2014-poverty-guidelines.

United States Department of Labor. "How the Government Measures Unemployment." Bureau of Labor Statistics, 2015. http://www.bls.gov/cps/cps_htgm.htm#unemployed.

Uradnik, Kathleen, Lori Johnson, and Sara Hower. *Battleground: Government and Politics*, Vol. I (A-H). Battleground Series, edited by Kathleen Uradnik, et. al. Santa Barbara: Greenwood, 2011.

VanDeMark, Brian. *Into the Quagmire: Lyndon Johnson and the Escalation of the Vietnam War*. New York: Oxford University Press, 1991.

Vanhoozer, Kevin J., et. al "God's Kingship in the OT and Jewish Thought." In *Dictionary for Theological Interpretation of the Bible*, edited by Kevin Vanhoozer, 420. Grand Rapids, Baker Book House, 2005.

Veterans Health Initiative. *Health Effects from Chemical, Biological, and Radiological Weapons*, 2003. http://www.publichealth.va.gov/docs/vhi/chem_bio_rad_weapons.pdf.

Vine, David. *Base Nation. How U.S. Military Bases Abroad Harm America and the World*. New York: Metropolitan, 2015.

Visser, Wayne. "CSR 2.0: From the Age of Greed to the Age of Responsibility." In *Reframing Corporate Social Responsibility: Lessons from the Global Financial Crisis*, edited by William Sun, Jim Stewart, and David Pollard, 231–252. Bingley, UK: Emerald Group, 2010.

Volkogonov, Dmitri Antonovich. *Autopsy for an Empire: The Seven Leaders Who Built the Soviet Regime*, edited and translated by Harold Shukman. New York: Free Press, 1998.

Volsky, Igor. "Paul Ryan Blames Poverty on Lazy 'Inner City' Men." *Think Progress*, March 12, 2014. Retrieved from: http://thinkprogress.org/economy/2014/03/12/3394871/ryan-poverty-inner-city/.

Wallace, Thomas P. *America is Self-Destructing: Wealth, Greed and Ideology Trump Social Justice and the Common Good*. Bloomington: AuthorHouse, 2013

Wallis, Jim. *On God's Side: What Religion Forgets and Politics Hasn't Learned about Serving the Common Good*. Grand Rapids: Brazos, 2013

Wal-Mart: The High Cost of Low Price, directed by Robert Greenwald. (2005, USA: Disinformation Company, 2005), DVD.

Warner, Judith. "The Women's Leadership Gap." Center for American Progress. March 7, 2014. https://cdn.americanprogress.org/wp-content/uploads/2014/03/WomenLeadership.pdf. Accessed March 2, 2017.

Watts, Steven. *Mr. Playboy: Hugh Hefner and the American Dream*. Hoboken: John Wiley & Sons, 2008.

Watson, Bruce. *Freedom Summer: The Savage Season of 1964 that Made Mississippi Burn and America a Democracy*. New York: Viking, 2010.

Weaver, Gina Marie. *Ideologies of Forgetting: Rape in the Vietnam War*. New York: State University of New York, 2010.

Weber, Laura E. "Gentiles Preferred: Minneapolis Jews and Employment 1920–1950." *Minnesota History*, 52, no. 5 (1991) 166–182.

Weil, Martin. "Duane 'Dewey' Clarridge, CIA Official Enmeshed in Iran-Contra Affair, Dies at 83." *The Washington Post*, April 11, 2016. https://www.washingtonpost.com/national/duane-dewey-clarridge-cia-official-enmeshed-in-iran-contra-affair-dies-at-83/2016/04/11/78979470-ff90-11e5-9203-7b8670959b88_story.html.

Weiner, Tim. *Legacy of Ashes: The History of the CIA*. New York, NY: Doubleday, 2007.

Weisberg, Harold. *Whitewash: The Report on the Warren Report*. New York: Skyhorse, 1965.

Weisman, Jonathan and Eric Lipton. "In New Congress, Wall St. Pushes to Undermine Dodd-Frank Reform." *New York Times*, January 13, 2015. https://www.nytimes.com/2015/01/14/business/economy/in-new-congress-wall-st-pushes-to-undermine-dodd-frank-reform.html?_r=0.

Weissmann, Jordan. "Newt Gingrich Thinks School Children Should Work as Janitors". *The Atlantic*, November 21, 2011. http://www.theatlantic.com/business/archive/2011/11/newt-gingrich-thinks-school-children-should-work-as-janitors/248837/.

Wells, Tom. *The War Within: America's Battle over Vietnam*. Lincoln: iUniverse, 2005.

West Side Story, directed by Jerome Robbins and Robert Wise (1961; Beverly Hills, CA; MGM, 2012), DVD.

Westheider, James E. *The Vietnam War*. Westport: Greenwood, 2007.

Wheaton, Bernard and Zdeněk Kavan. *The Velvet Revolution: Czechoslovakia, 1988–1991*. Boulder: Westview, 1992.

When AIDS was Funny, directed by Scott Calonico (2015; AD&D Productions Ltd., 2015). http://video.vanityfair.com/watch/the-reagan-administration-s-chilling-response-to-the-aids-crisis. Accessed March 2, 2017.

Whittier, Nancy. *The Politics of Child Sexual Abuse: Emotion, Social Movements, and the State*. New York: Oxford University Press, 2009.

Wilcox, Clyde. "Premillennialists at the Millennium: Some Reflections on the Christian Right in the Twenty-fist Century." In *The Rapture of Politics: the Christian Right as they United States approaches the Year 2000*, edited by Steve Bruce, et. al, 21–40. New Brunswick: Transaction, 1994.

Wilcox, Fred. A. *Scorched Earth: Legacies of Chemical Warfare in Vietnam*. New York: Seven Stories Press, 2011.

Wiley, Tabitha. *Original Sin: Origins, Developments, Contemporary Meanings*. Mahwah, NJ: Paulist, 2002.

Will, Emily Wade. *Archbishop Oscar Romero: The Making of a Martyr*. Eugene: Resource, 2016.

Willard F. Jabusch. "Whatsoever You Do." *Rise Up & Sing*, Vol. 9. Third edition. OCP, 2009.

Williams, Daniel K. *God's Own Party*. New York: Oxford University Press, 2010.

Wilson, Cary. *Your Brain on Porn: Internet Pornography and the Emerging Science of Addiction*. Kent: Commonwealth, 2014.

Winsboro, Irvin D. S. and Michael Epple. "Religion, Culture, and the Cold War: Bishop Fulton J. Sheen and America's Anti-Communist Crusade of the 1950s." *Historian*, 71, no. 2 (2009) 206–233.

Winters, Michael Sean. *God's Right Hand: How Jerry Falwell Made God a Republican and Baptized the American Right*. New York: HarperCollins, 2012.

Wirmark, Bo. "Nonviolent Methods and he American Civil Rights Movement 1955–1965." *Journal of Peace Research*, 11, no. 2 (1974) 115–132.

Wittner, Lawrence S. *The Struggle against the Bomb. One World or None. A History of the Nuclear Disarmament Movement through 1953*. Stanford Nuclear Age Series. Stanford: Stanford University Press, 1993.

Wood, Elisabeth Jean. *Insurgent Collective Action and Civil War in El Salvador*. Cambridge, UK: Cambridge University Press, 2003.

Woodard, J. David. *The America that Reagan Built*. Westport: Greenwood, 2006.

Woods, Randall Bennett. "Dixie's Dove: J. William Fulbright, the Vietnam War, and the American South." In *Vietnam and the American Political Tradition: The Politics of Dissent*, edited by Randall B. Woods, 149–70. Cambridge: Cambridge University Press, 2003.

———. *LBJ Architect of American Ambition*. Cambridge: Harvard University Press, 2006.

BIBLIOGRAPHY

———. *Quest for Identity: America since 1945.* Cambridge: Cambridge University Press, 2005.

World Trade Organization. "A Charter of Fair Trade Principles" 2009. http://www.wfto.com/sites/default/files/Charter-of-Fair-Trade-Principles-Final%20%28EN%29.PDF. Accessed March 10, 2017.

Yamauchi, Edwin M. "The Crucifixion and Docetic Christology. *Concordia Theological Quarterly*, 46, no. 1 (1980) 1–20.

Yoder, Jess. "The Protest of the American Clergy in Opposition to the War in Vietnam." *Today's Speech*, 17, no. 3 (1969) 51–59.

York, Herbert F. *The Advisors: Oppenheimer, Teller and the Superbomb.* San Francisco: W. H. Freeman, 1976.

Young, Kimberly. S. "Internet Sex Addiction Risk Factors, Stages of Development, and Treatment." *American Behavioral Scientist*, 52, no 2 (2008) 21–37.

Young, Ralph. *Dissent: The History of an American Idea.* New York: New York University Press, 2015.

Zeiler, Thomas W. *Dean Rusk: Defending the American Mission Abroad.* Wilmington: Scholarly Resource, 2000.

Zeitlin, Solomon. "The Essenes and Messianic Expectations: A Historical Study of Sects and Ideas during the Second Jewish Commonwealth." *The Jewish Quarterly Review*, 45, no. 2 (1954) 83–119.

Zinn, Howard. "Carter-Reagan-Bush: The Bipartisan Consensus." In *The Indispensable Zinn: The Essential Writings of the "People's Historian,"* edited by Timothy McCarthy, 41–65. New York: New Press, 2012.

Zubok, Vladislav. *A Failed Empire: The Soviet Union in the Cold War from Stalin to Gorbachev.* Chapel Hill: The University of North Carolina Press, 2007.

Zurcher, Louis A and George Kirkpatrick. *Citizens for Decency: Antipornography Crusades as Status Defense.* Austin: University of Texas Press, 1976.

www.ingramcontent.com/pod-product-compliance
Lightning Source LLC
Chambersburg PA
CBHW071017240426
43661CB00073B/2358